Market Power and Economic Welfare

Consulting Editor: **Donald J. Dewey,** Columbia University

Market Power
and
Economic Welfare

AN INTRODUCTION

William G. Shepherd
University of Michigan

Random House   New York

First Printing
98765432

Copyright © 1970 By Random House, Inc.
All rights reserved under International and Pan-American Copyright Conventions.
Published in the United States by Random House, Inc., New York, and simultaneously
in Canada by Random House of Canada Limited, Toronto.

Library of Congress Catalog Card Number: 75-99491

Manufactured in the United States of America.

Printed and bound by The Haddon Craftsmen, Scranton, Pa.

878,456

Preface

Some years ago, a senior colleague advised me that research on market structure was mostly "wrapped up and done." Soon thereafter another and younger friend, now a well-known specialist in the field, urged upon me that the "old" industrial organization field—by which he meant the issues which are covered in this book—was "dead."

If these opinions had been correct, this volume would have little more value than an almanac, surveying old and brittle facts, hardly worth my writing it or your reading it. But instead, in my own research and in the preparation of this book, I have found myself with fresh doubts and new facts (mine and others') on many basic issues. The result is a rather different perspective on what market power is and does. This field of study is in its adolescence, not senescence, and I expect the issues in this book to undergo much further rethinking, extension and empirical testing. In the meantime, it may be of value to think whole and carefully—if only provisionally—about what the directions of recent research have been, and about the special colorations which the lenses of early scientific research may impart. This is a hazardous experiment, for many of the issues are evaluative and many of the research results are in flux and controversial. The effort may turn out, in retrospect, to have been premature or unbalanced. I have not pretended to do an encylopedic treatment. The main hope has been to establish a perspective on the main features of the problem.

So this book is ventured as a broad summary and appraisal of its subject, a treatise in the format of a textbook. I have tried to include enough supporting detail—data, citations, and others—to fill out and establish the points made in the text, but without congesting the narrative. For students and perhaps colleagues, I hope that this material will whet the appetite for further study and revision. For the general reader, I hope the book will outline fairly and intelligibly the present state of knowledge—with all its gaps and margins of doubt—about this lasting problem.

As the research leading to this volume has evolved, I have had encouragement and perceptive advice from Shorey Peterson and John B. Lansing on many occasions. Frederick M. Scherer and Charles H. Berry have clarified a number of issues, and I am grateful also to John Perry Miller, Willard F. Mueller, Oliver E. Williamson, Thomas Saving, John M. Blair, Harold M. Levinson, Lee E. Preston, Paul W. MacAvoy, William S. Comanor, James S. Campbell, and Alister Sutherland for their helpful discussions of various points. I am particularly indebted to Donald J. Dewey for reading and criticizing the manuscript with patience and unflagging good humor and for reading the second draft once again after it was lost in the mail. The book owes much to his generosity and perceptiveness.

Several able research assistants, trained at the Research Seminar in Quantitative Economics at the University of Michigan, have included Barbara Moores, Barry Bosworth, and Toshiaka Taga. We were assisted in various parts of the research by arrangements with the Institute of Public Administration (now the Institute for Public Policy Studies) and the Computer Center at the University of Michigan, the Brookings Institution, and by research funds provided by the Ford Foundation. For permission to draw on earlier papers presenting some of the findings, I am indebted to editors of the *Review of Economics and Statistics*, *Southern Economic Journal*, *Antitrust Bulletin*, and *Oxford Economic Papers*.

For skilled typing of parts of successive drafts, I am grateful to Gloria Crosswait, Colleen Eccleston, Donna Nichols, Patricia Dapprich, and particularly Jacqueline Parsons. Michele Jarmak edited the final copy with unusual care and patience.

The inevitable publishing lag means that some recent research results cannot be included. On most points, the cut-off period has been the winter of 1969.

Much of this manuscript was completed before I took a position during 1967–1968 as Special Economic Assistant to the Assistant Attorney General for Antitrust in the U.S. Department of Justice. Some final revisions have resulted from my experience during this period. I am especially indebted to Donald F. Turner, Edwin M. Zimmerman, Robert A. Hammond, Lionel Kestenbaum and Donald I. Baker of the Antitrust Division at that time for their insight on a large number of competitive problems. But I have taken care to avoid disclosing privileged information, and I want particularly to absolve the Antitrust Division from any necessary connection with the views in this book.

The disclaimer applies also to the many other people and institutions that have given assistance. The point may sound conventional, but the help I have had from so many sides has been exceptional. And if my wife Theodora did not regard it as platitudinous, I would thank her too for making this book possible.

Ann Arbor

W. G. S.

Contents

Market Power and Economic Welfare

Chapter / **1**

Introduction

> There was a man of Sicily, who, having money deposited with him, bought up all the iron from the iron mines; afterwards, when the merchants from their various markets came to buy, he was the only seller, and without much increasing the price he gained 200 per cent.
> ARISTOTLE
> *Politics* (Book I, Chapter 12)

> Competition may not be the best conceivable stimulus, but it is at present a necessary one, and no one can foresee the time when it will not be indispensable to progress.
> JOHN STUART MILL
> *Principles of Political Economy* (1848)

This book is an attempt to convey the meaning, the scope, and the effects of monopoly power in advanced economies, particularly the United States. Few economic topics have stirred such hopes, fears, and disagreements as this one has, raising as it does the specter of power held in a few elite hands, of economic waste and exclusion, of damage to the free character of economic life. Although the problem is at least as ancient as the phenomenon of exchange, it has been of special and insistent concern in the United States for about the last century. A century hence, it will probably still be exciting both gloom and optimism.

Market power is the ability of a market participant or group of participants (persons, firms, partnerships, or others) to influence price, quantity, and the nature of the product in the marketplace.[1]   Acquired and rationally

---

[1] Alternatively, "A firm possesses market power when it can behave persistently in a manner different from the behavior that a competitive market would enforce on a firm facing otherwise similar cost and demand conditions."   (Carl Kaysen and Donald F. Turner, *Antitrust Policy* [Cambridge: Harvard University Press, 1959], 75.)   The key point is the discretion which market power provides in choosing among alternative price, innovation, investment and other strategies. Firms which have no such latitude do not possess market power.

exercised, market power may yield during its duration the commercial rewards of high and risk-free profits, as well as a wider range of social and political advantages. As this book will show, market power may be gained in many ways, and it may take a variety of forms. Its possible effects, too, cover a wide variety of economic and social conditions.

Market power may be sought and exploited directly for the rewards it yields; it may also arise more or less incidentally as a side effect of innovation or perhaps as an inevitable result of the imperatives of modern technology. Even when its origins are wholly laudable, it may frequently outlive them. Whatever its origins may be, market power *in itself* makes possible a restriction of output, raising of prices, retardation of technical progress, and further inequality in distribution.

There have now been several generations of debate and several decades of analysis and research on the monopoly problem in modern industrialized economies, yet there persists wide disagreement on the state of and prospects for competition in the United States and other nations. One would have expected the major improvements of analysis and quantitative research since the 1930's to have settled at least the main issues. Instead, very nearly the opposite has happened. Some regard market power as extensive and integral to a progressive economy; others view it as large and menacing, and therefore to be attacked root and branch; to still others it is slight and fleeting, of no real consequence. Actually, many of the latest arguments and concepts—technological imperatives of large scale, potential competition, the transience of market power, etc.—were common currency by 1900[2]. Some of the more recent "improvements" in analysis have yielded little new knowledge; some indeed have tended more to subtract from understanding. In addition, the evidence about market power has proven more difficult to prepare and evaluate than had been expected, too often serving merely as a hunting ground for the tendentious. Almost every "fact" has offered divergent, even contradictory, meanings; many clear "findings" have soon been reversed, some more than once; and every established point invites skepticism.

Accordingly, a number of public policies toward monopoly have lacked adequate guidance. In the United States, antimerger policies have grown more severe, but they have not been balanced by comparable actions to take apart existing concentration. Regulatory policies toward "natural-monopoly" utilities may no longer fit some of the newer competitive patterns, and regulation may also encourage utilities to extend their monopoly positions into other markets. The whole effect may be to stifle new competitive possibilities. Federal purchases and support of research and development in the last 20 years may have come to foster market power in many

---

[2] See, for example, Charles J. Bullock, "Trust Literature: A Survey and Criticism," *Quarterly Journal of Economics*, XV (February 1901), 167–217; and Shorey Peterson, "Antitrust and the Classic Model," *American Economic Review*, XLVII (March 1957), 60–78.

industries. A number of important new industries (such as nuclear power equipment, computer time-sharing) and changes (for example, in the status of the Post Office, or possibly the government's uranium enrichment plants) pose related questions. Abroad, too, public policies toward business have continued to grope and twist for lack of guidance.

There is wide agreement that market power has at least several forms, such as concentration, barriers against new competitors, vertical patterns, and the several others which will be explored in this book. But it has not been apparent exactly which elements do belong on the list, nor what their relative importance is. There has also been a growing fixation on concentration as "the" element of market power. Some of the rankings and interactions among the elements can be clarified by deductive reasoning. But factual evidence is also needed in order to place the elements of market power in correct perspective and to understand how they are related. Evidence is also essential for appraising whatever real effects of market power there may be.

This book looks both at concepts (Part I) and at evidence (Parts II and III) about market power. Chapter 2 briefly reviews the changing debates and concepts of competition since 1890, trying to put the present issues in perspective. This is peculiarly necessary because much of the present debate has been repeating, as if new, points which were aired at least 70 years ago, in some cases with rather more sophistication than is now common. Chapter 2 also notes the need to use a relatively expanded analysis in evaluating market power and its effects in actual markets. The main probable causes and forms of market power are noted in Chapter 3. Chapter 4 outlines the probable effects of market power on efficiency, progress, equity, and other conditions and attempts to specify the optimum market structure for promoting a "good," balanced economic performance; it also ventures to outline the probable natural structure that would evolve under common conditions underlying many markets. This permits a broad comparison between the "optimum" and the "natural" structure, to evaluate their divergence or similarity.

Part II appraises actual market power in the United States in the perspective of conditions found abroad. First, the changing role of the very largest firms—the corporate charmed circle—are evaluated. Two questions draw special attention in Chapter 5—are their scope and permanency increasing and why? Are they transcending competitive and profit motives toward a higher plane of social stewardship? The answers to these questions arise in part from the influence of financial markets on producing enterprises. Chapter 6, therefore, surveys structure in the principal markets for capital.

A four-chapter review of structure in other, nonfinancial markets follows. Manufacturing industries, which since the 1930's have been more closely measured than markets in other sectors have been, are inevitably a main focus of the analysis, but not exclusively so. Chapter 7 examines the structure within markets that is formally embodied in the lines of direct corporate ownership. This embraces several elements, including the familiar market shares and concentration ratios, asymmetry among the leading firms, and the extent to which these firms are aggregates of many smaller plants. Chapter 8 widens the focus to the softer quasi-structure of informal cooperation among companies via cartels and other direct agreements not to compete, joint directorships, trade associations, joint ventures, and the like. Barriers against new entry are also reviewed. Chapter 9 broadens the coverage still more to elements which are not strictly internal to (or relative within) the market. Such external elements include size relative to the total distribution of firms, diversification, and vertical patterns of several sorts.

The mosaic of facts in these five chapters permits a combined appraisal in Chapter 10 of those individual markets in which the composite structure probably clothes substantial market power. This leads in turn to an evaluation of the general scope of market power in this country and others. Chapter 10 also draws a broad comparison of actual market structures with "optimum" structure which was derived in Chapter 4.

Having outlined the character and extent of market power, the book next analyzes its probable causes (Chapter 11) and effects (Chapters 12 to 15). Economies of scale have long been studied as a main determinant of structure; market growth has gained recent attention as a possible solvent of concentration; various public policies may also be influential. Chapter 11 briefly reviews these and other possible determinants. The possible effects of structure range from niceties of allocational inefficiency to the gross structure of distribution and the rate and character of technical progress. The necessary starting point for appraising these is, in Chapter 12, the possible influence of market power on prices and profitability; is this influence usually large and lasting or slight and fleeting? This leads, in Chapter 13, to an estimate of the inefficiency in use of resources which market power may breed, and an exploration of whether structure affects market growth rates and business instability. In Chapter 14, technical change and distribution (of wealth, income, and individual opportunities) round out the book's survey of the main possible economic effects of market power. To lend further coherence and concreteness to this sequence of evidence, Chapter 15 draws together the main features of two leading situations of market power in the American economy; the computer and automobile industries.

A concluding chapter summarizes the main outlines of market power and its apparent influences on economic performance. It also notes several directions in which further research is most clearly needed. The policy implications (for antitrust, regulation, public ownership, and other public subsidy and purchasing activities) have been deliberately reserved for treatment in a later volume.

At this point, a brief word about general concepts may help to clarify how the approach taken here relates to the current structure-behavior-performance treatment of industrial organization.[3]   In the common analysis, market *structure* is assumed to determine the degree and directions of competitive *behavior* by firms.   This in turn affects the economic *performance* of the industry in efficiency, progressiveness, and other ways.   Following general usage, this book treats market structure and market power as overlapping but not coequal.   Market *structure* includes many elements, only some of which may directly embody market power—concentration, for example, ordinarily does embody market power, while the total number of firms often does not.   Market *power* usually takes concrete form in some combination of structural elements; but these various combinations of elements only suggest some degree of probability of market power, not a certainty or proof.   Some market power arises from " behavior "—actions, promises, or threats—without ever taking visible and systematic structural form, as Chapter 3 will explore.   Even though much of this behavior can be predicted from structure (or may be regarded as comprising *informal* structure), there is always some play and variation in the whole outcome.

Therefore, this book may best be viewed as an attempt to explore in some depth and detail the structural character of market power.[4]   The focus here on structure is not meant to deny the importance and diversity of behavior.   Rather the volume ventures to codify and appraise the relatively firm and systematic features of market power, as a first step toward comprehending the entire phenomenon.   This first step may seem to take too much of a structuralist approach, although I do not believe that it does.   In any event, the structural skeleton must be assembled before the behavioral flesh can be added on.

---

[3] See Joe S. Bain, *Industrial Organization*, rev. ed. (New York: Wiley, 1967).
[4] The approach is similar to that in Kaysen and Turner, *op. cit.*, with an expanded coverage of elements and effects.

PART I

Market Power
in Theory

Chapter 2

Changing Views
on Market Power
and Competition

In some cases the great company prefers to sell all the
goods that are required at a moderate price rather than to
invite rivals into its territory.   This is monopoly in form but
not in fact, for it is shorn of its injurious power; and the
thing that holds it firmly in check is *potential competition* . . . .
                              JOHN BATES CLARK
                              Essentials of Economic Theory (1907)

Of all forms of human conflict, economic competition
is the highest.   In no other form of conflict does success
depend so much upon production or service and so little upon
destruction or deception.
                              THOMAS NIXON CARVER
                              Essays in Social Justice (1915)

Concepts of competition and monopoly have proliferated in the fourscore
years since 1890, as analytical fashions and popular attitudes toward the
economy have come and gone from decade to decade.   Changing industrial
events (as they were or merely seemed to be) have shaped some of these
notions: "new competition," for example, is regularly rediscovered during
prosperous times.   There have been many conceptual fads, several major
shifts in emphasis, and some genuine analytical progress, even though most
of the current concepts (including potential competition) were matters of
common discussion as early as 1900.

Yet the nature and scope of market power and its effects are still subject
to great divergence of opinion.   This arises partly from the innate complexity
of the monopoly problem and from the ease with which one may see only a
part of it.   But the disagreements also reflect the fluctuations in debate and
in the economy, and the impressions created by research findings about the
problem.   To understand how the issues are now developing and what their

11

resolution may be, one must retrace their evolution.   For this purpose, the present chapter surveys the main changing views of competition in the United States during the last century.

EARLY VIEWS

The classical school of political economy had a lively concern for the evils of monopoly, whether created by public grants and other restrictions or by private pursuit of gain.   Yet before the first great wave of industrial combinations during 1897–1901 created "the monopoly problem" anew, market power was not regarded as a matter requiring systematic analysis beyond the simple and aberrant case of pure monopoly.   And as neoclassical analysis evolved after 1870 and industrial markets broadened to national scope, many economists and other observers came to regard markets as being, or becoming, essentially competitive.   The occasional city-wide traction trusts, price rings, and market corners here and there, notorious though they each might be, did not seem to require any special analysis, because they were thought to be just departures from the general rule.   Competition was regarded largely as the continuing evolution and interaction of enterprises organized by distinct persons, and was generally assumed to be efficacious.[1]

Industrial consolidation and growth from the Civil War to 1890 did create important cases of market power and abuses, the Standard Oil Trust being the prime instance.[2]   Antipathy to Eastern "moneyed cliques" and a handful of the more notorious Wall Street "villains," came to a focus in Populist struggles against the railroad interests during the 1880's.   But these were supervened by the traumas aroused by the trust wave of 1895 to 1904, which was actually only the peak of a five-phase development of the trust phenomenon.[3]

Public anxiety centered not only on the individual trusts, which were numerous enough, but also on their ties to major financial groupings and, even more broadly, on what seemed to be a tidal rise in the overall concentration of economic power.[4]   It was not just the seeming monopolization of scores of major industries and hundreds of others which stirred concern; in addition, the entire economy seemed to be entering into new and strange

---

[1] See Shorey Peterson, "Antitrust and the Classic Model," *American Economic Review*, XLVII (March 1957), 60–78, and the references to Alfred Marshall, J. B. Clark, and others cited there. Indeed, to some observers, such as Arthur Twining Hadley, *Economics* (New York: Putnam, 1896), Ch. 6; and Jeremiah Jenks, *The Trust Problem*, (New York: McClure, Phillips, 1900), the main need was to prevent the "evils" of excessive competition.

[2] Richard T. Ely, *Monopolies and Trusts* (New York: Macmillan, 1900); and Henry Demarest Lloyd, *Wealth Against Commonwealth* (New York: Modern Library, 1960).

[3] See William Z. Ripley, *Trusts, Pools and Corporations*, rev. ed. (Boston: Ginn, 1916).

[4] John Moody, *The Truth About the Trusts* (Chicago: Moody Publishing Co., 1904); and Donald J. Dewey, *Monopoly in Economics and Law* (Chicago: Rand McNally, 1959) and references cited there.

contours of financial and industrial power. Thus in 1904, as perceptive an observer as John Moody prophesied of the Rockefeller and Morgan financial groups:

> that they are harmonious in nearly all particulars, and that instead of there being danger of their relations ever becoming strained, it will be only a matter of a brief period when one will be more or less completely absorbed by the other, and a grand close alliance will be the natural outcome of conditions which, so far as human foresight can see, can logically have no other result. Around these two groups, or what must ultimately become one greater group, all the other smaller groups of capitalists congregate. They are all allied and intertwined by their various mutual interests.[5]

"Consolidation" was all the rage.[6] This provoked a major crisis of policy during the early 1900's. From the watershed decade of 1900–1910 stem the two major American policies toward monopoly: antitrust and public regulation of privately held utility firms.

Throughout this period, as in others, some of the most highly reputed economists found cause for satisfaction, not concern. By an ironic twist, the neoclassical marginalist revolution had come to orient leading theorists toward (near-) perfect competition.[7] While new developments in the economy seemed to be making monopoly inevitable in most industries, a strong conservative group of economists was persuaded that the opposite was true; or if it was not, that an adequate degree of competition would still somehow prevail. While public discussion and policy recognized that market power had many forms and sources, including its relation to absolute size and financial groupings, economists were coming to think of firms as functioning exclusively as members of individual and distinct markets, and, moreover, as numerous as the many trees "competing" in a forest, in Marshall's simile for market interactions. This, of course, reflected the special neoclassical concern with overall allocation, in an economy composed of an indefinite number of purely competitive markets, rather than with problems and prescriptions for individual markets in the real economy.

This basic division between images of market power in the economy has persisted, with changing details, down to the present day. The common view then was that: (1) new developments, especially in the supposed efficiency of

---

[5] Moody, *op. cit.*, 493.

[6] An excellent review is C. J. Bullock, "Trust Literature: A Survey and Criticism," *Quarterly Journal of Economics*, XV (February 1900–1901), 167–217. Bullock noted skeptically, "It is claimed that a combination can effect a saving in no less than twenty different directions; and the economy arising from such sources is declared to be great enough to give the trust a control over the market based solely upon superior efficiency, and to make competition 'hopeless.' For this reason it is held that such combinations may confer 'enormous' benefits upon society" (p. 191). Bullock urged skepticism of such claims.

[7] J. A. Schumpeter, *History of Economic Analysis* (New York: Macmillan, 1954); Bullock noted J. B. Clark's persistent optimism "that, while large-scale production is economical and giant industrial undertakings are to be the order of the day, competition is certain to continue, nonetheless" (p. 175). Clark was only one among many who were even more optimistic.

large enterprises, were making monopoly structure natural, inevitable, and desirable, and (2) monopoly power could have many sources, some of them outside of the industries in which firms mainly operated. Market power was attributed not only to concentration of control within individual markets but also (rightly or not) to connections and advantages from financial sources, predatory or cutthroat tactics of various kinds, collusion among companies, and advantages of size in and of itself in meeting competition from other firms.

These apparent threats to the competitive character of the economy were finally made tolerable by two major policy developments. One was public regulation, which was intended (with no small touch of optimism) to control "natural monopolies," as they were then thought to be, in the utility sector. The other basic change was in the posture of antitrust towards existing market power. After some early antitrust victories in 1911, the burden of proof that market power was harmful was, in effect, placed upon the antitrust agencies. Roughly speaking, the holders of market power came to be assumed to be innocent unless they could be shown to have gained their market power in an abusive way, or to have exercised that power unreasonably.[8]

Actually, many of the trusts soon lost their grip, such as it may have been, on the market. And economic growth appeared to continue through the 1920's, despite a moderate second merger wave, which filled out and cemented oligopoly structure in many industries (see Chapter 5). Accordingly, one could now lean both ways (as did most economists), believing both that competition was viable and that market consolidation and coordination yielded superior efficiency.

THE 1930's

The 1930's, however, broke this complacency, The Great Depression demonstrated the system's vulnerability to protracted stagnation. It also seemed through some eyes to expose a massive move toward concentration in many industries, as dominant firms survived while lesser firms were swept away. Industrial monopoly became one scapegoat of the depression, because many of the most depressed industries were those heavy goods sectors which had been most highly concentrated since the turn of the century. Their leading firms' market power was thought to enable them to avoid price cutting as demand declined, although price cutting might otherwise have restored them to full-capacity levels of production and employment. Therefore market power, as a cause of price rigidity, was blamed for at least accentuating the depression. Moreover, it appeared to be a spreading rot in the fabric of competitive capitalism itself. These fears were fed by some new empirical

---

[8] For an alternative view on this point, see Dewey, *op. cit.*

studies, purporting to demonstrate the march of monopoly in American industry, although efforts to prove that price rigidity was related to concentration were less successful.[9]

Concurrently, in 1932, there appeared Berle and Means' landmark volume, dealing with the role of large corporations in the economy.[10] Their lesson was twofold: (1) that the traditional character of corporate enterprise was fading because of a growing divorce between ownership and control, and (2) that there would be increasing dominance by giant corporations in the economy, on top of what they endeavored to show as an already large and growing share. This focused on the putative rise in *overall* economic concentration, largely apart from the structure of *individual* markets. Moreover, the rise of industrial giants seemed likely to eclipse further the role of high finance.

All of these parallel trends appeared to toll the knell on competitive capitalism as it seemed, in somewhat roseate retrospect, to have been. Unlike the 1897–1904 episode, new industrial changes now seemed to lead only to syndicalism and the Organic State, rather than to sheer efficiency. And this time much of the economics profession joined in the anxiety, inspired by new economic analyses of monopolistic and imperfect competition as common market conditions.[11] Attention soon focused on oligopoly, an area for theorizing which still defies clear solutions. In any event, the shock of recognition of the real world cast a pall of apprehension among economists. And the subject has not yet shed the atmosphere of crisis, prophetic—occasionally theological—dispute, and hyperbole.

HOPE REASSERTED

But pessimism did not last long. Empirical denials of the fact and relevancy of the administered price hypothesis appeared as early as 1937.[12] Systematic information about industrial concentration, assembled for the first time in 1939, appeared to reveal a great deal of oligopoly, but not very much extreme

---

[9] Arthur R. Burns, *The Decline of Competition* (New York: McGraw-Hill, 1936); Gardiner C. Means, *Industrial Prices and Their Relative Inflexibility*, Senate document 13, 74th Congress, 1st Session, (Washington, D.C.: U.S. Government Printing Office, 1935); Alfred C. Neal, *Industrial Concentration and Price Inflexibility* (New York: American Council on Public Affairs, 1942); and Richard Ruggles, "The Nature of Price Flexibility and the Determinants of Relative Price Changes in the Economy," in G. J. Stigler, ed., *Business Concentration and Price Policy* (Princeton: Princeton University Press, 1955).

[10] Adolf A. Berle and Gardiner C. Means, *The Modern Corporation and Private Property* (New York: Macmillan, 1932), reissued with additional material in 1968 by Harcourt, Brace & World.

[11] Edward H. Chamberlin, *The Theory of Monopolistic Competition*, 8th ed. (Cambridge: Harvard University Press, 1965); and Joan Robinson, *The Economics of Imperfect Competition* (London: Macmillan, 1933).

[12] Don D. Humphrey, "The Nature and Meaning of Rigid Prices, 1890–1933," *Journal of Political Economy*, XLV (October 1937), 651–666; Rufus S. Tucker, "The Reasons for Price Rigidity," *American Economic Review*, XXVII (March 1938), 41–54; and E. S. Mason, "Price Inflexibility," *Review of Economic Statistics*, XX (May 1938), 53–64.

concentration.[13]   The onset of World War II finished off what was already a dwindling public concern.   After massive study, the Temporary National Economic Committee, inaugurated by President Roosevelt in 1938, issued an insipid final report in 1942 to an uninterested public.[14]   Indeed, the War and the new Keynesian analysis helped to restore confidence that the economy would function efficiently if macroeconomic policy were properly managed.

In 1940, John M. Clark reasserted the earlier conservative view in the normative concept of "workable competition."[15]   "Workability" was an imprecise, elastic and variable criterion, embracing behavior and performance as well as structure, and it was capable of rendering acceptable nearly any industry situation.[16]   In some hands, as with the rule of reason doctrine after 1911, the concept came to mean that all industries (even those with maximal market power) were presumed to be acceptably competitive, unless concrete disproof were given, including a showing that a specifiable alternative situation would yield superior results.[17]   Clark's notion was soon adapted to policy purposes—industries in which competition, though imperfect, appeared to be "workable" might expect to escape antitrust attack.

Concurrently, Joseph Schumpeter advanced a more sharply etched and divergent alternative view of competition.[18]   Schumpeter sought to defend both large firms and some degree of market power within individual industries. In his view, the competitive process itself consisted of a series of *disequilibria*, caused by innovations by dominant firms.   Each innovation not only caused a disequilibrium by upsetting the existing pattern of production and market shares, but also was undertaken precisely in the expectation that the disequilibrium would yield monopoly profits to the innovating firm.   Prospects for monopoly profit induced innovation, which then caused disequilibrium, market power, and monopoly profits; but these in turn induced other large firms to undertake further innovations, which would soon take away the original innovator's advantage.   The monopoly profits actually gained by any of the series of innovations might be relatively small—surely smaller than the innovators hoped.   This innovation-monopoly-disequilibrium sequence

---

[13] National Resources Committee, *The Structure of the American Economy, Part 1: Basic Characteristics* (Washington, D.C.: Superintendent of Documents, 1939).

[14] K. Rawley, *The New Deal and the Monopoly Problem* (Austin: University of Texas Press, 1967).

[15] "Toward a Concept of Workable Competition," *American Economic Review*, XXX (June 1940), 241–256.

[16] As an indication of the eventual unwieldiness of the concept, see Stephen H. Sosnick, "A Critique of Concepts of Workable Competition," *Quarterly Journal of Economics*, LXXII (August 1958), 380–423.

[17] J. Markham, "An Alternative Approach to the Concept of Workable Competition," *American Economic Review*, XL (June 1950), 349–361.   Such an *ad hoc* criterion could not, of course, guide antitrust policy, in which each case serves as precedent for others.

"Workability" became a virtual preoccupation in the early 1950's, as nearly every specialist tried to breathe some systematic content into the concept.   Perhaps the definitive elaboration is in Clark's own *Competition as a Dynamic Process* (Washington, D.C.: Brookings, 1961).   Yet "effective" competition, as Clark now called it, was still too diffuse to provide a systematic basis either for describing or prescribing market forms.

[18] In *Capitalism, Socialism and Democracy* (New York: Harper & Row, 1942).

constituted the very heart of competition, in Schumpeter's view, and it generated benefits of technical progress far overshadowing any niceties of marginal misallocation caused as market power flickered on and off.

By contrast (as Chapter 3 will note), the neoclassical system of markets works toward a general equilibrium in which each firm has adjusted to its preferred profit position, and no further change is desired. Competition therefore is largely coequal with equilibrium. Technical progress, fast or slow, is not nearly so integral with this view of the economic process.

In fact (as Parts II and III will show), certain parts of the economy do correspond more closely with the Schumpeterian view than do others, which have relatively static conditions of production and adjustment. Therefore, one need not and *should* not necessarily choose outright between those two views of competition and progress. Nonetheless Schumpeter's point was of primary importance; it stresses that a view of competition framed entirely within the classical allocational framework may omit some of the most important elements of performance and, indeed, of market power and competition themselves.

John Kenneth Galbraith later extended Schumpeter's view, arguing that oligopoly offered perhaps the ideal setting for technical progress.[19] He also argued that oligopoly was inevitable, but that the countervailing power of buyers would usually arise and constrain oligopoly behavior. There followed (in 1954) a brief and acerbic debate over whether countervailing power could be relied on to arise systematically enough to neutralize most pockets of market power, and whether in fact the old and new holders of market power might themselves simply constitute a new, larger unit of unconstrained market power.[20] The verdicts of the profession appear to have been, respectively, "no" and "yes," but after 15 more years there has still been no adequate factual test of the possibilities.

At about this time (1950 to 1954), several exploratory empirical studies appeared purporting to show that competition in the American economy was both predominant and surviving, not small and shrinking.[21] Moreover, new studies of the status of the giant corporations in the economy showed little or no increase in their total share since the 1930's. They also created the notion of "turnover" among all large corporations *as a group*, and asserted that there was much insecurity within the top "ranks."[22] These and other empirical faggots fed the warming fires of optimism, which were already being fanned by the sustained industrial expansion since the War—an expansion which (helped by the Korean War) had exceeded most expectations. As it drew much blame in the 1930's for the collapse, competitive enterprise now came forward to claim much of the credit for the long postwar boom.

[19] John K. Galbraith, *American Capitalism* (Boston: Houghton Mifflin, 1952).
[20] American Economic Association *Papers and Proceedings*, XLIV (May 1954), 1–34.
[21] These studies are noted in Chapters 7 and 10.
[22] Chapter 5 will cover these points.

Meanwhile the study of industrial organization was evolving toward what has become a standard three-part basic schema: structure, behavior and performance. Most fully developed by Joe S. Bain, this analysis assumes that causation runs mainly from market structure through behavior to performance. It was generally recognized from the outset that such causation is not complete, and that some reverse influences—or interactions—may be important. Most systematic research now uses part or all of this framework, and in fact it has become something of a cookbook formula for dissertations on specific industries.

OPTIMISM AND OVERKILL DURING THE 1950's AND 1960's

During the 1950's the divergence of opinion about what market power is, and how much of it there is, widened further, as optimism waxed. One may venture to divide the discussants into several groups.

Taking up a concept current before 1900, Bain focused on potential competition as a possible moderating influence on the behavior of oligopolists.[23] In his view, oligopolistic firms might ordinarily restrain their monopolistic pricing enough to forestall entry by new competitors. If barriers to new competition were "high," market power and its effects could be great.[24] Indeed, Bain's eventual emphasis was that barriers *are* high in many industries. But paradoxically, Bain's stress on potential competition, together with the Schumpeterian view and the notions of workable competition, helped to foster what became known in the 1950's as the New Competition view of American industry. This impressionistic viewpoint stressed interproduct and interindustry competition and rivalry, from which no firms were thought to be wholly insulated. Though price competition might be lacking in oligopolies, there was confidence that *non*price competition (especially via new products) would be at least vigorous, and perhaps extreme. Even where structure was distinctly monopolistic, the behavior of dominant firms might be distinctly competitive. Giant enterprise, while possibly capable of restrictive behavior, was said to be more likely to behave competitively. And markets should be judged by their performance, not by their structure. Therefore, in this view, nothing could be more naïve or irrelevant than equating bigness with market power. And even bigness within an industry might betoken competitiveness—who can compete harder than a powerful corporation?

Far from being new, most of the points were revivals of notions from ancient decades, and they possessed little new relevance or force.[25] The

[23] "Pricing in Monopoly and Oligopoly," *American Economic Review*, XXXIX (March 1949), 448–464.
[24] Joe S. Bain, *Barriers to New Competition* (Cambridge: Harvard University Press, 1956).
[25] Edward S. Mason, "The New Competition," *The Yale Review*, Autumn, 1953, 37–48; George W. Stocking, "Saving Free Enterprise from its Friends," *Southern Economic Journal*, XIX (April 1953), 431–444; and Bullock, *op. cit.*

supposed primacy of "radical change," "dynamic processes," and the "imperatives of large scale" were, in the 1950's as in the 1890's, primarily a way of dismissing problems rather than exploring them. Change may seem to the impressionable to be pervasive, but its optimum relationship to market structure and to other goals is no simple matter. Yet some observers saw in all this a "new era" for business, in which antitrust could serve only to harrass efficient enterprises and damage the mainsprings of industrial progress.[26]

This train of thought also complemented the view of Berle and others about the modern corporation's social role.[27] Even where competitive pressure was lacking (despite the New Competitive view), large corporations might be relied upon to exercise social stewardship and make the right social choices in governing industry. Indeed, in a Spencerian view these enterprises had survived the competitive struggle and therefore were fit for statesmanship, and business leaders were regarded as well suited to the role of social arbiters and benefactors. This optimism was infectious, and indeed this view has continued as a major tenet of the business creed.[28] Whether or not it is valid, it has been influential; those many who view discretionary business power with misgivings have also stressed that it exists.[29]

As for the role of size, one can now see that it *was* important to counter the extravagant earlier claims that bigness invariably provides market power. Although the size of a firm relative to the total distribution of firms (and potential competitors) *is* commonly one element of market power, it is important to keep that role in perspective (as Chapters 3, 5, and 9 try to do). Yet the recent discussants were clearly guilty of overkill on the bigness question, with such assertions as this:

> Since the origin of that specialized but very broadly defined area of economic inquiry known as Industrial Organization, the more methodical and more rigorous practitioners of antitrust economics have struggled mightily to prove that there really was a difference between bigness and monopoly power to those less trained in the tools of economic analysis. In sum, "market power" and "bigness" are simply, like obesity and pregnancy, different conditions requiring different remedies.[30]

Overkill also occurred in the attempt to dispel earlier exaggerations that vertical integration might usually extend market power from one stage of

[26] For example, "Antitrust in an Era of Radical Change," *Fortune*, March 1966, 128–131.
[27] See Adolf A. Berle, *The Twentieth Century Capitalist Revolution* (New York: Harcourt, Brace & World, 1954); also Edward S. Mason, *The Corporation in Modern Society* (Cambridge: Harvard University Press, 1959).
[28] A current version is that only big business is capable of solving problems of racial discrimination and urban decay, and that it will actually do so; see Chapters, 5, 14 and 15.
[29] For example, Ben W. Lewis, "Economics by Admonition," American Economic Association, *Papers and Proceedings*, XLIV (May 1959), 384–398.
[30] Jesse W. Markham, "The Present War on Bigness: II," in *The Impact of Antitrust on Economic Growth* (New York: National Industrial Conference Board, 1965).

production to another.[31] In a setting of perfect competition, indeed, no leverage can occur, but only extremists would then assert that vertical integration may be presumed irrelevant to market power in real industries—on the contrary, it may have a large impact.[32]

Meanwhile, the main lines of antitrust policy, in what was widely thought to mark a distinct step forward, came to rely increasingly on horizontal market structure (particularly market shares) in defining market power. Market shares and trends in industry concentration increasingly took center stage in antitrust evaluations and decisions, and they seemed to provide a simple, direct, and concrete approach to defining and attacking market power. This has stemmed partly from the continuing publication by the Census Bureau of concentration ratios (for 1947, 1954, 1958, 1963, and 1966) across the whole spectrum of manufacturing industries. Another effect of this new emphasis was to tighten the focus of antitrust enforcement on industrial cases where, after all, concentration ratios are available and relatively easy to calculate. Yet there have been almost no direct efforts during the last 15 years to reduce concentration, only to restrain its rise through merger. This double standard toward mergers and existing concentration has had the effect of acquiescing in the positions of the established leading firms in highly concentrated industries.[33]

Skeptics and critics in the professional ranks have countered some of the more extravagant policy proposals of the optimists. Joel B. Dirlam and Alfred E. Kahn rejected performance as the sole criterion for antitrust policy, arguing rightly that it would paralyze action.[34] But most economists (especially those doing empirical analysis, including the present writer) have relied increasingly on concentration information. Perhaps the most important of these studies was by Carl Kaysen and Donald F. Turner in 1959.[35] In adopting a structural view of market power, and finding "close" or "tight" oligopoly to suggest unreasonable market power, they focused primarily upon formal internal structure, particularly market shares. Although Kaysen and Turner did take a hard line against these few elements of market power, they inevitably attenuated their policy position by framing market power in such simplified terms. Moreover, their main proposal—that tight oligopolies should be broken up at government initiative—was unlikely to

[31] Joseph J. Spengler, "Vertical Integration and Antitrust Policy," *Journal of Political Economy*, LVIII (August 1950), 347–352 and Robert Bork, "Vertical Integration and the Sherman Act: The Legal History of an Economic Misconception," *University of Chicago Law Review*, XXII (Autumn 1954), 157–201.
[32] See Bain, *Industrial Organization, op. cit.*, Chapters 9 and 10; and Walter Adams and Joel B. Dirlam, "Steel Imports and Vertical Oligopoly Power," *American Economic Review*, LIV (September 1964), 626–655.
[33] Donald J. Dewey, *op. cit.*; and John K. Galbraith, *The New Industrial State* (Boston: Houghton Mifflin, 1967), Ch. 16.
[34] Joel B. Dirlam and Alfred E. Kahn, *Fair Competition* (Ithaca: Cornell University Press, 1954).
[35] Carl Kaysen and Donald F. Turner, *Antitrust Policy* (Cambridge: Harvard University Press, 1959).

achieve any practical application, and indeed it has not, even with Turner himself directing the Antitrust Division during 1965–1968. So, paradoxically, this sharp attack on market power may have helped to narrow the foundations of antitrust policy and to weaken its potential grasp.

Meanwhile, perfect competition gained favor in the 1950's as the economist's usual assumption in framing general economic models. As elsewhere, theory interplays with reality, and this trend of analysis has promoted increasing confidence among economists that actual market activity (except perhaps for a few special cases) does approximate neoclassical competition in all essentials. This has been paralleled by fashions in theories of oligopoly. In the 1930's and 1940's, Paul M. Sweezy, William J. Fellner, Bain, and others had stressed the rigidities and cooperation which oligopoly might entail.[36] Yet, concurrently, the analysis of full-cost pricing assumed away interdependence among rivals, and possible rigidities and joint action among them.[37] In the 1950's William J. Baumol added to this the hypothesis that oligopolists commonly maximize their sales, or growth, rather than just profits; far from being restrictive colluders, they may be vigorous expansionists.[38] Moreover, many of those who still consider concentration a basis for market power (such as Bain) were hopeful that it will be heavily eroded by industry growth.[39] All in all, there has been growing confidence that collusion (and even formal cartels) is inherently futile, since participants have strong incentives to chisel. Indeed, it is now frequently asserted that most cooperative efforts are no more than feeble and transient.

The main drift of quantitative research has, partly inadvertently, reinforced these analytical predilections. Several possible effects of market power, such as those on profitability, price rigidity, and technical change, have shown up only weakly in the first results of exploratory analyses. Some others have, so far, shown no trace at all, even under fairly thorough study. Since much of the search for proof of effects is still in its infancy, these first returns can only be suggestive. Yet they have encouraged a growing belief that structural monopoly really *does* have little or no effect. These studies (including some by the present writer) have relied upon Census concentration ratios as the main indicator of market power, largely because those ratios are easily available. To those willing to believe that if one cannot measure X on the first try, then X doesn't exist, the scattered empirical findings have made it possible to "show" that concentration is inconsequen-

---

[36] Paul M. Sweezy, "Demand Under Conditions of Oligopoly," *Journal of Political Economy*, XLVII (August 1939), 568–573; and William J. Fellner, *Competition Among the Few* (New York: Norton, 1949).

[37] See R. B. Heflebower, "Full Costs, Cost Changes and Prices," in Stigler, ed., *op. cit.*, 361–396, and references cited there.

[38] See William J. Baumol, "On the Theory of Expansion of the Firm," *American Economic Review*, LII (December 1962), 1078–1087, and references cited there.

[39] Bain, *Industrial Organization, op. cit.*; the point is discussed further and tested in Chapter 11.

tial. Rightly or not (see Chapters 11–14), the research focus on concentration has encouraged nihilism.[40]

All this has put the traditional trustbusters (or "Populists," the current term of belittlement) on the defensive—perhaps deservedly so, perhaps not. In the cruelest irony of all, concentration ratios have boomeranged on them; whereas at first the ratios established how massive the concentration problem was, they are now commonly interpreted to suggest instead that concentration is only moderate and, more important, tolerable—possibly, even, *necessary* for industrial progress. Against this, the Populists, or true conservatives, have ventured two main counterattacks: (1) against administered prices (once again) as a sign of harmful market power, and (2) against conglomerates as a threat to competition. "Administered," or stable, quoted prices, are common in basic heavy industries, and these served as targets for a prolonged attack on pricing behavior in several major industries during the late 1950's by Senator Kefauver's Subcommittee on Antitrust and Monopoly.[41] Oddly enough, although most economists have remained unconvinced that such pricing patterns do prove the exercise of market power, administered prices are an article of faith (and of hope) at the highest levels of government in most advanced economies. Accordingly, major firms in major industries are regularly exhorted or pressured to adjust prices and other activities in line with the national interest, so viewed.[42]

More recently, the attack has shifted to conglomerate, or diversified, enterprise.[43] But, as yet, little evidence has been developed to prove the effect of conglomerate ties, either good or bad, beyond the vague and old-fashioned notion that the parent firm's "deep pocket" may cross-subsidize specific branches in "unfair" or "predatory" competitive tactics.[44] There are ample indications abroad, especially in Japan, that extensive diversification is at best a mixed blessing. Yet so far the attack on conglomerates as a threat to competition has stalled, perhaps fortunately so, for lack of empirical confirmation. The small burst of antitrust action against conglomerate

---

[40] Perhaps the most nihilistic is Donald J. Dewey, "Competitive Policy and National Goals: The Doubtful Relevance of Antitrust," in Almarin Phillips, ed., *Perspectives on Antitrust Policy* (Princeton: Princeton University Press, 1965). See also George J. Stigler, *Capital and Rates of Return in Manufacturing Industries* (Princeton: Princeton University Press, 1963); Arnold Harberger, "Monopoly and Resource Allocation," American Economic Association *Papers and Proceedings*, XLIV (May 1954), 77–87.

[41] U.S. Senate Subcommittee on Antitrust and Monopoly, Hearings and Reports on *Administered Prices* in the automobile, steel, and drug industries, Vols. 1–32 (Washington, D.C.: U.S. Government Printing Office; 1957–1961); see also Estes Kefauver, *In a Few Hands* (New York: Random House, 1965).

[42] Ben W. Lewis, *op. cit.*; and John Sheahan, *The Wage-Price Guidelines* (Washington: Brookings 1968).

[43] Corwin D. Edwards, *Maintaining Competition* (New York: McGraw-Hill, 1949); Stigler, *Business Concentration and Price Policies, op. cit.*, 331–360; and U.S. Senate Subcommittee on Antitrust and Monopoly, 88th Congress, 2nd Session, *Hearings on Economic Concentration, Part 1* (Washington, D.C.: U.S. Government Printing Office, 1964) and *Part 3* (1965), 1398–1426.

[44] For the best articulated skeptical view about the threat of conglomerates, see Donald F. Turner, "Conglomerate Mergers and Section 7 of the Clayton Act," *Harvard Law Review*, LXXVIII (May 1965).

mergers in 1969 has had to rely on general fears of overall concentration rather than on firm indications of their competitive role.

Evidently opinions and theory have seesawed since 1890, reflecting both changing (or seemingly changing) industrial events and developments in economic theory and its uses. The long trend has been to focus down to market shares and to look for empirical evidence that high shares do have an impact on market results. In proper perspective, these are sound developments, but they have recently been carried beyond moderation. The looseness and oversimplifications which arose during the 1950's led to more than a mere displacement of Cassandra by Pangloss. They have put careful and sophisticated analysts, testing concepts against complex reality, on the defensive via sweeping theoretical assertions. The rush to "test" concepts empirically has degenerated frequently into a sort of scientism, in which a lack of findings in a faulty test using slender evidence was asserted to disprove the existence of otherwise likely phenomena.

Ultimately, the main drift of expert opinion has been in three main, and convergent, directions: (1) Market structure is regarded mainly as a matter of concentration. (2) The natural structure and behavior of most markets are now commonly thought to be competitive in essential respects. (3) The lack of evidence of actual effect of concentration has suggested that structural monopoly, where it does exist, has few significant effects, except possibly in promoting technical progress.

In light of their origins, one must regard these views skeptically. There is good reason to review the empirical evidence on the whole topic of market power—its forms, determinants, and effects—as Parts II and III attempt to do. But first, and equally important, the elements which may comprise market power need to be examined conceptually and placed in some relation to each other and to their possible effects. That is the aim of the next two chapters.

Chapter 3

Determinants and Forms
of Market Power

It is not possible, nor will it ever be possible, by
calculating market shares, dividing price minus marginal cost
by price, or other hocus pocus, to present an unambiguous
measure of the degree of monopoly.   Market power has
many dimensions.

EDWARD S. MASON
" Market Power and Business Conduct" (1956)

The true elements of market power have been a matter of sharp and continuing debate, and opinions have often run to extremes.   This chapter's
outline of the main elements is therefore ventured with all due modesty as
a plausible framework upon which to arrange the empirical findings of
Part II.   These findings in turn may suggest further revisions in the concepts
of market power.

    This chapter also outlines the probable determinants of market power,
again in a preliminary spirit.   These outlines extend and embroider the
conventional neoclassical analysis of competition, monopoly, and oligopoly
in several ways.   The following brief review of that familiar analysis is
meant to point up what the extensions are and why they make sense.   Such
a review is also needed to define the effects of market power on prices, profits,
and efficiency, which will come in for measurement later in the volume
(Chapters 12 and 13).

ALLOCATION UNDER PERFECT COMPETITION AND MONOPOLY

Neoclassical analysis of allocation has customarily posited a variety of market shares for the firm—negligible in perfect competition, small in monopolistic competition, moderate in oligopoly, and total in monopoly— and then deduced the behavior in each setting.[1] The firm's share is usually taken as a given, set by costs or other determinants; market structure is then assumed to shape behavior via an essentially unilateral causation from structure to behavior.

The outcome under perfect competition has been known in all essentials since the work of W. Stanley Jevons and Leon Walras nearly a century ago. This outcome remains basic to an understanding of market power and its costs. Imagine that each market for inputs and outputs contains many small participants. Each has full knowledge and mobility to adjust quickly in maximizing its own welfare. None is large enough to affect the prices of the goods which it sells or buys. There are no barriers to movement in and out of markets. The firms are all small because it is most efficient to be so; "optimum" size (at which the average cost curve has a definite low point) is small relative to the whole market.

Now we focus our microscope on a single-product firm, which is producing in one of these competitive industries and buying its inputs (labor, capital, raw materials) in perfectly competitive factor markets. The firm's cost curves may be like those shown in Figure 3.1. At small levels of output, average cost is high, but it declines as the level of output increases. This reflects "economies of scale," as inputs are combined in technically appropriate proportions and levels. However, "diseconomies of scale" are encountered at still higher output levels, as (1) the fixed factor (space, a talented manager, etc.) is increasingly stretched thin or crowded by the other factors, or (2) sheer problems of disorganization and control loss arise. These, it is assumed, preclude the simple proliferation of more identical plants at constant costs. If such proliferation were possible, average costs might be constant over an indefinite range of size.

The differing costs at various output levels are reflected not only in average cost but also in marginal cost, which is at each output level the added cost of another bit of output. At the point of lowest average cost—often called the "optimum size"—marginal cost precisely equals average total cost, as shown in Figure 3.1.

These cost curves reflect the technical production conditions of the firm *and* the prevailing prices of the inputs which the firm uses. The use of each

---

[1] See, among others, Donald S. Watson, *Price Theory in Action* (Boston: Houghton Mifflin, 1963); William J. Baumol, *Economy Theory and Operations Analysis*, rev. ed., (Englewood Cliffs, N.J.: Prentice-Hall, 1966); Joe S. Bain, *Industrial Organization*, rev. ed., (New York: Wiley, 1967); William J. Fellner, *Competition Among the Few* (New York: Norton, 1949); and R. E. Kuenne, *Monopolistic Competition Theory: Studies in Impact* (New York, Wiley, 1967).

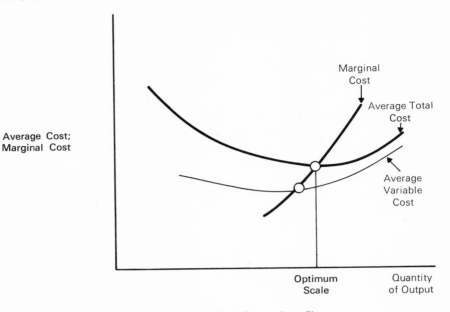

Figure 3.1 "Typical" Cost Curves for a Firm.

variable input (such as labor, machinery, or raw materials) will depend on the price of the *input*, its marginal productivity, and the price of output. Each input will be used up to the point at which its cost per unit (that is, the price paid for it) is no more than the value of the output it adds. If the price of the firm's output rises, or if technical progress increases the physical productivity of the input, the firm may use more of the input. A cut in the price of the input will also induce the firm to increase its use, and vice versa. At equilibrium, then, each input's marginal contribution to the value of the product just equals its price.

How much will this competitive firm produce? *Taking price as given,* the firm will produce just up to the point at which marginal cost equals the going market price. This output level yields the firm a maximum profit, or minimum loss; and it indirectly determines the amounts and combinations of inputs. If price goes down below average total cost but is still above average variable cost (such as at P_1 in Figure 3.2), the firm will produce at Q_1 in the short run, but will close down as soon as its fixed capacity wears out. If not even variable costs can be covered (P_2 in Figure 3.2), the firm will shut down immediately.

If market price rises above minimum average cost (at P_3) the firm will hire more inputs and expand output (to Q_3). At that point, the firm will reap some "excess" profits. The profits are "excess" because they are more than is necessary to say for managerial services and cover capital costs (interest plus a risk factor) in order to keep the firm alive over the long run.

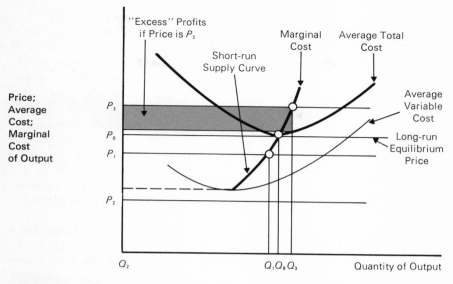

Figure 3.2 Output Choices by a Perfect Competitor, for Alternative Given Prices.

Yet under perfect competition, such "excess" profits may be stopped almost immediately. Because knowledge and mobility are perfect, other firms will immediately enter. The industry supply curve will accordingly shift out, and the equilibrium market price will decline until, in the long-run equilibrium, the price is at P_0 and all firms are producing at their optimum size.

In this all-competitive model, other markets also react in the same way to temporary jogs away from long-run equilibrium. Output will everywhere reach the "optimum" scale of production, and the marginal value of each factor in each use will equal its price. And at those margins, the value which society places on each good (shown by the *price* consumers are willing to pay for it) will be just equal to the society's real cost or sacrifice in producing that unit (as shown by its *marginal cost*). Accordingly the allocation of resources will be efficient: no readjustment at the margin, anywhere, could provide a net gain in total output and in total welfare. In every market, the price accurately reflects social value at the margin, and *market* costs precisely reflect the true cost to society of additional production.

This is the modern form of Adam Smith's "invisible hand," acting through decentralized adjustment under perfectly competitive market conditions. But this outcome is valid only within the confines of the underlying assumptions. This optimum may leave the distribution of wealth and income completely "unfair" (by whatever standards of "fairness;" see Chapter 4). It will ignore external effects of private behavior, thereby possibly causing divergences between *market* (or "private") costs and *real* (or "social") costs. Thus factories may pollute air and water, urban life may become intolerable, natural resources may be destroyed, etc., both because and in spite of competitive market activity. Also, the optimum will fail to provide for "public goods," such as education, roads, law enforcement, and—to use the ancient example—even lighthouses. Only within narrow limits, therefore, is the competitive optimum really optimum. Moreover, technological progress lies largely outside this competitive system. It may not be possible for an innovator to reap very large rewards for innovating. On the other hand, conditions do guarantee that once an innovation becomes available, for whatever reason, those who do not imitate it will succumb, because all others *will* imitate it.

The next step in reviewing allocation is to introduce monopoly into one market within the system. Imagine that all firms in one industry are brought under one owner, who also can in some way keep out all others. He will then, of course, reduce output and raise price in order to reap monopolist's profits; in earlier ages, this was "forestalling, engrossing, and regrating." In this polar case, the monopoly firms' demand curve is the total industry demand curve itself as shown in Figure 3.3. If all costs remain unchanged by this merger, the firm's marginal cost curve is the industry's former short-run supply curve. Since entry is now barred, this curve is now both the short- and the long-run marginal cost curve for this firm.

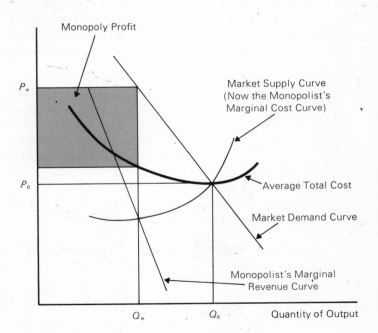

Figure 3.3   The Effects of Monopoly-by-merger.

The monopolist now has a "marginal revenue curve," showing the extra revenue he gets from selling each extra bit of output. It lies inside the down-sloping demand curve, as shown in Figure 3.3, because each extra unit sold knocks down the price on all the others; the added revenue to be gained from each is less than its price. Profits are highest at Q_m, at which marginal revenue equals marginal cost: the Q_m unit (and no more) is just "worth" producing. The resulting price is P_m and the monopolist pockets the profit shown by the shaded area. The conditions of efficient allocation no longer hold. Output is cut back to about half the former level, at which its price (benefit) now equals its marginal cost, and so the use of inputs is also cut well below previous optimum levels. By driving a wedge between social cost and social productivity, the monopolist causes an allocation which could be improved upon—that is, a misallocation.

In general, disproportional market power is associated with restriction of output and factor use below the levels consistent with efficient static allocation in the economy as a whole.[2] Society will gain if resources are reallocated toward greater output in monopolistic industries. The excess profits of monopoly are only a corollary of inefficient static allocation and are often a means for further protecting and strengthening market power. Those profits will also customarily increase inequality in the distribution of wealth and income.

The firm's market share may be only 50 percent or 10 percent, rather than 100 percent. This lesser market power will simply mean a proportionally weaker restriction of output and degree of misallocation, assuming all other competitors to be negligibly small. The excess profits will also be less, perhaps tending toward zero for very small shares under such so-called monopolistic competition.

INDETERMINACY UNDER OLIGOPOLY AND BILATERAL MONOPOLY

If other firms also have substantial shares, there results oligopoly, in which the few market leaders recognize their mutual interdependence. Each oligopolist must try to anticipate the reactions of the others to his own moves. But since this is all mutual, the outcomes of alternative strategies and actions are uncertain, and the resulting interactions may range from sustained warfare to the close cooperation of a "shared monopoly." This diversity of possible outcomes is deepened by the great variety of possible (1) oligopoly structures, differing in concentration, inequality among the leaders, and other elements, and (2) competitive attitudes and motives among

---

[2] If there is some degree of monopoly in all markets, the basic point still applies to industries which are unusually monopolistic: see Richard G. Lipsey and Kelvin Lancaster, "The General Theory of Second Best," *Review of Economic Studies*, XXIV (October 1956), 11–32. The full complexities of this question need not be explored for the present purposes.

the rivals. The range of possibilities is very wide, and the market may oscillate between the extremes.[3]

No general "theory" of oligopoly yet exists—there are only models for some of the many specific subtypes of oligopolies. One early model posits a pair of demand curves for the oligopolist, as shown in Figure 3.4. If rivals always respond to the firm's price adjustments, then the firm's demand curve has a lower elasticity than if rival firms never respond. The two demand curves therefore represent the indeterminacy faced by the oligopolist, and they show the outside limits of likely outcomes for this firm.[4]

If the oligopolist expects aggressive, hostile behavior from his rivals (that is, if he is pessimistic, or timid, or both), he may assume that rivals will follow his price cuts but not his price increases. These conjectures will lead him to behave as though his demand curve has a kink, as shown in Figure 3.4. Corresponding to this kink is an actual *discontinuity* in the composite marginal revenue curve. The firm, as always, sets output where marginal cost equals marginal revenue. Therefore, the discontinuity in marginal revenue at Q_0 means that the firm will choose Q_0 even though marginal cost may vary between MC_1 and MC_2. It also indicates that the firm's *output* will be relatively rigid. Note also that price will exceed marginal cost, perhaps substantially.

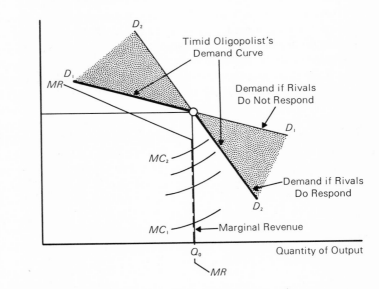

Figure 3.4   The Timid Oligopolist's "Kinked" Demand Curve.

[3] Fellner, *op cit.*; see also Bain, *op. cit.*, and Edward H. Chamberlin, *The Theory of Monopolistic Competition*, 8th ed., (Cambridge: Harvard University Press, 1965).
[4] See Paul M. Sweezy, "Demand Under Conditions of Oligopoly," *Journal of Political Economy*, XLVII (August 1939), 568–573; also Baumol, *op. cit.*

Kinked demand curve analysis treats the oligopolist as an independent, if timid, agent. The "kink" model is more fitted to a secondary oligopolist, or perhaps to one of several equal-sized dominant firms. Its defensive character would hardly suit a clearly dominant firm atop a group of smaller firms. The main available analysis for such firms concerns their choices between reaping profits now and maintaining their market shares. If barriers against new competitors (perhaps large firms eager to move in) are low, dominant firms may suffer and/or tolerate inroads if their prices are set high enough to extract all possible current profits. In fact, long-run profit maximizing may often lead dominant firms knowingly to yield their market shares, gradually or rapidly.[5] Yet, oligopolists may instead deliberately restrain prices in order to limit or forestall entry.

Another way of depicting the choices open to oligopolists is "game theory." Strategy toward rivals permeates many important oligopoly decisions; prime examples are automobile price and model changes and steel prices. The actual mixture of combat and cooperation will change as conditions change. Some of these conditions can be framed in models, illustrating the preconditions for price rings, wars-to-the-finish, and other sequences which actually crop up in oligopolies. Yet despite the high hopes which it inspired when it first appeared after World War II, game theory has not yet proven very helpful in analyzing and predicting behavior in actual markets.[6] Still another approach simply assumes away interdependence, holding that oligopolists may instead maximize their sales or their growth.[7] But each of these approaches treats only a facet, or special subtype, oligopoly, and many of these subtypes have hardly been touched. Therefore oligopoly still presents a range of indeterminacy between the competitive and monopoly outcomes.

To this point, the analysis has dealt with sellers, on the assumption that buyers are perfectly competitive and therefore passive toward sellers. Suppose instead that there is (to take an extreme case) but one buyer facing one seller. The outcome is, as under oligopoly, largely unpredictable.[8] The buyer's countervailing power may enable him to enforce a price as low as competitive sellers would have descended to; or the seller may prevail at the original monopoly price; or some sharing of the spoils may result. A monopoly (or oligopoly) position may be eroded by horizontal intrusion from competitive sellers, or "from the other side of the market by strong buyers." But Galbraith's claim, that "as a common rule, we can rely on countervailing power to appear as a curb on economic power" is subject to doubt, as was noted in Chapter 2 above.

---

[5] See Dean W. Worcester, Jr., "Why 'Dominant' Firms Decline," *Journal of Political Economy*, LXV (August 1957), 338–346, and his *Monopoly, Big Business and Welfare in the Postwar United States* (Seattle: University of Washington Press, 1967); also George J. Stigler, *The Theory of Price*, rev. ed. (New York: Macmillan, 1952), Chapter 13.

[6] A. G. Papandreou and J. T. Wheeler, *Competition and Its Regulation* (Englewood Cliffs, N.J.: Prentice-Hall, 1954), and Martin Shubik, *Market Strategy and Economic Theory* (New York: Wiley, 1959).

[7] Baumol, *op. cit.*, Chapters 13 and 14.

[8] See George J. Stigler, *The Theory of Price*, 3rd ed. (New York: Macmillan, 1966), 207–208.

From even this brief review of allocation theory under differing market conditions, one can note several special features of the analysis. First, market structure is assumed to embody crystal-clear lines of corporate identity and ownership. Minority control, informal groupings (no matter how tight), joint agencies, and other such line-blurrings are treated as special cases or as matters of enterprise "behavior." Second, structure is regarded as *given* for analytical purposes (*if* A-structure, *then* B-allocation), rather than as a changeable composite of elements which interact with each other and with "behavior." Third, each market is taken in isolation, as though its internal structure of market shares is all that matters. These simplifications are perfectly correct in framing a general analysis of allocation. But they are no less caricatures because they are deliberate.

Their lessons are forceful enough: monopolists may hold output to as little as half of the competitive level (if average costs are constant). A small degree of market power may have only slight impact, while oligopolists and bilateral monopolists may gyrate between shared-monopoly and extreme competitive outcomes. Since oligopoly comes in numerous forms and shades, no general results can be specified, apart from a loose relation between market concentration and degree of monopoly impact. Structure may, in any case, sharply influence both allocation and (by enriching monopolists) distribution. But, by contrast, the models derive no clear influence of structure upon technical progress, growth, and other economic goals; these stand largely outside the analysis.

POINTS OF EXTENSION

The elaboration, or application, of this body of theory in evaluating actual market power may extend in several directions. First, there are more forms than just market share in which a firm may seek, possess, and exploit market power.[9] Some of these are "informal," that is, not shown in formal and direct patterns of company ownership and control. Entry barriers are one of these; others will be noted shortly. They may be complex, as in the relative conditions of bilateral oligopoly.

Second, these elements tend to be plastic and partly substitutable. Firms seeking maximum market position and profits (virtually all firms) continually choose and adjust among them as their opportunities and constraints shift. As a prime instance of this, no rational firm goes all out in the long run to maximize its formal share in any market. This can be shown most simply by the firm's choice on the margin between two directions of market power: market share and cooperation with rival firms. A dominant firm will find it increasingly expensive to buy out the remaining small com-

---

[9] See also Carl Kaysen and Donald F. Turner, *Antitrust Policy* (Cambridge: Harvard University Press, 1959), and Bain, *op. cit.*, for the general framework.

petitors; as they grow fewer, each realizes its nuisance value and can hold out for it more steadfastly. Meanwhile, the net gains from swallowing them up decline progressively once the bulk of the market is in hand. The point beyond which further mergers do not pay may be well short of the entire market.[10] Because (absent perfect antitrust enforcement against collusion) cooperation with the fringe firms will also offer positive gains, the leading firm will find it most profitable to stop even before reaching this zero-net-gain point for mergers. If the aspiring monopolists move stealthily, of course, the unalerted small firms may sell out cheaply. But monopoly so gained may be short-lived; once known, it may attract new firms, which must be bought out or bought off in some way.

This margin between concentration and collusion will be at even lower market shares if there are several relatively equal leading firms. If any one of them moves to increase its share markedly, each or perhaps a coalition of the others can retaliate or threaten to retaliate smartly enough to make the first firm's move quite unprofitable. What happens when the leading group is asymmetrical (with one firm dominant) is discussed later in this chapter.

Third, the effects of market power are many—not just the efficiency which fits neatly in standard theory (plus possibly distribution). In addition, the internal efficiency of the firm may be weakened under market power.[11] Also, technical progress may be sharply affected; even if the effects are relatively weak, their long-run importance may transcend those of static misallocation.

Fourth, the causes, forms and effects of market power interact. This obvious point has been long recognized but has been recently underplayed. The costs of a firm may be influenced by its ability to extract low input prices. Profits (an "effect") may be used (as a "cause") to strengthen market power. In other ways, too, the unidirectional triad of causes-forms-effects may be too simple; and factual appraisals cannot expect to find clear evidence relating any two elements within this whole tissue of interrelations. As a conceptual matter, each form of market power—and each relation with an effect—can be understood as operating with the others held constant. When, as in fact, they all act simultaneously, the whole phenomenon is clearly complex even to visualize, much less to measure.

GENERAL FEATURES OF MARKET POWER

Market power is the ability of a market participant to influence price, quantity, and the nature of the product in the market. In its use of market power, as with all other activities of the firm, the firm's main aim usually

---

[10] See Donald J. Dewey, *Monopoly in Economics and Law* (Chicago: Rand McNally, 1959), 25–31.
[11] See particularly Harvey Leibenstein, "Allocation Efficiency vs. 'X-Efficiency'," *American Economic Review*, LVI (June 1966), 392–415.

is to improve and maximize its long-run profitability. A firm with market power will be able to reap—in the short run, the long run, or both—profits whose levels and degree of security are above those that can be reached under competition.

Market power is held by firms, but it is exercised in markets. It may arise from causes external to the market in which it is applied. Thus, it is not simply a feature of either the buying or the selling side of an industry. In fact, many enterprises operate at several vertically related market levels, including buying inputs, processing or combining them in one or more stages, and selling the resulting outputs or services. Market power may be gained and applied at any of these levels. The firm itself aims at widening the gap between its total revenues and total costs over some time horizon; this horizon may be as short as a month or a week (as in cornering a commodity) or as long as decades (as in many industrial markets). As J. B. Clark recognized long ago, net income may be enlarged either by adjusting prices or quantities sold, or by pushing down prices of inputs (as well as revising the quantity of inputs per unit of output, which is usually referred to as technical change).[12] For each such move, there are often many alternative strategies which the firm may use and combine.

Market power, therefore, may have several sources at various levels of the firm, a variety of (partly) interchangeable forms, and a number of different (ultimately observable) effects. We may infer the presence of market power from any of these—from its sources, forms, or effects—but ordinarily the forms are the most direct and reliable indicators. Market power is a matter both of strength and duration. Despite the growing emphasis on "permanent" market structure, great market power, briefly held, may be as significant as lesser market power which persists.

The sources and elements of structural monopoly may lie either within the market or outside it, although the rewards of market power are reaped within it. Market power may be gained by socially meritorious behavior of one sort or another (as through innovation which yields, as a side effect, net social benefits) as well as by a straightforward attempt to amass control. Moreover, firms possessing market power may often behave "competitively" —voluntarily or under threat—and they may frequently achieve "good" performance in one or several directions. Yet, the possibility, or even a proof, of good performance effects does not entitle one to believe (as some do) that market power does not exist.

Structural monopoly is essentially a matter of probabilities. The sources and elements yield market power only with some degree of likelihood; for example, high concentration in a market *probably* means high market power, but not *certainly* so. A careful observer will not expect to specify or to find elements which absolutely and immutably prove that market power is

---

[12] John B. Clark, *The Control of Trusts* (New York: Macmillan, 1901).

present. Since market power can assume many forms and many mixtures of these elements, the presence of any one or group of them only indicates with some *degree of likelihood* that market power is actually present; as Sherlock Holmes would put it, "the probability lies in that direction." Accordingly, the concepts of market power need *not* fit the conventional legal criteria for evidentiary proof in, say, antitrust prosecutions.[13] Moreover, the elements of market power may be perfectly real even though they may not be easily measurable themselves, either with existing or likely future data. Lord Kelvin's truth—that that which cannot be measured does not exist—must not be stretched too far or caricatured. Precise and easy measurability *now* is not a binding criterion on theory or research design (although it obviously is desirable and helpful for informing public policy).

DETERMINANTS OF MARKET STRUCTURE

Over the years quite a number of influences on market structure have been imagined, some rather general, vague, and variable, others quite precise. One general determinant may be the "growth stages" of industry. Actually there are two related versions: (1) that each industry progresses from monopoly to competition as it matures, and (2) that old industries shrivel into tight and collusive oligopolies.[14] The mechanism for change is, unfortunately, not clear. It cannot be just time, for industries "live" at different rates, some fast, some very slow indeed. Many industries insist on being reborn periodically with basic innovations. Indeed, some industries seem to do it backward; the automobile industry for example, has gone from low to very high concentration as it "matures."

As a second general determinant, one may expect stability of technical and demand conditions of an industry to encourage the development of market power. Conversely, uncertainty and change tend to corrode, both by upsetting established patterns and weakening the mutual responses which have been laboriously learned over time, and by holding out real or imagined possibilities to new entrants, who might otherwise stay out. However, one must not push the point too far; stability need not always breed market power, and really extreme degrees of uncertainty and change will usually be biased against survival of relatively small firms who may have thinner resources.

A third possible general determinant, the relative conditions of information in and outside the market, has by contrast a somewhat clearer role.

---

[13] This point is important, because much earlier analysis (such as of "workable competition") was limited by legal-economic traditions to framing competition essentially in antitrust terms, for guidance in enforcement proceedings. This not only mixed normative elements into a positive research problem; it also led to oversimplification.

[14] See U.S. Senate Subcommittee on Antitrust and Monopoly, 88th Congress, 2nd Session, *Hearings on Economic Concentration, Part 1* (Washington, D.C.: U.S. Government Printing Office, 1964), 138–41; also Bain, *op. cit.*

The more there is specialized knowledge and inside information about prices, sales, costs, and profits, both present and future, *within* an industry or group of firms, compared to relative ignorance and uncertainty *outside*, the more can insiders be expected to use this effectively in developing and maintaining market power. While this is clearest in the case of collusion among firms, as will shortly be noted, it is also true for monopoly positions which might be subject to intrusion if outsiders had more information. Moreover, greater inside information increases the degree of certainty and reduces the degree of risk for the favored firms, thereby directly improving their profit-risk conditions.

A final broad determinant is government policies, some of which may be quite decisive. These include research support, cash subsidies, controls, tax laws which favor mergers, defense supply contracts, antitrust measures, and many others. Antitrust may reduce concentration by direct attack; it may raise concentration indirectly by cracking down on collusion. Two other public policy approaches—public-agency purchasing and utility regulation—may have systematic effects worth noting briefly here.

The possible impact of purchases by public agencies has long been recognized, and this impact has increased massively during the last generation. The ability of government purchasing officers—particularly in the Defense Department, the National Aeronautics and Space Agency and the Atomic Energy Commission—to make or unmake market positions is now in some instances total, and it affects more than a few major industries, as Chapters 5, 9, and 11 will indicate. It affects, too, some of the very largest corporations, and it has yielded some instances of very high profitability. This is true also for the large array of purchases for domestic purposes at all levels of government. Highway construction, office and school building, equipment, and other sectors are influenced by the purchasing policies of public agencies. The placing of orders and the terms upon which they are set can influence market power, either reinforcing or neutralizing it.[15] Most public buyers (most notably the Defense Department) do not rate the promotion of competition among their suppliers as a primary aim, beyond having two sources of supply. Accordingly, an industry's heavy commitment to public purchases will often tend to indicate the presence of substantial market power.

Public regulation of utilities in this country has a curious and indirect effect. Such regulation ordinarily tries to set a "reasonable" profit-rate ceiling (such as 7 percent), which the utility firms are then entitled to earn on all capital permitted in their rate base. This provides an inducement for the utilities, so constrained, to expand their capital investment, either in real installations or by accounting maneuvers. It also dilutes their concern about the prices which they pay for capital equipment (and some other types

---

[15] See John K. Galbraith, *The New Industrial State* (Boston: Houghton Mifflin, 1967), and M. J. Peck and F. M. Scherer, *The Weapons Acquisition Process* (Cambridge: Harvard University Press, 1962). See also Chapters 5 and 11 below.

of purchases as well).[16]   This in turn enhances the market power obtainable in the utility *equipment* industries and the profit-risk rewards which they may reap.   By indirectly encouraging and rewarding collusion or monopolization in the supplying industries, commission regulation may foster market power in this group of industries.

The specific economic determinants of market power may include three main types.   First, economies of scale have been the most frequently discussed for over 80 years, and they are understandably claimed by spokesmen for all large and/or market-leading firms.   They may occur at all levels of operations: production on the factory floor, coordination among plant operations, R & D activities, marketing, or others.   They may be steep or mild; that is, the average cost curve (recall Figure 3.1) may slope down steeply or only slightly.[17]   The longer the down-slope extends the larger will be the "optimum size" of the firm.   This optimum size may take up the whole market, especially if markets are only local or regional; imagine for instance a modern steel works or atomic power system serving just Lichtenstein, or just Story County, Iowa.   But conversely, most of the economic case for big business and for high concentration in markets has always rested on the claim that technical economies of scale extend up to very large sizes, as Chapter 2 noted.

The cost advantages in a firm may be of two types: *technical* and *pecuniary*.   Only technical economies represent a genuine improvement in social efficiency.   Pecuniary economies simply increase a firm's profits at the expense of those earned by its suppliers or competitors.   In fact, many cost advantages of scale do reflect only bargain prices paid for inputs, rather than greater efficiency in turning inputs into outputs.   The usual assumption in theory is that all firms pay the same price for inputs, so that cost differences embody genuine differences in efficiency.   But pecuniary economies, from lower input prices, falsify such comparisons.

Many such pecuniary advantages stem from imperfections *in the markets for the inputs*—for raw materials, labor, and, above all, capital.   In the classic case, a large buyer will extract concessions from suppliers, who charge "standard" or even higher prices to the other, smaller buyers.   This is price discrimination—differing relations between prices and costs in different exchanges.[18]   The large buying firm may simply play off rival suppliers against one another, or threaten to make its own supplies.   Or the discrimination may come about entirely on the initiative of the sellers, who

---

[16] See F. M. Westfield, "Regulation and Conspiracy," *American Economic Review*, LV (June 1965), 424–443, and William G. Shepherd and Thomas G. Gies, *Utility Regulation* (New York: Random House, 1965), Chs. 1 and 9 and references cited there.
[17] Technical progress (an actual *shift* downward of the cost curve) differs in concept from economies of scale (moving *along* a given cost curve), though of course they are often mixed together in actual firms.   Technical progress is treated separately in Chapter 4.
[18] Price discrimination also frequently occurs with *uniform* prices for different-cost goods; but the basic element of cost-price difference is the same.

maximize their profits by dividing their customers and charging a different price to each group of customers. Many situations no doubt mix the two motivations. In any case, market power in the input markets can be the source of pecuniary economies of scale, and added market power, at the next level of markets. Usually such advantages are open mainly to larger firms—larger than other buyers, and larger absolutely.[19] Hence these are often called advantages of bigness per se, for they need not depend on the relative shares which a firm may hold in individual markets.

Of course, cheap inputs may reflect genuine cost savings on large orders, owing to less paperwork, longer production runs and more orderly planning by the seller. Yet discrimination may be mixed in; the discounts may exceed the cost differences. The prime example of this is the market for capital (or rather, the whole intricate network of financial submarkets wherein enterprises obtain investable funds on various terms). Competition cannot survive unless competitors can obtain investable funds; competitive markets for capital are essential to competition in all other sectors of the economy. Yet it is well known (as Chapters 6 and 11 will note) that the price of capital (interest payments and other) is fairly closely and negatively related to the size of the firm.

One partial reason for this is the economies of dealing in large financial batches. Another reason is that large firms can and do play off financial sources against each other more effectively. Still another reason is that larger firms tend to be more secure "risks," for a variety of reasons, including market leadership and diversification. Accordingly, a competent bank or investment firm will be drawn to the larger company; generally, the more favorable the firm's profit-risk position is, the less it will have to pay for its capital. This creates an "egg-and-chicken" circle. The advantage will be reinforced if a strong lender-borrower connection develops, for mere assured access by a firm to added finances will increase the deference of its rivals. It will also increase "entry barriers," by giving further pause to potential entrants.

Evidently the technical-pecuniary distinction among types of cost advantages is fundamental, even if it is often hard to draw it clearly in practical cases. The greatest difficulty arises when some costs—"overhead" costs—cannot be assigned to specific outputs.[20] This is the second determinant to be noted here. In such cases, the "economies" in the production of any one of the products may be impossible to evaluate, and the firm will also have considerable choice in pricing its various outputs. The resulting

---

[19] Yet, also, many small firms stay alive by fastening on such advantages, at a local level. The problem is complex. Advantages may be gained through largeness of *orders*, and also through sheer *company* size, which may increase the creditability of the buyer's threat to produce his own supplies.
[20] J. M. Clark, *Studies in the Theory of Overhead Costs* (New York: Macmillan, 1922), and W. A. Lewis, *Overhead Costs* (London: Allen & Unwin, 1948).

price discrimination will be both inevitable and a source of market dominance. Overhead costs are commonly thought to occur mainly in utilities such as electric power and telephones, but they may actually be only moderately important in some supposed utility operations, and other nonutility industries may have large overhead costs. Therefore overhead costs may be a determinant in a wide variety of markets.

The final determinant may be the rate of industry growth. Many observers have come to believe that growth erodes concentration and weakens collusion, while shrinkage tends to weed out small firms, thereby tightening concentration. In some eyes, growth is a major hope for checking concentration and destabilizing agreements. In a growing economy, time would be on the side of competition. Yet the mechanism by which this may occur has never been clarified, and collusion is more likely to crack under falling demand (perhaps then leading to mergers, if no antitrust constraint is applied), while it is superfluous when demand is expanding rapidly and causing fast growth.

The mix of these general and specific determinants will be important in shaping the degree and forms of market power that may emerge in individual instances. For example, weak scale economies combined with relative stability and a high ratio of inside-to-outside knowledge will strongly favor the development of collusion and other informal structure among independent firms, rather than their consolidation into a single, dominant firm. Evidently the possible combinations are numerous and complex.

INTERNAL MARKET STRUCTURE

its means

Certain specific elements of structure may be classed as "internal." Internal forms are those defined entirely by relative conditions inside the market; thus market shares are relative to the market and are independent of outside connections and of the absolute size of the firms in the market. Internal elements subdivide further into two sorts; those reflected in actual *formal* ownership and control of firms, and those based on *informal* cooperative patterns among firms. The meaning of these terms will grow clearer as the discussion proceeds.

Formal Structure

Assume that the market in question, whatever it is, can be properly defined. This would allow for true regional and local submarkets, and imports from other countries, as well as close substitutes (see Chapter 7). Some markets have clear and absolute boundaries, but many, or perhaps virtually all, have wide twilight zones. Yet, assume *arguendo* that a given market can be marked off.

In its narrowest definition, the internal structure of a market is the total pattern of shares held by the companies within it. This includes, presumably, shares on both the selling side and the buying side. Yet market shares on the selling side conventionally draw primary attention, on the assumption that the buyers have little market power (obviously a hazardous assumption).

While the general degree of market power held in the industry might be reflected by a concentration ratio for all the dominant firms together, the market power held by each one of them would be some function of its own market share in relation to the rest of the structure of the industry. Moreover, it would be the structure of the dominant firm or firms which would mainly matter, with only a minor role for the smaller fry.[21]

Thus, in addition to concentration ratios for all the leading firms together, one would need to know disparity of sizes *among* the dominant firms.[22] Generally, an asymmetrical oligopoly, dominated by one firm rather than having relatively equal-size leading firms, would involve a higher degree of market power. Although equal-size oligopolists might expect to attempt and possibly achieve considerable joint maximizing of profits, more definite control would be likely under and *within* a single dominant firm. Equal size among the market leaders makes cooperation riskier and its rewards smaller for each firm, compared with asymmetry.

To put it more broadly: if there is a distinct optimum size (owing to U-shaped cost curves), then all of the leading firms will tend to be that size. Disparity would involve inefficiency, from their being below the optimum level, or above it, or both. If, instead, costs are constant, then a dominant firm offers no social gain to offset the social cost of the market power it attains. There would be a net social gain from constraining firms to the minimum efficient size, or at least to greater equality of size.

Concentration may or may not stem from genuine economies of scale in production. That is, dominant firms may consist of one plant apiece or of many. This may normally influence their competitive relationships. So to market shares and disparity among the dominant firms, a third element can be added—the lack of divergence between plant concentration and company concentration (in other words, a lack of multiplant operation). The more the divergence, the more the concentration of firms would be based on a lot of smaller merged plants, rather than large firms with few plants or only one plant. This would suggest weaker economies of scale in production, which would in turn widen the possibilities of entry even by small competitors, and the ability of smaller efficient competitors to threaten or at least to discipline the larger firms. Less divergence means more market power; entry barriers are discussed further below.

---

[21] The small competitive fringe is often not a wholly trivial factor, but it normally will play no more role than a single firm with the same total share. Normally, indeed, that role will be much less, owing to the disparate aims and tactics of the fringe firms.
[22] See *Economic Concentration, Part 4* (1965), and Worcester, *op. cit.*

Informal Elements

What firms cannot attain independently or in opposition to each other, they may gain by cooperation. For each set of basic market conditions, there will be a natural margin between market shares sought by firms independently and the cooperation (or "shared monopoly") which is achieved among them. As was noted earlier in this chapter, this margin of concentration in a market will depend upon those factors which impel firms towards consolidation and those which favor cooperation.

To put it more generally, formal structure is usually embedded in a looser and softer structure of cooperative arrangements. These informal elements range from ironbound pacts down to diaphanous understandings, from enforceable contracts to nods and winks. The cartel, common abroad but illegal in the United States, comes in many varieties, including syndicates, joint selling agencies, systems for production quotas and plant closures, as well as price fixing. Short of outright cartels, an infinite gradation of shared-monopoly and cooperative policies are possible, including interlocking directorships, joint ventures among competitors, and trade associations. Not all of these create market power, but they frequently provide an essential focus or vehicle for cooperation. Particularly where antitrust constraints are weak, informal structure may be important, in some cases more so than formal structure.

Successful collusion (that is, making a high price stick) depends on keeping members in line and keeping new competitors out.[23] This can best be done if:

1 Firms in the market are few (concentration is at least moderate) so behavior can be easily policed.
2 Their costs are similar, otherwise their gains from cooperation would diverge and interests would clash.
3 Transactions are quickly and fully made known *within* the cartel, so that retaliation against chiselers can be swift and sure.
4 There is full secrecy (of behavior and profits) from outside view, so that no outsiders will be attracted.
5 Various specific barriers can be erected, such as control of essential raw materials, patents, etc.
6 Customers are many and small, or not fully intent on minimizing the price they pay (as may be the case with public agencies or regulated utility firms).

The mark of a fully effective cartel is the pooling and dividing of its members' *profits*. Weaker rings have to settle for dividing up sales in the market, which leaves profits to be reaped separately and invites chiseling.

Cooperation usually freezes the market shares of members, in contrast to the flux one would expect under active competition. Therefore cooperative

---

[23] See Dewey, *op. cit.*, 18–23.

behavior may usually be inferred from a high rigidity of *formal* structure over time, even without any tangible evidence of collusive devices. Therefore, stability of market shares over a period of time is a useful index of informal structure.

The other important element is barriers against new entry.[24] These have many possible sources, including such specific devices as patents and controls over a limited raw material. Scale economies may make it necessary for an entrant to come in on a large scale. The capital required for such entry may be difficult or impossible to raise, especially if the industry is very large and capital-intensive. This is accentuated by the natural expectation that such large entry will provoke aggressive retaliatory tactics by the existing firms. Such prospective retaliation discourages the providers of funds for potential entrants, as well as the entrants themselves. Despite their rather intangible and therefore informal character, entry barriers are a major element of market power.

EXTERNAL ELEMENTS OF MARKET STRUCTURE

For any given internal market structure, market power can also be influenced by certain conditions which may be regarded as external to "the" market itself. Although some of these conditions play complex roles, their influence upon market power is often clear and strong.

These elements principally include: size relative to the total distribution of firms, the extent and incidence of diversification, and certain vertical relationships. Not all of these are of equal weight, and for some of them, especially vertical ones, the probability of influence on market power may be moderate or low.

Size Relative to the Total Distribution of Firms

Chapter 2 noted the peculiar turns in the debate about size; overcondemned by the early critics, size was said to be wholly irrelevant in the zealous rebuttals of the 1950's. This recent overkill has led economists, in rather lonely unanimity, to deny vigorously an elemental truth of business life. Size alone does not constitute market power; bigness is *not* bad per se. But size is unequivocally an element, often an important one, in market power.

It is not the absolute dollar amount of assets of the firm which matters, but rather the relative position of the firm in the whole array of enterprises. Small and middling size firms must regard many larger firms as potential competitors: some of the very largest firms face no such danger. Large

---

[24] See especially Joe S. Bain, *Barriers to New Competition* (Cambridge: Havard University Press, 1956).

firms can threaten countermeasures against potential entrants which would be inconceivable on the part of smaller firms facing large, determined entrants. To illustrate, a given market structure will involve more market power if it occurs in the automobile industry than in the toy car industry. What firm of $100 million or even $1,000 million in assets (perhaps 50th to 500th in size among industrial firms) could successfully enter the U.S. automobile industry in scale? Which such firm could *not* easily dominate toy cars by direct entry or merger? Clearly, for a given set of other structural elements, larger size will usually mean greater market power.[25]

As a related matter, larger firms often (even usually) obtain lower input prices than smaller firms can (as was noted just above; see also Chapter 11). This is in part because of true economies of bulk sales, which the lower prices merely reflect. Also, large buyers often enjoy lower prices from sellers, either by pressure or as part of the seller's voluntary maximizing of his own profits. These advantages of size are perhaps clearest in the case of financial markets, as noted above. This may both cause and reflect the large firm's greater average degree of market power and lesser risk, but the result is still the same, and it helps insure that relative size is an element of market power.

Diversification

Firms diversify for many reasons.[26] Tax laws favor mergers, including conglomerate ones. Diversity may enhance a firm's total financial stability as fluctuations of its parts tend to even out (this is only a financial balancing; the real employment levels in a firm's individual divisions may fluctuate as much as they would in separate companies). A firm in a shrinking industry may branch into growth industries as a means to keep growing or even to survive. Research often grows in new, unexpected directions. Some inputs may be used for disparate outputs—brand-name advertising, for example. Antitrust fears may lead a dominant firm to forage elsewhere for growth and investment opportunities. Indeed, the tighter the antitrust constraint against increased market shares, the more will excess internal resources (especially profits) accrue and seek outlets.

There have been doubts that diversification will affect market power, but in some circumstances it clearly can. Since the issues are still under active debate, they may deserve exploring here in some detail.[27] It is generally recognized that the holding or acquisition of a firm by a larger one

---

[25] See also the important paper by Marshall Hall and Leonard W. Weiss, "Firm Size and Profitability," *Review of Economics and Statistics*, XLIX (August 1967), 319–331.

[26] For reviews of these reasons, see Michael Gort, *Diversification and Integration in American Industry* (Princeton: Princeton University Press, 1962), and G. E. Hale and Rosemary D. Hale, *Market Power: Size and Shape Under the Sherman Act* (Boston: Little, Brown, 1958), Ch. 6.

[27] This section draws on material in James S. Campbell and William G. Shepherd, "Leading Firm Conglomerate Mergers," *Antitrust Bulletin*, XIII (Winter 1968), 1361–1382.

may usually improve its competitive situation and widen its possible strategies, perhaps sharply.[28] The debate centers on what, and how extensive, these changes may be. Two broad kinds of competitive advantages resulting from the connection may be (somewhat artificially) distinguished: (1) added access to productive nonfinancial resources, such as managerial talent, transportation capacity, or research capabilities, which may improve the firm's technical efficiency; and (2) access to competitive advantages unrelated to real nonpromotional economies, such as a longer line of credit on better terms, brand-name transfers, and opportunities to acquire other inputs at reduced prices.

The most common among the second group is the financial or pecuniary advantage: the achievement by the acquired firm of access to more liquid funds at lower cost and freer from outside supervision and constraints than would otherwise be available. Put another way, outside parentage may provide the branch with at least some of the advantages of relative size (noted in the section just above). In certain circumstances, where the parent firm's financial resources are much larger than those of the branch, the result may approximate what has rather crudely been called a "deep pocket." Even in intermediate instances, with the two entities more on a financial par with each other, the financial effect is widely recognized and counted on in business affairs. Some economists go so far as to deny its presence altogether, but that denial usually is based on unrealistic assumptions about the degree of perfection in capital markets.

One important indication of the financial advantages is the well-known fact that interest rates on loans tend to vary inversely with firm size.[29] This would suggest both (1) that a larger parent firm directly opens substantial financial advantages to a smaller branch, and (2) that two relatively equal-size partners mutually gain (though less sharply) by merging into a larger single entity.

In addition to lower costs of capital, the financial advantages include a greater availability of capital to the branch, when compared to its independent possibilities.[30] The whole financial effect will vary from case to case, and in unusual instances it may be relatively small. But it will almost invariably be present in some degree, and it is probably substantial in some

---

[28] I am here setting aside, as special (though not trivial) cases, those takeovers which merely result in a financial gutting of the acquired firm.

[29] See Federal Reserve Board, *Studies of Bank Loan Rates in 1955 and 1957* (Washington, D.C.); also F. R. Edwards, "The Banking Competition Controversy," *National Banking Review*, III (September 1965), 1–34, and references cited there; also S. H. Archer and L. G. Faerber, "Firm Size and Cost of Externally Acquired Equity Capital," *Journal of Finance*, XXI (March 1966), 69–83.

[30] See especially Hall and Weiss, *op. cit.*; also Ezra Solomon, ed., *The Management of Corporate Capital* (New York: Free Press, 1959), and Myron J. Gordon, *The Investment, Financing and Valuation of the Corporation* (Homewood, Ill.: Irwin, 1962). The point is reinforced by the common business view that internal funds are "cheaper" than external funds. Even if this were an incorrect view (a matter of some theoretical dispute), the fact that it is widely held would be sufficient in the present context.

cases. It would be manifestly incorrect to expect the opposite—that (apart from exceptional cases) firms are financially *weakened* by being held or acquired by firms possessing market power and earning monopoly profits.

The two main types of advantages are partly overlapping, and both kinds of advantage may be present in any given instance, with the effect of strengthening the branch and widening its competitive opportunities. But only the first type adds unambiguously to efficiency, as well as adding to market power; the second type tends only to enlarge market power, without the saving economic graces.

One problem for evaluation here is to recognize the probable tradeoffs between the main effects, which offer varying competitive costs and benefits.[31]

In the view of some observers, the first kind of transfer clearly predominates among conglomerate ties. Yet no clear evidence that these transfers have been actually caused by conglomerate ties has ever been put together (see Chapter 5).

To some observers, the second group of effects appears certain to predominate.[32] Indeed, Edwards and others expect conglomerate ties to foster repeated predatory initiatives, funded via cross-subsidizing among the branches. This they regard as likely to occur from "sheer size," even if *none* of the branches possesses market power individually. Yet systematic evidence that such cross-subsidized predation actually occurs—*and* that its costs outweigh possible net gains in productivity—has not yet been gathered, and it may well never be.[33]

Therefore, the extreme optimistic and pessimistic views of conglomerate connections are both unsubstantiated as yet, and the problem of tradeoffs between the two kinds of advantages accruing to branches cannot be fully resolved. There remains, however, a reasonable middle ground: (1) that the connection may ordinarily strengthen the branch firm via access to two main sorts of added resources and (2) that the purely market-power-increasing effect will vary directly with the market power held by the parent firm in other lines, or the parent firm's own financial resources alone. Therefore, if the branch is among the leaders in its industry, its external backing unquestionably *increases* structural monopoly. If it is in the second echelon, its backing tends to equalize it with larger firms (indirectly reducing asymmetry) and so reduce structural monopoly. Of course if *all* of the leading firms are merely branches, then the relative effect may be neutralized; but

---

[31] The distinction between only two basic types of advantages is admittedly crude. Further refinement of the kinds of advantages, their incidence and net economic value, may be less important than the leading firm-lesser firm distinction, which is noted shortly: *that* distinction substantially obviates the need for a more refined economic treatment of the competitive advantages.
[32] Corwin D. Edwards, in *Economic Concentration, Part 1;* John M. Blair, "The Conglomerate Merger in Economics and Law," *Georgetown Law Journal* (Summer 1958), 632–662; and *Economic Concentration, Part 1* and *Part 2* (1965), 77–109, 203–219 and 651–673.
[33] *E.g.,* Donald F. Turner, "Conglomerate Mergers and Section 7 of the Clayton Act," LXXVIII (June 1965), 1313–1346.

market power will be greater all around because all are, in effect, larger, relative to the whole distribution of firms.

Diversification's role therefore has two subelements; *incidence*, the branch's standing in the industry, and *extent*, the parent firm's market power elsewhere.[34] A conglomerate firm made up of market-leading branches clearly holds market power; a conglomerate merger uniting leaders in separate markets clearly adds to market power by tending to entrench both parts. Whether the parent firm will encourage or support the branches in predatory tactics (via cross-subsidizing, which however is not *always* predatory) cannot be foretold, but this capacity will often exist and the very possibility of its use may customarily alter behavior throughout the market, perhaps shifting it substantially.

Vertical Elements

Although vertical elements may enter into structural monopoly, their roles are complex and equivocal. Prices under bilateral monopoly (or oligopoly) are not determinate, and the outcome may range between pure competition and pure monopoly. A new monopolist or oligopolist may often arise to countervail an original position of market power, thereby pressing it toward competitive outcomes, but this is not a certain result. It is true that a firm's market power will often stem from input-price advantages which it can gain only because its suppliers have market power and are able to discriminate in price. In such cases, the vertical relation to structural monopoly among suppliers strengthens, not neutralizes, market power in the industry in question. This helps explain why sellers with market power may discover that "countervailing power" is developing among their buyers. But it does not assure that the total result will be less monopolistic than the original situation.

Vertical integration's effect on market power may also go either way, much as with diversification. Its net effect depends upon both its magnitude and its *incidence*. If it focuses in dominant firms at both levels, it is almost certain to raise power at both levels. By contrast, if it involves mainly secondary firms at either or both stages, its net effect may be to reduce market power.[35] Yet this second situation may be an unstable one, for dominant firms cannot be expected to refrain for long from vertically integrating when their rivals have already done so.

A rise in market power through vertical integration is particularly likely when there are economies of scale or effective collusive arrangements

---

[34] For similar reasoning, see also John Narver, *Conglomerate Mergers and Market Competition* (Berkeley: University of California Press, 1967) and the White House Task Force on Antitrust Policy, *Report*, July 5, 1968 (Washington, D.C.: mimeographed, issued May 20, 1969 by the Department of Justice).

[35] See, among others, Walter Adams and Joel B. Dirlam, "Steel Imports and Vertical Oligopoly Power," *American Economic Review*, 1964, 626–655, and references cited there.

at the prior market level. Also, if the integrating firm can preempt a scarce input, such as ore, or locational rights, the integration may directly increase market power. This merely reflects the fact that vertical relationships may involve a severe degree of struggle between large buyers and sellers, and either party may gain substantially by embracing both sides of the market and then dealing vertically with firms which are competitive at the other level. Finally, integration may raise entry barriers by increasing the total capital which a new entrant (now necessarily at two levels) will need. This effect will vary with size and capital-intensity. These conditions favorable to market-power gains through vertical integration may not be common, and so such integration is not ordinarily thought to be a major or systematic route to increased market power. Nonetheless the possibilities are there, in the appropriate situations.

In summary, structural monopoly has a number of elements, formal and informal, internal and external. They probably include (1) market shares and asymmetry and fewness of plants among formal elements within markets; (2) barriers to entry and the whole range of cooperative arrangements which comprise informal or "soft" structure (and which stability of market shares reflects), and (3) primarily relative size, diversification and vertical patterns among external elements. Within certain limits, which will vary from case to case, firms may choose among these elements in seeking market power and its rewards. And the presence or absence of any one element does not prove the presence or absence of market power, while a combination of several elements may indicate with a high degree of probability that market power is present.

Evidently, these elements may interact. Do they tend to reinforce each other, or to serve mainly as mutually interchangeable forms, so that the mass of industry is a rather smooth pudding of only moderate or slight market power? To put the question another way, can one possibly define a "natural" composite of structural elements which is likely to evolve under common conditions of markets? We will explore these questions in theory (Chapter 4) and fact (Chapters 7–10). But first the probable effects of market power on performance are reviewed in Chapter 4. This will suggest an "optimum" market structure which can be compared with the possible "natural" structure.

How Market Power
May Affect Performance

Monopoly, besides, is a great enemy to good management, which can never be universally established but in
consequence of that free and universal competition which
forces everybody to have recourse to it for the sake of self-
defense.

ADAM SMITH
The Wealth of Nations (1776)

Market performance may provide many different benefits. These include
efficiency within enterprises, and smooth and rapid adjustments of the whole
economy toward the optimum allocation of resources (but without creating
large external costs). Further economic goals are stability, growth, and
technical progress. Finally, market activities may promote a fair sharing
of economic rewards, and avoid impairing social, political, and cultural life.

Market power may either hinder or promote each of these objectives in
varying degrees. A composite of many elements, a hydra with many and
changing heads, market power also has many possible effects, some small,
some large. This chapter can endeavor to note only the main probable
effects. Since the one composite (market power) may touch upon the other
composite (performance) in many ways, one cannot hope to do more than
sum up the primary possibilities here.

In evaluating performance, one must compare the real outcome with
what might reasonably have been expected, and then try to determine how
much of the gap between actual and opportunity was caused by market power.

This speculative sort of exercise is not easy to do well, but it is important to try (as Chapters 12–15 do). It may be possible to improve on the pure doubt and partisan assertions which otherwise would prevail.

This chapter looks first at the direct effects on financial quanta: on prices and profits. Second are the "real" economic effects, on allocation, stability, growth, and technical change. Third are the equity and social effects, including fairness, opportunities, and cultural patterns. Some of the more familiar items need only brief mention here, whereas others (especially technical change and distribution) need more. The problems in forming sound total judgments about actual performance are then summarized. Finally, an attempt is made to define "optimum" and "natural" market structures, under varying circumstances, and these are then compared.

PRICES

Market power enables two main changes in prices: (1) toward higher *levels* than otherwise would occur, and (2) discriminatory differences in the *structure* of specific prices to separate customers.

More strictly, market power shifts upward the whole probability distribution of prices which the firm may profitably set, both raising the average and extending the possibilities for really high prices. Whether or not firms actually choose to raise prices to squeeze out every drop of profitability in the short or long run, the possibility of doing so is there. This possibility, even if not directly exploited, may condition the behavior of competing firms, through their anticipation of what the original firm could do *if* it chose to. When market power is obtained through collusion, it shifts upward the collective probability distribution of prices and shrinks the probability range of lower prices by preventing price wars and other "destructive" competition. Of course, as Chapter 3 noted, firms may choose to limit prices (and profitability) so as to avert new entry. Or they may, instead, take their profits now, letting entry come as it may. In so doing, they would find their market share dwindling: this would be another interaction between structure and its "effects."

As for price structure, the upward shift in actual prices may not be uniform to all customers. This is because market power often enables firms to discriminate in prices among their customers, as one tactic toward maximizing overall profits. Buyers with relatively inelastic demands will be charged higher prices than those with relatively elastic demand. Indeed, prices to elastic-demand buyers may be well below the competitive levels. This will in turn have corollary effects in reducing competition among the buying firms by making inputs relatively cheaper to the larger ones. Market power at one level therefore usually tends to create market power at the next level. In any case, it alters the price structure from what would otherwise prevail in the absence of market power.

PROFITABILITY

The real prize of market power is of course more profit. Indeed, if market power did not confer this prize, it would hardly be sought as unremittingly as it is. In popular discussions, sustained high profits are often taken as a sign of superior performance; to the economist, they suggest also—and often *instead*—the exercise of market power, and possible danage to economic performance.

Firms seek profits both as a reward and as a means for gaining still more market power and future profits. Profits, the residual revenues after costs have been met, are of course the paramount indicator of a privately-owned enterprise's health and strength. But profits are usually difficult to appraise. It is useful to point out a number of often-neglected features of profits.

1. The degree of profitability is best evaluated as a *rate of return on capital* invested in the business. Profits as a sum or as a percentage of *sales revenue* have virtually no significance for showing the firm's degree of profitability. After all, only a fool would invest in or attribute market power to a company *just* because its ratio of profits to sales was high.

2. There are quite a few ways of defining both profits (that is, net income) and assets, and actual firms display a perfect maze of different accounting concepts, procedures, and illusions. Therefore, actual measurements and comparisons of profits have always been in some degree difficult and controversial. Also, the actual profitability of distinct products and divisions in larger firms is usually kept secret; ordinarily only companywide data are published. Naturally, those who attain high profits (especially through market power) will not brandish them before society, but will instead endeavor to moderate them and clothe them in other guises, through accounting adjustments and honorific relabeling (for example, payments for "good will").

3. In addition, profits tend over time to become capitalized as costs ("rents," in economic terms). The key profitable factors—a superior executive, inventor, or possibly a cheap input—may bargain for higher payments, or a "cost" item labelled "good will" may be inserted in the accounts. All in all, many changes in accounting profits have no real economic meaning, and many true changes in profits are masked in reported accounts.

4. Profitability has long been known to have at least two main dimensions: rate of return and security (or nonriskiness). Generally the mass of investment decisions reflects preferences for risk-avoidance, and so secure profits (secure against downward fluctuations) are preferred to risky profits. If competition tends to equate marginal profitability conditions in equilibrium, it is really in terms of profit rates *adjusted* for differences in risk. Thus, in long-run equilibrium, some competitive but unstable "(risky") industries might have high average profit rates in any given period, and vice versa.

Raw profit rates, therefore, are only a partial indicator of profitability, and should not be expected to correlate closely with market power.

5. While a firm's real capital stock has a fairly clear and stable value, the value of its outstanding shares of common stock may gyrate at every whim and tremor of the market. Therefore the motives of and rewards reaped by the stockholder "owners" may differ from or even clash with the motives of the firm's managers or profitability of the firm itself. Thus a corporation's profit-risk results may be spectacular, while its stock, already bid up in anticipation, is a poor buy. This peculiarity suggests that the capital market exerts continuing pressures, even on secure large firms, to maximize profits. Implications of this for the corporate conscience are noted in Chapter 5.

6. Except for the polar case of pure monopoly, industry-wide profits are a poor indicator of the profits attained through market power. One must isolate those firms (or parts of firms) which actually possess market power. Attempts to relate industry structure to "industry" profits are hazardous, particularly for middle-range and loose oligopoly (see Chapter 12).

7. Finally, the true margin of profitability is not the direct rate of return, which usually ranges between 7 and 20 percent. Instead it is, to use a rule of thumb, the margin of return *above* the interest rate on riskless funds, such as Treasury bonds or, in Britain, consols. If the bond rate is 7 percent, a firm's rate of return of 7 percent would in fact be no net return at all as a reward to risk capital and possible market power. At 10 percent, the net return would be only 3 percent, while 16 percent would really yield a net return of 9 percent, or three times as much. It is these net returns to which the market value of common stock is particularly sensitive. This basis of evaluation is used in Chapter 12; it is essential in appraising the true degree of difference among differing rates of return.

Altogether, profitability is a treacherous hunting ground for evidence about performance; it is subtle in concept, difficult to measure and ambiguous to interpret.

X-INEFFICIENCY AND MISALLOCATION

Market power may cause waste of resources in at least three main distinct ways:

First is "inefficiency" *within* individual enterprises, rather than in allocation among them. The security and relatively high profits gained by a monopoly position may permit and encourage the firm to slacken or develop other forms of inefficiency in the usual business sense.[1] In theory this slippage need not occur, because firms may profit-maximize with equal ardor

---

[1] It is perceptively discussed by Harvey Leibenstein in "Allocative Efficiency *vs.* 'X-Efficiency'," *American Economic Review*, LVI (June 1966), 392–415.

in every situation, under the watchful eye of informed shareholders and the capital market generally. But, in fact, firms (undeterred by theory) have often responded to success by slowing, softening, and maximizing among other preferences. The degree of this softening may be nearly impossible to measure, because it simply soaks up some part of the profits, often leaving them looking very low indeed. Even so, it may be important and is frequently visible enough.

Second is the overall static misallocation, analyzed in Chapter 3 as distortion away from the marginal conditions of efficient allocation among all markets. The degree of restriction may be as much as one-half of competitive output levels, in theory. The overall burden of this can only be assessed on an economy-wide scale (as it is in Chapter 13). The loss may, at a minimum, be only the net loss in consumer surplus between the actual allocation and the optimum, the famous triangle shown by A in Figure 4.1.[2] This net loss is bound to be rather small, as well as exceedingly difficult to discover. Yet in fact the impact in a modern economy may be much larger. Market power may contribute to the economy's inability to achieve full employment, price stability, and an equilibrium balance-of-payments position simultaneously. The *total* loss in output and unemployment from these constraints may be entirely, or at least partly, treated as a cost of market

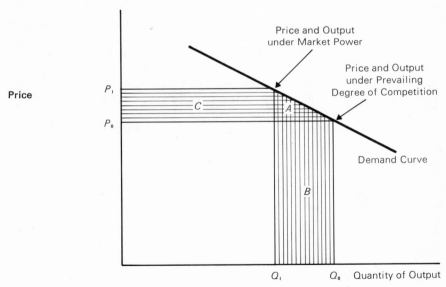

Figure 4.1 Alternative Misallocation Burdens and Equity Costs Under Market Power.

2 Price P_0 is assumed to reflect the same degree of competition as is prevalent in the rest of the economy. The gap betweeen P_0 and P_1 then reflects the net excess market power in the industry in question.

power. That would be, in the limit, the total of *A* and *B* in Figure 4.1. The point is explored further in Chapter 13.

A third possible form of misallocation is excess advertising. Market power can be created by increases in product differentiation, which is often sought through advertising expenditure and effort.[3] Moreover, market power in turn makes it possible to increase product differentiation further, again through advertising and other sales effort. In certain conditions of oligopoly, much of this advertising, a form of nonprice competition, is likely to be of a mutually neutralizing, standoff sort, with no technical or social benefits at all. To this extent, and in those particular industries, market power will then have the effect of a waste of resources in futile advertising activity. This possibility, which was most intensively debated in the 1950's, is probably highest in those relatively few industries with the favoring conditions *and* a high intensity of advertising.

GROWTH AND FLUCTUATIONS

Misallocation under market power may also slow the rate of national economic growth by requiring restrictive policies which reduce investment. On the other hand, theory predicts no clear impact of market power upon growth in specific industries. Thus, for example, a monopolist in aluminum may "build ahead" of demand precisely in order to preserve its monopoly; or, as in steel, it may not. Monopolists in brand-new industries may restrain growth in order to "skim the cream" off the market; but the entry this induces may (at least eventually) offset the restrictive "effect."

In any case, an industry's growth rate is not usually a good criterion of its performance. Expansion requires additional resources, which have alternative uses in other industries or activities. While one may view the sustained 8 percent yearly growth of the electric power industry with satisfaction, one would not wish it to rise to 50 or 150 percent yearly, even though that might be within the economy's capabilities. It is only in comparison with what might have been expected, and with the alternative uses of the resources, that growth is germane at all to industry performance. Apart from this, there are practical difficulties in measuring and appraising growth patterns—is it growth in sales, employment, net output, real net output, etc., which matters? Growth is, therefore, not a performance standard for *individual* industries, despite its prime importance in *national* economic performance.

---

[3] See William S. Comanor and Thomas A. Wilson, "Advertising, Market Structure and Performance," *Review of Economics and Statistics*, XLIX (November 1967), 423–440. For a counter-view, see Jules Backman, *Advertising and Competition* (New York: New York University Press, 1967).

Fluctuations in output and employment are frequent and sharp in some industries, but rare in others. Such instability is costly, and it breeds instability in other industries. Accordingly, stability is usually regarded as an element of good market performance. During the 1930's, as noted in Chapter 2, there were accusations that price rigidity in monopolistic industries accentuated the declines in output and employment. In the late 1950's, the complaints recurred, this time attacking "administered prices" in a few major industries for holding steady or even rising during recessions. In both cases, the rigidity against cuts, supposedly made possible by the market power of major steel, automobile, and other oligopolists, was seen as a mechanism by which market power aggravated industrial fluctuations.

Technical problems in defining stability (in frequency and amplitude of fluctuations) and measuring it are fairly straightforward, though not negligible. The real problem is in setting the benchmark for normative appraisals. Heavy producers and durable goods industries are inherently more unstable than others, owing to the familiar accelerator effect. But the degree of each one's "inherent" instability may defy close estimation, as Chapter 13 notes in reviewing the evidence.

TECHNICAL CHANGE

In recent years, technical change has taken center stage as an important possible impact of market power and as a standard of industrial performance. Yet the net gains from technical progress—and, particularly, from market power's effect on it, either way—are difficult to conceptualize and to measure. Some observers therefore dismiss innovation as a useful criterion for appraising market power; others insist on its supremacy.[4] Here there is space only to mention, first, the categories and benefits of technical change, and, second, the main likely effects of market power on them.

Technical change can be classified in at least three different directions:[5]

1. There are usually three stages to an innovation and the resulting adjustments: first, *invention*, the creation of a new idea or system; next, *innovation*, the actual embodiment of the idea in the productive processes of a firm; this usually causes, third, *imitation* by other firms, either by precise copying of the innovation or by close simulation of it. The sources of each of these stages and the influences on them may be quite different. In trying to evaluate the sources and achievements of technical advance, one would need to apportion them among these three stages.

---

[4] For the negative view, see Joe S. Bain, *Industrial Organization*, 2nd ed. (New York: Wiley, 1968); and Joel B. Dirlam and Alfred E. Kahn, *Fair Competition* (Ithaca: Cornell University Press, 1954). On the positive side, consult the references in Dirlam and Kahn's book.

[5] See R. R. Nelson, ed., *The Rate and Direction of Inventive Activity* (Princeton: Princeton University Press, 1962); J. Schmookler, *Innovation and Economic Growth* (Cambridge: Harvard University Press, 1966); and E. Mansfield, *Industrial Research and Technical Change* (New York: Norton, 1968).

2. Another important classification of technical change is between *product* innovations and *process* innovations. Though many innovations do not fall entirely into one category or the other, the distinction is an important one. The two kinds of innovation stem from different incentives and have different impacts in the marketplace. Certain competitive conditions will favor one kind, others will favor the other. Moreover, the total benefits of the two kinds of innovation may differ markedly.

3. Technical change may also alter the combinations in which inputs are used, as with labor-saving or capital-intensive techniques. Many innovations probably favor one factor or the other. For example, the net effect of much recent innovation is commonly thought to be labor-saving. Yet an evaluation of technical progress must deal with gains in *total* productivity, not just for any one input, such as output per man-hour or per machine.

If innovation is biased, its measurement becomes more difficult, even with the best of statistics. Moreover, as Chapter 14 will note, the data for making actual indexes of technical change are scanty. Several ways of measuring technical change have been proposed, but most of them are incomplete or defective. For example, the number of patents generated by an enterprise may bear some relation to its actual rate of innovation. But many patents are trivial, especially if they are developed simply to give a close approximation to another firm's major innovation; and many other patents are used to block competitive innovation or for other tactical purposes, rather than being used constructively. Employment of scientists, another common indicator, actually shows only one *input* for innovation, not the efficiency in converting that input into technical advances.

The normative evaluation of technical progress—that is, how "good" the performance of it is—is relative. The opportunities for innovation vary. We do not really expect much innovation to occur in some industries, such as cotton gray goods, cottonseed oil, and bricks. Yet in some other industries, one rightly expects the returns from research and the resulting rate of technical progress to be high. A high rate of actual innovation *compared* to what might normally have been expected is the real test of excellent technical progress. The "norm" is not easy to specify.

Moreover, it is not only the relative rate of innovation which matters, but the *net* benefits accruing from innovation. Innovations ordinarily have costs, and they also have impacts, not all of which are net benefits. This problem has three main features. First, innovation ordinarily follows expenditures on Research and Development. Yet R & D can be wasteful, with little net result, rather than highly fertile. It is the net productivity of R & D that matters. More precisely, R & D expenditures should normally be undertaken up to, and not beyond, the margin at which their net benefits (that is, their net rate of return) justify the expenditures. R & D can therefore obviously go too far, or not far enough, in any specific case. Moreover, R & D spending may focus unduly on one stage of activity (such as imitation) or on one type of innovation (such as minor product innovation), and fall short of its true potential productivity.

Second, any significant innovation will displace some factors in that firm or in others, and it may displace other products as well. These external effects properly belong in any overall judgment of the net benefits from any innovation. In some cases, the short-run impacts may be severe, such as in highly labor-saving innovations. Short-run difficulties should not be permitted to halt long-run beneficial adjustments; yet a full assessment of innovation requires a broad totaling of its negative and positive effects.

Third, international trade possibilities may be important. Much innovation may simply duplicate gains abroad, which are already available (or would be, if trade barriers were cut) to the economy through foreign trade. Of course, if foreign-exchange reserves are extremely short, then import-saving innovations may offer additional net benefits, but that is a special point not affecting the general principle.

Evidently, technical progress is hard to appraise. No simple listing of patents, of research spending, or of innovations will suffice. Even so, it may be possible to make rough practical judgments.

Now, in any case, how may market power influence technical change? There can be little doubt that market power has some effects on the rate and direction of invention, innovation, and imitation, and upon true technical "progress" by normative standards. But these effects may vary widely from case to case, depending on the specific conditions of the industries and technical possibilities, and on the specific forms in which market power arises. The following three specific points explore some of the complexities.

First, it is probable that most innovators (as distinct from inventors, some of them eccentric and civic-minded) do so out of the hope of gain. There are also counter-influences to innovation, which limit the possible gains to any and all initiators. On the other hand, there are major routine sources of invention (including universities) which function at least partly autonomously, even in the absence of unusual expected gains.

Now, better profit-risk results are the prime payoff to market power. The gains to an innovator, therefore, must be in higher profits, lower risk, or both. A technical change which carries great risk must presumably offer correspondingly higher profit rewards. A sure innovation with little risk entailed needs to offer only modest profit gains. Indeed, if risk is low enough (as under some patents), even a subnormal profit-*rate* expectation may be quite sufficient to call forth the innovational effort!

Put generally, for each potential technical advance there may be an *optimum* configuration of market structure and profitability rewards, yielding the best performance in creating, installing, and diffusing a new technique. In some cases, there may be a range of alternative, equally effective market structures for any given technical change. These optima will vary from case to case, and assertions about them are hazardous. Thus one could not safely say that either no market power or unlimited market power will always optimize technical change. And, for another example, the patent device's protection and rewards may grossly diverge from optimum conditions for some or all innovations.

Second, the sources of invention are varied. Do they come from the fertile minds of lonely geniuses, the humdrum outpourings of routine activity in large research laboratories, or, perhaps, from hard-pressed smaller firms whose survival requires innovation? In either case, how important are monetary inducements of competitive threats in calling forth the new ideas and their practical embodiments? One possibility is that the flow of inventions is essentially autonomous, and that the market environment and structure influence only how rapidly these inventions will be embodied in innovations, as well as how fast imitation will occur.

Third, a related element is the possibility that there are true economies of scale in R & D activities themselves. If such economies of scale are extensive, this could promote concentration, both in individual industries and in overall patterns. Yet even so, much research could be performed by specialized research enterprises, selling their services to producing companies of all sizes.

Generally speaking, varying market structures imply complex mixtures of inducements and counter-inducements for technical change.[6] These may arise in fairly predictable fashion. For example, innovation by a very small firm in a large market may promise only small gains if the innovation can be imitated quickly (or even slowly) by the rest of the market. Indeed there has been some confidence that oligopoly provides a superior market structure for technical progress, because the innovator realizes at least a major share of the total benefits to the industry and moreover will be strongly induced to innovate both as a means of nonprice competition and as a defense.[7] Therefore, society may benefit from the special pressures and inducements of oligopoly, which drive oligopolists to rapid innovation as a major form of competition. Moreover, the other oligopolists, being capable of comparable innovative effort, can and will develop close imitations of the original innovation fairly quickly, so that the innovator is unable to exploit his novelty fully or retard further change.

There are many subissues in this interweaving of threats and inducements, but some general probabilities can be outlined. First, where R & D-scale economies are not controlling, tight oligopoly will usually be inferior to loose oligopoly as a setting for innovation. The competitive pressures to perform R & D efficiently and to put inventions into practice (rather than

---

[6] See, *inter alia*, F. M. Scherer, "Research and Development Resource Allocation Under Rivalry," *Quarterly Journal of Economics*, LXXXI (August 1967), 359–394.
[7] John K. Galbraith, *American Capitalism*, rev. ed. (Boston: Houghton Mifflin, 1956) and recall Chapter 2's discussion of Schumpeterian competitive processes.

wait to initiate) will be sharper. The ability of a dominant firm to retard innovation will not be present.

Second, symmetry and asymmetry among industry leaders will usually foster quite different results. In symmetrical oligopoly, all leading firms are under pressure to innovate as a means (defensive and offensive) of non-price competition. Innovation would also destabilize efforts at collusion, by causing cost and motivational differences among the firms.[8] Under asymmetry, the smaller leaders *must* innovate to offset the input-price and other advantages of the dominant firm, while the dominant firm may adopt a passive role, imitating rather than inventing or innovating.

Finally, the character of the possible innovations may strongly influence the eagerness or reluctance of the firm to carry them out under alternative market structures. Easily imitated product innovations or process innovations might encourage firms mainly to be imitators rather than to make the effort of innovating, except under secure monopoly. Under oligopoly, all of the firms may mutually, though not collusively, hold back from the original effort at innovation. That is to say, even a supposedly "optimum" market structure for innovation may be biased towards certain types of innovation and away from others.

DISTRIBUTION

Fairness or equity in distribution actually has two separate dimensions: (1) *actual* patterns of income and wealth held by people at each point in time, and (2) the structure of *opportunities* for future improvement. Debate usually concentrates on the actual patterns, which, after all, can be directly measured and to some degree (slighter than usually thought) changed by social policy. Yet the structure of opportunities may be more important in some ultimate sense, and may influence the "fairness" of any given *actual* pattern. Thus, actual inequality may seem fairer if (1) everyone previously had a fair chance to strike it rich, and/or (2) everyone now has a fair chance to do so.

Broadly speaking, the actual degree of inequality among income and wealth levels will be increased by market power. That is, market power is ordinarily attained and exploited by relatively few members of society (as managers and/or owners), and their enrichment ordinarily involves a relative, and not always small, decrease in purchasing power on the part of those who face higher prices as consumers, possibly lower prices as suppliers, and lower returns as competitors. The direct redistribution is shown by area C

---

[8] But, by the same token, the oligopolists may be induced to try to refrain from innovations which would upset the cooperative *status quo*. Such mutual restraint will be easier to achieve or enforce under tight oligopoly than it is under loose oligopoly.

in Figure 4.1. Since this amount is usually shifted from the many to the few, market power will almost always tend to increase inequality in actual income and wealth.[9] Whether this is good or bad in itself and whether it may have desirable incentive affects for certain kinds of effort are matters of debate, and are also related to the structure of opportunities.

This structure embraces in itself at least three main elements. There is, first, the array of *kinds* of competitions or races open to citizens. Each of these competitions will favor certain talents (artistry, guile, patience, affability, calculation, persistence, coordination, exactitude, oral advocacy, combativeness, physical beauty, gentleness, capacity for indignation or drudgery, etc.). Some entrants will find few or no competitions open for their particular talents and preparation. Market power has the effect of rewarding or accentuating certain kinds of traits, particularly (and obviously) those which are useful in developing and perpetuating market power. Generally, these include a certain degree of skill and tenacity in perceiving economic possibilities, in acting upon them, and in negotiating and other organizational skills. Ordinarily, too, a strong orientation toward monetary rewards is necessary; and market power is rarely attained and exercised without some capacity for aggressive and hostile behavior toward specific competitors (and, often, suppliers).

The second element in the structure of opportunities is the start—equal or unequal—which the participants have. Wealth (and market power), once established, generally favor the access of relatives and children of the holders of market power to high financial rewards themselves. In this sense, market power tends to skew opportunities toward relatively few. This need not apply, however, when the holder of market power is a large and impersonal organization, as many modern corporations are. In such cases the existence of market power may provide relatively impersonal and "objective" access for most participants, as long as the managers refrain from indulging other preferences and prejudices.

The third element is the degree of disparity in the rewards meted out. This economic differential between winners and also-rans (presidents and janitors, oil executives and gas station operators) may in fact be relatively slight, with only a small increment gained by the winners. Or the differences may be sharp, with very high first prizes. The larger the spread, the more likely it is that the resulting effect on distribution will be toward inequality. The effect of market power in this direction is fairly clear; it does tend to widen the desparity among the prizes attained by the competitors, and by sellers and buyers. In contrast to the family farm and the filling station, where the rewards differ but not by enormous amounts, market power on a

---

[9] The exception is the small-scale monopolist selling to the wealthy. This is not a trivial possibility; many local service trades in affluent communities play this role. It is, however, a relatively interstitial and small-scale process, which—as will be noted in Chapter 14—has bred none of the substantial fortunes.

large scale holds out the possibility of extremely high rewards for some, compared to the low or negative results for others.

A special case is the problem of racial and ethnic discrimination. It is often said that competition is color-blind, while monopolists have the opportunity to apply prejudices of their own or of their workers against one minority group or another.[10] Yet, instead, it may be the secure large firm with a "corporate conscience" which is most likely, perhaps certain, to take practical steps toward equal opportunity.[11] Probably it is in financial markets, in the access to enterprise capital, that discrimination may be most critically reinforced or dissolved. Which structure of financial markets would best promote equal opportunity? Would it be impersonal competitive processes, or benevolent, powerful investment sources? Here, evidently, is a problem of distribution which a competitive economy might have been expected to solve. There are others, also.

In any case, the *actual* distribution of income and wealth tends to be disequalized by market power. For the most part, this would go against the grain of traditional standards of fairness in the United States, though not in all other countries. The structure of *opportunities* may derive mixed and ambivalent effects from market power, in terms of performance. Some people will praise the opportunity for great enrichment which market power may offer to citizens of even the humblest origins. They may also esteem the impersonal ladders to executive and other occupational success which many large corporations are said to offer. But others point out that each monopolist preempts opportunities for leadership and independence, which otherwise might be open to many competitors. Indeed, Schumpeter, the arch-defender of modern capitalism (as he envisioned it to be), foresaw in darkest colors the absorption of competitive opportunities into giant private bureauracies. Evidently, the net effects of market power on economic opportunities are likely to be at least partly negative. The net effect depends both upon specific conditions in each case *and* upon the observers' own ethical preferences.

COMPETITION AND BROADER PATTERNS

Market power usually alters the character and reduces the reach of competition itself, making of it a ponderous and closed bargaining sequence, with exclusion and control as the main aims. To many thoughtful observers, this is a loss at least as great as the damage to narrow economic performance.[12]

---

[10] Gary S. Becker, *The Economics of Discrimination* (Chicago: University of Chicago Press, 1957).
[11] Edward S. Mason, ed., *The Corporation in Modern Society* (Cambridge: Harvard University Press, 1959) and *Fortune* (January 15, 1968) offer sober and optimistic views, respectively, on this possibility.
[12] See *inter alia*, Henry Simons, *Economic Policy for a Free Society* (Chicago: University of Chicago Press, 1948); and Corwin Edwards, *Maintaining Competition* (New York: McGraw-Hill, 1949).

On the other hand, this same competition is widely condemned, especially abroad, for the strife and selfishness it is said to foster. It imposes uncertainty, it undermines social cooperation, and it enshrines the Gradgrind and Babbitt, while trampling upon the gentler virtues. These are not frivolous charges, and competition can easily become lopsided or run to excess, so that monopoly, properly controlled, might be preferable in many cases to competition. The problem is not a simple or easy one. But in advanced economies, within a setting of tolerably adequate social programs, market power's net impact on competitive processes is likely to be on the negative side.

Another possible effect of economic performance is on "economic freedom." Certain market structures and patterns of behavior are more coercive and autocratic than others. And more scope for individual discretion is ordinarily preferable to less. Therefore some observers equate competition with maximum economic freedom. Yet, in a complex social setting, freedom has complex meanings. Market power enlarges the area of choice for those who hold it, at least partially at the expense of those lacking it. Yet an unchecked, anarchistic, remorselessly *competitive* process may also offer certain types of "freedom" to a relatively few participants in maximum degree, while suppressing it for most others. Therefore, discussion has advanced in recent years beyond the notion that competition is in some fashion necessarily or precisely correlated with freedom. Even so, market power is ultimately more likely to narrow the scope for independent choice than to widen it in most situations.

Finally, attitudes and motivations in the marketplace can pervade the entire culture and civilization in which they occur. These effects can color the entire society for good or ill. For example, the large and secure enterprise has been viewed disapprovingly as a breeder of docility, narrowness, and acquisitiveness. It has also been viewed as the source of social leadership, whereby the scramble of competitors for mere survival may be transmuted into the secure affluence and social mediation of enlightened industrial statesman. These and other possible patterns are of great importance to the whole fabric of social and cultural life.

APPRAISING THE EFFECTS OF MARKET POWER

Evidently, market performance is a changeable mosaic of disparate elements, each complicated in itself. Forming a rounded judgment of market power's effects and of industry performance is difficult, even apart from the scarcity of reliable evidence, because one must combine these elements on some basis of priority and importance. Each observer will have his own weighting system, or scale of values, and some will weigh the performance elements entirely differently from others. Some will be appalled by a small retardation of innovation in industry X. Others will extol industry X for its internal efficiency or exemplary hiring of minority-group citizens. The gaps in available evidence, which become evident in Chapters 12–15, simply accentuate this fundamental problem.

In addition, the observer must assess not only what, in a positive sense, has actually *happened*; he must also evaluate these positive findings against normative criteria, that is, what might reasonably have been *expected*. This in turn requires further information about industry potential, much of it of an essentially speculative character. Such speculations are unavoidable in any normative evaluation; and they are thoroughly implicit in all common dialogue about industry performance.

These difficulties are of course not much, if at all, greater than those of many other fields of social inquiry, such as the determinants of crime, adultery, or alcoholism. And, though the purist may flinch at imprecise calculations, it is important to do them as well as possible, because there is no shortage of partisan claims about performance and its relation to market power.

Despite the foregoing difficulties, it may be possible to outline approximately the sorts of market structures which may be best for engendering good performance. There are tradeoffs involved; one structure may feature efficiency, another progress, another fairness. But the main alternatives do cluster around a fairly limited and convergent range of elements, as will be seen.

The next section outlines what the main features of such an optimum structure may be. Will *actual* structures tend spontaneously to coincide with, or evolve toward, this *optimum* structure, or, by an unkind fate, will they tend to converge on some structure which generates an inferior performance, in some or all directions? These questions have underlain the whole debate about competitive trends in the economy since before 1890. The answer, if one can be found, is obviously important. The following sections explore which "natural" structures may be expected to emerge under common conditions and compare them with the probable "optimum" composite.

OPTIMUM STRUCTURE

A balanced mix of performance goals would (in the American setting at least) include efficiency, technical progress and competition itself, with possibly lighter stress on fairness and stability. In other societies, there would be different relative weights. It would be pseudoscientific to try to calibrate precise weights for these elements. Even so, the main outlines of "optimum" structure are fairly clear.

The most interesting and general case for analysis is one of relatively constant average costs of production and research for all sizes of firm. In such a case, *any* internal market structure will yield minimum real cost (except for X-inefficiency, which would be greater as market power is greater). The optimum structure in this General Case would be, broadly, loose (low-concentration) symmetric oligopoly, with weak, informal structure, and small or only moderate absolute size and other external elements of market power. Too-low concentration would run the risk of retarding those innovations which are at least partially induced. Zero market power could impose intolerable insecurity upon many or most competitors. But high concentration or cooperation would affect pricing, foster X-inefficiency, and retard innovation. Asymmetry would (generally) provide less innovation and more collusion than would symmetry.

In short, all of the elements of market power could be present, but each in small or moderate degree. The larger any one element of market power might be, the lower the others would need to be. Thus, the larger the industry (steel, automobiles, oil, electrical equipment, chemicals), the lower would concentration, leading-firm diversification, or barriers to entry, etc., need to be. High concentration, high barriers, and high leading-firm diversification in a large industry would be nonoptimal, under the assumptions of the general case. For a typical moderate-sized market, four-firm concentration might range from 25 to 40 percent, *assuming* approximate symmetry among the leading five to ten sellers, low barriers to entry, and no other strong elements.

Other cases are more specialized, with more obvious and familiar lessons. One may define an Optimum Size Case, in which there is a distinct minimum-cost (efficient) size of firm, but with gentle down and up slopes in the average-cost curve, much like the shape of a loose clothesline. In this case, efficiency alone would prescribe this lowest point for the firm's size (and market share). But if the resulting concentration sharply exceeded or fell short of loose oligopoly, then some marginal sacrifice of efficiency might be warranted, in order to promote technical progress and other goals. This is especially true if the scale economies (the downslope of the cost curve) are gentle or uncertain. The optimum structure depends on the tradeoff among the elements, of which minimum cost is only one. Of course, if the economies or diseconomies were steep (as they are often claimed to be), they may be controlling. If this dictates tight oligopoly, it is then especially important to minimize the other elements of market power. Note that one would then expect all leading firms to be equal at that optimum size, with little or no asymmetry among them.

Minimizing the other elements of market power is especially important in the old-fashioned Natural Monopoly Case, where efficient size embraces the entire market. Many utilities may be of this sort, including local electric power distribution, gas, telephones, water, and sewage. To neutralize this internal market monopoly, it would be appropriate to go to some lengths in order to minimize absolute size, diversification into leading positions in other markets, and vertical integration into leading positions at other levels. For example, it might be optimum for power distribution companies to be as small and localized as scale economies permit (no holding companies), not diversified into other lines, and not vertically integrated into making electrical apparatus. It would also be wise to scrutinize their purchasing policies closely, lest X-inefficiency weaken their efforts to enforce competitive pricing among their suppliers.

All in all, optimum structure is defined by several simple propositions, which combine and mutually trade off in rather complex ways. In general terms, optimum structure is as close to loose oligopoly as scale economies permit (in terms of gradients), leading firms are always approximately symmetric, entry barriers are low, cooperation is held to a bare minimum, and other external elements are weak, except where they are needed to neutralize or supplement scale economies. Scale economies or diseconomies are controlling only when their gradients are steep. Financial markets must have similar optimum structure, or optimum structures in other markets may tend to decay into unduly monopolistic structures.

NATURAL STRUCTURE

Chapter 2 noted how widely views on natural structure have diverged, from John Moody's unified financial and industrial galaxies to the recent optimistic view that competitive structure is pervasive. Theory yields a variety of specific predictions, but the main outlines of natural structure can be defined fairly clearly.

In the General Case, (with constant costs), loose oligopoly is possible, but ordinarily it may be expected to coalesce into tight oligopoly. This is both because of input-price advantages and the greater profits available from achieving market power. Pure monopoly, though possible, will not usually emerge, even if entry barriers are high; instead, as noted earlier, a concentration-collusion margin may usually evolve, short of pure monopoly and mixing oligopoly and cooperation. If cooperation is proscribed, the margin will be at higher levels of concentration. The partly collusive oligopoly will be tight, unless cooperation is so effective as to make high concentration unnecessary. Asymmetry is almost certain to appear, possibly in extreme degree; symmetry is unstable in the circumstances, because there may be disproportionate gains in being the dominant firm. There is no reason to expect such tight, asymmetric, collusive oligopoly to be systematically neutralized by any or all of the external elements. In fact, leading firms may usually become associated with diversification, either by branching into new growth fields or by being taken over by larger firms.

In the Optimum Size Case, leading firms will converge on the efficient size, except that at least one firm will usually go beyond it into the range of rising costs. It will accept (and be able to sustain) this relative inefficiency to the degree that its extra size confers added input-price and market-power advantages. This leading firm (or firms) will fight incursions by lesser firms, both using and protecting its advantages. The followers will settle at efficient scale, or less, and they may very probably rely also on innovation to sustain their less-advantaged position. The leading firm (or firms) may then adopt a relatively passive, imitator's role in technical change, partly because its larger market share reaps it a larger reward for any improvement it may preempt, buy out, or imitate. The net total of innovation will, however, be less than it would be if all were at the optimum size.

This asymmetric structure has two special features. It is inferior to symmetry in both the efficiency and the innovation it yields. And it embodies perpetual inner strain between the leading and secondary firms. Each secondary firm would like to displace the dominant firm, but none may be able to, or dare to mount a frontal campaign to do so. Some fairly strong informal structure is also probable in such tight oligopoly. There is no reason to expect external elements to neutralize this structural monopoly, rather than strengthen it.

The direct effect of natural-monopoly cost conditions is, naturally, a one-firm market. Vertical integration, both backward and forward, is also likely, partly in defensive anticipation and partly as an outlet for the profits accruing as the monopoly exploits its advantages. These profits may also find more diverse uses, and such diversification will be perhaps even more luxuriant if standard rate regulation is imposed on the firm (as Chapter 3 noted). Generally, the original monopoly will serve as the nucleus for a variety of additional elements of market power. Early electric utility development in the United States illustrates some of these possibilities; telecommunications presently does, too.

All in all, the general contours of natural structure emerge fairly clearly. The degree of structural monopoly will usually exceed the levels prescribed by economies of scale—in some cases greatly so. Where it does not, collusion will be relatively strong. The various structural elements cannot be relied upon to neutralize each other; on the contrary, many of them will tend to reinforce. If there is any single "natural" structure for the most general case, it is tight, asymmetrical, collusive oligopoly, possibly reinforced by external elements. This hypothesis is not meant to imply a rigid matrix; there will obviously be variations in it, departures from it, and slow evolution toward it in individual cases. Also, it may be under steady pressure and threats from potential entrants and from the forces of industry growth and general technical change. Nonetheless, both logic and probability suggest it as the main archetype of natural structure.

COMPARING NATURAL AND OPTIMUM STRUCTURE

Apparently optimum and natural structure may tend to diverge, though in degree rather than in kind. Natural structure will usually be more market power than optimum structure would prescribe. Internal market structure will probably be tighter, more asymmetric, and more collusive than would be best for performance; constraints on collusion may simply induce higher formal market power; and external elements are at least as likely to reinforce as to neutralize the internal market elements.

This is not a contrast between polar opposites, between monopoly versus competition, as has been feared from time to time. Nor is it an invariable pattern. Both natural and optimum structures will usually be intermediate and complex cases. But the various elements may usually reinforce, rather than neutralize, market power. Unless extra constraints are added, structural monopoly may go beyond optimum levels and patterns in most markets. Moreover, specific constraints (such as against collusion) may simply alter the composition of structural monopoly, not shrink it.

Among questions for factual analysis two stand out. (1) Is market power, in general terms, as significant as the analysis of natural structure suggests? (2) Does the specific composition of structural elements tend to coincide with what may be the natural archetype: tight, asymmetric, collusive oligopoly, with external elements probably reinforcing? The next six chapters try to outline answers to these and related questions.

Market Power in Fact

Chapter /**5**

The Setting, with
Particular Attention
to Large Firms

There are but few exceptions to the rule, that large
private firms, though far superior to public departments, are
yet, in proportion to their size, no less inferior to private
businesses of a moderate size in that energy and resource,
that restlessness and inventive power, which lead to the
striking out of new paths.

ALFRED MARSHALL
"Some Aspects of Competition" (1890)

The numbers are not great; we may think without error
of most work being done by five or six hundred firms. This is
the part of the economy which, automatically, we identify with
the modern industrial society. To understand it is to understand that part which is most subject to change and which,
accordingly, is most changing our lives.

JOHN KENNETH GALBRAITH
The New Industrial State (1967)

The setting for market activity includes the whole array of enterprises, from smallest to largest. Industrial firms are only a minority of this array, as Table 5.1 shows. Yet the largest of these firms have come to dominate popular and expert ideas about trends in the whole economy. They may indeed be the heart of trustified monopoly capitalism or, instead, Schumpeter's swarm of struggling, creative behemoths. According to much of the recent literature, these firms are now (1) the essential core of the economy; (2) gradually increasing their total share; (3) subject, nonetheless, to risk and flux; (4) increasingly diversified; (5) fed on government purchases and R & D support; (6) the proven archetype for efficient organization; and (7) newly vested with broad social concerns. These points bear on the status of market power in several important ways, and so this chapter briefly reviews evidence about them. On some points the data are far from precise and the inter- pretations must be tentative, but the scope and character of large enterprises can still be fixed in fairly clear perspective.

TABLE 5.1 SECTORS IN THE U.S. ECONOMY

Sectors	Percent of National Income Originating in Each Sector		Employment, March 1968 (thousands)	Number of Private Enterprises, 1965 (thousands)		
	1950	1967		Sole proprietorships	Active Partnerships	Active Corporations
Agriculture, forestry and fisheries	7.3	3.4	3,537	3,225	128	28
Mining			585	36	15	13
Construction	7.1	6.2	3,306	705	58	113
Manufacturing	31.6	30.2	19,345	186	37	186
Transportation	5.6	4.0				
Communication	1.4	2.0	4,265	297	18	60
Electricity, gas, and sanitary services	1.6	2.0				
Wholesale and retail trade	17.0	14.8	13,778	1,854	235	440
Finance, insurance, and real estate	9.1	10.8	3,036	539	249	388
Services	9.0	11.5	10,300	2,208	169	188
Government, public firms, and rest of world	10.3	15.1	12,215	—	—	—
Total	100.0	100.0	70,367	9,078	914	1,424

SOURCES: Adapted from U.S. Bureau of the Census, *Statistical Abstract of the United States, 1968,* (Washington, D.C.: U.S. Government Printing Office, 1968), Tables 464, 317, and 682.

MERGERS AND LARGE FIRMS IN EARLIER DECADES

Although many large railroad and other enterprises were formed between 1850 and 1890, the main mass of large "modern" corporations first emerged from the "trust movement" of 1897–1901. This wave of mergers, some of them embracing scores of competitive firms at a stroke, formed near-monopolies in a variety of big and little industries: in 1904 John Moody counted over 300.[1] Large overall concentration in the economy emerged together with high concentration in individual industries: Chapter 2 has noted that the virtue, the economic inevitability, of "consolidation" was widely asserted; monopoly appeared to be the natural structure of industry.

This first merger wave (Figure 5.1 shows the number of manufacturing and mining mergers) was paralleled by similar waves in Canada, England, and other countries.[2] There have been two later waves in the United States,

---

[1] John Moody, *The Truth About the Trusts* (Chicago: Moody Publishing Company, 1904).
[2] See H. W. Macrosty, *The Trust Movement in British Industries* (London: Longmans, 1907).

neither of them with the dramatic (if rather transient) impact of the 1897–1904 outburst. The 1920's wave, which like the first wave was generously laced with promoters' manipulations, tended to combine secondary firms, cementing oligopoly structure in a range of industries. The latest wave continues growing, although a series of antitrust challenges in early 1969 seems to have checked it sharply, possibly permanently. Mergers have been increasingly "conglomerate" in character; a reasonable appraisal (Table 5.2) is that as much as 80 percent of recent mergers are "conglomerate." Mergers are also numerous outside the manufacturing sector. The trade and services sectors averaged over 400 per year during 1961–1967.

Yet the role of mergers in creating large firms dwindled from 1901 to the 1950's.[3] Differing industry growth rates caused most shifts in the ranks

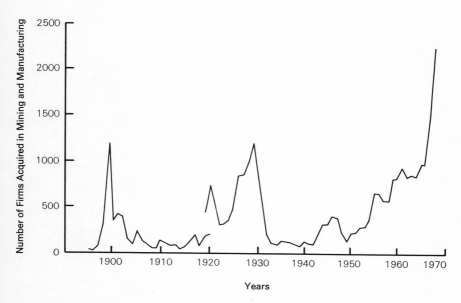

Figure 5.1   Number of Mergers in U.S. Mining and Manufacturing, 1895–1968

SOURCES: Data for 1895–1920, Ralph L. Nelson, *Merger Movements in American Industry, 1895–1956* (Princeton: Princeton University Press, 1959), Table B-7; for 1919–1940, Willard L. Thorp, "The Merger Movement," in *The Structure of Industry*, Temporary National Economic Committee, Monograph No. 27, (Washington, D.C.: U.S. Government Printing Office, 1941), Part III, pp. 231–234; for 1940 to the present, U.S. Cabinet Committee on Price Stability, *Studies By the Staff* (Washington, D.C.: U.S. Government Printing Office, 1969). The Nelson and Thorp series are not entirely comparable, and so they are not spliced.

---

[3] See J. Fred Weston, *The Role of Mergers in the Growth of Large Firms* (Berkeley: University of California Press, 1953). Among major present progeny of earlier mergers are General Motors, Standard Oil, General Electric, U.S. Steel, Bethlehem Steel, Union Carbide, Chrysler, RCA, I.T.&T. and, of course, the Bell System, and almost all of the largest banks.

TABLE 5.2 DISTRIBUTION OF LARGE MANUFACTURING AND MINING ACQUISITIONS BY TYPE AND BY PERIOD OF ACQUISITION

Type of Merger	1948–1953			1954–1959		1960–1966		1967		1968		
	Number	Percent of number	Percent of assets	Number	Percent of number	Number	Percent of number	Number	Percent of number	Number	Percent of number	Percent of assets
Horizontal	18	31	39	78	25	69	13	14	9	14	7	4
Vertical	6	10	17	43	14	82	15	13	8	17	9	7
Conglomerate:	34	59	44	193	61	387	72	128	83	161	84	89
Market extension	4	7	2	20	6	31	6	—	—	7	1	6
Product extension	27	47	39	145	46	276	51	94	61	113	59	39
Other	3	5	3	28	9	80	15	34	22	47	24	43
Total	58	100	100	314	100	538	100	155	100	192	100	100

SOURCE: Adapted from Willard F. Mueller, Statement on *The Status and Future of Small Business*, Hearings before the Select Committee on Small Business, U.S. Senate, 90th Congress, 1st Session (Washington, D.C.: U.S. Government Printing Office, 1967), Table 11; and Cabinet Committee on Price Stability, *Studies by the Staff* (Washington, D.C.: U.S. Government Printing Office, 1969).

of large firms during 1900–1950.[4]   Many firms, such as the Central Leather Co., the seventh ranking industrial enterprise in 1909, rode shrinking industries into oblivion.   Many such shifts, or "turnover," are of little account, since below the top 10 or 20 firms the gradations in size are rather small, and therefore small size changes can yield large and virtually meaningless shufflings in "rank."   Also, since many of the early trusts were obviously overextended from the start, many of their declines were predictable.   In any event, the degree of shifting faded steadily during the period.[5]

It is a safe guess—but still a guess—that overall concentration in the manufacturing sector changed little either way during 1900 to 1950.[6]   There were large rises in some utility sectors (electricity, gas, telephones) and in retail trade.   Therefore, for the whole economy, the large firm share was probably steady or only gently rising.

PRESENT STRUCTURE

That there are relatively few large firms among many middling ones and swarms of little ones is, of course, inevitable.   Appendix Table 1 shows it, for the whole economy and for the main sectors.   It also shows that large firms are far from ubiquitous, even in manufacturing—prominent, yes; a "core" of the economy, perhaps, or at least of part of the economy.   But in some sectors, and in many industries (as Chapter 7 will note), medium-size and smallish enterprises predominate.   Moreover, many large firms are mainly holding companies, setting no model for the size of producing enterprises.   Appendix Table 1 also shows that large manufacturing firms do not stand alone; banks, insurance and other firms are even bigger in certain financial respects.

Moreover, almost all of the very biggest manufacturing firms are either (1) in mature, standardized-product industries (automobiles, oil, steel) or (2) real or quasi-holding companies.   As Appendix Table 2 shows, these account for almost all of the largest 25 firms, which are those over $2 billion in assets and about 100,000 in employees.   There is little evidence for the common notion that the very largest firms are models or prototypes for the whole variety of manufacturing enterprise, let alone for those in other sectors. One may put it even more definitely; largish size (up to about $2 billion sales or assets, or 100,000 employees) may be common for operating firms in many manufacturing industries, but larger instances are so distinctly specialized types as to verge on oddity.   This view is borne out by patterns abroad

---

[4] Seymour Friedland, "Turnover and Growth of the Largest Industrial Firms, 1906–1950," *Review of Economics and Statistics*, XXXIX (February 1957), 79–83.

[5] Norman R. Collins and Lee E. Preston, "The Size Structure of the Largest Industrial Firms, 1909–1958," *American Economic Review*, LI (December 1961), 986–1011.

[6] Morris Adelman, "The Measurement of Industrial Concentration," *Review of Economics and Statistics*, XXXIII (November 1951), 269–296.

(see Appendix Table 4). The large firms are mostly oil or steel producers (such as Royal Dutch Shell and the German Finsider) or quasi-holding companies (such as Unilever and Mitsubishi); and two of them represent industry-wide *public* ownership of the British and French coal industries. The prototype role of large enterprises is, therefore, at best, unproven. This point may go against the grain of the recurring merger fever in Western Europe and Japan, to create firms which can "stand up to the American giants." In fact the "stand up to" case is largely empty (except possibly for several special situations); a handy tool for aspiring monopolists to use on acquiescent governments.[7]

POSTWAR TRENDS

In the manufacturing sector, large firms have steadily and substantially enlarged their share since 1947. As Figure 5.2 shows, the rise has been faster than the "glacial pace" which 1909–1947 witnessed, and its pace

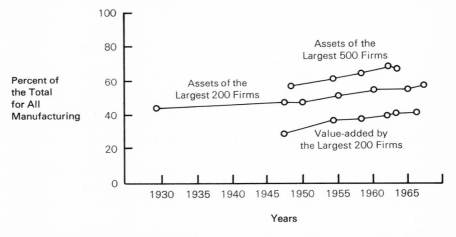

Figure 5.2. Trends of Overall Concentration in U.S. Manufacturing, 1929–1967

SOURCES: Data on assets in the largest 500 firms, Charles H. Berry, "Corporate Bigness and Diversification in Manufacturing," *Ohio State Law Journal*, XXVIII (Summer 1967), 402–426; assets in the largest 200 firms, U.S. Cabinet Committee on Price Stability, *Studies by the Staff* (Washington, D.C.: U.S. Government Printing Office, 1969), p. 92; value-added by the largest 200 firms, U.S. Bureau of the Census, *Annual Survey of Manufacturers, 1966*, M66(AS)-8, Supplement (Washington, D.C.: U.S. Government Printing Office, 1968), Part 8.

---

[7] U.S. Senate Subcommittee on Antitrust and Monopoly, 90th Congress, 2nd Session, *Hearings on Economic Concentration, Part* 7 (Washington, D.C.: U.S. Government Printing Office, 1968), 3682–3706.

may have increased during 1966 and 1967.[8]   The trend in the economy as a whole is not conclusively known, for lack of statistics.   The relative expansion of the service sector, whose units are mostly small-scale, might even have offset the rise in the manufacturing sector.   Yet, at least in utilities and finance (see Chapter 6), there has been increasing concentration, so that the trend for the whole economy is probably rising.

Four main causes for this probable rise have been suggested.   One is mergers.   These have had some impact in railroads, electric and telephone utilities, and banking.   They have also had a substantial influence in manufacturing, even though most of the very largest firms have had to tread more lightly in pursuing mergers because of increasing antitrust constraints.   As Table 5.3 shows, mergers have equalled one-seventh of the asset growth of

TABLE 5.3   MERGERS DURING 1948–1965 BY THE 200 LARGEST MANUFACTURING CORPORATIONS OF 1965

Size of Acquiring Corporation	Number of Acquisitions	Total Acquired Assets ($ billion)	Assets Acquired as a Percent of		Asset Growth 1948–1965
			1948 Assets	1965 Assets	
20 largest	183	2.6	10.4	2.8	3.9
21–100	1,286	11.7	55.1	15.3	21.1
101–200	1,223	7.2	78.4	19.7	26.5
All 200	2,692	21.5	39.0	10.6	14.5

SOURCE: Adapted from Willard F. Mueller, Statement on *The Status and Future of Small Business,* Hearings before the Select Committee on Small Business, U.S. Senate, 90th Congress, 1st Session (Washington, D.C.: U.S. Government Printing Office, 1967), Table 4.

all the top 200 during 1948–1965; below the very top firms, the fraction goes as high as one-fourth.[9]   Moreover the fractions are rising recently, as the merger wave has quickened.   During 1960–1967, the mergers by the largest 100 and 200 industrials have just equalled the margin by which those firms' *total* share of assets increased; lacking those mergers, the overall degree of industrial concentration might have remained constant.[10]   Yet mergers are not a fundamental explanation (why, in fact, have they occurred?), and they

[8] Cabinet Committee on Price Stability, *Studies by the Staff* (Washington, D.C.: U.S. Government Printing Office, 1969) 45–49, 69–81.
[9] Morris Adelman has noted that in many cases much of the merger growth would have occurred anyway by internal expansion, if the mergers had been prevented.   (*Economic Concentration, Part 1* (1964) 226–227).   But, conversely, many mergers may have led on to further internal growth which, without the merger, would *not* have occurred.   The whole question, being partly speculative, cannot be decided without further research.
[10] Cabinet Committee on Price Stability, *op. cit.,* 78–79.

have been unevenly scattered. Many industries and large firms have gone almost untouched by them, so far.

A second cause for the rise is that high growth rates in some big industries boosted the total large-firm share to some extent, as they probably did in the 1909–1947 period; one may single out oil, automobiles, aircraft, electronics, and computers. Yet by contrast, steel, meat, copper, and other slow growers have exerted a downward pull. The total effects are not precisely known; they have probably been important, but less so than in previous decades.[11]

A third possible source is government as the sponsor of much industrial research and development (R & D), and as the largest single buyer of industrial output. Table 5.4 shows that federal funds (chiefly through the Defense Department and the space agency, NASA) have been paying for a majority

TABLE 5.4 INDUSTRIAL PATTERNS IN R & D FUNDING, 1962 AND 1965

Industries	Federal funds as a Percent of total funds		Amount of Federal funds 1965 ($ million)	Total Funds as a Percent of Industry Sales, 1965
	1962	1965		
Food and kindred products	4	1	1	.4
Textiles and apparel	*	*	*	.4
Lumber and products	*	*	*	.5
Paper and products	—	—	—	.7
Chemicals and allied products	22	14	190	4.2
Industrial chemicals	21	16	147	4.6
Drugs and medicines	2	*	*	5.9
Other chemicals	40	*	*	2.3
Petroleum	7	16	69	1.2
Rubber products	23	15	25	1.9
Stone, clay and glass products	*	3	4	1.6
Primary metals	7	4	8	.8
Fabricated metal products	19	11	17	1.4
Machinery	30	23	258	4.1
Electrical and communication	63	62	1,978	9.4
Motor vehicles and transport	28	26	326	3.1
Aircraft and missiles	89	88	4,500	28.0
Instruments	46	32	125	6.2
Other manufacturing	*	2	1	.7
Nonmanufacturing	75	71	255	—
Total	57	55	7,759	4.3

* Not separately available, but included in total.
SOURCE: Adapted from National Science Foundation, *Basic Research, Applied Research, and Development in Industry, 1965* (Washington D.C.: U.S. Government Printing Office, 1967).

[11] Since (as Chapter 8 will note) turnover of firms *within* major industries has been small, industry growth rates have at least played some role in shaping over-all concentration.

of the R & D done by industrial firms; indeed in some of the fastest-growing major industries, for nearly all of it. For many of these industries, too, public programs take a large share of output (as Chapter 9 will note). Yet the incidence of this within the whole group of large companies is only partial and uneven; this will be explored further toward the end of this chapter. Moreover, many defense suppliers have gone from feast to famine, while overall concentration has continued steadily upward. Therefore, public sponsorship has probably had only a limited direct upward effect on overall concentration. Although it is extremely important for more than a few very large firms, it is equally true that a wider spread of federal R & D support and of purchasing could probably have weakened or checked the relative rise of the very largest firms (see also Chapter 11).

Fourth, the largest firms may simply enjoy superior efficiency, as most of their managers understandably believe—and some European observers echo. It is true (as Chapter 12 will note) that the largest firms are unusually profitable, both in rates of return and relative security. In 1964, actually a rather lean year for them, the 20 largest industrial firms had 25 percent of the sector's assets and 32 percent of the profits after taxes. Rates of return (after tax) on invested capital have been averaging as much as 12–15 percent, year in and year out, for many of the largest firms. Of the 500 largest, only about 2 percent have shown losses in any given recent year, and most of these rank below 300th. Similarly, since 1959 none of the 50 largest banks, utility or insurance firms, or the largest 30 retailers, has shown even a transient or small financial loss in any year. These patterns are reflected in the financial ratings assigned to firms by investor services; these ratings are unmistakably (though not uniformly) correlated with company size. This has reinforced the enthusiasm with which some observers equate bigness with efficiency, and the largest firms are frequently regarded as being both archetype and the most advanced state of private enterprise generally.[12]

Yet all this says nothing conclusive about true efficiency. The high profitability may reflect pecuniary rather than technical economies, as Chapter 3 cautioned. And the very biggest firms are mostly special cases, rather than a general type. As noted above, nearly all of them are either (1) steady inhabitants of relatively older, standardized industries, such as oil, steel, automobiles, meatpacking, and banking, and/or (2) virtually holding companies, such as most of those in electronics. These two types account for most of the top 25 industrial firms; and those over $2 billion in assets; and those over 100,000 in employees. Moreover, as later chapters will explore,

---

[12] Recall Chapter 2; the classic affirmation is in Joseph A. Schumpeter, *Capitalism, Socialism and Democracy* (New York: Harper & Row, 1942); see also, among others, A. D. H. Kaplan, *Big Enterprise in a Competitive System*, rev. ed. (Washington, D.C.: Brookings, 1964); John Kenneth Galbraith, *American Capitalism* (Boston: Houghton Mifflin, 1956), and *The New Industrial State* (Boston: Houghton Mifflin, 1967); David A. Lilienthal, *Big Business–A New Era* (New York: Harper & Row, 1953) and Adolph A. Berle, *The Twentieth Century Capitalist Revolution* (New York: Harcourt, Brace, & World, 1954).

many of the largest firms do—as dominant firms in major industries, and buying in imperfect markets for inputs—probably get pecuniary gains (plus federal research support). All in all, very large size is hardly the proven archetype. Indeed, if one holds aside the two special types of largest American firms, much of the supposed size "gap" between American and large foreign firms fades away.

Much is often made of "turnover" among the largest firms, as a disproof of "entrenchment and rigidity of big business leadership."[13] This would be mostly irrelevant to market power exercised in separate markets, and the triviality of most turnover among lesser-ranking firms has already been mentioned above. Turnover "among the giants" might reflect Schumpeterian processes, though that really requires study of turnover within industries (see Chapter 8).

For whatever meaning it may yield, overall turnover in manufacturing has been lower since 1945 than in previous decades, and much of it has stemmed from relatively predictable industry growth rates (see Appendix Table 2).[14] Defense purchases have been another large influence on some firms (mainly in aerospace), and mergers have had an appreciable effect on those below the very top, particularly during the 1960's. In banking, insurance, and even retailing, the ranks have been remarkably stable (that is clearly shown in Appendix Table 3), particularly in the face of rapid growth during two decades. If Schumpeterian processes are at work, they must have been mostly internalized and directed by the largest manufacturing and financial firms.

Yet, massive and semipermanent though they may seem, the largest corporations do not stand apart from and above the rest of the economy. They engage, at all levels, in trade and technical associations and related joint contacts. There are also complex networks among the directorates of these and other firms, knitting virtually all of the larger firms into other industries and financial sectors.[15] In addition to these informal relations among firms,

---

[13] A. D. H. Kaplan, *op. cit.*, 123.

[14] During the relatively stable pre-Vietnam years of 1955–1963, 18 firms rose by five or more rungs into or within the top 50 industrials. They included 4 aircraft companies (Lockheed, North American, Boeing, and United), 5 companies with electronics activities (IBM, General Telephone, I.T.&T., Sperry Rand, and General Tire and Rubber), and 4 oil companies (Socony Mobil, Texaco, Standard Oil of California, and Continental).

Of 1955's top 50, 21 dropped five or more notches by 1963. These included five steel firms (Bethlehem, Republic, Jones and Laughlin, Armco, and Inland), four rubber companies (Goodyear, Firestone, U.S. Rubber, and B. F. Goodrich) and three oil companies (Sinclair, Cities Service, and Sun Oil).

[15] Antitrust Subcommittee of the Committee on the Judiciary Staff Report, House of Representatives, 89th Congress, 1st Session, *Interlocks in Corporate Management* (Washington, D.C.: U.S. Government Printing Office, March 12, 1965); also Federal Trade Commission, *Report on Interlocking Directorates*, (Washington, D.C.: U.S. Government Printing Office, 1951); and House Select Committee on Small Business, Preliminary Report, 85th Congress, 1st Session, *Interlocking Directors and Officials of 135 Large Financial Companies of the United States*, H. Rept. No. 1278 (Washington, D.C.: U.S. Goverment Printing Office, 1957); and a major recent study, Committee on Banking and Currency, House of Representatives, 90th Congress, 2nd Session, *Commercial Banks and Their Trust Activities: Emerging Influence on the American Economy*, Staff Report for the Subcommittee on Domestic Finance (Washington, D.C.: U.S. Government Printing Office, July 8, 1968).

there are the directorates held in virtually all of the large corporations by members of the largest banks, investment concerns, and insurance companies. These personal contacts are, in turn, merely part of the amorphous but pervasive market for corporate control.

In any case, virtually all of the giant corporations are woven into a loose but all-embracing tapestry of face-to-face, familiar, stable relationships. These links are neither randomly made nor quickly changed.[16] Most of them simply draw on the best corporate experience, but some of them cement buyer-seller connections, while others bring the policies of competing firms into indirect contact, through side-by-side directorships. In any case, the larger financial units have traditionally had intimate, supervisory access to the large firms, and they will continue to have it. To them an industrial statesman heading one of the world's largest corporations may be just another successful manufacturer.

Many of the same large-firm patterns of rising share, stability, and financial interweaving are found in other industrialized countries, but are etched in more sharply. In Western European economies (and still more so in Japan), the largest firms hold even larger shares than in the United States. And large-firm shares have been rising in Britain and Germany in recent years.[17] After a rise during 1954–1959, the 50 largest German industrial companies further enlarged their share of total industrial shipments from 30.6 percent in 1959 to 38.9 percent in 1966. The three largest Japanese combines—Mitsui, Mitsubishi, and Sumitomo—have complete or partial control of at least 17 percent of assets and profits in the entire Japanese economy (not just in manufacturing), and their share has probably been rising.[18]

Much of the recent merger wave in Europe is in professed reaction to American entry via merger in many industries. These responses are widely said to be needed in order to match or "stand up to" large American firms. That this need is exaggerated has been noted above. There are other, more plausible, rationales, including "fighting company" tactics by some American firms abroad and the public R & D support channelled to many large American firms in research-intensive industries. Against these real and imagined threats, merger is at best a partial answer. Nevertheless it is occurring, helping to create large European firms and trans-Atlantic oligopoly on rather a new scale.

On another point of comparison, the supervisory connections of major financial groups are generally closer and more stable and exclusive in Western

---

[16] *Interlocking Directors and Officials.* As an additional example, the Antitrust Division in 1968 required General Motors, Ford, and Chrysler to drop some directors who represented small overlaps. But in deference to these established positions, it allowed two years for phasing some of them out.

[17] *Economic Concentration, Part 7,* 3490–3491, 3688–3696.

[18] Eugene Rotwein, "Economic Concentration and Monopoly in Japan," *Journal of Political Economy,* LXXII (June 1964), 262–277; and Eleanor Hadley's discussion in *Economic Concentration, Part 7,* 3508–3534.

Europe and Japan than in the United States. For example, "major Swedish businesses all fall within certain well-defined groups, connected either with banks, or with family groups—or both."[19] The re-formation of combines in West Germany and Japan, arranged largely by the larger banks, has left the banks with an unusually central role. Yet there have also been many "take-overs" by new promoters, and American firms have moved into some large markets.[20] Broadly speaking, large American firms are—in their rising share, stability, and, possibly, financial ties—moving toward patterns which have been common abroad. Ironically, the patterns abroad are being accentuated partly in response to various policies and initiatives by the American firms.

DIVERSIFICATION

Conglomeration actually embraces multiregional (for example, a string of dairies) as well as multiproduct operations. It can be achieved by internal growth, as well as by merger; also many spin-offs—which amount to decon-glomerations—occur without the fanfare attending mergers. For all these reasons, the recent rise of conglomerate mergers does not *prove* that a trend toward conglomerate enterprise exists. Moreover, much corporate control is subsurface, through gradations of partial holdings. In some cases, the holdings are so small as to escape outside detection entirely (as also occurs in financial markets; see the next chapter). Yet in other cases, full formal control of a branch may be diluted by a deliberate company policy of decen-tralizing decisions to autonomous divisions. The data on diversification which follow are accordingly sketchy at best, but the main outlines do emerge fairly clearly. An analysis of conglomerate patterns for *individual* industries is held over to Chapter 9.

First, is diversification *extensive* among large firms? Broadly speaking, it is, and not only in Japan. In 1950, as Table 5.5 shows, most of the very largest American firms were multi-*industry* enterprises, some of them exceed-ingly so. The degree of product-class (5-digit) diversity was, naturally, even greater. In both 1958 and 1963 nearly one-quarter of the employment in the 200 largest firms was in (2-digit) industry groups *other* than their primary ones; in certain groups the share was much higher.[21] Moreover, the larger firms are very much (though not uniformly) more diversified than smaller ones. It is important to recognize that by far the greater part of

[19] "Big Business Galaxy," *The Economist* (Oct. 28, 1967).
[20] See J. H. Dunning, *American Investment in British Manufacturing Industry* (London: Allen & Unwin, 1955); and J. H. Dunning and W. G. Jensen, *The Role of American Investment in the British Economy*, Broadsheet 507 (London: Political and Economic Planning, February 1969). See also *Economic Concentration, Part 7*, (1968), 3692–3693.
[21] *Economic Concentration, Part 1*, 85; and U.S. Senate Subcommittee on Antitrust and Monopoly, *Concentration Ratios in Manufacturing Industry, 1963: Part II* (Washington, D.C.: U.S. Govern-ment Printing Office, 1967), Table 24.

TABLE 5.5 DIVERSIFICATION IN LARGE AMERICAN FIRMS, 1950

Number of Industries in which a Company had an Establishment	All 1,000 Largest Forms	Firms Ranked by Value of Shipments		
		1–50	51–500	501–1000
Over 20	7	7	—	—
16–20	10	8	2	—
11–15	25	5	20	—
6–10	122	15	90	17

SOURCE: Adapted from Federal Trade Commission, *Industrial Concentration and Product Diversification in the 1,000 Largest Manufacturing Companies: 1950*, (Washington, D.C.: U.S. Government Printing Office, 1957), Table 21.

present conglomerate patterns is of long standing; the mergers of the 1960's have only added marginally to an extensive preexisting situation. Moreover (as Chapter 9 will indicate) the preexisting diversification has involved leading positions in large industries far overshadowing those involved in the recent mergers.

There is rather less diversification in large British enterprises. Most of it is focused in the very large firms, and there has been virtually no conglomerate merger activity of the recent American sort.[22] In Japan, secrecy and gradations of intercompany controls preclude any precise estimates, but there is no doubt that diversity within the main combines is unusually great. Their subsidiaries are in all reaches of the economy—finance, trade, shipping, services, mining, insurance, and utilities, as well as in manufacturing.[23]

Second, has diversification by large firms been increasing? Again, broadly speaking, it has, though not uniformly. The wave of conglomerate mergers in the United States does not, in itself, prove an increase in "conglomeration," for reasons noted above. Also, the net growth of diversification may have lagged behind general economic expansion, and it may have been focused in only a few industries (which will be examined shortly).

Yet some such trend is clear from other evidence, covering mainly large firms.[24] One study has noted increasing diversification between 1929 and 1954.[25] During 1954–1958 the number of multi-industry firms increased

[22] U.K. Board of Trade, *The Report on the Census of Production for 1958* (London: Her Majesty's Stationery Office, 1963), Part 135, Table 19.
[23] In 1955 the three largest combines probably had control of at least one firm in at least 51 out of a sample of 64 major industries. The probable number of industries for each combine were: Mitsui, 37; Mitsubishi; 32; and Sumitomo, 37. See Rotwein, *op. cit.*, 268–71; and Miss Hadley, *op. cit.*, and sources cited there.
  There are numerous extreme instances of conglomerates outside Japan as well. In 1965, the I.T.&T. Corporation contained 430 separate boards of directors. Unilever, Ltd. embraced 500 companies in 50 countries, with a wide array of products and trading operations.
[24] See *Economic Concentration, Part 1*, 155–80, 223–48, and *Part 2* (1965), 745–77.
[25] Michael Gort, *Diversification and Integration in American Manufacturing Industry* (Princeton: Princeton University Press, 1962).

59 percent. Joel Dirlam's review of the 100 largest industrials during 1930–1963 shows increasing diversification in all but a few.[26] During 1950–1962, there was a rise in the proportion of the 1,000 largest manufacturing firms shipping large numbers of 5-digit products.[27] Charles Berry has shown beyond any doubt that diversification of the 500 largest industrials rose during 1960–1965.[28] And the sharp rise in large conglomerate mergers during 1966–1968 strongly suggests that the rise is continuing. This increasing diversification may provide most of the explanation how overall concentration has risen substantially since 1947 while intra-industry concentration has been rising only slightly (see Chapter 7).

By contrast, most recent British mergers have been within industries; of 74 large mergers in 1967, for example, 70 "fell within the purchasing company's existing product range."[29] In later 1967 and 1968, a set of large mergers, almost entirely horizontal, cropped up on shipbuilding, electrical goods, computers, automobiles, and banking.[30] Elsewhere in Europe, and in Japan, too, conglomerate mergers have recently been relatively less important than in the United States. Of course, in recent years, American firms have injected conglomerate elements into many European markets via their own entry across the water. American holdings in European industries are substantial and growing, and they cluster heavily in the largest American firms. As of 1966, 25 firms had about 60 percent of all American investment in Europe; the next 166 had only about another 20 percent.[31] Therefore, the degree of diversification among all of the leading firms in European markets is really rising more than the evidence about European firms alone would suggest.

Third, are diversification and its recent increase *focused* in a few specialized industry groups? They are, but only in part, and decreasingly so. In the United States, large-firm diversification is pronounced for companies in chemicals, fabricated metals, electrical and other machinery, rubber, aerospace and electronics, and food products, among others. Indeed, the chemicals area is essentially a grouping of conglomerates, facing each other in hundreds of submarkets. By contrast, most oil and steel companies have avoided diversification, although there have recently been some recent mergers into adjacent fuels and metals. Diversification is relatively low (with exceptions) in textile products and lumber products.[32] In Britain, diversification is most prominent in chemicals, machinery, electronics, and

[26] *Economic Concentration, Part 2*, 745–777.
[27] *Economic Concentration, Part 1*, 156–160.
[28] Charles H. Berry, "Corporate Bigness and Diversification in Manufacturing," *Ohio State Law Journal*, XXVIII (Summer 1967), 402–426, especially 424–426 and Table 11.
[29] H. B. Rose and G. D. Newbould, "The 1967 Takeover Boom," *Moorgate and Wall Street* (Autumn, 1967).
[30] See *Economic Concentration, Part 7*, including the author's discussion at pages 3688-3696.
[31] *Ibid.*, and references cited therein.
[32] *Economic Concentration, Part 1*, 83–85; *Part 2* (1965), 745–777 and 973–976; *Concentration Ratios, 1958: Part II*, Table 34; and *Concentration Ratios, 1963: Part II*, Table 24.

aircraft, but not in textiles, lumber products, autos and foods.[33]   In Japan, diversification is pervasive, but control is often attenuated.

Typically then, the incidence of diversification is broad and changeable. Certain chemicals and metal fabricating industries and the aerospace sector may be more prone to diversification. But there are no standard or "natural" patterns. This is further shown by the changing pattern of new diversification in recent years, some of it occurring in or moving into industries previously untouched by it. Some causes of these changing patterns will be noted in the more detailed analysis in Chapter 9.

GOVERNMENT PURCHASES

Much of the "military-industrial complex" or "new industrial state," if they exist at all, must inhere in the purchases of the Defense Department, the National Aeronautical and Space Agency, and the Atomic Energy Commission.   These, the really big federal purchasers, are summarized in Table 5.6.

TABLE 5.6   PROCUREMENT BY DEFENSE, NASA, AND AEC

	Fiscal Year	
Agency	1966 ($ million) (Percent)	1967 ($ million) (Percent)
Defense prime contracts		
Procurement Total	33,533	39,219
100 Largest	21,400	25,693
R & D contracts Total	5,323	6,067
100 Largest	(4,900)	(5,600)
NASA Total	5,032	4,651
100 Largest firms	3,714	3,578
AEC Total industrial contractors	1,643	1,594
30 Largest	1,448	1,443
Total: Amount	45,531	51,531
As % of the value of industrial shipments	(9.3)	(10.0)

NOTE: Figures in parentheses are estimated.
SOURCES: Adapted from Defense Department, *100 Largest Prime Contracters* and *500 Largest R & D Suppliers;* N.A.S.A., Annual Procurement Report; AEC, *Financial Report* (all Washington, D.C.: U.S. Government Printing Office, published annually); U.S. Bureau of the Census, *Statistical Abstract of the United States 1968*, (Washington, D.C.: U.S. Government Printing Office, 1968).

[33] U.K. *Census of Production, 1958, op. cit., Part 135*, Tables 14–18.

That the total amounts are large should occasion no surprise. Their incidence in heavy goods and aerospace industries is also well known, although some of the details below indicate an even greater role in some industries and firms than is commonly recognized.

Yet the impact of these purchases on the largest firms *as a whole* is probably relatively moderate. During fiscal 1964 through 1968, for example, the 25 largest manufacturing firms secured military prime contracts for supplies equalling only about 3 percent of their total sales.[34] The big prime contracts have focused increasingly in firms, especially in aircraft and electronics, ranking below the very largest. The profits, growth, and relative positions of many of the very largest firms lie largely outside specific federal contracting policies (although subcontracting does spread the participation).

Yet the aerospace subsector does contain many large firms with extreme involvement in defense supply. For the 25 industrial firms gaining the most military contracts in fiscal 1961–1962, these contracts equalled nearly half (45 percent) of their entire 1962 sales. By 1965 this reliance had declined, but only slightly, to 39 percent. Within these 25 firms, the 8 aircraft and 3 electronics firms are the extreme group, averaging 62 percent. For the rest, defense supply averaged no more than 17 percent of sales. By 1968 the proportion for all 25 had declined further to 23 percent; but if one holds aside General Motors and Ford as special cases, the proportion for the rest is 36 percent.

To put the situation in clearer focus, one must look at individual companies. For this purpose, Appendix Table 5 indicates the role of direct federal spending in a selection of 48 of the largest manufacturing firms during 1965–1967. The selection includes those clearly engaged in what might be called "R & D-intensive" or "innovation-orientated" industries, such as electronics and aircraft, rather than primary metals, textiles, oil, lumber products, and the like. The classifications are rather arbitrary, and they may be in error in some details, but they do suffice to indicate the broad patterns.

The purchases focus sharply in aerospace, electronics, communications, ships, weapons, construction, and certain services, as Appendix Table 5 indicates. This is further shown by Table 5.7, which shows the industrial distribution of military procurement in 1966–1967. In its partial incidence, this may be well short of the ubiquity which "military-industrial complex" connotes. Yet the purchases are clearly a significant (if not dominant) factor for a number of firms and industries that have long posed antitrust

---

[34] This is evident from *The 500 Largest U.S. Industrial Corporations* (New York: *Fortune*, 1964–1968); and U.S. Defense Department lists of the *100 Companies and Their Subsidiary Corporations Listed According to Net Value of Military Prime Contract Awards* (Washington, D.C.: U.S. Government Printing Office, issued annually in December); the data for 1966 can be found in U.S. Congress, Joint Economic Committee, 89th Congress, 2nd Session, *Background Material on Economic Impact of Federal Procurement–1966* (Washington, D.C.: U.S. Government Printing Office, 1966).

TABLE 5.7 DISTRIBUTION OF DEFENSE
PURCHASES BY
"COMPETITIVE" STATUS,
FISCAL YEAR 1967*

Product or service	Total ($ millions)	Percent of Total:	
		Code 5 Purchases	Codes 3, 4 and 5 Purchases
Airframes	5,495	29.0	81.2
Aircraft engines	1,548	21.4	83.5
Other aircraft	459	56.6	69.3
Missile systems	3,710	45.2	90.2
Ships	1,512	28.2	30.4
Combat vehicles	441	52.1	56.9
Non-combat vehicles	585	10.7	10.8
Weapons	325	74.9	75.8
Ammunition	3,027	71.8	75.2
Electronic–communication equipment	2,549	54.0	67.1
Petroleum–products	1,180	9.6	9.6
Textiles–clothing	577	0.7	0.7
Military building supply	109	30.3	32.0
Subsistence	41	14.6	14.6
Construction	1,260	7.7	22.6
Construction equipment	122	17.2	26.2
Photographic equipment	53	41.6	68.1
All other equipment	584	25.4	31.5
Services	2,076	39.0	43.7
Total	25,656	37.5	62.2

NOTE: The competition codes are described by the Defense Department as follows
(See also Appendix Table 6):
0—Formally advertised for competitive bidding.
1—Negotiated: "price competition." More than one price quote was available.
2—Negotiated: "design and technical competition." Price was not the decisive factor.
3—Negotiated: "Follow-on" (extension) of a code 1 contract without further competition.
4—Negotiated: "Follow-on" of a code 2 contract without further competition.
5—Negotiated directly with a single source. No attempt at competition.
* For detail, see Appendix Table 6.
SOURCE: Adapted from unpublished Defense Department listings and compilations.

questions; these are especially computers, telephone equipment, automobiles, electrical equipment, aircraft and engines, and photographic supplies.

Fluctuations in purchasing may have had some destabilizing effects on supplier firms, including perhaps those in aircraft. In fact, much of the turnover among the "ranks" of all of the large firms has reflected changes in aircraft and related products.[35] For example, there were 18 firms ranking in the 50 largest in the pre-Vietnam years of 1955 to 1963 which rose in rank

[35] See also M. J. Peck and F. M. Scherer, *The Weapons Acquisition Process* (Boston: Division of Research, Graduate School of Business Administration, Harvard University, 1962).

by 5 places or more. Among these 18 risers, half were aerospace firms ranking among the 25 largest defense contractors. Yet there is little flux in several other sectors; for example, Western Electric's and General Electric's procurement and R & D contracting operations have moved steadily. As will also be noted below, many contracts are renewed and enlarged routinely. For that matter, many firms get an effective lock on future contracts for major systems at the outset by doing the R & D, work often paid for by a defense R & D contract.

Under Secretary McNamara, since 1961, the Defense Department has shifted toward "competitive" contracting procedures.[36] Table 5.7 shows that even this effort has been only partially successful, at best.[37] The Defense Department assigns contracts among 6 competition categories, or codes. Only code 0 fits the strict notion of competitive procurement, with formal advertisement and competitive bids. All other categories were negotiated contracts. On code 1 purchases, there were "at least two price quotes" to choose from; code 2 purchases involved a "design and technical competition," and price was not usually a deciding factor. These may or may not involve genuinely competitive conditions. Codes 3 and 4 are merely renewals of contracts in codes 1 and 2, respectively. Code 5 includes all contracts which no stretch of purchasers' imagination could assign elsewhere; no effort was made to approach more than one supplier. Defense Department staff advise taking the classifications with a large grain of salt. Thus the large construction consortium in Vietnam has found its way somehow into code 4, even though it has been largely a chosen instrument from the start. Most of the contract renewals in codes 3 and 4 are so routine as to qualify for code 5 status. Even many of the quasicompetitive code 1 and 2 purchases were foregone conclusions, owing to R & D contracts which put one competitor ahead.

Code 5 is no doubt a gross underestimate (or an extreme lower-bracket estimate) of true "sole-source" procurement. Codes 3, 4 and 5 together may give an upper-boundary estimate of effective sole-source buying, but even they may understate the true amount. As Table 5.7 shows, "sole-source" contracting was at least 37 percent and probably 50–65 percent of total defense prime contracts which were let in fiscal year 1967. The shares are highest in aerospace, as is well known, but they are also surprisingly high in ships, combat vehicles, weapons, ammunition, electronic and communication equipment, military building supply, photographic equipment, and services. In these lines one would have expected that the greater interchangeability of products would have led to low shares, if there really had been a determined effort to limit sole-source purchasing.

---

[36] Background Materials," *op. cit.*, 1966.
[37] For an extremely critical treatment of the competitive character and impact of defense spending, see U.S. Joint Economic Committee, 91st Congress, 1st Session, *The Economics of Military Procurement* (Washington, D.C.: U.S. Government Printing Office, 1969).

Appendix Table 7 shows the amount of code-5 contracts for each of those large firms in Appendix Table 5 which had significant amounts of code 5 purchases. Even understating sole-source purchases as they do, these data suggest that noncompetitive purchases are a significant fraction of business for more than a few large firms. The code-5 share exceeds 10 percent (which might usually suggest perhaps 20 percent of true sole-source purchases) in 17 of the firms.

NASA purchasing follows the same basic pattern, on a smaller scale. The AEC does not attempt classifications, but many of its contracts have by now acquired a sole-source character.

The lesson from all of this appears to be crystal clear. Quasi- and non-competitive public procurement continues to be a substantial problem, which has hardly been touched despite recent efforts by Secretary McNamara and supposed surveillance and pressure by the Antitrust Division and allied groups. The Vietnam buildup during 1964–1968 almost certainly accentuated the problem, by enlarging purchases rapidly under conditions of haste.

GOVERNMENT SUPPORT OF RESEARCH AND DEVELOPMENT

The more fundamental effect of these agencies upon competitions probably stems from their support for R & D and related activities by private firms.[38] This has helped open the so-called technology gap between U.S. and foreign firms in several R & D-orientated industries, such as communications, nuclear power, aircraft, electronics, and electrical equipment. Table 5.4 showed that federal R & D support has been very large indeed in these and some other industrial areas, and it has been over 55 percent of *all* industrial R & D in recent years. It is extremely concentrated; almost exactly 50 percent of all defense R & D contracting in fiscal year 1967 went to 10 firms. Appendix Table 5 gives detail for some large firms. Many contracts for NASA and the AEC actually involve an extensive R & D component, yielding results which the contractor can apply in other markets. Therefore it makes sense to include them in evaluating R & D-related activities.

Appendix Table 5 indicates that, even by itself, federal funding of R & D and related activities is a significant percentage of total *sales* for many of these large firms. For many of these firms, presumably, the government pays for virtually all R & D activity. This may be appraised with the help of Table 5.4, which shows R & D as a percentage of sales for individual

[38] In Galbraith's view, "The great innovating process in our society comes from this massive outpouring of Federal funds. And these go ... overwhelmingly to the big firms." See Subcommittees of the Select Committee on Small Business, U.S. Senate, 90th Congress, 1st Session, *Planning, Regulation and Competition* (Washington, D.C.; U.S. Government Printing Office, 1967), 32. See also Richard R. Nelson, Merton J. Peck and Edward Kalachek, *Technology, Economic Growth and Public Policy* (Washington, D.C.: Brookings, 1967); and Edwin Mansfield, *The Economics of Technological Change* (New York: Norton, 1968).

industries. Thus General Electric's R & D-related Federal contracts were 10.2 percent of sales in 1966–1967 and Western Electric's were 17.2 percent (Appendix Table 5); for the electrical equipment and communication industry as a whole, *all* R & D funds in 1965 were 9.4 percent of net sales (Table 5.4). Although the precise details are arguable in some instances, the general pattern is fairly clear. Research and innovation in many of the largest firms *are* being fed by the federal government. The large-firm focus of R & D support programs is also clear from a variety of sources.[39] Although the government is not an R & D sponsor for all large firms, the sponsorship is evidently a major, if not dominant, source in most R & D-intensive industries.

This may of course confine competitive possibilities in these growing and formative industries. At the least it reduces, if not blocks, the chances that dominant firms will be challenged by new competitors via major innovation in a range of industries. This must temper optimism that medium and lesser firms can discipline or displace leading firms by means of a greater R & D productivity.

CORPORATE MOTIVATION

Much of the foregoing contradicts the notion that the largest firms form some sort of new archetype of efficient organization for productive and innovative enterprise. What about the new view of corporate motivation—that the large firms are actually (or latently) really quasisocial entities which can, should, and do serve as economic arbiters and stewards of the public interest?[40] Free from close pressure of market forces and dealing on a spacious scale, these firms may indeed possess wide latitude in their decisions, which in turn have heavy economic and social impacts. Workers, consumers, and investors are all affected by managerial choices about prices, wages, dividends, research, product development, expansion, and the rest. In addition, stockholders may have so little real control, and profits may be so great, that the managers are largely free to rise above mere profitmaking and don the mantle of statesmanship. As Chapter 2 noted, "What this all seems to add up to is the existence of important centers of private power in the hands of men whose authority is real but whose responsibilities are

---

[39] Nelson, Peck, and Kalachek, *op. cit.*, and references cited there.
[40] Adolf A. Berle, Jr., *American Economic Republic* (New York: Harcourt, Brace & World, 1963). The development of Gardiner C. Means' views is shown in his *Pricing Power and the Public Interest* (New York: Harper & Row, 1962). See also Ben W. Lewis, "The Effectiveness of the Federal Antitrust Laws," American Economic Association, *Papers and Proceedings*, XXXIX (May 1949), 703–709, and "Economics by Admonition," in *ibid.*, LIX (May 1959), 384–398. The biggest academic impact of the thesis is perhaps shown by Edward S. Mason, ed., *The Corporation in Modern Society* (Cambridge: Harvard University Press, 1959), in which the authors take the transformed corporation as a fact, not a possibility.

For dissents, see Earl F. Cheit, *The Business Establishment* (New York: Wiley, 1964), and Shorey Peterson, "Corporate Control and Capitalism," *Quarterly Journal of Economics*, LXXIX (February 1965), 1–24.

vague."[41] Though some view these "self-perpetuating oligarchies" with dismay, many observers are now satisfied or at least hopeful that the "corporate conscience" will generally guide the managers to perceive and serve the larger public interest, thanks in part to frequent admonitions from public officials. Nearly all agree that managerial latitude really is wide.

Yet this view reflects mainly the *externalia* of corporate power, to the exclusion of the real and, subjectively, very forcible pressures on the "managerial elite." The dispersion of share ownership and management's clockwork control—except for comic interludes—at the annual company meetings are largely irrelevant to the real motivations of the large-firm executives. There are powerful business pressures which are imposed on them, in a personal sense, by the network of mutual ties and financial supervisors at the boardroom level. But the real pressures stem ultimately from the financial markets—especially the stock market. They are reinforced by the relative absence of nepotism in most of the giant firms, the rich prizes commonly awaiting the executives who make it to the top and the many goals of executives beyond their own firms. For these reasons, the intense business pressures stoically talked of by executives in even the largest firms are truer to life than the homespun, social-steward images accepted by admiring or alarmed observers.

The stock market is quite crucial in this respect, even though its original importance as a channel for savings and a source of external funds for businesses has dwindled in recent decades. The current market price of common stock (relative to general stock price trends) is the supreme index of company performance. It sums up all of the heterogeneous dimensions of company performance in one indicator. It is publicly known, widely and instantaneously. It reflects (though not entirely) the composite, informed, and objective judgments of the many major personal and institutional investors.[42] It is intimately known to the managers and directors themselves, many of whom have large personal holdings and stock-option bonuses at stake.

Yet, more important than all this, is the happy and fundamental peculiarity that stock prices are *prospective*; they move to discount expected future performance, good, bad, or mediocre. Excellent management can push a stock to new highs, but without continued excellence the price will fall. Equally, the fruits of new monopoly advantages or other windfalls tend to be immediately discounted ahead, so that even an assured market dominance or an airtight patent will not usually free the executive for civic statesmanship.

Therefore, as a rule, the stock market is very much like a treadmill, helping to enforce commercial standards on publicly-traded firms of all sizes.

---

[41] Mason, *op. cit.*, 4. See also John K. Galbraith, *The New Industrial State* (Boston: Houghton Mifflin, 1967).

[42] Large institutional holders, including mutual funds, hold substantial blocks of every large corporation's stock. Their appraisals are informed and influential; see Chapter 6.

In its effects, it is remarkably like the bonus systems for managers in soviet-type economies. By overfulfilling their planned targets, these managers get both (1) bonuses and (2) higher targets for the next period. Of course, this may also encourage them to moderate their successes from year to year.

In this country, the ratchet effect imposed through the discounting process of the stock market is a fundamental force in modern business. It is normally impervious to public spirit, the "corporate conscience" and all the other honorific items in the new analysis of motivation. Moreover, its influence, applied firsthand by the financial and intercorporate peers, filters down through the ranks. In some cases, executive promotion may be influenced by family, school, ethnic and other connections (as will be noted shortly). But with the spread of so-called professionalized management, especially in the large firms, the competition for advancement undoubtedly follows "business" lines in all essentials. Second- and third-level managers compete by seeking profits and growth, not by demonstrating their ability to inject social issues and charitable giving into their companies' business affairs. In many cases, these competers are in charge of subsidiaries, some of whose common stock is still outstanding, so that the ratchet effect operates directly on them.

The stiffness of the intracorporate competition is naturally enhanced by the large size of the winners' prizes. By any standards, and even after taxes, they reach high levels, to say the least, in many of the larger corporations (see Chapter 14). Moreover, even the very highest corporate managerial posts are well below the top of the business ladder. Their occupants are subject to commercial pressures and inducements from still higher peer levels. The supervision by the directors and the prospects of gaining directorships and other advantages will usually induce strong commercial motivation even in those who have ascended to what may seem, from Main Street, to be the apex of the business world.

Therefore, the transformation and social stewardship of the corporate giants may fairly be regarded as largely mythical. The evidence for them has always been meager and superficial. That the mass of shareholders may be "disenfranchised" and "passive" matters little, because there are other, pervasive, direct pressures on managers, virtually all day, every day. Of course the large firms do have social impacts which are of deep concern for public policy. The potential effects on, for example, regional stagnation or racial discrimination from a determined effort by large corporations could be substantial. Or, for an even more direct example, the total benefits of improved drugs may be unusually large; but leading managers of drug companies have not been in the vanguard in developing ways to diffuse those benefits. In general, one may expect to look in vain for tangible evidence that the higher managerial ranks seriously entertain these possibilities, or, in all candor, think of themselves as possessing the latitude to do so.

This is attested nicely, to take another example, by a recent Presidential request that large firms become involved in training and hiring the hard-core unemployed. When in 1967 the 500 largest firms were individually approached, "23 agreed to help, 29 refused, and 85 said they were interested."[43] The remaining 363 apparently made no response at all. In 1967, amid much favorable comment, insurance firms offered to take $1 billion (perhaps 1 percent of their total portfolios) in loans for urban ghetto housing. Backed by federal government guarantees, the returns on these loans would be about as good as on Treasury bonds, which the insurance firms already hold in large amounts. That such a small shift in portfolios at little or no financial sacrifice, has evoked wide praise (and no little self-congratulation) suggests that current criteria for social contribution by business are distinctly, and realistically, on the low side.

Toward racial discrimination in employment, where the large firms' impact could be great, their performance has particularly belied the myth of corporate stewardship. The 100 largest industrial and service firms with headquarters in New York were surveyed in 1967. Their employment of Negroes and Puerto Ricans in white-collar jobs—the best single indicator of corporate nondiscrimination—lagged behind every other category of enterprises: smaller firms, other sectors, nonprofit entities, etc.[44] The firms' headquarters even lagged behind their own subunits' performance in other cities; this would further suggest that there is nonpecuniary maximizing in this direction at upper levels of large firms, rather than affirmative nondiscrimination. Moreover, there were wide variations among the 100 firms; although 45 had no Negroes at all in managerial positions, in 5 firms Negroes held over 3 percent of such posts. There was no shortage of qualified applicants in New York City, since large numbers were employed by the various other entities. In addition, anti-Jewish discrimination at executive levels of large firms, not only in New York City, has been shown to be substantial.[45]

These patterns may fall far short of some recent claims and hopes for the social contribution of large enterprises toward easing economic discrimination, but that should not be surprising. By cultural and socioeconomic background most corporate managers are not prepared for or strongly interested in understanding and solving the social problems which may be involved only peripherally in their business dealings. Even if they were oriented toward social action, all the direct pressures on them go the other way. The civic activities engaged in by many executives are usually

---

[43] *Washington Post*, Dec. 1, 1967.
[44] U.S. Equal Employment Opportunity Commission, *White Collar Employment in 100 Major New York City Corporations* (Washington, D.C.: U.S. Government Printing Office, January, 1968), 582–620. Oddly, firms which had pledged "affirmative action in minority employment" (under the "Plan for Progress") had markedly lower Negro representation than did nonparticipants.
[45] U.S. Equal Employment Opportunity Commission, *Restricted Membership at the Management Level: Exclusion of Jews from the Executive Suite* (Washington, D.C.: U.S. Government Printing Office, January, 1968), 653–690, surveys a variety of studies.

of a personal sort, and may indeed be viewed as personal makeweights to the commercial demands of their real work. Despite much postprandial rhetoric and earnest exhortation, the strength of appeals to the "corporate conscience" is usually an accurate index of the lack of one.

In summary, the largest corporations occupy a large and growing share of activity in the American economy, as in most other advanced economies. In world markets, too, American corporations often play a major role, despite efforts by various European and Japanese corporations to attain comparable size. The degree of turnover among these firms has been steadily declining over the decades, so that now it is unusual for a very large corporation to slip very far or very fast. In view of their relatively mild degree of risk, these corporations continue to be exceptionally profitable.

Among middle-range firms there has been some recent increase in the degree of diversification, although many of the very largest firms were already well established as conglomerates with leading positions in major industries. All in all, diversification is focused in a number of industrial sectors, rather than widely spread. Defense contracting also is focused fairly narrowly, though it accounts for much of the modest turnover among all of the largest manufacturing firms. A large share of corporate innovation—nearly all of it by a number of large corporations in some industries—is paid for by the government.

There is only limited substance in the view that the very large corporations provide an archetype for business enterprise generally. And the new industrial state may reasonably be estimated as covering less than 15 percent of the national economy, a significant but not dominant segment. As for the supposed new character of the modern corporation, it is largely a myth. Commercial pressures are still pervasive, even in the largest corporations. The background and tasks of the corporate manager are rarely conducive to a career of industrial statesmanship. The record of social contribution by large firms bears this out. Commercial motivations to attain and use market power are, if anything, even stronger than they have been in the past.

Chapter 6

Financial Markets

Therefore, viewed as a whole, we find the dominating influences in the Trusts to be made up of an intricate network of large and small groups of capitalists, many allied to one another by ties of more or less importance, but all being appendages to or parts of the greater groups, which are themselves dependent on and allied with the two mammoth Rockefeller and Morgan groups. These two mammoth groups jointly (for, as pointed out, they really may be regarded as one) constitute the heart of the business and commercial life of the nation, the others all being the arteries which permeate in a thousand ways our whole national life, making their influence felt in every home and hamlet, yet all connected with and dependent on this great central source, the influence and policy of which dominates them all.

JOHN MOODY
The Truth About the Trusts (1904)

Money is more than just another input, along with labor, raw materials, and semifinished goods. Access to capital is a key source of market power, or of new entry to destroy it. Therefore, the conditions in financial markets may influence competitive possibilities throughout the economy, as Chapter 3 noted.

American financial markets are probably more competitive than those in any other country. Yet this standard of comparison is rather low. Financial markets may still run to tight oligopoly. The leading sources of funds may tend to be generally aligned with larger firms and with leading firms in individual markets, and, therefore, the entry and growth of new competition in many industries may be disadvantaged. These possibilities, which have long been discussed but never definitively settled, are explored in this chapter.

The two natural focuses of interest are banking (a source of interest-bearing credit) and the markets for corporate stock (a source of equity or venture capital). Banks also play a dual role—as deposit holders and short-term lenders to enterprises and as managers of over $225 billion of assets now held in their trust departments. The lending is large; the trust accounts are even larger, holding perhaps 20 percent of all common stocks outstanding.

OVERALL STRUCTURE

The prominence of financial groupings at the turn of this century was noted in Chapter 2.[1] Yet, by the 1920's the role of the great financial groups was slipping; by 1940 their dominance had been deeply eroded. Since then, they have held their positions in underwriting and some other specialized areas, but it now makes sense to look primarily at such entities as commercial banks and insurance firms in analyzing market power in financial markets.

Overall concentration, for what it may indicate, is about twice as high in banking as in manufacturing. The 10 largest banks held about 30 percent, and the 50 largest nearly 50 percent of commercial bank assets in 1966; whereas the 50 largest manufacturing firms accounted for 38 percent of manufacturing activity in that year. Insurance is still more highly concentrated; the 3 largest had 36 percent of all life insurance company assets in 1967, and the 10 largest had 61 percent.[2]

The share of the largest banks has been rising since at least 1930; the asset share of the 10 largest rose from 19 percent in 1955 to 30 percent in 1966.[3] In insurance, the share of the largest firms may have slipped slightly from 1955 to 1967, but probably not by much.

In both sectors, the degree of stability in market shares has been high (see Appendix Tables 2 and 3). In banking, most shifts in shares have reflected (1) mergers, rather than competitive upheavals, and (2) differing regional growth rates (for example, New England compared with California). Stability in life insurance positions is particularly striking in light of the rapid growth during the last decade.

In other advanced economies, the share of major banking and insurance interests is even proportionately larger and the rankings are even relatively more stable.[4] Moreover, recent mergers are further raising concentration,

---

[1] See also Daniel J. Baum and Ned B. Stiles, *The Silent Partners: Institutional Investors and Corporate Control* (Syracuse: Syracuse University Press, 1965).

[2] See *The 500 Largest U.S. Industrial Corporations* (New York: *Fortune*, 1968); and Institute of Life Insurance, *Life Insurance Fact Book* (New York: 1968).

[3] See also D. and C. Alhadeff, "Growth of Large Banks, 1930–1960," *Review of Economics and Statistics*, XXXXVI (November 1964), 356–363; and Federal Deposit Insurance Corporation, *Annual Report, 1966* (Washington, D.C.: U.S. Government Printing Office, 1967).

[4] See U.S. Senate Subcommittee on Antitrust and Monopoly, 90th Congress, 2nd Session, *Hearings on Economic Concentration, Part 7*, (Washington, D.C.: U.S. Government Printing Office, 1968); and *The Economist*, (February 18, 1968), for discussion and comparisons of some European countries and Japan. Also, on Britain, see the U.K. National Board for Prices and Income, *Bank Charges*, Report No. 34, Cmnd. 3292 (London: Her Majesty's Stationery Office, 1967).

especially in Britain.[5] As a dilutant to this rise, there have been important moves by some American banks into many local and national banking markets abroad.

INDIVIDUAL FINANCIAL MARKETS

There are detailed and systematic data only for banking markets. Defining these markets poses the usual difficulties. For banking services affecting the majority of local production and commerce, the markets are local. For other services, especially those for large firms, the markets may be regional or national in scope.

On any reading, concentration in these markets tends to be relatively high, ranging from tight oligopoly up to near-monopoly. Table 6.1 shows both large and small metropolitan areas; four-bank ratios average 68.5 percent. In the smaller areas, two-bank ratios average 71.9 percent. Local concentration, under controls created during the 1930's, is much higher than it was in earlier decades.[6] There have been some changes in local concentration since 1939, with a slight downward national trend.[7] Yet even the largest declines have left concentration quite high. And concentration has stayed about steady or has risen in about half of the cities, even over a 28-year span. Very probably, only a virtually total antitrust ban on significant banking mergers since the early 1960's has prevented a significant rise in concentration.[8]

Asymmetry also tends to be high in local banking (see Table 6.1). In the largest cities, the leading bank averages more than four times the size of the fourth-ranking bank. In small cities, the leader averages 70 percent larger than the second bank. Entry barriers are usually very high, thanks mainly to state and national banking policies governing branching and the chartering of new banks.

These entry barriers and the economies of scale that largely proscribe very small banks mean that the smaller cities are not a good test of the "natural" market structure hypothesis outlined in Chapter 4. By contrast, the largest cities provide a better test, despite the recent limits on mergers; entry is not so nearly closed and scale economies do not prescribe more than

---

[5] *Economic Concentration*, Part 7, 3680–3696.

[6] Deane Carson and Paul H. Cootner, "The Structure of Competition in Commercial Banking in the United States," in Commission on Money and Credit, *Private Financial Institution* (Englewood Cliffs, N.J.: Prentice-Hall, 1963), 77–79; and J. M. Guttentag and E. S. Herman, *Banking Structure and Performance*, Institute of Finance, Graduate School of Business Administration, *The Bulletin*, No. 41/43 (New York: New York University Press, 1967).

[7] Among the 46 largest cities, four-bank concentration fell more than 5 points in 23 and rose by more than 5 points in 10. Statistical laws alone would have predicted a tendency to decline, since most ratios were already not far from the upper boundary of 100 percent.

[8] See also the articles collected in The Administrator of National Banks, *Studies in Banking Competition and the Banking Structure* (Washington, D.C.: U.S. Government Printing Office, 1966).

TABLE 6.1   BANKING STRUCTURE IN
             THE LARGEST AND
             SMALLEST CITIES, 1966

17 SMSA's with IPC* Deposits over $1 billion	Total IPC Deposits ($ million)	4-Bank Concentration Ratio (Percent)	Ratio of Largest Bank to Fourth Largest Bank
New York	20,540	58.1	1.8
Chicago	7,012	53.4	4.2
Los Angeles	5,350	79.5	3.7
Philadelphia	3,392	56.9	1.8
San Francisco	2,840	82.0	5.4
Boston	2,708	66.5	3.9
Detroit	2,669	78.1	8.2
Pittsburgh	2,075	88.2	6.8
Washington, D.C.	1,920	54.1	2.2
St. Louis	1,729	46.2	5.7
Houston	1,714	58.6	4.5
Cleveland	1,661	87.1	2.7
Newark	1,500	62.1	3.1
Dallas	1,434	70.6	10.1
Minneapolis-St. Paul	1,158	58.0	6.7
Atlanta	1,021	81.9	2.8
Baltimore	1,006	83.7	1.7
Averages for the 17		68.5	4.4

21 SMSA's with IPC Deposits under $50 million	Total IPC Deposits	2-Bank Concentration Ratio	Ratio of Largest Bank to Second Largest Bank
Averages for the 21	39	71.9	1.7

* SMSA refers to Census standard metropolitan areas; IPC refers to individuals, partnerships and corporations.
SOURCE: Adapted from Federal Deposit Insurance Corporation, *Concentration Ratios by Metropolitan Areas* (Washington, D.C.: F.D.I.C., annual).

medium size, which may be relatively small in the largest-city banking markets. Therefore, the relatively high concentration and asymmetry shown for large cities in Table 6.1 do lend some support to the possibility that tight asymmetrical oligopoly is "natural," even when it can no longer be attained by merger alone. This point is diluted to the extent that the banks in these cities are engaged in markets of regional and national scope.

In addition to this formal structure, there are a variety of other informal relations among banks. Mutual stockholding or indirect controls among banks are found in a number of important urban and state banking markets.[9]

[9] Committee on Banking and Currency, House of Representatives, 90th Congress, 1st Session, *Control of Commercial Banks and Interlocks among Financial Institutions* (Washington, D.C.: U.S. Government Printing Office, 1967).

Also the banks have traditionally engaged in cooperative activity and semi-self-regulation, which limits certain competitive activities as well as new entry. This cannot be shown metrically, and it does vary from city to city, but it is nevertheless important. One reflection of it is the low degree of change in relative positions among banks (apart from mergers) in most cities. Abroad, these informal structural elements are usually even more extensive and influential.[10]

RELATIONS WITH NONFINANCIAL FIRMS

In supplying funds to firms and constraining their decisions, financial markets operate partly as anonymous forces and processes. In addition, there are specific relationships between the financial enterprises and the firms they serve. These specific ties introduce or reflect imperfections in the otherwise competitive and impersonal functioning of financial markets. It is safe to say that the pervasive family and interest groupings still found in Sweden, Japan, France, and, to some extent, Britain no longer exist at the core of the American economy.[11] Yet there are long-lasting and tangible relationships, particularly among the largest financial and industrial enterprises. Boards of directors of nearly all of the largest firms contain members of the largest banks, investment banks, and insurance firms.[12] A large number of indirectly "interlocking" directorships results from these positions. These arrangements are, as was noted earlier, neither randomly made nor frequently changed.

Transactions patterns follow similar lines. They represent close and intimate working relationships, involving disclosure of company conditions, detailed counseling, and personal loyalties. Not surprisingly, such relationships are changed only in unusual cases. One study found that between 1945 and 1955 only one-third of a sample of firms changed their primary banking connection, and in most of these cases the change was made only by marginal reshuffling among existing connections.[13] It is true that such multiple balances and other connections do provide the larger firms with a significant amount of leverage for playing banks against each other in order

---

[10] On Britain, see Bank Charges, *op. cit.*; collusive arrangements (such as not taking a loan applicant who had been rejected by another bank, a rule still in force; *The Economist*, February 18, 1968) have caused the main banks to suffer steady declines in their shares of all banking activities, and have led them to lag in new innovations. See also Hadley's discussion of Japan in *Economic Concentration, Part 7*.

[11] See *Economic Concentration, Part 7*; also "Big Business Galaxy," *The Economist*, October 28, 1967, xx–xxi.

[12] U.S. House Subcommittee on Antitrust, Committee on the Judiciary, 89th Congress, 1st Session, *Interlocks in Corporate Management*, (Washington, D.C.: U.S. Government Printing Office, 1965); and Committee on Banking and Currency, House of Representatives, 90th Congress, 2nd Session, *Commercial Banks and Their Activities*, 2 vols., Staff Report for the Subcommittee on Domestic Finance, (Washington, D.C.: U.S. Government Printing Office, 1968).

[13] See Lawrence L. Werboff and Marvin E. Rozen, "Market Shares and Competition Among Financial Institutions," in Commission on Money and Credit, *Private Financial Institutions* (Englewood Cliffs, N.J.: Prentice-Hall, 1963), 265–331.

to gain favorable terms. Yet here, too, the patterns are stable, and the banks and other financial entities are not passive.[14] And the net effect—that large firms usually gain better terms than smaller firms—will be equally real whether it arises from impersonal processes or individual advantages.

What is true of the overall distribution of firms may be expected to apply also to the differential status of firms within their industries. The leading firms deal more steadily and intimately with larger financial entities than do their lesser competitors. Even where a large bank may deal with both, this may only tend to limit its support for competitive initiatives among them.

THE PROBABLE FINANCIAL EFFECTS

Market power and financial advantages are so mutually related that it is not possible to disentangle their cause-and-effect roles in any precise way. But the advantages of relative total size do appear to exist. The unit cost of loans varies inversely with the size of loans and the size of borrowers.[15] This reflects in some degree the lower costs of making large loans and the existence of some scale economies in banking, but that is not all there is to it. Market power held by banks appear to yield them appreciable extra profitability.[16] They and other major sources of funds have leeway as well as incentives to offer advantages to attractive borrowers, whose security may arise from large relative size and/or their leading and profitable positions in individual markets. The advantages include both lower costs of capital and greater amounts of it. Evidently the conditions of security and favorable financial terms are mutually reinforcing, in some degree.

These advantages are reflected in such indicators as the financial ratings of firms compiled by the various investor services. These ratings, which also influence the avaliability of funds, are highly correlated with company size and leading market positions. Another hint can be seen in the patterns of institutional holdings of common stocks. Such holdings represent some of the largest and best informed factors in the market. Table 6.2 summarizes the number of institutional investors with holdings of various-sized industrial firms at a recent date. The holdings cluster in the larger firms, possibly more than the volume of shares would cause. It may be more significant that

---

[14] Thus, Morgan Stanley and Co., a major underwriter of industrial bonds, has as steady clients 7 of the 10 largest industrial firms and 11 of the next 40 (*Fortune*, February, 1968, 184–186).
[15] See, among others, the Federal Reserve Board's *Business Loan Studies for 1955 and 1957* (Washington, D.C.: U.S. Government Printing Office); and S. H. Archer and L. G. Faerber, "Firm Size and Cost of Externally Acquired Equity Capital," *Journal of Finance*, XXI (March 1966), 69–83.
[16] Hints of this are in F. R. Edwards, "Concentration in Banking and its Effect on Business Loan Rates," *Review of Economics and Statistics*, XLVI (August 1964), 294–300; and Franklin R. Edwards, "The Banking Competition Controversy," *National Banking Review*, III (September 1965), 1–34, and references cited there.

TABLE 6.2 INSTITUTIONAL HOLDINGS IN MAJOR INDUSTRIAL FIRMS, JANUARY 1968

Ranks Among the Largest Industrial Firms (by total sales)	Average Number of Institutional Investors Holding Common Stock
1–9	706
50–59	213
100–109	85
200–209	107
300–309	49
400–409	19
491–500	22

SOURCES: Adapted from *The 500 Largest Industrial Corporations* (New York: *Fortune*, June 15, 1968), and Standard and Poor's *Stock Guide*, (New York: Standard and Poor's, January, 1968). The patterns at any given time reflect some degree of randomness.

individual variations around the general pattern almost wholly reflect market positions within industries. In each group, the firms with unusually high numbers of institutional holders are also leading firms in individual markets. Evidently, once again, there are recognized financial advantages to both relative size and individual market positions. In fact, institutional holdings cluster sharply in the 50 or so largest issues traded on the New York Stock Exchange. Moreover, such holdings comprise up to 40 percent on average of these companies' issues.[17]

EQUITY AND EFFICIENCY

Several particular influences of financial markets deserve mention at this point. The distribution of wealth may be affected in two ways by market power in financial markets. One way is indirect, via market power which may be increased in other markets. Where such power is slight and fleeting, its rewards are small, with little effect on wealth holdings; conversely, the effect may be large in some cases. The second way is direct, arising from imperfections in capital markets which provide special advantages to some participants. On these two planes, imperfections in financial markets may appreciably accentuate the inequality of wealth.

Although upwards of 25 million persons in the United States now own at least one corporate share, most of these shares are in relatively few hands.[18]

[17] Baum and Stiles, *op. cit.*, 53–66.
[18] Victor Perlo, "People's Capitalism and Stock Ownership," *American Economic Review*, XLVIII (June 1958) 333–347; R. J. Lampmann, *The Share of the Top Wealth-Holders in National Wealth, 1922–1956* (Princeton: Princeton University Press, 1962), and Ferdinand Lundberg, *The Rich and the Super-Rich* (New York: Lyle Stuart, 1968).

Much of this concentration arose during 1870–1930 from the creation of market power in a range of major industries.   Stock ownership is substantially more concentrated than ownership of most other major kinds of assets. Recently, certain institutional holdings have risen, and many of these (such as pension funds) can be considered to be holdings on behalf of those in relatively lower wealth and income levels.   Yet still other of these are merely indirect forms of holdings for larger personal investors.   Therefore, from early years, financial markets have contributed to the formation of much of the inequality of wealth in recent generations.

Given this skewed distribution of holdings, market movements in recent decades (and particularly since 1947) have increased the relative asset shares of the wealthiest groups.   A random selection of stocks would have returned about 9 percent yearly during 1946–1960, and would have more than quadrupled in value from 1948 to 1962.   Of course, this broad movement has not sprung from market power—in financial or other markets—and the resulting increase in wealth inequality might reflect only the initial inequality of holdings, entirely apart from possible imperfections in financial markets.

But these imperfections accentuate the disequalizing effect.   They enlarge the gains to market power generally, as an indirect effect.   And, as a direct effect, they focus the realization of these gains, because larger holders or their agents (often institutional investors) usually have better direct knowledge of short- and long-term influences on stock prices, compared to the small investor, who relies mainly on public information.   This problem of "insiderism" has been dramatized recently by several major actions brought by the Securities and Exchange Commission; in each case, large gains were apparently made by insiders.[19]   These cases are probably only the extreme tip of a very large iceberg, for insider problems arise virtually unconstrained in almost all enterprises.[20]   One further influence is the traditional aversion of bank trust departments to small accounts; this has effectively excluded millions of small holders from access to informed investment management.[21]

Informed holders have traditionally followed the adage to "sell on the news;" smaller holders (perhaps 23 million of the 25 million) have been likely to buy.   The larger holders have done even better than average in the rising market, and the smaller holders have done correspondingly less well.[22]

---

[19] See *The New York Times*, September 1, 1968, Financial Section.
[20] For an account of the ineffectiveness of public regulation of insiderism, see "Inside the Insiders Report," *Forbes*, March 1, 1968.
[21] *The Wall Street Journal*, January 31, 1969.   Traditional minimums for accounts have ranged from $100,000 to $500,000.
[22] For a view dissenting from the consensus on this point, see Irwin Friend, "Romance versus Statistics in the Stock Market," *Proceedings, Business and Economic Statistics Section*, American Statistical Association, 1964, 178–185; also H. G. Manne, *Insider Trading and Stock Market* (Glencoe: Free Press, 1966). Manne concedes the point made here–differential information and gains–but argues that no other clearly practical arrangement will promote entrepreneurship as well as he believes the present system does.
  For a survey of insiderism in other countries, see *The Economist*, May 13, 1967, 701–702.

Moreover, the differential is even sharper when the market turns down; experienced traders can usually gain in a falling (or a churning) market as effectively as on a rising one, contrary to the common experience of the small holder. Therefore, the interruption of the postwar bull market in 1962 and the erratic movements since then have not necessarily reversed the differential effect.[23]

The effect of these and related patterns has emerged in recent computations showing a rise in the inequality of wealth since the early 1950's.[24] Of course, capital values of other types of assets—including farmland, urban sites and structures, and inventories—have also tended to rise, but most of them not so far or fast. Moreover, their personal ownership patterns are less concentrated than are those of stock ownership.

These imperfections and disequalizing effects are not necessary in order to gain the possible *efficiency-enforcing effects* within large firms and in product markets. Indeed, the strength of commercial pressures upon the giant corporations, noted earlier in Chapter 5, are more effective the *more* competitive are financial markets. Reduction of market power in financial markets would therefore promote both equity and efficiency, perhaps substantially.

One further implication of these patterns is that stock ownership inevitably entangles the public interest more closely with the price levels of individual stocks. No fewer than 25 million shareowners are concerned about the prices of their shares, whether their holdings are minute or massive. Many of the firms so owned are intimately and continually involved in antitrust enforcement activities, regulatory proceedings, subsidy programs, public buying of goods and R & D services, and other public policies. Some of them are in many of these all of the time. All of these public actions affect share prices, often adversely, and it is idle to suppose that the framers and administrators of public policies can wholly ignore these effects; indeed, they do not. Congress acted speedily in 1962 to protect shareholders from any possible adverse share-price effects of the Dupont-General Motors antitrust decision. This, of course, protected, along with innocent recent purchasers, all of those long-term holders and heirs who presumably had benefitted from the antitrust infraction. If the dissolution of existing firms (however dominant their position) has now virtually disappeared from the antitrust arsenal, it is largely because of its potential downward impact on share prices.[25] Moreover, protection of share prices has become something between an

---

[23] By 1969 such specialized trading (particularly in short sales) has given rise to no fewer than 125 hedge funds, trading almost exclusively for large investors and partnerships. These represent perhaps the furthest development of informed speculation able to gain regardless of market movements. Whatever their useful arbitrage function may be, such activities clearly widen the differential gains among investors. See *The New York Times*, April 23, 1969, p. 55.
[24] Lundberg, *op. cit.*, and references cited there.
[25] Donald J. Dewey, *Monopoly in Economics and Law* (Chicago: Rand McNally, 1959).

important constraint and an implicit requirement of regulatory policies toward public utilities, such as electricity and telephones. These pressures toward governmental involvement are, for good or ill, likely to intensify as shareholding spreads still further. They constitute a set of additional, indirect effects of financial markets upon market structure in the rest of the economy.

Chapter 7

Other Markets:
Formal Internal Structure

To begin with, I think that it is the better opinion that
popular rumor, going now as ever to extremes, has exaggerated
some features of the movement towards combination and
monopoly, even in America.

ALFRED MARSHALL
" Some Aspects of Competition " (1890)

This article may be summarized in three statements.
(1) The American economy is highly concentrated. (2) Concentration is highly uneven. (3) The extent of concentration
shows no tendency to grow, and it may possibly be declining.
Any tendency either way, if it does exist, must be at the pace
of a glacial drift.

MORRIS A. ADELMAN
"The Measurement of Industrial Concentration" (1951)

We come now to evaluate the degree of market power in individual markets
throughout the rest of the economy. Despite all efforts to condense and
enliven, this will require us to wade through rather more statistics and details
than the usual reader finds to be a sparkling treat. Following the usage in
Chapter 3, the various elements are grouped in three parts: formal internal
structure in this chapter, informal elements in Chapter 8 and external
elements in Chapter 9. Chapter 10 brings these components together for a
summary appraisal.

Over several decades the study of formal structure—primarily concentration—has matured to the point of brittleness, as Chapter 2 outlined. From
a youthful overconcern with transient monopolies (grain corners, utility
pyramids), some researchers have now swung over to an apparent fixation
on permanent concentration. Only those market shares which *last*, it is

said, reflect market power.[1]   Both of these extremes are wrong; monopoly may be short-lived yet substantial (and how short is short?).   Yet appraising flux in structure remains a difficult and subtle task, even in the unusual cases where there is complete factual evidence.   Those concerning themselves only with permanent structure will rate market power far lower than do those who are impressed even by briefly held market positions.   The correct perspective probably lies in between, where every observer will naturally claim to be.   Yet clearly the recent literature has moved distinctly toward a permanent-structure preoccupation.   This in itself explains much of the postwar revival of confidence that most markets are competitive in all essentials.

THE EXTENT OF CONCENTRATION

By usage, convenience, and good sense, one begins with concentration ratios. They are simplicity itself—the share of the leading firms in their industry (usually the four largest firms).   Thus, U.S. Steel, Bethlehem, Republic, and Armco made just 49 percent of the value of shipments of steel products in the U.S. in 1966.   The Census, forbidden since the mid–1800's to disclose data on any single firm, publishes four-firm ratios; indeed, disclosure rules have been interpreted to dictate that the ratios *must* cover no less than four firms.   This naturally frustrates researchers, who could learn much from studying the more detailed patterns; but Congress and the Census Bureau are steadfast against disclosure.[2]

Most research has focused on ratios for Census "four-digit" industries; for example 2011, meat packing; rather than 20, all food products; or 20111, fresh or frozen beef.   Four-digit industries have come to be regarded as about the right average degree of detail, but many Census four-digit industries are either too inclusive (embracing scores of disparate products) or too narrow. Most often they are too inclusive, lumping together separable products and distinct regional submarkets; thus, the national ratio of 14 percent for newspapers obviously masks very high local concentration.   In some cases imports, not included in the ratios, cause concentration in total sales to be lower than the ratios state; for example, U.S. automobile-output concentration is now over 99 percent, but imports reduce the sales ratio for the country to about 90 percent.   This is more important in other countries, where imports usually bulk larger in a wider range of markets.

Yet if these blemishes can be corrected, a good concentration ratio is a

---

[1] For example, see George J. Stigler's Preface to *Business Concentration and Price Policy* (Princeton: Princeton University Press, 1955), and Carl Kaysen and Donald F. Turner, *Antitrust Policy* (Cambridge: Harvard University Press, 1959), 78.   There have even been attempts to construct "change-adjusted" concentration indexes for long periods.   Moreover, most research has come to draw heavily on the prepared concentration ratios; as will be noted, these tend to mask some of the extremes and short-term holdings of market power.

[2] By comparison, Japan publishes market shares for each firm, and Britain, Canada, and Australia present ratios for the three leading firms.

powerful datum. It shows the degree of few-firm leadership directly and unmistakably. And it shows changes in market power with special clarity. Thus, the market power shown by a ratio of 53 or 63 percent may be a matter for debate, but a rise in ratio from 53 to 63 (without large changes in other structural elements) strongly suggests rising market power.[3] The other great virtue of the ratios—their abundant availability—is also, of course, an invitation to their over-use.[4]

At any rate, how much concentration is there? Since most utilities are clear- or near-monopolies, while much retailing tends toward atomism, the real question is where the majority of markets may lie in between, toward high or low concentration? Is monopoly, tight oligopoly, or loose oligopoly prevalent? The latest set of official ratios for U.S. manufacturing industries is summed up in Table 7.1 and Figure 7.1. Industries concentrated more than 40 percent account for only about two-fifths of economic activity (that is, 42.4 percent of value-added). Really high-concentration industries (above 70 percent) appear to embrace only 15.5 percent, and the miniscule 1.6 percent in industries with concentration above 90 percent seems to clinch the point—monopoly, or anything approaching it, now seems to be rare. Of the approximately 420 industries, concentration is reported to be below 40 percent in about 250, accounting for 58 percent of all value-added. "Average" concentration appears to be about 39 percent. Loose oligopoly verging on monopolistic competition appears to be the rule.

Abroad, industrial concentration has appeared to be rather higher than this. Comparisons are difficult, for the British, Canadian, Australian, German, and Japanese sets of ratios are less complete and are checkered with differing definitions of industry boundaries. Also, there are a number of major cases, including light bulbs, telephone equipment, automobiles, computers, steel, copper, lead, and glass, where American concentration is generally *higher* than elsewhere.[5] Still, the cumulative weight of official

---

[3] There have also been attempts to devise "summary" indexes of concentration, reflecting the whole structure in one number. These attempts have been largely futile so far, despite some ingenious attempts; see Stigler, *op. cit.*, especially 57–100 and 119–140; and Morris Adelman, "Comment on the 'H' Concentration Measure as a Numbers-equivalent," *Review of Economics and Statistics*, LI (February 1969), 99–101. In fact, every index has some bias: none is ideal or neutral. A summary index giving "equal weight" to all firms in an industry will over-weight trivial ones; an index focusing on the leading firms may (at least in some industries) under-weight small but effective fringe competitors. There is no wholly "scientific" way to ascertain the correct balance.

[4] Full sets of ratios for U.S. manufacturing industries are available for 1947, 1951, 1954, 1958, 1963 and 1966 on a standard basis, and for many industries for 1935; they are published in U.S. Subcommittee on Antitrust and Monopoly, *Concentration Ratios in Manufacturing Industry, 1963* (Washington, D.C.: U.S. Government Printing Office, Part I, 1966; Part II, 1967). The most recent set of ratios is in U.S. Bureau of the Census, "Value-of-Shipment Concentration Ratios by Industry," *Annual Survey of Manufactures, 1966*, M66(AS)-8 (Washington, D.C.: U.S. Government Printing Office, 1968).

[5] See Joe S. Bain, *International Differences in Industrial Structure* (New Haven: Yale University Press, 1966); Gideon Rosenbluth, *Concentration in Canadian Manufacturing Industries* (Princeton: Princeton University Press, 1957); and W. G. Shepherd, "A Comparison of Industrial Concentration in the United States and Britain," *Review of Economics and Statistics*, XL (February 1961), 70–75.

TABLE 7.1 PERCENTAGE SHARES OF TOTAL U.S. MANUFACTURING VALUE-ADDED IN 1966 THAT OCCURRED IN INDUSTRIES OF VARIOUS DEGREES OF CONCENTRATION

Degree of concentration in the largest four firms	Shares of Value-added, according to		
	Raw Census Concentration Ratios 1958	Raw Census Concentration Ratios, 1966	Adjusted Concentration Ratios, 1966
90–100	2.1	1.6	17.0
80–89	2.0	2.4	9.0
70–79	9.4	11.5	8.0
60–69	4.1	5.8	15.1
50–59	13.1	7.5	14.7
40–49	7.3	13.6	14.7
30–39	13.0	10.8	9.7
20–29	22.5	27.2	9.1
10–19	19.0	13.7	2.3
0–9	7.5	5.9	0.4
70 and higher	13.5	15.5	34.0
40 and higher	38.0	42.4	78.5
"Average" degree of concentration	37.2	39.0	60.3

SOURCE: Calculated from data in U.S. Senate Subcommittee on Antitrust and Monopoly, *Concentration Ratios in Manufacturing Industry, 1963, Parts I* and *II*, (Washington, D.C.: U.S. Government Printing Office, 1966); and U.S. Bureau of the Census, "Value-of-Shipment Concentration Ratios by Industry," *Annual Survey of Manufacturers, 1966*, M66(AS)-8 (Washington, D.C.: U.S. Government Printing Office, 1968).

data has convinced many observers that concentration is lower, on average, in the United States than it is abroad.

But if one adjusts the raw reported ratios to reflect genuine market concentration more accurately, the picture changes. Many industries in this country contain distinct local or regional submarkets in which genuine concentration exceeds the national ratio. Prime examples include milk, bread, newspapers, cement and concrete, brick, oil, and steel products.[6] Other Census "industries" contain many separate, noncompeting markets;

[6] In *Concentration Ratios*, 1963, *Part II*, there are regional and local ratios for many of these spatially fragmented industries—see Tables 25 and 26.

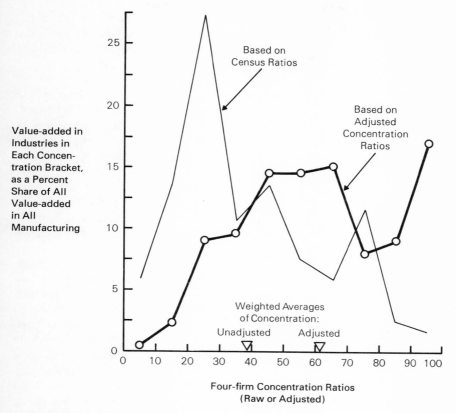

Figure 7.1 Concentration Patterns in American Manufacturing Industries in 1966

examples include drugs, photographic equipment, and more than a score of catchbin residual categories, such as "organic chemicals, not elsewhere classified."[7] Finally, imports need to be entered in some of the ratios too. These are slight or absent in most American markets; but abroad, imports are a major element in many, if not most, major industries.[8] Many of these adjustments can only be rough approximations, and it is wiser to avoid them unless the raw ratio is clearly wide of the mark. The 1966 U.S. ratios were adjusted by the author where necessary to represent the "average" degree of concentration in relevant markets, allowing for spatial submarkets and

[7] See in *Concentration Ratios*, 1963, *Part I*, Table 4. Also, some Census industries are too narrow, though these are fewer.
[8] See U.S. Tariff Commission, *Imports* (Washington, D.C.: U.S. Government Printing Office, December 1966), Table 1, 1–10. Also, B. N. Vaccara, *Employment and Output in Protected Manufacturing Industries* (Washington, D.C.: Brookings Institution, 1960).

divisions among noncompeting products as well as import competition.[9] Some 225 of the 417 Census industries needed adjusting; in each case care was taken to be on the low side.[10]   Although other researchers might differ on details, they would probably reach the same general results.

These corrected ratios confirm concretely what has been suspected all along: concentration is actually well above the official ratios.   The weighted average in American industries is probably about 60 percent, not 39 percent. Outright monopoly still looks unusual, and only one-sixth of activity is in industries with four-firm concentration above 90 percent.   But extremely *low* concentration is even rarer; industries below 20 percent concentration account for only 3 percent of manufacturing activity.[11]

Oligopoly of varying tightness is prevalent, if not quite ubiquitous. More than three-fifths of activity is in those 199 industries concentrated more than 50 percent.   This is a little higher proportion than Kaysen and Turner's reestimates indicated; even so, they, too, found oligopoly to be "preponderant."

Actually, near-monopolies and duopolies are fairly numerous and prominent in manufacturing, even apart from the familiar utility quasi-monopolies. Western Electric is the sole supplier of equipment to its parent, the Bell System, which includes 84 percent of American telephones and virtually all long-distance operations.   General Motors is reported to make over 80 percent of all buses and locomotives.   General Motors also makes over 70 percent of medium and high-priced cars sold in the U.S. and Canada; and its 55 percent share of *all* cars, plus Ford's 25 percent and Chrysler's 17 percent, has turned the auto industry into an unusually tight oligopoly.   IBM has held over 70 percent of the main computer industry since its beginning, both in the United States and worldwide, after holding 90 percent of tabulating equipment (see Chapter 15).   Campbell makes about 90 percent of canned soups.   Gillette has regained most of its traditional 75 percent of razor blade sales.   A number of major drugs are essentially monopolies held by virtue of patents.   Photocopying is a virtual monopoly, as are many local newspapers.   In many other, lesser products (such as chocolate candy, cymbals, postage meters, and city directories, for example) there are also near-monopolies, some of them not at all temporary.

---

[9] Carl Kaysen and Donald F. Turner, *Antitrust Policy* (Cambridge: Harvard University Press, 1959), also offered a detailed adjustment of industry ratios as of 1954.   Although the basic considerations were the same as those used here, they adjusted "industry" definitions, rather than adjusting the ratios for *given* industries.   The two approaches are not inconsistent, and they reach similar findings.   Similar results are also reached in Leonard W. Weiss, "Average Concentration Ratios and Industrial Performance," *Journal of Industrial Economics*, XI (July 1963), 237–254, for 2-digit industry groups. Weiss' ratios average lower than those reported in Table 7.2, but their ordinal patterns are similar.

[10] The individual ratios are in Appendix Table 8; some of them are also shown in Appendix Table 9.

[11] Moreover, it is mostly confined to a few industry groups.   Over half of the industries below 20 percent concentration are in group 23, Wearing Apparel; almost none are in the heavy industry groups.

Duopolies (ranging between monopoly and tight oligopoly) are even more common. The main aircraft, aircraft engine, and propeller markets are essentially duopolies. Nuclear power equipment was first a monopoly, and then a duopoly, until General Electric and Westinghouse were unable to expand production capacity fast enough; currently they hold "only" 75 percent.[12] The other two "entrants," oddly enough, are Combustion Engineering, and Babcock and Wilcox, which have held nearly all of the power boiler market (including nuclear) for many years. A number of other electrical products, particularly larger ones, verge on duopoly. The U.S. sulphur industry has been a virtual duopoly for decades—so have small arms and ammunition, heavy turbogenerators, several categories of photographic equipment, construction equipment, and pipelines for petroleum and chemical products. Synchronous satellites are now made principally by a very small number of electronic equipment firms. News services are essentially a duopoly. Recall also that somewhere between 37 and 63 percent of military procurement is effectively "sole source," approximating something between duopoly and monopoly in many cases.

This is enough to indicate that near-monopoly and duopoly—both of which go well beyond what a *four*-firm concentration ratio of 90 or 99 shows—are frequent and firmly based even in some of the biggest industries. Some of these are "new" R & D-based industries, but many of them are not, and their structure is often durable (for example, automobiles, computers, buses, sulphur) or tightening, rather than eroding. These extreme cases have been masked by the four-firm concentration ratios and therefore deemphasized. Even the "adjusted" ratios tend to underplay them by lumping them with "mere" tight oligopolies.

The subsectors of industry vary sharply in concentration, as Table 7.2 shows. High concentration is rare in textiles, clothing, lumber products, furniture, leather, and other miscellaneous industries. In heavy industries such as chemicals, oil, metals, machinery, automobiles, and aircraft, high concentration is common. It is also frequent in other, less capital-intensive sectors, including foods, printing and publishing, glass and stone products, and instruments.

As for concentration abroad, any adjustments of the ratios would have to be more complex, involving large changes for (1) import competition and (2) realignment of "industry" definitions. Although I have not ventured a dragnet reestimate for this volume, nor has anyone else, the net effect of revisions in the foreign ratios would probably raise the overall level of ratios only marginally, if at all. For example, many Canadian, British, and European industries face substantial import competition, and trade among

---

[12] U.S. Atomic Energy Commission, *The Nuclear Industry, 1967* (Washington, D.C.: Atomic Energy Commission, 1968). Many other nuclear power subindustries are either near-monopolies or duopolies; see Arthur D. Little, Inc., *Report on Competition in the Nuclear Power Equipment Industry*, (Washington, D.C.: Atomic Energy Commission, 1969).

TABLE 7.2 DIFFERENCES AMONG U.S. INDUSTRY GROUPS IN THEIR ADJUSTED CONCENTRATION IN 1966

Industry Group	Total Value added ($ billion)	Percent Share of Total Value-added in Industries with Concentration Ratios of					Weighted Average of Concentration Ratios (Percent)
		0 to 19	20 to 39	40 to 59	60 to 79	80 to 100	
20 Food and kindred products	24.9	0	18.6	44.4	30.8	6.2	55
21 Tobacco manufacturers	1.9	0	0	15.4	5.4	79.2	83
22 Textile mill products	8.0	0	43.5	45.9	9.3	1.3	44
23 Apparel and related products	9.2	49.8	39.7	7.5	3.0	0	23
24 Lumber and wood products	4.8	4.9	28.6	64.2	2.3	0	43
25 Furniture and fixtures	4.0	2.1	77.7	20.2	0	0	34
26 Paper and allied products	9.4	0	50.7	35.5	7.7	6.1	44
27 Printing and publishing	13.3	0	46.2	8.4	12.9	32.5	56
28 Chemicals and allied products	22.8	0	1.7	21.3	46.5	30.5	71

29 Petroleum and coal products	4.7	0	0	13.3	86.3	0.4	68
30 Rubber and plastics products	6.3	0	40.1	27.5	32.0	0.4	49
31 Leather and leather products	2.4	12.1	6.0	80.5	1.4	0	44
32 Stone, clay, and glass products	8.4	0	4.6	24.9	32.5	38.0	71
33 Primary metal industries	20.9	0	6.4	19.6	18.2	55.8	75
34 Fabricated metal products	15.8	8.4	12.3	54.3	16.3	8.7	51
35 Machinery	26.8	0	31.9	25.5	30.1	12.5	55
36 Electrical machinery	23.4	0	7.0	42.2	34.5	16.3	61
37 Transportation equipment	29.2	0.3	2.3	10.7	6.8	79.9	83
38 Instruments and related products	6.4	0	0	49.5	14.5	36.0	67
39 Miscellaneous manufacturing	4.3	0.9	38.8	35.5	21.6	3.2	48
Total	247.0	2.7	18.8	29.4	23.1	28.0	60

SOURCE: Calculated from data in U.S. Senate Subcommittee on Antitrust and Monopoly, *Concentration Ratios in Manufacturing Industry, 1963, Parts I and II* (Washington, D.C.: U.S. Government Printing Office, 1966); and U.S. Bureau of the Census, "Value-of-Shipment Concentration Ratios by Industry," *Annual Survey of Manufactures, 1966,* M66(AS)-8 (Washington, D.C.: U.S. Government Printing Office, 1968).

Common Market countries may have an even greater effect (the possible countereffects of cartel activities are discussed in the next chapter). Indeed, some of the heavy industries have a large, if not pervasive, multinational component; shipbuilding, oil, primary metals, certain chemicals, and electrical equipment are prime examples. In these, "dominant" home producers are often only modest factors.

Some further oblique light on multinational patterns vis-à-vis concentration is cast by Table 7.3, which estimates how far American firms have

TABLE 7.3 PROBABLE U.S. SHARE OF SHIPMENTS IN SPECIFIC INDUSTRIES IN THREE EUROPEAN COUNTRIES IN 1965 (PERCENTAGE)

France, 1963		Britain, 1964		West Germany, 1965	
Petroleum refining	20	Refined petroleum		Petroleum	30–35
Razor blades and		products	over 40	Glassmaking	about 40
safety razors	87	Computers	over 40	Automobiles	30–40
Cars	13	Cars	over 50	Electrotechnical	
Tires	over 30	Carbon black	over 75	Industries	10–20
Carbon black	95	Refrigerators	$33\frac{1}{3}$–50	Electronics, control	
Refrigerators	25	Pharmaceuticals	over 20	instruments, and	
Machine tools	20	Tractors and agricultural		data processes	85–90
Semiconductors	25	machinery	over 40	Rubber	about 20
Washing machines	27	Instruments	over 15	Paper making	about 20
Lifts and elevators	30	Razor blades and		Chemicals	10–20
Tractors and		safety razors	about 55	Cosmetics	about 20
agricultural				Pharmaceuticals	10–15
machinery	35				
Telegraphic and					
telephone					
equipment	42				
Electronic and					
statistical machinery					
(of which					
computers=75%)	43				
Sewing machines	70				
Electric razors	60				
Accounting machines	75				

SOURCE: Adapted from Christopher Layton, *Trans-Atlantic Investments* (Paris: Atlantic Institute, 1966).

directly entered several major European markets. In many cases, they have gained large shares; in many cases, too, other countries' firms also have entered. To some extent, such direct entry is an alternative to shipping in products, and it injects external competitive elements (see also Chapter 9 below). Whatever its ultimate meaning, it suggests that foreign concentration ratios may warrant further downward adjustments to reflect the breadth of relevant markets and competitors.

Pending a complete review, one cannot yet be *entirely* sure that concentration in American industrial markets is generally and significantly higher than levels found abroad.[13] That it is in a majority of cases is probable; that it is not less is almost certain. This conclusion may surprise some readers, who are accustomed to thinking of American markets as being decidely more competitive than those abroad. They may well be right; concentration is only one element of market power. Yet concentration clearly does, by any sensible appraisal of the information, appear to be no lower in relevant American markets than in foreign ones; it is probably higher.

There remains the question suggested by Chapter 4's discussion of natural structure—does oligopoly tend to be loose or tight? At the least, one may say that tight oligopoly is more prevalent than has come to be commonly thought. Nearly half of manufacturing activity is in industries concentrated over 70 percent, and quite a few major industries verge on duopoly or monopoly. Only 19 percent of activity is in clearly loose oligopolies, clustering between 20 and 40 percent concentration. Moreover, as Chapter 11 will discuss, quite a few industries would probably have higher concentration if there were no antitrust constraints. The tendency toward tight oligopoly may not be overwhelming, all in all, and it varies among industry groups, as Table 7.2 shows. But it is strong enough to reject the opposite hypothesis, that loose oligopoly is the natural form (except perhaps in textile and wood-products industries); and it lends at least moderate affirmative support to the view that tight oligopoly is the natural structure under common conditions.

Outside manufacturing, we need to look chiefly at utilities (including transportation), primary products, distribution, construction, and services. Each of these is diverse, some nearly beyond any summary description. But some basic patterns of concentration are fairly clear.

Despite the tradition (which was never wholly correct) that they are "natural monopolies," some utilities face some rivalry.[14] Gas and electricity do complete strenuously for some custom, particularly for larger residential and industrial contracts; but this is only partial rivalry among duopolists. There was in 1968 and 1969 an outside chance that the Bell System's virtual

---

[13] In 1951, unadjusted British and American ratios showed roughly the same extent of concentration: see W. G. Shepherd, "A Comparison of Industrial Concentration in the United States and Britain," *Review of Economics and Statistics*, XLIII (February 1961), 70–75. Though British concentration has risen since then [see W. G. Shepherd "Changes in British Industrial Concentration, 1951–1958," *Oxford Economic Papers*, XVIII (March 1966), 126–132, and U.S. Senate Subcommittee on Antitrust and Monopoly, 90th Congress, 2nd Session, *Hearings on Economic Concentration, Part 7* (Washington, D.C.: U.S. Government Printing Office, 1968), 3688–3696] the scissors effect of adjusting American and British ratios would probably at least offset that.

[14] See among others, William G. Shepherd and Thomas G. Gies, *Utility Regulation* (New York: Random House, 1966).

monopoly of land-based telephonic service might be changed to some form
of partial rivalry with a separate satellite system. Yet even this unlikely
departure from past monopoly would go no further than a partial duopoly,
with strong elements of mutual reliance.[15]   Railways and some urban transit
systems have undergone the sharpest erosion of any utility monopoly, but
even this has left large sections of traffic highly concentrated.[16]   Airlines
range from duopoly on lesser routes to moderate oligopoly on some major
routes.[17]   Most municipal services—water, sanitation, transit—are actual or
virtual monopolies, whether publicly or privately run.

Among primary products (apart from agriculture), some, such as many
metal ores and sulphur, have high concentration.[18]   Some coal markets
have tended to move from loose toward tight oligopoly in recent years.[19]

Many subtrades in retail and wholesale distribution tend toward loose
but spatially fragmented oligopoly, especially in larger cities.   But in certain
lines concentration is high in the relevant markets: examples are book
wholesaling, automobile dealers, and lumber merchants.   Construction is
mainly a set of local and regional oligopolies split among such types as
residential, commercial, and highway construction.

Services come in all market types, not just near-atomism.   Hotels,
theaters, and hospitals exist as tight oligopolies in many cities.[20]   Others,
such as laundries, restaurants, home services, and professional services,
usually have low concentration.

Patterns (or nonpatterns) like these are also common abroad, though a
few frequent differences can be noted.   Some utilities are more geographically
unified—that is to say, they are more complete monopolies.   Urban and
airline transport are one example; postal and domestic telecommunications
are commonly both in the Post Office; and electricity, gas, and broadcasting
are usually more unified.   Coal is one public enterprise in both France and
Britain.   By contrast, retail distribution is generally less concentrated,
especially because the supermarket mode of grocery distribution has only
begun to develop.

---

[15] See William G. Shepherd, "Communications: Regulation, Innovation and the Changing Margin
of Competition," in William Capron, ed., *Technological Change in the Regulated Industries*
(Washington, D.C.: Brookings, 1970,).
[16] See J. R. Meyer *et al.*, *The Economics of Competition in the Transportation Industries* (Cambridge: Harvard University Press, 1959).
[17] See Richard E. Caves, *Air Transport and Its Regulators* (Cambridge: Harvard University
Press, 1962).
[18] Many, such as copper, iron, oil, and many raw chemical inputs, are influenced by vertical and
joint venture patterns, discussed in Chapters 8 and 9.
[19] Reed Moyer, *Competition in the Midwestern Coal Industry* (Cambridge: Harvard University
Press, 1964).
[20] Thus the eight leading accounting firms audit about 80 percent of all publicly held companies
in the United States, as of 1968.   They audit 468 of the 500 largest industrial corporations, and
96 of the largest 100.   Indeed, the four leading accounting firms audited 285 of the largest 500
and 62 of the largest 100 industrial firms.   See *Fortune*, June 15, 1968, 178–79.

TRENDS AND CHANGES IN CONCENTRATION (MAINLY IN MANUFACTURING)

The "trend" of concentration has been a matter of special interest since the 1930's. Even monopoly may be tolerable if it is fading; even moderate oligopoly may arouse concern if it is tightening. True trends, if they persist long enough, do eventually bring great changes. Yet true trends (if they exist!) are usually hard to discern, often even in retrospect. Although the subject has lent itself to overzealous—perhaps pathological—debate in the past, it does deserve a careful look.

There are primarily three questions to be answered here. First, what was the trend in concentration during the long premodern interval, from about 1880–1890 to 1945–1950? Second, has there been an overall trend since then—upward or downward? Third, does concentration in *individual* industries tend to change very much and very systematically as time passes? In particular, does high concentration in any given market tend to last or to fade quickly?

First, consider the long trend. Nobody really knows whether the pre-1880 period was the Golden Age of Competition or just an era (like most previous eras) of local near-monopolies. Most markets were tightly local, with few producers. Water and rail transport development after the Civil War sharply widened most industrial markets, and some observers regard the trust movement as merely as reversion toward pre-1860 degrees of market power.

In trying to specify the long trend of American concentration, one needs to start *before* the merger wave of 1897–1904. Rather than fixing the modern outlines of industrial structure, as some believe, this wave created scores of near-monopolies, many of which were aberrant and abortive.[21] Their later shrinkage demonstrated their intrinsic flimsiness.[22] Also, many of these trusts embraced only narrow lines and submarkets, not entire industries.

It may be most correct to envision a trend from 1880–1890 to 1945–1950 which was basically steady and sluggish apart from relatively transient episodes in 1897–1904 and the 1930's. This trend was almost certainly upward; this follows from the probable constancy of concentration between the 1900–1910 decade and 1945–1950.[23] Actually much of this apparent constancy reflects the lack of definitive evidence about 1900–1910, rather than the existence of positive proof. Systematic, reasonably comparable data on industry concentration go back only to 1935; 1890–1910 is a matter of archaeology; pre-1890 is a matter for statistical paleontologists.

---

[21] See, for example, Shaw Livermore, "The Success of Industrial Mergers," *Quarterly Journal of Economics*, L (November 1935), 69–96.
[22] See also A. S. Dewing, "A Statistical Test of the Success of Consolidations," *Quarterly Journal of Economics*, XXXVI (November 1921), 84–101.
[23] Virtual constancy for 1909–1947 has been widely agreed since Morris Adelman's "The Measurement of Concentration," *Review of Economics and Statistics*, XXXIII (November 1951), 269–296.

Apart from sheer discovery problems, there is a basic bias in comparing the numbers for 1900–1910 and 1945–1950. The relatively simple industries (leather, wire nails, tobacco, matches) grasped at by the trusts had, by 1945–1950, proliferated and been replaced by much more complex and diverse aggregations. Ratios for 1947 "industries," embracing more product-type and geographical submarkets, were bound to be lower even where true market structure was the same. This is one reason why large adjustments in modern concentration ratios are, as we have seen, needed, but it is not really possible to adjust the 1900 data as systematically. Since the strength of this bias is not precisely known, one concludes only that it raises the probability that concentration rose at least marginally during the long period.

Trends in other sectors were mixed, except for utilities and food retailing. The patchwork of local electric, gas, and telephone systems grew and merged into virtual sectional and national monopolies during the period. This stemmed both from enlarging technology and the spread of exclusive franchising under public regulation. The national telephone (and telephone equipment) monopoly was virtually complete by 1890, but its hold on communications had greatly increased by 1950 with the relative fading of the telegraph and the Bell System's new preemption of microwave transmission. Conversely, new modes of passenger and freight haulage had reduced concentration in most transport markets. In food retailing, the spread of the supermarket chains created oligopoly in almost every locale.

Now consider, second, the modern period. From 1947 to the middle 1960's, manufacturing concentration has probably edged up significantly. One must use unadjusted census ratios, with all their quirks, to appraise the trend; whatever their other faults may be, these ratios will ordinarily reflect the *direction* of change fairly reliably. The fraction of manufacturing employment and value-added that was in high-concentration industries shows a slight rise from 1947 to 1958.[24] A further slight but definite increase in concentration probably occurred from 1958 to 1966, as Table 7.1 indicates; the weighted average of concentration rose from 37.2 to 39.0 percent. This partly reflected faster growth by the larger high-concentration industries, for there were 138 industries over 50 percent concentrated in 1958, but only 124 in 1963.

This rather steady rise in concentration is not massive, and it hardly parallels the continuing growth in the total large-firm share.[25] Such a

---

[24] From W. G. Shepherd, "Trends of Concentration in American Manufacturing Industries, 1947–1958," *Review of Economics and Statistics*, XLVI (May 1964), 200-212; and Morris A. Adelman, *Economic Concentration, Part 1* (1964), 325.

The 1958–66 interval is complicated by changes in the Census definitions of about half of the industries between 1958 and the 1963–66 data. Table 7.1 reflects the naive assumption that, since the number of industries is approximately constant throughout, the fineness of industry definitions is approximately equal. Other calculations, based on subsets of constant-definition industries, give roughly the same finding of a mild rise during 1958–66; see Sanford Rose, "Bigness is a Numbers Game," *Fortune* (November 1969), 112–114.

[25] However, there was some tendency for the largest firms to increase their market shares, at least during 1947–1954. See Ralph L. Nelson, *Concentration in the Manufacturing Industries of the United States: A Midcentury Report* (New Haven: Yale University Press, 1963), 14, 90–108.

divergence between the trends in overall- and in individual-industry concentration probably has two main roots. First, the corporate giants may simply have inhabited the faster-growing industries.[26] Or, second, the much-publicized conglomerate diversification by the large firms across industry lines (explored in Chapters 5 and 9) might have caused the disparity. Both causes were probably at work, though their exact role has not yet been resolved.[27] To some extent, there were rises in consumer-goods-industry concentration, and declines in producer-goods industries.[28] But these do not explain the total shifts.

Concentration appears to be rising even more rapidly in at least some other advanced economies. In Britain during the 1950's there was a significant upward shift, and a wave of recent mergers has probably helped to raise concentration further.[29] In Germany, too, there has been an upward drift which has been substantial in some cases.[30] The trend in France is probably up, especially in the last several years. Evidence from Japan is mixed, and at least one observer has concluded that concentration has tended to decline.[31] The interpretation of these changing patterns involves some ambiguities, especially in the case of Japan, where conglomerate ties are particularly important. Yet, rising concentration has evidently been the common, if not the universal, experience of industrial economies in recent years; in none of them has there *clearly* been a decline.

Third, within the whole trend of concentration generally, how do individual industries fare? In particular, does oligopoly concentration, once attained, tend to persist or dissolve? If it dissolves—under competitive intrusions or from voluntary yielding of shares by leaders who are intent solely on extracting profits *now* (as Chapter 3 discussed)—then market power under tight oligopoly may be judged slight and fleeting. If it persists, then it suggests entrenchment and rigidity.[32]

This question clearly lends itself to a factual test. A reasonable test would cover the period 1947–1966, for which four-firm concentration ratios (with their admitted defects) are available. Lacking any obvious standard,

---

[26] This explanation also requires that these fast-growing, large-firm industries have no greater concentration than average. This seems unlikely at first blush, and yet the Census reports surprisingly low *raw* concentration ratios for such fast-growing, large-firm industries as oil (four-firm ratio of 32 in 1958), inorganic chemicals (34), drugs (27), and aircraft equipment (27).

[27] Nelson, *ibid.*, finds little of the diversification element during 1947–1954. Yet the main divergence in overall and industry trends has come since 1954.

[28] Willard F. Mueller, *The Celler-Kefauver Act: Sixteen Years of Enforcement*, Antitrust Subcommittee, Committee on the Judiciary, House of Representatives, 90th Congress, 1st Session, (Washington D.C.: U.S. Government Printing Office, 1967).

[29] See *Economic Concentration Part 7*, 3688–3696. The largest rises have been in aircraft, electronics, automobiles, computers, banking, textiles and shipbuilding; others are planned.

[30] See *Economic Concentration, Part 7*, 3486–3501. The rise during 1954–1960 alone was about 10 percent of the average degree of concentration.

[31] See Eugene Rotwein, "Economic Concentration and Monopoly in Japan," *Journal of Political Economy*, LXXII (June 1964), 262–277, and Eleanor Hadley's discussion in *Economic Concentration Part 7*, 3508–3528.

[32] See *Economic Concentration, Part 1*, 66–72, 104–105, 136–149, 265–277; *Part 2* (1965), 637–50.

one may arbitrarily take a change (rise or fall) by more than 10 percentage points as clearly significant.   Anything less than 10 points over a 19-year span would be less than 1/2 point per year and could be regarded as a mild or random shift, or possibly a mere error in measurement.

Setting an unbiased industry coverage is more difficult.   "Oligopoly" is complex, both in concept and in fact.   One cannot just take all high-concentration industries from Census tables, for this would include many nonoligopolies and exclude many true oligopolies (whose reported ratios often understate true concentration, as we have seen).   As an expedient, one may choose those industries which have come to be viewed as oligopolies, by common consensus based on the whole structure.   The industries in Appendix Table 9 represent a listing of 35 such "consensus oligopolies."[33] They yield a fairly definite answer—oligopoly concentration persists.   There was no "significant" change for 29 of the 35 industries.   There were four significant rises as against two declines, and these rises were generally bigger than the declines.[34]   Of the two declines, one (electric motors and generators) at least partly reflected antitrust action.   The other one (aircraft engines) reflects a statistical quirk, since in fact the industry is approaching a duopoly condition; in any event, it is largely controlled by defense procurement policy.   Even computers is largely a statistical illusion; in the tabulating and electronic computer markets taken separately, IBM's shares have held roughly at 90 and 75 percent, respectively (see Chapter 15).   In some other industries (synthetic fibres, light bulbs, photographic equipment, flat glass, soaps, cereals) declines which might have been expected failed to materialize and rises occurred instead.

Concentration was not entirely rigid.   There were many smallish shifts, both up and down.   But in the face of large postwar changes and growth over two decades, oligopoly concentration has proven to be durable, even in the tightest oligopolies.[35]   There is little support here either for Stigler's hypothesis that oligopolists yield up their market shares or Worcester's prediction that dominant firms decline (as discussed in Chapter 3).   Although one can eke out examples that fit both predictions, there are more and bigger counter-examples,   At the least, the main body of evidence suggests that tight oligopoly and near-monopoly, once attained, tend to persist.

One may compare this with changes in a sample of 29 "oligopolies" in Japanese manufacturing (similar but not necessarily the same as the ones in

[33] See W. G. Shepherd, "Trends of Concentration in American Manufacturing Industries, 1947–1958," *Review of Economics and Statistics*, XLVI (May 1964), 200–212.
[34] Twelve of the industries did not even change by more than 5 points; of those changing by 6 to 10 points, the 8 rises just about balanced the 9 declines. Of those 9 declines, at least four (cane sugar, cigarettes, tin cans and transformers) reflected antitrust or other public policy measures.
[35] See also *Economic Concentration, Part 1*. A concurring view is reached in the *Report* of the White House Task Force on Antitrust Policy, July 5, 1968 (Washington, D.C.: mimeographed, issued May 20, 1968).   Further discussion of causes of concentration levels and changes is given in Chapter 11.

the American sample).[36] Average five-firm concentration for the group was 74 in 1949. Ten of the industries showed constant or rising concentration from 1949 to 1962. But, in contrast to the stable American ratios, concentration declined in 19 of the Japanese oligopolies; 12 of the declines were of 10 concentration points or more. Major declines included sugar (down 20 points), cotton fabrics (21 points), paper (27 points), synthetic fibers (19 points), petroleum products (35 points) and cameras (16 points). Yet among *all* Japanese industries, concentration did not decline markedly, so these declines did not merely reflect a general shift. Altogether, American oligopolies appear to be distinctly stable and solid by comparison.

ASYMMETRY AMONG LEADING FIRMS

For any given set of other structural features, the degree of monopoly and probability of collusion may be higher if leading firms are sharply unequal than if they are coequal (as Chapter 3 noted). Long recognized to be important (as "single-firm domination"), such asymmetry has receded in recent discussion, partly because four-firm concentration ratios hide it. Indeed, as Chapter 3 noted, most discussions now routinely assume that oligopoly is a grouping of equals; and oligopoly theories and general discussions now hardly recognize or analyze asymmetry as a major element of market structure.[37]

Yet even a casual look at major oligopolies (such as automobiles, petroleum, chemicals, steel, computers, electrical equipment, appliances, photographic equipment, commercial banking, and insurance) suggests that sharp asymmetry is, if not the rule, at least exceedingly prominent. What about the whole range of industries? Fortunately, the iron grip of Census disclosure rules was briefly loosened enough to give a cross-section glimpse of asymmetry in 1950.[38] An "index of disparity" of size among the leading four firms was computed for each industry, and though the index is rather esoterically constructed, it will do in sketching the magnitudes involved.[39] In many cases it can be partly updated with data from non-Census sources (see Appendix Table 8).[40]

If each firm is about twice the size of the next largest (for example, market shares of 50, 25, 13, and 6 percent—similar to the automobile industry

---

[36] Drawn from the Japanese Fair Trade Commission, *Report on Industrial Concentration* (Tokyo: Fair Trade Commission, 1968).

[37] Except Worcester, *op. cit.*, and Blair in *Economic Concentration, Part 4* (1965).

[38] Federal Trade Commission, *Industrial Concentration and Product Diversification in the 1,000 Largest Manufacturing Companies: 1950* (Washington, D.C.: U.S. Government Printing Office, 1957).

[39] "The index of disparity is the average deviation of the value of shipments among [the four] leading firms, expressed as a [ratio to a] tenth of the average value of their shipments," *ibid.*, 131.

[40] See also Worcester, *op. cit.*, Ch. 6.

now), the index stands at approximately 5.0. This would be sharp asymmetry, by any view. In fact, the index was 5.1 on the average for *all industries* in 1950, and of course it ranges much higher in many industries. Among the industries with exceptionally great asymmetry are locomotives, drugs, glass, tin cans, steam engines and turbines, communications equipment, instruments, as well as the major oligopolies already noted in Appendix Table 8.

Only for Japan are comparable data about asymmetry available. These show asymmetry to be much more moderate than in the United States. Among all 169 industries, the leading firm is no more than 25 percent larger than the next largest firm in nearly half of the cases. In only 24 cases is the leader more than twice as large as the next firm. Appendix Table 10 shows the main Japanese patterns.

Japanese industries may be more symmetric because cooperation is more widely permitted there; and yet from smaller markets one would have expected, on the contrary, to find greater asymmetry. In any event, does asymmetry (in Japan, America, or elsewhere) tend to be high in industries whose concentration is high, or vice versa? If the correlation were negative, it would suggest that these two structural features are in some degree offsetting, or interchangeable. If they were positively related, it would suggest that concentration tends to be reinforced by asymmetry.

In fact, asymmetry is fairly closely and positively correlated with concentration in both American and Japanese industries.[41] There are many exceptions, but the overall pattern is unmistakable, both from statistical analysis and major cases. One may ordinarily expect the leading firms in a highly concentrated industry to include a "dominant" member (or two).

DIVERGENCE BETWEEN COMPANY AND PLANT CONCENTRATION

Firms may develop a multiplant character for technical reasons of efficiency, especially in industries which are geographically decentralized because transport costs of inputs or outputs are high relative to processing costs. However, a multiplant condition may simply reflect mergers or other actions to achieve market power and purely pecuniary gains, as when the older trusts were formed overnight from scores or hundreds of plants. Even (or especially) in a decentralized industry, with similar plants scattered throughout the country, there may be little or no genuine technical superiority in multiplant operation.

---

[41] Analysis of all four-digit American industries showed a correlation coefficient (r^2) of .29 between 1950 asymmetry and 1954 concentration; this is significant, at least by statistical criteria. This is based on official concentration ratios; use of adjusted ratios would involve dubious methodology, since 1966 is rather distant from 1950.

Therefore, high divergence poses at least a question about the genuine technical efficiency of multiplant firms, especially if they are the dominant firms. The suspicion is heightened if high divergence occurs in a tight asymmetrical oligopoly, because there is a higher probability that the dominant firm has achieved its position through the private advantages of simply controlling many plants, rather than through technical superiority. Especially in such cases, the burden of skepticism lies against the multiplant firm, especially if its number of plants is much higher than that of any other firm in the industry.

As for market power, divergence may also suggest that entry is easy, because an entrant needs to build or buy only a relatively small plant. If so, this would generally indicate lower market power, even though in some cases a high nationwide divergence in an industry could mask a series of small local markets into which no such easy entry is possible.

Divergence in American industries shows several clear patterns, even though the evidence is incomplete.[42] First, divergence is rather low, averaging between 25 and 30 percent (depending on how one assigns weights in computing the average). It is naturally low in low-*concentration* industries, but most of these industries are, by definition, of less concern about market power. Second, plant concentration dwindled perceptibly and widely during 1947–1958, and more moderately during 1958–1963; that is, industry sizes grew faster than their large-plant sizes. It follows that, third, divergence increased appreciably during 1947–1963, and is probably continuing to do so, since decentralization is growing while company concentration is still edging upward.[43] Fourth, divergence is not closely linked, either high or low, with specific industry groups. There is only a moderate clustering of high divergence in food and tobacco products, chemicals, and some machinery lines.

All this draws special attention to the industries which combine high (reported) concentration with high divergence. One may take four-firm concentration of 40 percent (unadjusted), and eight-firm-plant divergence of 30 percent, as reasonable benchmarks for "high." For example, electric lamps had eight-firm concentration of 96 percent, but eight-plant concentration of 46 percent. Such industries numbered 32 out of the known 166 in 1947–1958, but they had as much as 30 percent of value-added in those 166 industries in 1958. All those with divergence below 10 percent numbered 70, but their value-added was also about 30 percent of the sample's total.

The 30 high-divergence cases as of 1958, shown in Appendix Table 11, repay closer analysis. These industries have shifted moderately toward higher

---

[42] Data have been reported for 1947, 1958 and 1963. For 1947 and 1958 there are data only for 166 of the 443 industries (and only partially even for some of the 166); these cover 45 percent of total value-added. For 1963, there are 328 industries covering 75 percent of manufacturing shipments. The data are reported in *Economic Concentration, Part 4*, 1720–1731; and *Part 6* (1967), 3373–3379. One must proceed carefully, for in many industries plants have disparate activities.
[43] These two points are also made by John Blair, *ibid.*, 1541–1551.

divergence during the whole 1947–1963 period; 17 rose while 14 fell and the risers' $13.1 billion of value-added was more than twice as great as the decliners' $6.0 billion. The risers included such prominent cases as cigarettes, tires and inner tubes, glass containers, tin cans, motors and generators, electric lamps, and motor vehicles and parts. In cases such as these, divergence may mainly reflect market power in the multiplant leading firms, rather than ease of entry, because there has been little entry (see Chapter 8 also). Divergence fell mainly in "older" industries (such as meat-packing, explosives, cottonseed oil, sugar refining, and copper rolling).

No less (and no more) than 18 industries had high concentration and very low divergence in 1958. These, shown in Appendix Table 12, were mostly medium-heavy engineering industries, such as elevators and locomotives. In fact, the really giant industries are strikingly absent, though it is their supposed scale economies which have been most publicized. This suggests that there may be distinct limits on economies of scale at the plant level (to be explored in Chapter 11). Perhaps there is something like a general ceiling on the efficient plant size.

In any case, the high-concentration, high-divergence industries comprise an important special group. Moreover, the phenomenon appears to be growing; such industries are increasing in number and their divergence is accentuating. The next chapter will consider entry barriers more broadly. By contrast, the 18 high-concentration, low-divergence industries are rather few and small. These, the core of the case for scale economies in production as the root of high concentration, had only 1.5 percent of all manufacturing activity. In 1963, of 328 industries for which data are available, only 27 had four-firm concentration above 50 percent and divergence below 10 percent. These 27 had only $9.2 billion in shipments, only about 3 percent of all shipments.[44] Altogether, the high-concentration, low-divergence cases form a small and special group.

At the risk of hardening likelihoods into assertions, one may draw from this chapter the following broad outline of formal market structure. The predominance of oligopoly is affirmed, particularly in the manufacturing sector. Near-monopoly and duopoly occur in a number of important and lesser cases. Relatively tight oligopoly seems more common than loose oligopoly, which is found mainly in a few subsectors. American concentration is more likely to be higher, compared to advanced economies abroad, than lower.

These patterns reflect a gradual but continuing rise in concentration over the long period of American industrial evolution.[45] The great merger wave of 1897–1904 and the retrenchment of the 1930's were, in this perspective, relatively transient episodes. The gradual rise in manufacturing concentra-

---

[44] *Economic Concentration, Part 6*, 3374.
[45] This rise has occurred despite antitrust constraints on many industries; but it may recently have been accentuated by other public policies, as Chapter 11 notes.

tion seems to be continuing since World War II, though not as rapidly or forcefully as in Britain, West Germany, and France.

Looking within the totals, one finds that high oligopoly concentration has tended to persist during the 1947–1966 period. Either postwar economic changes have been weaker than is popularly said, or oligopoly, once attained, is much more stable than is commonly thought.

As for asymmetry, it is commonly high in U.S. industries, much higher than in Japanese industries. Therefore, most American industries have moderate or heavy dominance by the largest firm or two. A cadre of approximately equal leading firms is unusual, if not quite a curiosity, in this country; in Japan, near-equality is much more common. Asymmetry and concentration are correlated in both countries, weakly among all industries but strongly in a number of major industries.

Divergence between company and plant concentration is high in a sizeable group of industries. In many fewer cases, and few of them of major importance, does high company concentration rest directly on high-plant concentration; these probably account for less than 3 percent of industrial activity. High divergence in high-concentration industries appears to be accentuating slightly, judging at least by 1947–1963 changes.

On balance, the common state of American industry appears to be moderately tight, asymmetric oligopoly, and the most important exceptions are toward still higher concentration. The high averages, and the numerous extreme cases, suggest that there is substantially more concentration in the economy than has been thought since the middle-1950's. Moreover, divergence patterns suggest that leading firms are increasingly composed of numerous plants rather than of large plants prescribed by scale economies. These patterns are broadly consistent with the natural structure hypothesis of Chapter 4; that formal structure tends toward tight asymmetric oligopoly even if this may take the leading firm beyond the minimum scale required for technical efficiency.

Chapter 8

Other Markets:
Informal Structure

In Adam Smith's time England was full of trade
combinations, chiefly of an informal kind, indeed, and
confined to very narrow areas; but very powerful within
those areas, and very cruel.

ALFRED MARSHALL
"Some Aspects of Competition" (1890)

Formal market structure is usually embedded in an informal structure of
arrangements and understandings among enterprises. Price rings, conspiracies, and quasi-agreements—how pervasive and powerful are they?[1]
Collusion is latent in every oligopoly, and in the pessimistic 1930's it was
thought to be strong. More recently this suspicion has subsided, and a
number of observers and spokesmen now urge that covert collusive pacts
(and even many officially tolerated cartels abroad) are fragile, fleeting, and
ineffective. Although administered prices and price leadership reflect some
degree of tangible or tacit cooperation, the late Senator Kefauver's attack
on them during the 1950's was greeted largely by public and professional
indifference. Even when major price-fixing episodes have come to light,
such as the 1950's conspiracies in electrical equipment and broad-spectrum
antibiotics, they have been regarded as isolated oddities.

---

[1] See especially William J. Fellner, *Competition Among the Few* (New York: Knopf, 1949), for
analysis of the conflicting oligopoly motivations.

How extensive is informal structure? Does it usually reinforce, being strongest where formal structure is most monopolistic? No simple and precise answers are possible. After all, every market mixes sweet and sour, coalitions and clashes. Often "agreements" merely veil struggles. Co-operation can take many forms, of varying visibility. Only some of these forms are reviewed here, and even for these the evidence is often sparse, especially in this country where price fixing may land its perpetrators in jail. Even so, some fairly clear patterns do emerge. Those noted here include:

1 barriers against new entry
2 cases and patterns of known agreement
3 measures of the degree of turnover among leading firms
4 interlocking patterns of directorships (direct and indirect)
5 trade associations
6 joint ventures

BARRIERS TO ENTRY

The barriers against entrants include mainly scale economies, capital and advertising requirements, distribution networks, key resource inputs, and any other factor which an outsider must have in order to enter.[2] Even when all economic factors favor entry, a key patent (as in drugs) or a legal franchise or quota may provide a shield. All of these elements vary and interlace, so that in most industries no mechanical evaluation of them is possible. Clearly, most utilities and finance have high or absolute barriers, based both on technology and publicly granted franchises (which often exclude entry far more than technology justifies, such as in television and railroads). Most retail and other services have low barriers. Some minerals are tightly controlled, some not. But most professional services have clear entry barriers. Also, automobile and some other dealers are partly protected by franchises, and some entertainment services, such as professional sports, have collectively managed entry controls.

For manufacturing industries, Bain made approximate ratings of barriers for 20 industries in the early 1950's, using broad categories of very high, substantial, and moderate-to-low barriers. The following list expands and updates the coverage to about 1969, using a variety of sources, indications, and admittedly informal weightings. "Entry" is defined as a substantial move into a market, not the mere gaining of a toehold or market niche, which is usually possible in any industry. The list deliberately focuses on the clearer cases, leaving out a large number of other industries, most of which would probably have relatively low barriers.

---

[2] See Joe S. Bain, *Barriers to New Competition* (Cambridge: Harvard University Press, 1956).

Very High Barriers to Entry

Distilled liquors
Wood Pulp
Newspapers
General periodicals
Drugs
Soaps
Explosives
Glass and glass products
Automobiles
Aircraft and parts
Photographic supplies

Steel
Copper
Tractors
Computers
Copying equipment
Heavy electrical equipment
Electrical lamps
Telephone equipment
Buses
Locomotives
Shipbuilding

Substantial Barrier to Entry

Cereals
Flour mixes
Bread
Sugar
Soft drinks
Cigarettes
Lumber
Paper
Periodicals
Gypsum products
Metal cans
Typewriters

Books
Gases
Organic chemicals
Inorganic chemicals
Synthetic rubber
Toilet preparations
Fertilizers
Petroleum refining
Tires and tubes
Aluminum
Heavy industrial machinery
Large household appliances

Moderate to Low Barriers to Entry

Meatpacking
Flour
Canned fruits and vegetables
Woolen and cotton textiles
Clothing
Brick and tile
Small metal products

Wooden furniture
Corrugated containers
Printing
Footwear
Cement
Foundries[3]

Tariffs and import quotas form a special type of barrier, which excludes foreign but not domestic entry. The exact height of such trade barriers is not known, partly owing to their conceptual complexity, and no survey of them can be presented here.[4] Appendix Table 13 does note approximate tariff rates and other import controls for those industries which clearly have substantial market power. Many industries are also protected by explicit

---

[3] Adapted from *ibid.*, 276–299. The order of industries within each barrier category is the same as in the Census standard industrial classification; it is not meant to suggest rank differences in barriers.

[4] See B. N. Vaccara, *Employment and Output in Protected Manufacturing Industries* (Washington, D.C.: Brookings, 1960); B. Balassa, "Tariff Protection in Industrial Countries: An Evaluation," *Journal of Political Economy*, LXXIII (December 1965), 573–594; and H. G. Grubel and H. G. Johnson, "Nominal Tariff Rates and United States Valuation Practices: Two Case Studies," *Review of Economics and Statistics*, XLIX (May 1967), 138–142.

import quotas (such as in oil and sugar) or implicit controls (such as "Buy American" and other provisions sheltering telephone and electrical equipment and virtually all producers of military goods).

AGREEMENTS AND CARTELS

Cooperation at its strongest binds the participants with contracts enforceable by law. Cartels of this sort have proliferated abroad, some of them created at direct government initiative in order to "rationalize" their industries, others springing wholly from private enterprise. At the other extreme, in the United States, collusion affecting price is illegal outright and must go underground to function.

Cartel arrangements may subordinate company autonomy in many ways, ranging to virtual consolidation. Almost every conceivable device has been tried at some time and place, both here and abroad, and many still persist by the thousands.[5] One can only guess at the tens of thousands of price-affecting agreements which are extant at any one time in local, national and international markets and range from detailed and ironbound pacts down to futile and vague attempts "to hold the price line." Some involve a common sales organization, such as those called "syndicates" in Germany.[6] Others incorporate the pooling of members' profits. Some cartels exercise control to close down "excess" or "uneconomic" members. Weaker cartels simply assign production quotas to members, with varying power and means of penalizing renegades and chiselers. American price rings have usually relied on schemes for rotating orders among the members, in line with "agreed" shares (often agreed only after much strife).[7] American conspiracies, being illegal per se rather than enforceable by law, are usually fairly fluid, with some members leaving and re-entering as the balance of their own interests shifts. Most price agreements, published or secret, claim some other praiseworthy goal, such as stable prices, rationalization of industry capacity, standardization, or orderly marketing. Whatever their benefits in these respects, the agreements invariably attempt to raise prices and improve profitability. Therefore, such horizontal arrangements almost always qualify as genuine elements of market power.

[5] For example, over 2,500 restrictive agreements have been registered under the Restrictive Practices Court in Great Britain since 1956 (and only 12 of them have been found to serve the public interest); see Alister Sutherland, "Economics in the Restrictive Practices Court," *Oxford Economic Papers*, XVII (November 1965), 385–431; and *Registrar of Restrictive Trading Agreements*, Cmnd. 3188 (London: Her Majesty's Stationery Office, 1967). See also U.S. Senate Subcommittee on Antitrust and Monopoly, 90th Congress, 2nd Session, *Hearings on Economic Concentration, Part 7* (Washington, D.C.: U.S. Government Printing Office, 1968).
[6] J. P. Miller, ed., *Competition, Cartels and their Regulation* (Amsterdam: North Holland, 1962), 195–196. Syndicates often extend to all purchases of member companies as well: see *Economic Concentration, Part 7*.
[7] Such conflict was common in the American electrical equipment price rings, even though they worked effectively for many years. It also infests many seemingly tight cartels abroad.

No census of these elements can be attempted here, especially because it is hard to tell which arrangements are firm and which are soft or even wholly ineffectual. Yet the main patterns are fairly clear and well known. Where cartels and restrictive agreements are not explicitly illegal, they are nearly ubiquitous. Abroad, one may roughly distinguish three broad categories: government-sponsored cartels, international cartels, and others (the great majority).

Government sponsorship is always tricky to interpret, because often the real initiative and control for a cartel lie with industry. For example, early railroad regulation in the United States may have served mainly to shore up the railroads' own rate cartel.[8] Often the government—or, rather, some small branch within it—merely acquiesces to the industry's own organization (usually declared to be only "temporary"). Many "depression" and "rationalization" cartels have cropped up in Japan since 1950, with varying degrees of effectiveness. The approximately 20 such cartels operating with official status during 1964–1967, setting quotas for members' production, were virtually the same as purely private cartels.[9] Rationalization cartels were widespread in Britain and Germany during the 1930's; the purely private ones differed little from those ostensibly formed at governmental behest.[10] America's abortive experiment in industry-wide "codes" under the National Recovery Administration during 1933–1935 proved at least two points: (1) virtually every industry has under its surface a boiling urge to fix prices (particularly during slack demand), and (2) not even government support could make a cartel work in low-concentration industries under depression conditions.

Another prime example of industry-government collaboration in enforcing cartel patterns are the production controls and import quotas in the U.S. oil industry. The pure waste from this is at least several billion dollars yearly.[11]

Official fostering or tolerance of cooperative "rationalization" has occurred in almost all sorts of industries, under almost all sorts of conditions, but usually it centers on loose-oligopoly manufacturing industries undergoing severe temporary or long-run shrinkage. Tight oligopolies ordinarily can create self-policing cartels with only official acquiescence and occasionally without it. Lesser structural monopoly (such as in textile products and coal) requires stronger governmental support in enforcing quotas and preventing

---

[8] This point is advanced by Paul W. MacAvoy in *The Economic Effects of Regulation* (Cambridge: M.I.T. Press, 1966).
[9] See *The Oriental Economist*, March 1965, 131–134, and March 1966, 145–160, and *Economic Concentration, Part 7*, 3508–3546.
[10] See Robert A. Brady, *The Rationalization Movement in German Industry* (Berkeley: University of California Press, 1933). One of the least successful among many rationalization programs in Britain was in the coal industry, which, like so many schemes for changing an industry, froze it instead.
[11] See Alfred E. Kahn, "The Depletion Allowance in the Context of Cartelization," *American Economic Review*, LIV (June 1964), 286–314.

"demoralization." This can be seen in present Japanese, British, and continental policies toward controlling and restructuring certain industries.[12] Yet even tight oligopolies frequently are affected, such as the British aircraft industry and the French and Japanese steel industries.

International cartels gained notoriety during World War II, mainly because they had hindered the development of several strategic goods (explosives, synthetic rubber, and others) by member firms in the United States and Britain.[13] Cartels were "most common and most powerful" in such relatively loose oligopolies as chemicals, radio apparatus, electrical appliances, photographic equipment, business machines, iron and steel, nonferrous metals, glass, and optical instruments.[14]

The current status of these cartels is one of the larger voids in economic research.[15] A few other known international arrangements can be added to the probables, including the airline and ocean-freight cartels. Although these display frequent signs of internal dissension, they have been generally stable and effective. Many of the older international divisions have faded as large American and West European enterprises have interpenetrated national markets, especially in major consumer and producer durable-goods. Yet the scarcity of present evidence does not indicate in any positive way that international cartels have faded away.

Among all other arrangements, there is infinite variety outside the United States. Over 2,500 written restrictive agreements have been registered (many of them since discontinued at least formally) in Britain since 1956, under the Restrictive Practices Act.[16] Holland had 1,401 registered restrictive agreements in 1961. In Germany, "119 horizontal agreements had become legally enforceable," including a variety of export term-fixing, rebate, and other cartels, plus 9 syndicates (which verge on complete consolidation).[17] Norway had about 700, Denmark about 2,000, and Sweden about 900 schemes

---

[12] See *Economic Concentration, Part 7.*
[13] See *inter alia,* Corwin D. Edwards, *Economic and Political Aspects of International Cartels,* Subcommittee on War Mobilization of the U.S. Senate Committee on Military Affairs, 78th Congress, 2nd Session, (Washington, D.C.: U.S. Government Printing Office, 1944), and George W. Stocking and Myron J. Watkins, *Cartels in Action* (New York: Twentieth Century Fund, 1946).
[14] George W. Stocking and Myron J. Watkins, *Cartels or Competition?* (New York: Twentieth Century Fund, 1948), 109.
[15] See the broad survey by Corwin D. Edwards, *Cartelization in Western Europe* (Washington, D.C.: U.S. Department of State, 1964), and *Economic Concentration, Part 7.* In 1969 a major informal restrictive arrangement in world steel markets was created at the initiative of the U.S. steel industry and with the full and public assistance of the U.S. government. It was arranged by the State Department and will be monitored by the U.S. Customs Bureau. "Never before in the history of U.S. trade relations has the U.S. government negotiated directly with private foreign companies to obtain from them a voluntary cutback on their exports to the U.S." "Steel's Newest Puzzle" (*Business Week,* February 1, 1969, 17–18).
[16] In many cases, looser agreements have taken their place: see *Economic Concentration, Part 7,* 3680–3696.
[17] Political and Economic Planning, *Cartel Policy and the Common Market* (London, 1962), 21–27. There were registered also 200,000 resale price maintenance contracts. See also Miller, *op. cit.,* 194–196.

ranging from "guiding" arrangements to formal cartels.[18]   Among all these, the most successful cartels and controls have focused in mining and heavy manufacturing industries with standardized products and cyclical fluctuations.   Controls are weakest in lighter industries with (1) lower concentration, (2) differentiated products, and (3) heterogeneous cost patterns.[19]

In the United States, many local trades are outside the interstate reach of the antitrust laws; others, both local and national, are specifically exempted or cartelized under governmental programs.   Such local trades commonly include laundries, real estate, commercial banking, insurance, movie theaters, and many performing services, such as those of plumbers, travel agents, morticians, and taxi drivers.   Professional sports are presently exempt from effective antitrust action.   In these trades, agreements are commonplace, though of varying concreteness.   Most major insurance markets are virtually self-regulated under the haven of state-commission jurisdiction since 1945.

Self-regulation of prices is more explicitly sanctioned in most of the "professions," including nearly all medical, dental, nursing, hospital, and other health services, and many areas within higher education.   Indeed, one may put it more generally; the elite prefer not to compete, at least not via price.   Instead, they regulate their markets through strong informal structure at local and national levels.

In more extreme cases, a government agency itself administers the controls, often primarily in the producers' interests.   This is found especially in the production of petroleum, sugar, and fluid milk.[20]

What about the whole underworld of hidden cooperation, ranging from joint pacts to "conscious parallelism"?   Those that work best and longest are, almost by definition, least known.   Indirect hints (such as rigid market shares: see the next section) are often the only evidence there is.   Major price-fixing convictions may pinpoint some past instances, but probably not the present ones.[21]   These cases have focused mainly on the same sorts of basic oligopolies in which, abroad, cartels and restrictive agreements are common.   Also, in such industries—for example, steel products, chemicals, petroleum products, electrical equipment, and instruments—identical bids for public agency contracts are most frequent.[22]   Indeed (as Chapter 3 noted), public agencies and regulated private utilities are singularly likely to

---

[18] *Ibid.*, 63–71.
[19] *Ibid.*, 200–208.
[20] See Kahn, *op. cit.*; Melvin de Chazeau and Kahn; *Integration and Competition in the Petroleum Industry* (New Haven: Yale University Press, 1959); and Geoffrey S. Shepherd, *Marketing Farm Products*, 5th ed. (Ames: Iowa State University Press, 1965).
[21] Yet in these, unless the basic conditions favoring collusion are altered, cooperation usually persists on a muted level.
[22] Attorney General of the United States, *Reports on Identical Bidding in Public Procurement* (Washington, D.C.: issued annually since 1962).

encounter price fixing among suppliers in all countries.[23] All of the indirect indicators are slippery and debatable, but they do suggest the industries in which collusion is most probable.

Generally, then, horizontal arrangements among competitors appear to be most common and effective in moderate oligopolies with standardized products and similar cost patterns. Agreements are particularly effective when the main customers are public agencies or regulated firms. They are unnecessary where formal structure is very tight, and weak where concentration and entry barriers are low.

STABILITY AMONG THE LEADING FIRMS

Successful cooperation will—while it lasts—usually hold company shares virtually constant. Such constancy may be used to infer cooperation, even when direct evidence is lacking. Constancy might also stem from vigorous but stalemated competition, as all competitors strain and "succeed" equally. But such a running standoff is relatively improbable. The greater the stability, the higher is the probability that overt or covert cooperation exists; a churning among the leading firms could suggest active competition, no matter how monopolistic the structure seems to be.[24]

Encouraged by the possibility that such turnover may dominate all other elements of market power, several researchers have devised indexes of turnover. The best is probably still Michael Gort's index of market-share stability among the 15 leading firms, computed for 205 industries.[25] It is true that the indexes cover only 1947 to 1954 and there are no absolute criteria for rating actual indexes as "high" or "low."

Yet the numbers are clear enough to reject the possibility that turnover has been, or still is, a pervasive scrambler. The indexes indicate a higher degree of stability than an earlier study, for 1937–1939, had suggested.[26]

---

[23] See Fred M. Westfield, "Regulation and Conspiracy," *American Economic Review*, LV (June 1965), 424–443, and the author's Chapter 9 in Richard E. Caves and Associates, *Britain's Economic Prospects* (Washington, D.C.: Brookings, 1968). As of 1967, 1900 damage suits had been brought by utilities following the 1961 electrical equipment price-fixing convictions, plus more than 100 major suits concerning aluminum cable and brass tube and pipe; Frederick B. Lacey, *Problems Raised for Utilities by the Continuing Wave of Price Fixing Cases and Treble Damage Actions*, Speech to Briefing Conference on Gas and Electricity Power Law, (Washington, D.C., February 17, 1967), mimeographed.

[24] See Jules Backman, *Advertising and Competition* (New York: New York University Press, 1967) and *Competition in the Chemical Industry* (New York: Manufacturing Chemists Association, 1964).

[25] Michael Gort, "Analysis of Stability and Change in Market Shares," *Journal of Political Economy*, LXXI (February 1963), 51–63. The index is simply the coefficient of correlation (r) between the market shares of the top 15 firms in 1947 and 1954. If the shares were wholly shaken up during 1947–1954 the r might go to 0; if they stayed exactly the same (or all changed in the same proportion) the r would rise to its maximum of 1.0.

[26] The earlier study, by Crowder for the Temporary National Economic Committee, is summarized in George J. Stigler, ed., *Business Concentration and Price Policy* (Princeton: Princeton University Press, 1955), 93. Gort also noted a difference, but minimized it.

Even during the drastic changes of the 1947–1954 period, leading-firm shares changed little in most of the industries, even by this sensitive index.[27]   An index (r) of .9 or above may be regarded as very high, with little more than slight flutterings among the top firms; one below .5 would unquestionably be low.   Of the industries, stability actually exceeded .9 in 111 and was below .5 in only 20.   In fact, the index was .99 or above—which is just about absolute zero in turnover—in no less than 20 industries, including some of the largest and best known oligopolies.[28]   This group also had extraordinarily high concentration (even by the official ratios)—an average of 74 percent, as against 38 percent for all industries.   Moreover, many prominent, stable oligopolies, including iron and steel mills, oil, and glass, were not covered at all in the study.   The data included in Appendix Tables 9 and 13 further suggests that turnover among oligopolists tends to be slight.

Such instability as there was also clustered strongly in just a few industry groups, especially in clothing (which had 9 of the 20 indexes below .5), lumber, and furniture.   By contrast, high indexes were common in food processing, tobacco products, paper and paper products, rubber, stone, clay and glass; fabricated metal products; electrical machinery (12 of 14 were over .9); transportation equipment; and instruments.

There are no fixed criteria for evaluating turnover, but these indexes suggest that its role in reducing market power is small and spotty.   In the 15 years of relative normalcy since 1954, the pressures making for turnover probably have been less than they were during 1947–1954.   Moreover, stability is positively (though not overwhelmingly) correlated with concentration and asymmetry.[29]   All of this places the burden of proof upon those who maintain that market power in concentrated industries is really low because of turnover in the top ranks.   Turnover is particularly weak where formal structure is most monopolistic.

Although turnover indexes have not been calculated for the years since 1954, there is enough scattered information to suggest that turnover has not quickened since then in major oligopolies.[30]   A recent attempt to show high turnover in a sample of seven industries succeeds instead in giving the opposite impression.[31]   Leading firm shares have declined moderately in cigarettes,

---

[27] The index is probably *too* sensitive, since it weights changes in, say, the 15th firm as heavily as those in the very largest.   Therefore minor changes at the industry fringe could pull down the index, even though the shares of the dominant firms stayed the same.

[28] Included were automobiles, electric motors and generators, steam engines and turbines, aluminum rolling and drawing, light bulbs, tin cans, sugar refining, ball bearings, photographic equipment, and sewing machines.

[29] Between stability in 1947–1954 and concentration in 1947, the correlation coefficient in an analysis of 203 industries is .53; between stability and the disparity index (see Chapter 7) it is .28. Both are positive and "significant" in a statistical sense.

[30] Including soaps, oil, tires, glass, steel, copper, computers, electrical equipment, telephone equipment, shipbuilding, photographic supplies, automobiles, buses, locomotives, synthetic rubber and insurance.   Some of the instances of large turnover are man-made, by antitrust action, (as in cigarettes, aluminum, and metal cans).

[31] Backman, *Competition in the Chemical Industry, op. cit.,* 106–120.

soda pop, and razor blades; but in cereals, soup, tires, and electrical hand appliances the market shares have been nearly rigid.

Evidently, a steadiness of both concentration (recall Chapter 7) and individual market shares prevails in most American markets. By contrast, Japanese industries are generally less rigid, in both respects.[32] British and continental patterns have not been analyzed, either here or elsewhere, but it is known that there have been some large shifts following American entry into a number of major industries.

INTERCONNECTIONS AT THE DIRECTOR LEVEL

A variety of intercompany relationships at the boardroom level were noted in Chapters 5 and 6. The widespread "horizontal" interlocking directorates among competitors have shrunk since the Clayton Act made them illegal in 1914.[33] But many remain, and there are also many indirect connections, some of which probably influence competitive behavior.[34]

Direct vertical ties—mutual directorships between buyers and sellers— are frequent, especially in larger companies in the more prominent few-firm industries.[35] By any realistic view, these are likely to affect the patterns and terms of transactions. Yet since these arrangements are not against the law, no body of case evidence about their effects has been developed.

"Indirect" contacts among competitors, through joint directorships in other firms, are also abundant. The effects of these are, of course, more tenuous and variable than those from direct connections. The same may be true of the many directorships held by financial houses in competing large firms.[36]

Since large corporations and capable executives are finite in number, some overlapping of directorships is inevitable. But the overlappings in many of the major highly concentrated industries go further in systematic and stable ties than one would expect to be necessary for achieving efficiency in using directoral talent. Moreover, it would be irrational to expect those involved to pass up all opportunities for realizing gains from the relationships.

---

[32] See Fair Trade Commission, *Report on Concentration Ratios in Manufacturing Industries* (Tokyo: Fair Trade Commission, 1968).

[33] U.S. House Subcommittee on Antitrust, Committee on the Judiciary, 89th Congress, 1st Session *Interlocks in Corporate Management* (Washington, D.C.: U.S. Government Printing Office, 1965).

[34] *Ibid.*; and Federal Trade Commission, *Report on Interlocking Directorates* (Washington, D.C.: U.S. Government Printing Office, 1951). There is nothing new in these ties, as the survey by the National Resources Committee in 1935 and the mass of earlier literature show.

[35] The pervasiveness of these contacts in some industries is, by any standards, extreme. Some of the large corporations do have a smaller variety of directorship contacts than others.

[36] *Interlocks in Corporate Management, op. cit.*; and Subcommittee on Domestic Finance, Committee on Banking and Currency, House of Representatives, 90th Congress, 2nd Session *Commercial Banks and Their Trust Activities*, 2 vols. (Washington, D.C.: U.S. Government Printing Office, 1968).

And the wide range of contact, whatever its effects on direct competition, is likely to soften "potential" entry and competition from other large firms.

Among the variety of industry patterns, one basic pattern is consistent; it is the largest companies which have directors from the largest financial firms, as Chapter 6 noted. Among the largest entities, these arrangements are often nearly permanent. This informal element, related also to absolute size, would usually enhance the market power of the leading firms within individual industries.

TRADE ASSOCIATIONS

Trade associations and related "technical" cooperative activities may also promote cooperation, but they present a wide range of activities whose effects are uncertain. There are thousands of such associations in the United States: hardly any important industry lacks at least one.[37] In 1961, the Department of Commerce reported a total of 13,000 trade associations— nearly 2,000 of them national, 3,000 state and regional, and 8,000 local. Employment for "specialists in association management" was reported to be 30,000 and "rapidly increasing."[38] The outlawing of price agreements has shrunk the cooperative role of trade associations compared to the 1920's, when they were often officially blessed by the Federal Trade Commission. Yet one notes that "technical" trade meetings were the locus of the electrical price conspiracies of the 1940's and 1950's.[39] Moreover, the purely informational publishing of transactions and prices by associations may substantially influence the scope of price cutting and related competitive tactics.

The possible informational advantage of trade associations for competition are obvious enough. Yet, associations which collect and disseminate information about prices may hinder or forestall price shading by competitors, so that price-information services may in some instances serve more to reinforce and to police collusive arrangements than to undercut them. The net direction of these affects will vary from case to case. Moreover, some trade associations may strengthen the smaller firms against the larger ones. And many associations are formed to exert countervailing power against monopolistic sellers (for example the purchasing associations to which many independent grocers belong).

Despite the variety of their possible roles and effects, trade associations are germane to informal structure. Self-government usually requires a

[37] For example, see Temporary National Economic Committee, *Trade Association Survey*, Monograph No. 18, (Washington, D.C.: U.S. Government Printing Office, 1940), and George W. Stocking, "The Rule of Reason, Workable Competition, and the Legality of Trade Association Activities," *Workable Competition and Antitrust Policy* (Nashville: Vanderbilt University Press, 1961), 18–118.
[38] U.S. Department of Commerce, *Directory of National Asosciations of Businessmen* (Washington, D.C.: U.S. Government Printing Office, 1961).
[39] Richard A. Smith, *Corporations in Crisis* (New York: Doubleday, 1963), 113–166.

staffed organization. Of industrial trade associations in the United States in 1960, some 70 major ones had full-time staffs of over 40 persons, with several over 400.[40] Such organizations, even without supporting regional and local subunits, were engaged in extensive activities, and some of them undoubtedly affected competitive relationships. All of them comprise, to some extent, informal structure. They are focused in certain industries— particularly lumber and wood products, electrical products, textiles, aerospace industries, and alcoholic beverages. The very largest ones are in utilities, all branches of transport, and, above all, the many lines of insurance. About local associations, little is known systematically, but most local trades (such as laundries, coal, real estate, and construction) have frequent meetings and other cooperative customs and arrangements.

These trade association patterns are not closely related to concentration or other formal structural elements. There is some tendency for associations to be minimal in the very highly concentrated industries, for obvious reasons. Also, where industry structure tends to be atomistic, trade associations tend to be merely nominal. Generally speaking, large and active associations are common in industries with concentration in the medium range, such as textiles, lumber, coal, oil, and some branches of insurance. The relation with turnover is equally diffuse. On one hand, in textiles there is a good deal of turnover, while textile trade associations at all levels are relatively numerous and active. On the other hand, in insurance, relatively little turnover is combined with important trade associations. Whether trade associations reinforce stability or stability breeds trade associations cannot yet be established with any assurance.

JOINT VENTURES

"Joint ventures," set up and shared by otherwise competing firms, pose another informal, intercompany basis for market power. They are found extensively in, among others, the steel, copper, oil, and chemical industries.[41] The 70 or more joint ventures in the steel industry give it a much more tightly knit form and outlook than bare concentration ratios show—more like 3 major entities than 10 or 15. There are about 65 joint-venture oil pipelines. To take two of the largest ones, all of the largest 11 U.S. oil

---

[40] *Directory of National Associations of Businessmen.* This includes only national associations. Many local and regional associations also are large and influential, but there is virtually no systematic evidence about them. Often national associations in an industry are nominal precisely because the local or regional associations are the effective unit of self-government, as in medical and hospital services.

[41] See for example Daniel R. Fusfeld, "Joint Subsidiaries in the Iron and Steel Industry," American Economic Association, *Papers and Proceedings*, XLVIII (May 1958), 578–587. A defense of joint ventures in the chemical industry is in Jules Backman, *Competition in the Chemical Industry, op. cit.*; see also Stanley E. Boyle, "The Joint Subsidiary: An Economic Appraisal," *Antitrust Bulletin*, VI (Spring 1962), 303–18.

firms are organized into two joint-venture pipelines running from Texas to the East coast: the Colonial and Plantation pipelines.[42] The Colonial partnership (which is closed to outsiders) has a broad range of exclusive and collaborative features which are unnecessary to the pipeline's financing and operation. Its total equity financing ($38 million) could have been easily handled by any one of the leading oil firms, by other enterprises, or by consortia. Chemicals joint ventures are also small compared to the resources of the cooperating firms.

Though such ventures may give some technical advantages and may even promote new competition and innovation in some cases, their potential for coalescing interests into informal structure is perfectly clear. Joint ventures producing raw materials inputs (as in iron, copper, other metals, and chemicals) tend to stabilize and mutually control these supplies. This not only mutually constrains existing competitors; it helps exclude possible entrants. Research on them—as on so many other areas—is still in its infancy, but most joint ventures appear to be undertaken by large firms and to be relatively small.[43] That is, they usually are not really necessary in order to provide adequate capital. This would emphasize their anti-competitive effects, as focal points for cooperation rather than as sources of new competition.

Even more important cases of joint ventures and consortia among competitors are increasingly common in international markets. In copper, electrical equipment, chemicals, and other basic materials, there are major ventures linking American and foreign firms which in other respects are competitive.

This chapter has shown that on some elements of informal structure, the evidence yields only hints rather than conclusions, variety rather than patterns. Yet the hints are consistent enough, cumulatively, to indicate that informal structure is both important and fairly systematically related to formal structure.

Entry barriers are high in many major concentrated industries. Explicit agreements are common abroad, especially where they can be enforced by law. Where they are illegal, one cannot say with assurance what alternative arrangements are in force. But generally speaking, collusion occurs in much the same industries as cartels occur abroad. These industries are, generally, heavy manufacturing industries with moderate concentration, with relatively standardized products and uniform costs, and with large sales to public agencies or regulated firms. These fit the conditions posited in Chapter 3 for successful collusion.

---

[42] Plantation includes Standard Oil of New Jersey, Standard Oil of California and Shell; Colonial (completed in 1965) includes Gulf, Texaco, Standard Oil of Indiana, Sinclair, Pure, Cities Service, Phillips, Mobil, and Continental.

[43] Stanley E. Boyle, "An Estimate of the Number and Size Distribution of Domestic Joint Subsidiaries," *Antitrust Law and Economics Review*, II (Spring 1968), 81–92.

Whatever its forms, informal structure seems to yield a remarkable stability of market shares among industry leaders. Apart from a few special subsectors, informal structure emerges from the stability coefficients and other data as something almost tangible itself. And it tends to reinforce concentration and asymmetry, not to even it out. Patterns of indirect boardroom relationships and joint ventures lend further consistency to this outline. In partial contrast, trade associations tend to compensate for low formal structural monopoly.

Informal structure may exert less influence on performance than does formal internal (and external) structure. And in international perspective, some of the American patterns are relatively mild. Yet they remain substantial in many markets; informal structure is a major feature of most moderate to tight oligopolies, and it generally accentuates formal structure.

Chapter 9

Other Markets:
External Elements

A large concern usually must show a regard for the
strength of other large concerns by circumspection in its
dealings with them, whereas such caution is usually unnecessary
in dealing with small enterprises.   The interests of great
enterprises are likely to touch at many points, and it would
be possible for each to mobilize at any one of these points a
considerable aggregate of resources. . . .   Hence there is an
incentive to live and let live, to cultivate a cooperative spirit,
and to recognize priorities of interest in the hope of reciprocal
recognition. . . .   This aspect of the power of large concerns
becomes more conspicuous as the diversity of operations
becomes greater, that is, as the likelihood that the large
concern has monopoly power in any particular market
becomes less.

CORWIN D. EDWARDS
"Conglomerate Bigness as a Source of Power" (1955)

External elements of market power are, like the internal patterns, varied and
often intricate.   On some of them, there is little concrete evidence to work
with.   Yet it is possible to discern some of their main outlines and relations
to other elements.   In keeping with the analysis in Chapter 3, this chapter
focuses on relative size, diversification and vertical patterns.

RELATIVE TOTAL SIZE

There are primarily two measurable ways in which relative size may relate to
a market.   First, the industry as a whole may simply be large or small.   The
larger it is, the more a given degree of concentration would normally yield
market power, via entry barriers and other effects.   Second, the leading
firms in it may be among the largest in the entire economy; to put it another
way, some fraction of its activity may be accounted for by firms that rank
among the very largest in the whole economy.   The higher this "large-firm"

fraction is, the more will the leading firms enjoy the advantages of relative size and the less will they be subject to the threat of new entry. These two elements are closely related but not identical.[1]

For American manufacturing industries, the evidence on relative size and internal structure is less complete than has been thought. Total industry size obviously varies greatly (for example, in 1963, from $40 million of shipments of lampshades to more than $25 billion of shipments of automobiles), and it is quite definitely related inversely to the official nationwide concentration ratios.[2] Actually this "relation" may be largely an illusion, since (as Chapter 7 showed) reported concentration ratios are far off the mark in many industries. The "adjusted" ratios cannot wholly clarify this, because many of them submerge the true size of local and regional markets in their national totals.

Still, there remains a weak presumption that (if scale economies play a large role, or at least a more influential role than diseconomies of scale) larger markets are less concentrated than smaller ones. From this and from general observation, one may conclude that industries which are both large and internally monopolistic are relatively unusual.[3] In the United States the most prominent instances of this include automobiles, aircraft, chemicals, drugs, oil, steel, computers, telephone and telegraph apparatus, photographic equipment, heavy electrical equipment, major banking, insurance and, of course, most "utility" industries. In Canada, the instances are fewer: automobiles, agricultural implements, railway rolling stock, cotton yarn and cloth, aluminum, cigarettes, oil, and utilities.[4] The main cases in Britain include automobiles, iron and steel, chemicals, electrical equipment, aircraft, insurance, banking and, again, utilities.[5] All in all, relatively few industries stand out in all three countries, and the same is probably true in other industrial economies also.

Next, large-firm shares range from low (7 percent in textiles) to very high (94 percent in aircraft); they change very little; and they showed no appreciable trend between 1958 and 1963.[6] They are highest in the heavy

---

[1] A high large-firm share could stem from some combination of large industry size with high concentration (aircraft, rubber) or extraordinary size with medium concentration (oil, steel).
[2] A recent analysis is in Ralph L. Nelson, *Concentration in the Manufacturing Industries of the United States* (New Haven: Yale University Press, 1965); and U.S. Senate Subcommittee on Antitrust and Monopoly, *Hearings on Economic Concentration, Part 1*, 88th Congress, 2nd Session (Washington, D.C.: U.S. Government Printing Office, 1964), 266–268.
[3] See also B. Peter Pashigian, "The Effect of Market Size on Concentration," *International Economic Review*, X (1969), in process.
[4] See Gideon Rosenbluth, *Concentration in Canadian Manufacturing Industries* (Princeton: Princeton University Press, 1957), 117–120.
[5] See W. G. Shepherd, "A Comparison of Industrial Concentration in the United States and Britain," *Review of Economics and Statistics*, XLIII (February 1961), 70–75; *Economic Concentration, Part 7* (1968), 5680–5696; Joe S. Bain, *International Differences in Industrial Structure* (New Haven: Yale University Press, 1966); and B. Peter Pashigian, "Market Concentration in the United States and Great Britain," *Journal of Law and Economics*, XII (1969), in process.
[6] See U.S. Senate Subcommittee on Antitrust and Monopoly, *Concentration Ratios in Manufacturing Industry: 1963*, Part II (Washington, D.C.: U.S. Government Printing Office, 1967), Table 33. The only clear rises were in soaps, engines and turbines, and instruments.

producers' goods industries, including of course most of the industries just listed above. Large-firm shares are strongly and positively correlated with reported concentration in American industry (and more loosely with adjusted concentration).[7] These shares also correlate positively (though less closely) with stability of company shares within industries, a prime indicator of informal structure (recall Chapter 8).[8] In other words, there is less turnover among leading firms when those firms are among the nation's biggest, or are branches of them.

DIVERSIFICATION

Chapter 3 has noted that diversification's role in market power has two separate elements: its *incidence* and its *extent* (that is, whether the owned branch is a leading or lesser firm, and how much market power the parent has). Accurate and full evidence on these patterns would not be difficult for the Census Bureau to compute, and it could go far to clarify the real causes and effects of diversification. But such data are only now beginning to be prepared, and in rather tortuous forms. The broad outlines of diversification were noted in Chapter 5. Now we will try to assess its extent and incidence within individual industries.

Its extent ranges from very great, particularly in chemicals and electronics, to very small. In the United States, large-firm diversification is prominent in fabricated metals, electrical and other machinery, rubber, aerospace and electronics, chemicals, and food products, among others. Indeed, the chemicals and electronics industries are essentially groupings of conglomerates, facing each other in a great many submarkets. By contrast, diversification has been much less in a number of oil and steel firms, and it has been relatively low in textile products, lumber products, and tobacco products.[9] In Britain, diversification is most prominent in chemicals, machinery, electronics, and aircraft, but not in textiles, lumber products, automobiles and foods.[10] In Japan, diversification is pervasive.[11] In India, the Tata and Birla complexes dominate a series of fledgling major industries.[12]

Very broadly speaking, diversification in the United States is associated with concentration, especially in the industries *from which* firms branch. Though its absolute extent has been increasing, (especially in certain sectors

---

[7] The degree of correlation (r) with the official ratios is .53, which though statistically highly "significant" is far from a complete covariance.
[8] This correlation coefficient is .28, which is also statistically "significant."
[9] *Economic Concentration, Part 1*, 83–85; and *Part 2* (1965) 745–777 and 973–976. But some oil and tobacco firms have recently shifted strongly toward diversifying.
[10] U.K. Board of Trade, *Census of Production, 1958* (London: Her Majesty's Stationery Office, 1963) Part 135, Tables 14–18.
[11] *Economic Concentration, Part 7*, 3508–3534.
[12] *Washington Post*, April 8, 1968.

such as book publishing, tobacco products, and meat packing), many industries remain virtually untouched by it.   Even so, diversification now appears to be rather more extensive in the United States than it is in Western Europe (except probably Italy), though it is still far less than in Japan.[13]   Yet many Japanese conglomerates exert only weak control over their subsidiaries, in many cases much weaker than is customary in American diversified firms.[14] Therefore the more extensive diversification in Japan may generally have less total influence on market power.   Diversification is limited by law in some American regulated sectors, including banking and certain power and transportation utilities.   Yet even in these cases the boundaries have been eroded, especially with the rise of holding company devices in recent years.   And, by contrast, public ownership of utilities in some other countries may have tended to freeze the traditional segmentation by inhibiting diversification by those public corporations.[15]

On incidence—is diversification focused primarily in leading or lesser firms?   If the latter, then its net effect could be to neutralize market power. The evidence gives only hints, but they are definite and consistent.   One may look first at the incidence of the very largest firms in markets.   In 264 product classes out of the total of 926 in 1950, at least one of the 1,000 largest firms was among the leading four producers, even though (1) those shipments were less than 10 percent of all of the firm's shipments and (2) this product was outside the firm's primary industry.[16]   During 1929–1954, out of some 370 product additions by Gort's sample of 111 large firms, no less than 116 brought the companies into the leading eight producers in 1954.   In more than half of these 116 cases, the entered industry was of high concentration.[17] There is no reason to expect that these patterns have changed more recently, although there have been many conglomerate acquisitions of lesser firms.

In 1958, a majority (550) of all 1,014 product classes had a branch of at least one of the 100 largest companies among its four leading firms.   But less than one-tenth (86) of the product classes had one or more such branches among its *next* four firms and, at the same time, none in the top four.   In 1963, the patterns were much the same.[18]   Therefore, one may fairly conclude that branching by these firms tends to reinforce market power, rather than to neutralize it.   This tendency toward leading positions is more pronounced in the more concentrated industry groups (recall Chapter 7).

---

[13] In Italy, a complex array of activities is held by Instituto per la Ricostruzione Industriale (IRI); see M. V. Posner and S. J. Woolf, *Italian Public Enterprise* (London: Duckworth, 1967).
[14] *Economic Concentration*, Part 7, 3508–3552.
[15] See, among others, the present author's treatment in Richard E. Caves and Associates, *Britain's Economic Prospects* (Washington, D.C.: Brookings, 1968), Chapter 9.
[16] Federal Trade Commission, *Industrial Concentration and Product Diversification in the 1,000 Largest Manufacturing Companies: 1950* (Washington, D.C.: U.S. Government Printing Office, 1957), 41–42.
[17] Michael Gort, *Diversification and Integration in American Industry* (Princeton: Princeton University Press, 1962), 128–131.
[18] *Concentration Ratios, Part II: 1958*, and *1963*, Tables 30 and 18, respectively.

Some parallel hints emerge from a new set of data about the degree of specialization by leading firms in 1963. These data make it possible to single out those concentrated industries in which a significant share of the leading firms is made up merely of branches of firms which are primarily in other lines. A reasonable benchmark for this situation would be at least half of the eight leaders' total market share consisting of branches of "outside" firms. Some 50 industries so qualified in 1963, out of all 199 industries with adjusted four-firm concentration of 50 percent or higher.[19] Thus, in at least one out of every four highly concentrated industries, the leading firms are mostly branches of larger diversified firms. These 50 industries produced $13.8 billion of value-added in 1963, which was 9.7 percent of the value-added in all of the 199 concentrated industries. This indicates that the 50 were relatively small industries, as indeed they must be, compared to the larger industries in which the parent firms primarily exist. Therefore the sample is biased toward underestimating the extent of leading firm diversification. Even so, the $13.8 billion is not small, especially since the test uses a benchmark which isolates only the clearest cases. Moreover the test here ignores the effective outside-market ties which many hold via branches in regional submarkets in the "same" industry.

There is also strong evidence that recent diversification by large firms has not strongly eroded structural monopoly. This sheds further light on entry barriers (recall Chapter 8). Some new entry by branching or merging of established firms does of course occur, as Charles Berry has recently shown.[20] During 1960–1965 the average degree of entry by large firms into two-digit industry groups averaged 18 percent (and exit averaged 14 percent).[21] This 18 percent represents a Schumpeterian sort of entry, and Berry correctly stresses that such entry can be critically important in appraising market power.[22]

Yet the *incidence* of this entry is as important as its average *level* (which in fact appears to be relatively modest—well short of the "radical changes" seen by some). Does such entry focus on the major structural monopolies, as they are shown by the other elements? On the contrary, as Figure 9.1 indicates, such entry is *inversely* related to concentration (and, therefore, to most of the other elements). Cross-industry entry by large firms is at its

[19] Based on *ibid*, 1963, Table 22, and Appendix Table 8.
[20] Charles H. Berry, "Corporate Bigness and Diversification in Manufacturing," *Ohio State Law Journal* (Summer 1967), 402–426.
[21] This is the number of large firms (among the 500 largest) which had plants in industry group X in 1965, but not in 1960, *as a percent* of all firms with plants in industry group X in 1965. For example, of 186 firms (among the 500 largest) with chemicals plants in 1965, 21 had not had such plants in 1960. The index of entry is therefore 11 in this case. The indexes are calculated from data in Berry, *ibid*. Exit is based on firms with plants in 1960 but *not* 1965.
[22] To be precise, one must note that a Schumpeterian process could proceed, in the pure case, with no visible change in company population or industry coverage. "Creative destruction" could occur by destruction of asset values by innovations of continuing firms, rather than by entry, shifting, or death of actual firms. Yet one may expect such internal processes to generate at least some observable changes among firms, and these changes may serve as a first approximation in trying to measure the force and direction of the process.

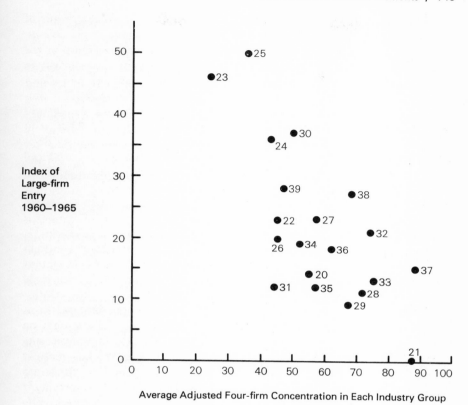

Figure 9.1 Concentration and Entry by Large Firms in U.S. Manufacturing, 1960–1965 (Percentage)

NOTE: The number by each observation is the Census Standard Industrial Classification code number for the industry group (for industry group names, see Table 7.2).
SOURCES: The index of large-firm entry is computed from data in Charles H. Berry, "Corporate Bigness and Diversification in Manufacturing," *Ohio State Law Journal*, XXVIII (Summer 1967), 402–426; the index is the number of firms (among the 494 largest) which had at least one plant in the industry group in 1965 but not in 1960, as a percent of all large firms with plants in the industry group in 1965. Concentration data are drawn from Table 7.2, *supra*.

weakest in such tight oligopoly areas as chemicals, metals, petroleum, transportation equipment, machinery, electrical equipment, and cigarettes. It reaches substantial proportions precisely in those groups (apparel, lumber products, and furniture) whose structure is, as has been shown, already particularly competitive.

Given present data, one can hardly envision a more pointed test of the role of large-firm entry and diversification. The findings are unusually clear; they confirm the reinforcing character of structural elements, and they go against the grain of the Schumpeterian view of entry and diversification. Creative destruction apparently destroys the hapless rather than the strong.

Moreover, Berry shows that entry by large firms during 1960–1965 into new industries was mainly into leading positions. And during the recent surge of mergers, a large number has combined firms already in leading positions.[23] All in all, the evidence clearly leans toward the predominance of leading-firm ties. There is no reason to expect these patterns in manufacturing industries to be reversed in other sectors. If anything, they are likely to be even stronger (as in food retailing and hotels, where multimarket chains tend to be among the largest sellers in each local market). On the whole, the incidence of diversification in American industries and trades may well be more weighted toward leading firms than it is in Japanese industries. In any case, the American patterns are relatively clear and they probably represent stronger control of subsidiaries.

A final indication of patterns in diversification is given by international branching by American firms into European national markets. As noted in Table 7.3, many producer and consumer durable-goods industries in Europe contain substantial firms which are really branches controlled from across the water. In most cases the net effects are probably procompetitive. This is chiefly because many of the branches are below the largest size in the industry, and because many of them inject different and more aggressive managerial attitudes, which upset the patterns mutually evolved by domestic firms. Moreover many of these markets are essentially or partly pan-European, and so concentration and the American branches' positions are often much less than in each country separately.[24]

VERTICAL INTEGRATION

As Chapter 3 noted, bilateral monopoly has long been thought to occur only rarely, and with unstable, indeterminate results. "Countervailing power" is likewise commonly regarded as a sporadic occurrence, rather than the self-generating offset which Galbraith seems occasionally to envisage. Such vertical relationships, where they do occur, would no doubt influence market power and behavior. The result could range from a mutual neutralization of market power to a cooperative, stable, joint position with much price discrimination.

In fact, Chapter 4 noted that market power may be expected to breed more structural monopoly in the next level of production, mainly through

---

[23] See James S. Campbell and William G. Shepherd, "Leading-Firm Conglomerate Mergers," *Antitrust Bulletin*, XII (Winter 1968), 1361–1382.
[24] See *Economic Concentration, Part 7.*

differential prices favoring large buyers. And, indeed, bilateral market power occurs frequently. Some cases were enumerated by Galbraith; these focus on retailing chains as powerful buyers of many consumer goods (except automobiles and petroleum products). In producer goods, automobile companies as purchasers of steel are Galbraith's main example (but with no proof that the countervailing power actually neutralizes market power in the steel industry). Among other possible examples are tire manufacturers as buyers of tire cord and fabric, automobile companies and chain retailers (such as Sears) as buyers of tires, newspaper chains and major magazines as users of paper, makers of electric and communications equipment as buyers of copper wire, oil companies as purchasers of drilling and refining equipment, and various labyrinthine patterns within the chemicals industries. Some similar patterns can be found commonly abroad, also.

Though bilateral market power occurs often, it is far from universal. In many main markets, the buyers are mostly fragmented, disparate, and competitive. In these cases, the evolution of countervailing power (comparable to the "original" market power) should neither be hoped for nor feared. Presently such cases include automobiles, computers, buses, nuclear power equipment, cereals, newspapers, periodicals, some chemicals, soaps, synthetic fibers, petroleum products, glass products, cement, plumbing fixtures, farm equipment, light bulbs, instruments, medical supplies and photographic equipment. Many of these important cases also include some degree of vertical integration by dominant firms at one or both levels. This appears to be sufficient to forestall the development of countervailing power in many cases. Moreover, it tends to encourage bilateral monopoly situations, where they do occur, to lean toward vertically cooperative (not mutually offsetting) behavior.

Where vertically integrated firms are dominant at one or more levels of production (particularly at the earlier stages of production), this is likely to contribute to market power. Instances of this are relatively few but important. In the United States, they include steel, aluminum, flour products, copper and most other metals, wood pulp and paper products, some chemicals, glass, and petroleum products. Abroad, the phenomenon is also common in metals industries.

On the more general question of whether integration is related to internal structure, there appears to be no clear answer. Nelson and Miller have found no significant relationship between the degree of integration and levels or changes in concentration.[25] But both of them have used *unadjusted* Census concentration ratios and proxy variables for integration and so the question about actual concentration remains open.

---

[25] Nelson, *op. cit.*, 78–83, 93–99, 105–108; Richard A. Miller, "Vertical Integration and Monopoly Power" (1968, mimeographed).

TABLE 9.1 INDUSTRIES SELLING HEAVILY TO PUBLIC AGENCIES AND REGULATED UTILITIES, 1966

Industry	S.I.C. Code Number	Value of shipments ($ m)	Major public-agency purchasers	Major regulated-utility purchasers
Highway construction	1611	(7,500)	Federal and State	
*Armaments	19	6,461	Defense Department	
Pharmaceutical preparations	2834	4,432	Defense, hospitals	
Explosives	2892	469	Defense	
Petroleum refining	2911	18,742	Defense	Airlines
Steel pipe and tube	3317	1,072		Natural gas
Nonferrous wire drawing and insulating	3357	3,711		Electric
Safes and vaults	3492	92		Banks
Fabricated pipe and fittings	3498	463		Natural gas
Steam engines and turbines	3511	867	TVA, federal power projects	Electric
Computing and related machines	3571	4,833	Defense, other departments	Airlines, Electric, telephone
Electrical measuring instruments	3611	1,020	Defense	Electrical
Transformers	3612	1,053	TVA, federal power projects	Electrical

Product	SIC code	Amount	Public sector	Private sector
Switchgear and switchboards	3613	1,549	TVA, federal power projects	Electrical
Current carrying devices	3643	811	TVA, federal power projects	Electrical
Noncurrent carrying devices	3644	673	TVA, federal power projects	Electrical
*Communications apparatus	366	10,030	Defense	Telephone, airlines
*Combat vehicles	37174	(400)	Defense	
*Aircraft, missiles, and parts	372	17,564	Defense	Airlines
*Shipbuilding and repairing	3731	2,239	Defense	
Locomotive and parts	3741	701		Railroads
Railroad and street cars	3742	1,695		Railroads
Scientific instruments	3811	749	Defense	
Optical instruments and lenses	3831	332	Defense	
Surgical and medical instruments	3841	360	Hospitals	
Surgical appliances and supplies	3842	769	Hospitals	
Photographic equipment	3861	3,286	Defense	
Research and development	7391	(5,000)	Defense	
Total		(96,873)		

NOTE: Figures in parentheses are estimates.

* Indicates that Defense "sole source" purchases (Chapter 5) are a substantial element in sales.

SOURCES: Adapted from Walter Isard and Gerald J. Karaska, *Unclassified Defense and Space Contracts: Awards by County, State and Metropolitan Area, United States, Fiscal Year 1964,* (Philadelphia: World Friends Research Center, 1965); and U.S. Bureau of the Census, *Annual Survey of Manufacturers, 1966,* M66(AS)-1 (Washington, D.C.: U.S. Government Printing Office, 1968).

SPECIAL BUYER TYPES

Following the arguments in Chapter 3, we look at two main types of buyers—public agencies and regulated utilities.[26]   As Chapter 5 noted, a large share of these purchases departs from competitive conditions.   The effects of these purchases, especially those made by the Defense Department, filter throughout the economy, through primary, secondary, tertiary, and still further ranks of subcontractors.   Yet it is mainly for *primary* suppliers that public buying (and regulated-utility purchases) may affect market power and profitability.   Presumably (but not conclusively) subcontracting is conducted under more or less standard commercial pressures and motivations.

Accordingly, it is germane to list, as in Table 9.1, the most prominent industries which sell heavily to such buyers.   The list concerning public agencies is fairly short and narrowly focused in certain sectors, primarily aircraft, weaponry, and equipment.   In addition, military construction has become large in certain areas.

This group overlaps extensively with the regulated-utility and nonprofit suppliers, which are even more tightly clustered in the capital-goods sectors. Electrical equipment has gained the greatest publicity and notoriety in this respect, but there are other important industries also, including communications, railroad, and medical equipment.   Airlines use aircraft and fuel; natural gas courses through pipes; communications equipment is large and diverse, and most of it is purchased by a monopoly system (Bell) from its own subsidiary (Western Electric).

Nearly all of these industries in Table 9.1 have, in the last three chapters, displayed at least several of the conventional elements of structural monopoly. Undoubtedly, the mixture of cross-incentives and pressures differs for each case.   But in any event, the industries are fairly numerous and, both individually and collectively, substantial.   They accounted in 1966 for about one-sixth of all industrial shipments.

In other countries the utilities tend to be publicly owned, and therefore the rate-base incentives to permit monopolistic equipment pricing might be thought to be absent.   Yet even there, public buyers seem to have been as tolerant as some of their regulated American colleagues.   In Britain, at least, the telephone and electricity systems have not been aggressive purchasers, probably to the detriment of efficiency among the suppliers.[27]

In summary, external market features—particularly industry size and large-firm share, diversification, integration, and special buyer types—range between high and low extremes, and focus in fairly definite subsectors.   With

---

[26] Subsidized industries as buyers, such as shipbuilding, also rate inclusion on principle, but they are rather rarer and harder to trace.   Tax treatment of oil holdings and discoveries also favors inclusion of oil drilling equipment as a special case.   These and other mixed cases would deserve coverage in a comprehensive survey.

[27] See Caves, *op. cit.*, Chapter 9.   Drug purchasing by the National Health Service has also been relatively nonaggressive.

the possibly weak exception of industry size, they tend broadly to occur together with other elements of market power. This continues the broad tendency toward reinforcement among structural elements which was noted in Chapters 7 and 8.

Diversification appears usually to strengthen structural monopoly rather than to offset it. Other external elements, including vertical structure, lack of countervailing power among buyers, and special buyer types, are evidently substantial for certain industries, especially certain types of heavy equipment. Most of these elements converge on a fairly distinct group of industries, which are noted in the next chapter.

Chapter 10

A General Summary
of Market Structure

Competitive industries have their monopolistic aspects;
monopolized industries have their competitive aspects. The
situation in both fields is constantly in a state of flux. The
most that can be said today is that competition is far too
common to justify the thesis that the competitive system is
approaching extinction, and that monopoly is far too common
to justify its treatment as an occasional exception to the
general rule.

CLAIR WILCOX
Competition and Monopoly in the American Economy
(1940)

The main available pieces of the structural jigsaw puzzle have now been
assembled in separate boxes, ready to be combined into one summary picture.
This will point up the industries and markets in which market power is
probably substantial. In addition to suggesting the scope and incidence of
market power, it may also indicate the main lines of "natural" market
structure. As a further check, we will look at manufacturing industries
which appear to have low market power, to see if they show any common
patterns or recent systematic changes. Finally, the special group of industries
with a large element of overhead costs will be briefly noted.

THE INDUSTRIES AND MARKETS

If an industry contains several or all of the main elements of market power,
its leading firms are likely to possess a significant degree of market power.
There are no agreed uniform criteria for weighting the importance of the

various elements, and as we have seen all too clearly, the information that can be mustered about the elements ranges from imperfect to totally absent. Is concentration more important than leading-firm diversification; are entry barriers more important than acquiescent customers? Accordingly, the detailed industry listings in Appendix Tables 13 and 14 have to represent rough-and-ready estimates of the cumulative importance of the disparate structural elements. Yet for most of the included industries the evidence is tolerably clear, and little hedge or apology is needed. Appendix Table 13 in particular includes only industries for which the positive evidence is relatively strong. The coverage in that table probably understates the extent of substantial market power, since information on some of the elements (turnover, collusion, diversification) is sparse or missing, and this has undoubtedly kept some industries off the list.

Altogether, Appendix Tables 13 and 14 offer a reasonably reliable and conservative estimate of market power in the United States, particularly in the manufacturing sector. Although some of the data are less current than one would prefer, the main outlines of the whole problem have probably changed little, except to grow moderately in some directions. At the least, the groupings convey the main extent and forms of market power in recent years, and they indicate approximately the dimensions which a more comprehensive listing would take.

Table 10.1 singles out some of the most prominent examples of market power (apart from utilities), showing major firms in each.[1] Some of these broad groupings depict the competitive situation more accurately than do the narrower four-digit industries in Appendix Table 13. Most of these major industries combine large size, asymmetry, and high concentration. Although the shifting of market shares over the years has been substantial in some cases (chiefly aircraft, aluminum, and metal containers), much of it has been caused "artificially" by antitrust and procurement policies. In others (such as electrical goods, steel, telephone equipment, and photographic equipment), market shares continue to be stable. The 21 manufacturing industries alone account for nearly $80 billion of value-added in 1966, or nearly a third of all manufacturing activity.

THE EXTENT AND TREND OF MARKET POWER

Market power now assumes a rather different and larger shape than recent professional commentary has suggested. This reflects the adjustment of

---

[1] In one of the utility sectors, of course, is that largest of all monopolies, the Bell Telephone system (which includes Western Electric), with assets over $40 billion. There is the large partial monopoly of the Penn-Central railroad, among quite a few other quasi-monopoly railroads. The local, state, and regional quasi-monopolies in the power sector include particularly Consolidated Edison in New York, Pacific Gas & Electric and Southern California Edison in California, and Commonwealth Edison in Chicago. Table 10.1's focus on manufacturing is not meant to minimize the importance of these other prominent cases.

TABLE 10.1 MAJOR AMERICAN
MARKETS WITH
SUBSTANTIAL MARKET
POWER, 1968 (APART
FROM UTILITIES)

Markets and Leading Firms	Net Assets in $ million	Approximate Share of These Firms in Relevant Markets (Percent)
Industrial		
Telephone equipment		80–90
Western Electric	2,721	
Motor vehicles		90–100
General Motors	14,010	
Ford	8,953	
Chrysler	4,398	
Computers		70–80
IBM	6,743	
Heavy electrical equipment		70–80
General Electric	5,744	
Westinghouse	2,271	
Petroleum refining		40–50
Standard Oil (N.J.)	16,786	
Texaco	8,687	
Gulf	7,498	
Mobil	6,872	
Iron and steel		50–60
U.S. Steel	6,391	
Bethlehem	3,060	
Armco	1,633	
Republic	1,608	
Drugs		70–80
Am. Home Products	680	
Merck	488	
Pfizer	735	
Lilly	457	
Soaps, etc.		60–70
Procter & Gamble	1,612	
Colgate	531	
Lever	238	
Industrial chemicals		60–70
DuPont	3,289	
Union Carbide	3,209	
Dow	2,312	
Monsanto	1,895	

TABLE 10.1—*continued*

Markets and Leading Firms	Net Assets in $ million	Approximate Share of These Firms in Relevant Markets (Percent)
Aircraft engines		90–100
General Electric	5,744	
United Aircraft	1,358	
Aircraft		80–90
Boeing	2,186	
McDonnell-Douglas	1,335	
General Dynamics	866	
Flat glass		50–60
P.P.G. Industries	1,095	
Libby-Owens-Ford	385	
Aluminum		80–90
Alcoa	2,192	
Kaiser	1,371	
Reynolds	1,197	
Copper		60–70
Anaconda	1,685	
Kennecott	1,541	
Phelps-Dodge	654	
Photographic supplies		60–70
Eastman Kodak	2,565	
Tires and tubes		70–80
Goodyear	2,377	
Firestone	1,883	
Uniroyal	1,121	
Photocopying		70–80
Xerox	906	
Dairy products		60–70
Borden	1,023	
National Dairy	948	
Carnation	456	
Metal containers		80–90
American Can	1,337	
Continental Can	1,073	
Cereals		60–70
General Mills	505	
Kellogg	286	
Soup		90
Campbell	560	

TABLE 10.1—*continued*

Markets and Leading Firms	Net Assets in $ million	Approximate Share of These Firms in Relevant Markets (Percent)
Air transport		*
United	1,797	
Pan American	1,458	
American	1,418	
TWA	1,160	
Television broadcasting		80–90
CBS	(671)	
NBC	n.a.	
ABC	(320)	
Commercial banking		
New York		40–50
First National City	19,355	
Chase Manhattan	19,014	
Manufacturers Hanover	9,202	
Chicago		40–50
Continental Illinois	6,302	
First National	5,746	
California		60–70
Bank of America	23,961	
Security Pacific	5,711	
Wells Fargo	4,734	

NOTE: Figures in parentheses are estimates.
* Not applicable, because markets are primarily intercity and vary greatly in concentration and company shares.
SOURCE: *The 500 Largest U.S. Industrial Corporations, Fortune,* May 15, 1969.

concentration data, as well as a broadening of coverage to include the several main elements of market structure. From this more inclusive perspective, the economy does appear to contain more structural monopoly in a variety of sectors than the recent literature (with its special statistical emphases) has come to suggest. As far as the estimates are reliable, they suggest that markets with substantial market power accounted in 1963 for at least $171 billion, or approximately 41 percent, of national income arising in market activity.[2] Now, obviously, no great precision can be claimed for these estimates, either in their details or in their totals. But they do offer a reasonable minimum estimate of the present scope of substantial market power, ranging probably between 35 and 45 percent of market activity.

[2] Appendix Table 13's 94 industries with substantial market power had 45 percent of all manufacturing value-added in 1966 ($115 billion of a total $251 billion). The other sectors come very close to the same proportion, as shown in Appendix Table 14 and discussed in that table's footnotes.

Tight or moderate oligopoly concentration—mingled and reinforced in most cases with other structural elements—is a common form, if not the common form, of market structure. It is especially prevalent in much of manufacturing, finance, and—with uneven incidence—transport and utilities. Moreover the extent of genuine monopoly and duopoly emerges as quite high, perhaps not less than was commonly recognized in the years before concentration ratios took center stage.

These recent patterns offer instructive comparisons with the several earlier estimates of the extent of monopoly. Perhaps the most thorough and sophisticated treatment was by Clair Wilcox, dealing with conditions in the 1930's.[3] Although he was reluctant to advance any global estimate, Wilcox did suggest that neither monopoly nor competition was prevalent, and he took pains to portray the extensive array of highly monopolistic industries.

The two other main efforts at global estimates were by George Stigler and Warren Nutter.[4] Both of them relied heavily on Wilcox's material, and both narrowed the focus down primarily to concentration. In addition, they included some debatable classifications of utility industries as effectively competitive under regulation, a distinctly optimistic—in some cases downright unrealistic—assumption, according to present indicators.

On the basis of these and related assumptions, Wilcox's evidence was transmuted in Stigler's and Nutter's hands into estimates which put the "monopolized" or effectively "monopolistic" share of industries at about 20 percent. Both concluded that the economy was essentially competitive, with only a small monopolistic fringe. These reestimates contributed to the postwar revival of optimism, which was outlined in Chapter 2.

The present estimates may be regarded as reaffirming the earlier analysis and evidence in Wilcox's treatment. No less than 35–45 percent of economic activity, including the critically important financial sector, is carried on in the presence of substantial market power in varying forms. A more direct comparison with Wilcox's own original estimates can be seen in the Appendix Table 13, where the industries rated as "monopolized" by Wilcox are marked with asterisks. The main patterns have evidently changed little, except for the growth of such new major industries as aircraft, electronics, and some machinery and household durables.

In addition, structural monopoly has apparently been increasing steadily and appreciably over the whole range of markets since World War II. Concentration has been edging up on an average, and in individual cases it has been remarkably impervious to erosion, especially in tightly oligopolistic industries. Overall concentration, in the very largest manufacturing companies, has risen rather faster during the postwar decades. Diversification

---

[3] Clair Wilcox, *Competition and Monopoly in the American Economy*, Monograph 21, Temporary National Economic Committee (Washington, D.C.: U.S. Government Printing Office, 1940).
[4] George J. Stigler, *Five Lectures on Economic Problems* (London: Macmillan, 1949); and G. Warren Nutter, *The Extent of Enterprise Monopoly in the United States, 1809–1939* (Chicago: University of Chicago Press, 1951).

has also increased, and it tends to focus in leading firms, rather than in smaller ones. These trends are apparently continuing. Even if there have been no parallel and additive shifts in the other elements, the degree of market power in the United States must have been rising significantly, perhaps substantially.

In a world perspective, market power in the United States is probably not less than is common in other advanced economies, and it may be substantially greater. The mingling of structural elements—especially concentration, entry barriers, asymmetry, relative size, diversification, and the impact of public buying and utility regulation—in the United States suggests that market power is at least roughly comparable to that in Western European economies and Japan, if not generally higher. Many important market-power positions abroad are now under public ownership, and not only in the utility sectors.[5] Moreover, as Chapter 7 noted, import competition is generally much more potent abroad than in U.S. markets; indeed, much potential competition abroad is from relatively secure American firms. True, overall and market concentration have recently been on the rise in Britain, Germany, and France, probably more sharply than in the United States. But this has been at least partly offset by the entrance—or threats of it—by American firms into European and other markets, especially in consumer and producer durables industries. Also in many industries American firms enjoy R&D support and public protection which are not available to foreign firms.[6]

The American economy is, therefore, neither unique nor even more advanced than other countries in the competitive character of its markets, although the scale and the mix of elements no doubt differ in details. Informal structure (especially restrictive agreements) and financial interconnections are probably more important abroad than in the United States. And structural monopoly may be rising at a faster rate in Western Europe than in the United States; but there are also counterpressures and disciplining factors which are less stringent in the United States.

NATURAL STRUCTURE

What of Chapter 4's hypothesis that markets may commonly tend toward asymmetric, tight, and collusive oligopoly, with some substitutability among the various structural elements? The evidence is (though with exceptions) at least broadly consistent with this, much more than with the alternative

---

[5] In France and Italy, particularly, public ownership in various manufacturing industries is large and diverse. See, for example, M. Shanks, ed., *The Lessons of Public Enterprise* (London: Cape, 1963) Ch. 17. Many of these are R&D-intensive industries which offer the richest prospects for growth and profitability in the next several decades.
[6] See U.S. Senate Subcommittee on Antitrust and Monopoly, *Hearings on Economic Concentration, Part 7*, 90th Congress, 2nd Session (Washington, D.C.: U.S. Government Printing Office, 1968), 3441–3534, 3682–3706.

hypothesis of symmetrical loose oligopoly. Indeed, it is partly a tribute to independent business traditions and attitudes, to changing postwar conditions, and to the longer-lasting effects of antitrust enforcement that structural monopoly is not even greater than it is in the United States.

The broad drift of changes in structure during the postwar years appears to affirm further the tendencies toward the tight oligopoly structure. Consider the 94 manufacturing industries listed in Appendix Table 13, plus (for completeness) all others with concentration over 70 percent in 1947. In only 14 of these did concentration decline by so much as 10 points or more during 1947–1963. These 14 still reflect market power: 11 of them are still in Appendix Table 13, and the other 3 came very close to inclusion. Most of these 14 declines can be explained by special factors, such as government policy measures toward synthetic rubber, cigarettes, aluminum, aircraft, and aircraft equipment. Apparently, structural monopoly, once attained, tends to stick, unless it meets some extraordinary jolt. A prime reason for this may be the manner in which public agencies buy supplies and R&D work (see Chapters 5 and 11). And the apparent vulnerability of Japanese oligopoly concentration contrasts sharply with American stability.

But though market power appears generally to be a major characteristic of the modern economy, it is not omnipresent. It is particularly focused in heavy manufacturing industries (listed roughly in order in Table 10.1), certain utilities, and the major financial markets. More than would be predicted a priori, the structural elements tend to reinforce each other, rather than to fill in or average out the gaps in each other. Therefore, market power is neither hopelessly ubiquitous nor hopelessly great; and many "concentrated" markets are so small and easily entered that effective market power in them is slight. Therefore, attention and policy measures can quite correctly be focused on the prime cases, such as those in Table 10.1; and a major program to reduce market power could have a moderate and distinct scope.

INDUSTRIES WITH LOW STRUCTURAL MONOPOLY

The relatively few industries with few or none of the structural elements of market power deserve a separate look, to see what common characteristics they may have and whether they represent a stable condition. Low concentration emerged in Chapter 7 as an unusual phenomenon, confined mainly to the clothing and wood products industries, most agricultural products, and certain services and trades.[7] Evidence on the other structural elements has not altered this basic pattern. Consider the 130 manufacturing industries with 1947 concentration ratios of 25 percent or less. Of the 53 which had stability indexes, most (but not all) showed high turnover. Large-firm shares

---

[7] Of 35 industries with adjusted concentration below 20 percent in 1963, 20 were in clothing.

for most of the 130 industries were much smaller than the average. The same can be said of the mass of small-scale local service trades; though many of them have serious imperfections in information (as in repair services), many of them have low concentration, high turnover, easy entry, and few vertical or conglomerate ties.

Most of these markets involve nearly uniform products or services, which are also undergoing relatively little innovation. Commonly, as in printing and forging, plant size can be small, while improved transportation has steadily widened the intercity competition among local suppliers in many of these industries. This has concurrently eroded the rewards to entry by really large corporations, even as sidelines.

Some of these industries do appear to be evolving toward increased structural monopoly. Among the 130 industries with concentration below 25 percent in 1947, concentration had risen by 5 or more points by 1966 in approximately 40 of them.[8] In about 20 industries, the rise was 10 points or more. These rises much exceeded the scattering of declines among the 130 industries (such declines of course being rather small), and many of them occurred in the clothing and other low-market-power industries. Although the preponderance of rises may not be surprising, it does represent a fairly widespread shifting. It hints that oligopoly may emerge even in sectors where it has tended to be uncommon in the past. This hint should be set beside the more definite indications that structural monopoly, once it is evolved, does not appear to wither rapidly. Perhaps this dual process explains the continuing rise in concentration. A main source of competitive structure may be "new" industries, which might lose their initial tight structure as they develop (recall Chapter 4). Yet in recent decades, the "new" and growing industries have mostly been of the sorts (aircraft, electronics, telephone equipment, consumer durables, producers' equipment, health services) where tight oligopoly or virtual monopoly are common and where expansion has *not* eroded structural monopoly.

OVERHEAD-COST, R&D-INTENSIVE INDUSTRIES

What about the role of "new" industries, which might be expected to evolve away from monopoly as they develop in their life cycle (recall Chapter 3)? The last two decades have witnessed many instances of this, such as the ballpoint pen and color television, and others are now in progress. Yet many of the declines have been less than would have been expected. And in still other important cases the "natural" erosion has been staved off entirely. In these cases, tight oligopoly and virtual monopoly have persisted. In most of these cases there are major elements of pricing based on overhead

---

[8] These appraisals cannot be exact because of revisions in some industry classifications.

costs, federal R&D support and related policies, or patents. In some instances two or more influences are at work, as when some firms' federal R&D work forms a mass out of which many products are drawn. The main such hardcore instances so far have been computers, nuclear power equipment, telecommunications equipment, various electronic equipment, photocopying equipment, aircraft, and aircraft engines (see Chapter 15 concerning computers). Insurance firms, in their dual role of insurers and investors, also share some of the overhead-cost pricing features. In some cases, such as multiple-access data processing, there is a danger that a new industry will be frozen permanently into monopoly, as a regulated utility seeks to enlarge its range of protected activities.[9]

All in all, the downward tendency of concentration in major "new" industries has not been as widespread as might be expected, especially since most of these industries are growing extremely rapidly. Life-cycle tendencies evidently can be checked or reversed by other factors, either industrial or political, particularly in the presence of a large overhead-cost element.

---

[9] See the filings in the Federal Communications Commission inquiry on this matter (Docket No. 16979, March 5, 1968), especially the submission by the Antitrust Division of the Department of Justice.

PART III

Causes and Effects of Market Power

Chapter /**11**

Determinants of
Market Structure

Yet fish there be, that neither hook nor line,
Nor snare, nor net, nor engine can make thine:
They must be groped for, and be tickled too,
Or they will not be catch'd, whate'er you do.

JOHN BUNYAN
The Pilgrim's Progress (1684)

If we examine the actual rise and structure of trusts, we
shall always find the economy of large-scale production
supported by some more certain basis of monopoly. These
supports may be provisionally classified as follows:—
1. Superior access to raw materials.
2. Superior control of means of transport and distribution.
3. Differential advantages in production or marketing due
   to patents, trade marks, special processes.
4. Public franchises, licenses, or other privileges bestowing
   monopoly or restricting competition.
5. Tariff legislation.

J. A. HOBSON
The Evolution of Modern Capitalism (1926)

The patterns shown in Chapters 5–10 have not just happened, by the play of
chance or economic caprice. Random elements do intervene, but in many
markets the structure evolves systematically, often tightly molded by underlying determinants. To an appraisal of these determinants, which were noted
in Chapter 4 and at various later points, we now turn.

There are at least several alternative kinds of determinants (recall
Chapter 3). One is *technical* economies of scale, in production, distribution,
innovation, and selling activities. Another is purely pecuniary gains to
scale and to market leadership. Still another may be industry life cycle,
which includes the possible influence of growth rates. All of these will shape
both natural and optimum industry structure. In addition to these economic
determinants, a variety of public policies may intervene, such as R&D support, procurement, and antitrust. These will be discussed in the first section,
in order to clear the scene for appraising the economic determinants.

But first one must emphasize that there are two serious limitations on an empirical survey of this sort. One is that the analysis must be incomplete, because it must focus mainly on "permanent" structure—therefore it misses much of the shorter-term market power. Moreover, it also misses much of the continuing adjustments *among* structural elements.

The second limitation applies also to all of the statistical testing in Chapters 11 through 14. Attempts to measure the causes (and effects, as in the next three chapters) of market power will usually understate what is being measured. This downward statistical bias has several causes. First, the evidence is incomplete, especially where firms have an interest in secrecy. Therefore, some evidence of market structure simply lies hidden, inpenetrable by all research. Other bits of evidence—being averages, incomplete, or not well fitted to the concept being measured—mask much of the true variation. Second, it is still the old and stale problems, now partly solved, which get attention and investigation. Therefore the most abundant and seemingly the best data tend to cluster on industries and firms which (often *because* of the attention) have now lost much of their monopoly bite, rather than on new cases of market power with sharp effects. Third, market processes eat away differences, especially those which are given publicity. This is especially clear for cost differences, which tend to fade away in time. It has also proven true of abnormally large profits, when they occur.

For reasons such as these, the causes and effects of market power are extraordinarily elusive to statistical investigation; even groping and tickling the data will not catch some of the statistical fish. Even tight existing relationships may show only traces under numerical analysis. And inaccurate data may falsely suggest relationships that do not exist. This warns against relying exclusively upon the calculator or computer. It also cautions us that many of the faint statistical hints may actually represent patterns which are much more distinct than the data at hand can show.

PUBLIC POLICY INFLUENCES

Perhaps the oldest governmental influence on market power is the tariff. Although the tariff may never really have been the Mother of all Trusts, we have seen (in Chapter 8 and Appendix Table 13) that it is often an important element. The formal tariff rates do not seem to be statistically associated with concentration or other structural elements. Moreover (as Chapter 7 noted), quotas and related trade barriers often create more severe restrictions than the tariff rates suggest, while relatively high tariffs on major imported inputs may undercut the supposed protection from tariffs on finished goods which use those tariffed imports as raw materials. In any event, trade barriers have been an important element in markets in many countries, particularly since the 1930's.

Public funding of R&D probably has a deep influence on many of the science-intensive industries. Chapter 5 has indicated that it focuses sharply in a relatively few large firms, in some cases providing nearly all R&D funds. In fact, in a majority of major R&D-intensive industries, public R&D funds have been clustered more tightly in the leading firms than are private funds. Such industry groups include chemicals, petroleum products, machinery, electrical equipment, vehicles, and instruments.[1] The reasons why such support centers on leading firms are relatively simple—ease and security of contracting—and one may also note that the public support is usually not much more concentrated than are the companies' own funds. It may also be true that some federal R&D work has little direct spillover into commercial use.[2] But much of it does have some direct payoff, and the total R&D volume is often so large that the indirect benefits from it must often be substantial. Moreover, the R&D contract has very often paved the way for the procurement contract and for subsequent renewals, for many small contracts as well as for a parade of major items.[3] Probably, public R&D funding has tended strongly to strengthen and stabilize leading-firm positions in many R&D-intensive industries.

The stabilizing effect of procurement is further attested by the degree and pattern of sole-source buying, shown in Appendix Table 6. Even at the high-water mark of competitive procurement in 1966–1967, much the greater mass of purchasing was still on an essentially noncompetitive basis, and not just in aerospace industries. This may tend to strengthen leading firms, reducing the prospects for natural erosion of leading positions via innovative and other efforts by lesser firms. Even if these lesser firms are much more fruitful in R&D (see below), federal procurement and R&D support may handily offset this. Moreover, foreign competition is not even a remote disciplining factor in most of these national-security items.

Various other policies tend to strengthen American sellers in some world markets.[4] These include "Buy American" restrictions on some equipment imports, plus influence over some purchases for the international satellite communications network. Also, United States agencies control some of the technology and production in the nuclear fuel cycle and for a wide range of military and related items. Current problems in the balance

---

[1] U.S. National Science Foundation, *Basic Research, Applied Research and Development in Industry, 1965*, NSF 67–12 (Washington, D.C.: U.S. Government Printing Office, 1967); see also Appendix Table 5 for data on some individual firms, and in Table 14.1 below.
[2] Richard R. Nelson, Merton J. Peck, and Edward Kalachek, *Technology, Economic Growth and Public Policy* (Washington, D.C.: Brookings, 1967); and Edwin Mansfield, *The Economics of Technological Change* (New York: Norton, 1968).
[3] Merton J. Peck and Frederic M. Scherer, *The Weapons Acquisition Process* (Boston: Division of Research, Graduate School of Business Administration, Harvard University, 1962); also H. O. Stekler, *Structure and Performance in the Aeorospace Industry* (Berkeley: University of California Press, 1966); and John K. Galbraith, *The New Industrial State* (Boston: Houghton Mifflin, 1967).
[4] See U.S. Senate Subcommittee on Antitrust and Monopoly, 90th Congress, 2nd Session, *Economic Concentration, Part 1*, (Washington, D.C.: U.S. Government Printing Office, 1968), 3687–3706.

of payments have evoked many more-or-less calculated attempts to proscribe import competition.

In all of these ways, public policies now tend to enlarge and harden market power, particularly in R&D-intensive industries. Parallel efforts by countries abroad (in many cases in response to American policies) often exert only minor counter-effects. In America the main offsetting policy initiative may be antitrust enforcement. Over the course of decades, antitrust measures have helped to reduce market power in several industries–notably aluminum, tin cans, meatpacking, cigarettes, and petroleum. Informal structure is limited, as noted in Chapter 8, perhaps well below levels which are common abroad. This has probably promoted concentration in the United States more than trivially, by shifting upward the preferred concentration-collusion margin in many industries. Antimerger policies may recently have slowed rising concentration in some industries, but this is still very recent and probably well short of the major effect which some have asserted, and it has not arrested the general rise (recall Chapter 10). Moreover, the constraints on horizontal and vertical mergers may have induced some expansion in conglomerate merger activity, which (as Chapter 9 suggested) has tended to have an anticompetitive incidence. Also, since about 1952, antitrust has largely abandoned attempts to make changes in established structure, even where structural monopoly would appear to warrant it. Prime examples of potential candidates for action are automobiles, steel, and the vertical tie between Western Electric and the Bell operating subsystems. Though one would be unduly harsh to call it a "charade," antitrust policy has now largely acquiesced in, and therefore ratified, existing market structure.[5] Therefore it is not a strong specific offset to other public policies which accentuate market power in a range of major markets.

The whole effect of these policies probably extends abroad as well, inducing added concentration in a variety of European industries.[6] Much of the continuing merger activity, often under strong governmental pressure, reflects efforts to "stand up to" American firms. Yet many of these U.S. firms enjoy heavy government support, or have long been ripe for antitrust action. To this extent, American policies are ultimately fostering structural monopoly abroad beyond what is, by any reasonable estimate, necessary or appropriate.

Evidently, in any event, public policies intermingle with economic determinants of structure in many of the most important and controversial industries. The foregoing summary has not filtered out the policy effects,

---

[5] See the exchange among John K. Galbraith, Willard F. Mueller, Donald F. Turner and Walter Adams in *Planning, Regulation and Competition*, Hearing before U.S. Senate Subcommittees of the Select Committee on Small Business, 90th Congress, 1st Session (Washington, D.C.: U.S. Government Printing Office, 1967).

[6] See *Economic Concentration*, Part 7, 3682–3706, and references cited there; also John Sheahan, *Promotion and Control of Industry in Postwar France* (Cambridge: Harvard University Press, 1962).

nor perhaps could even a comprehensive effort; but it has indicated that the following review may not be able to factor out clearly the purely economic causes. With this warning, we turn first to technical economies of scale, and then to pecuniary economies.

ECONOMIES OF SCALE

In Production and Distribution

One would like to plot out, for each industry, clear average-cost curves for plants and firms, reflecting efficient operations at each level of production. These curves, like those in Chapter 3, would show both the range and steepness of scale economies and diseconomies in the various activities (production, distribution, and innovation) of the firm. Otherwise, the possible "technological imperatives" cannot be accurately appraised. It would then be relatively easy to judge, in each case, how far scale economies could explain some elements of structural monopoly and what the marginal costs or gains of less concentration might be.

Despite its seeming simplicity, this research task bristles with conceptual and empirical difficulties. Only since the 1930's have there been scientific attempts to measure scale economies, and the results of these have been slender. From the 1890's to the 1930's (as Chapter 2 noted), scale economies were commonly asserted to be both steep and extensive, thereby favoring a high degree of consolidation and unification. Yet this presumption rested mainly on armchair belief and self-serving claims, rather than on systematic evidence. Recent research has, by contrast, seemed to suggest that there is a range of "optimum" or "minimum-average-cost" scale, usually beginning at sizes that are, in relation to the total market, very small.[7] The continuing coexistence of both small and large firms in most industries lends this finding added plausibility.[8] Accordingly, many observers now assume that there is an approximate parity of efficiency, or constant costs—neither economies nor diseconomies over a large size range, in most industries. By the same token, the cases *for* and *against* concentration have both been diluted, since internal efficiency appears not to be affected very much either way.

Yet much of the evidence for this is, as we will now see, sparse and controversial. Most of it lumps together technical and pecuniary advantages, and deals with plants rather than entire firms. Moreover, the search for "minimum efficient scale" has drawn off attention from *dis*economies in higher ranges of output. Such diseconomies may be, as Chapters 3 and 4 noted, at least equally important for market power and public policy.

---

[7] Joe S. Bain, *Barriers to New Competition* (Cambridge: Harvard University Press, 1956); T. R. Saving, "Estimation of Optimum Size of Plant by the Survivor Technique," *Quarterly Journal of Economics*, LXXV (November 1961), 569–607.
[8] G. J. Stigler, "The Economies of Scale," *Journal of Law and Economics*, I (October 1958), 54–71.

Three different techniques for measuring scale economies have been tried since research began in the early 1930's.[9] The first method simply plotted out cross-section data on company size and average cost.[10] Unfortunately, average costs usually proved hard to measure and to assign to individual products. Also, all firms—efficient and inefficient—usually were included, and so the resulting descriptive, retrospective "cost curves" did not depict minimum attainable costs in an efficiency sense; that is, they gave little normative information useful for public policy. Moreover, no effort was made to winnow out the pecuniary (input-price) advantages of scale. Finally, and most crushing of all, cost differences tend over time to be wrung out, as quasi-rents are capitalized into costs and losses are written off.[11] Inevitably, measured cost curves will look flat, as indeed the studies reported time after time; but this may be mostly an economic illusion. This problem does not apply to marginal costs (which however are virtually immeasurable directly), but the studies focussed only on average costs.

In a second and more direct approach, Joe Bain canvassed managerial estimates of "optimum" scale of new plants, and of possible economies of multiplant operations (as of 1950). In most of his 20-industry sample, "optimum" plant scale turned out to be only a sliver of total industry size; the cost curves appeared to be flattish; and there was no strong evidence of multiplant economies. In most of the industries (and especially oil refining, flour, metal containers, tires and tubes, shoes, cement, steel, gypsum products, and soaps), concentration was well in excess of what efficient technology apparently prescribed. These estimates have become fixed points of reference in the literature on the subject, but they are few and increasingly out of date. And they may overstate the range of "optimum scale," because those interviewed would naturally declare their own size to be efficient, no matter what that size may be.[12]

Since 1958, a third approach, the survivor technique, has been advanced, purporting to yield efficient estimates for hundreds of markets, not just in manufacturing but in virtually all sectors.[13] The technique simply postulates that if firms of size x are surviving (or increasing in number), this proves their "efficiency" in all essential activities. Here is a twentieth-century version of Spencerian industrial evolution indeed! Such an acid test of "efficiency"

---

[9] This section is condensed from my, "What Does the Survivor Technique Show About Economies of Scale?" *Southern Economic Journal*, XXXVI (July 1967), 113–122.

[10] See National Bureau of Economic Research, *Cost Behavior and Price Policy* (Princeton: Princeton University Press, 1943); also J. Johnston, *Statistical Cost Analysis* (New York: McGraw-Hill, 1960).

[11] See Donald Dewey, "The Ambiguous Notion of Average Cost," *Journal of Industrial Economics*, X (July 1962), 31–37; and Martin Bronfenbrenner, "Imperfect Competition on a Long-Run Basis," *Journal of Business*, XXIII (April 1950), 81–93.

[12] This point was suggested to me by Donald Dewey.

[13] The proximate origin may be George J. Stigler, *op. cit.*; but an earlier study on the 1930's used the technique on a large scale. See Willard L. Thorp and Walter F. Crowder, *The Structure of Industry*, Monograph 27, Temporary National Economic Committee (Washington, D.C.: U.S. Government Printing Office, 1941), Part I, Ch. 2, 19–57.

embraces location, research, and all the rest, not just production activity on the plant floor. It avoids the profit-rent-capitalization problem by using readily available Census data on plant sizes. The technique has been applied to 137 manufacturing industries already, and its results are gaining wide acceptance. It deserves close scrutiny.

These strengths are also weaknesses; what *is* is by no means necessarily what *ought to be*. One might almost as well use trends in actual market structure as a basis for prescribing the optimum structure, rather than merely predicting the natural structure. Survival of a size group of plants or firms may reflect pure pecuniary advantages or any number of socially dubious activities, instead of technical efficiency. This defect is most severe in just those industries where market power is greatest (such as automobiles, computers, telephone equipment, drugs, and aircraft), for which normative estimates of scale are needed as a guide for public policy. A financially robust, dominant firm may or may not be technically superior; that is precisely the question which cannot be assumed away.

Morover, the technique yields no information on the *gradients* of economies and diseconomies, which also must be known in gauging the net costs and benefits of public action toward market power. Finally it runs afoul of some practical problems; for one, only labor-size data about plants are available, so the estimates are likely to be distorted by trends in labor-saving innovation. Thus a decline in the largest plants (as shown by number of workers) might reflect simply labor-saving innovation which shrinks the labor "size" of all plants, not a true shrinkage in the production size of plants.

The upshot is that survivor estimates are weak in concept and, so far, mostly unreliable in statistical results. Odd statistical results are frequent. Despite a number of ambitious attempts, only a handful of tolerably consistent estimates have been made, few of them for the really interesting and important industries.[14]

Consequently the relatively reliable evidence now existing on scale economies in firms is confined mainly to Bain's findings. They hint that concentration far exceeds purely technical requirements in the majority of industries. They also indicate how overwhelmingly ignorant we are about current conditions in nearly all markets, even after three decades of studies. Upon such slender statistical reeds has turned the whole debate over size and efficiency, and it apparently must continue to do so for some years more, at least.

Yet, survivor results may be a relatively reliable way of indicating minimum efficient sizes. On this point their specific results are crystal clear—in the great majority of industries, efficient scale in plant production is reached at small, even miniscule, shares of the industry. Thomas Saving, for example, found that in over 70 percent of his industries by number (86 percent by share

---

[14] See Shepherd, *op. cit.*, for a survey of these findings in detail.

of employment), "minimum optimum" plant size is less than 1 percent of industry size. Even if these estimates understate by half, plant efficiency still seems to provide no justification for most concentration in American industry.

There are still other straws in the wind, casting doubt on the relative efficiency of the largest units. In a large number of industries, there has been a decided shift away from large plants. This was hinted in Chapter 7's discussion of plant-company divergence. There is more direct evidence as well.[15] Of a sample of 133 important industries, 78 showed declines in the share of the largest plants during 1947–1958, despite the constancy in total manufacturing employment.[16] Apparently there are strong pressures in many industries toward smaller employment size of plants; these pressures may stem from changes in relative transportation costs and in methods of information processing, both of which have recently encouraged greater decentralization of economic control.[17] Also the labor-saving bias of much innovation is undoubtedly at work. Even so, these downward shifts appear to be significant, especially since they bear no apparent relation to levels or changes in concentration. In fact, concentration has been steady or rising in many of the industries in which the shrinkage in large plants has been greatest.

Over the whole range of two-digit industry groups, the large-plant share declined in a majority (11 out of 19), including the heavy-industry groups (oil, tires and tubes, metal products and machinery).[18]

Among individual industries, the instances of rising large-plant share are clustered in only eight of the larger four-digit industries, especially cigarettes, pharmaceutical preparations, aircraft, and scientific instruments. When these eight industries (plus two "new" defense industries—guided missiles, and sighting and fire-control equipment) are removed, the share of the largest-size plants in *all* other industries declined marginally, rather than rose. This handful of industries forms a decidely atypical group. Their value-added grew much more rapidly than the average. And, directly and indirectly, many of them are heavily involved with defense procurement and other public policies. Despite their shift toward larger plants, concentration declined in several of these industries.

To put it at its mildest, rising relative plant size has not clearly led to increased concentration. Nor have declines in large-size plants exerted close and powerful downward pressure on concentration. Distinct changes in plant concentration have often been roughly paralleled by shifts in company

---

[15] The most prominent single example is the automobile industry, in which new plants are smaller than older ones, even though many of the newer plants produce models for several different divisions; see also Chapter 15. In steel, new and efficient plants are being built on a very small scale; see *Business Week*, "The Mini-Mill: Steel on a Budget," March 29, 1969, 66–70, for one account of this.

[16] These are discussed more fully in Shepherd, *op. cit.*

[17] These factors are discussed in *Economic Concentration, Part 4* (1965) through *Part 6* (1967).

[18] Based on U.S. Bureau of the Census, *Census of Manufactures, 1947* and *1963*, (Washington, D.C.: U.S. Government Printing Office, 1949 and 1965 respectively). Significant rises in large-firm shares occurred in tobacco, clothing, furniture and primary metals.

concentration, as Chapter 7 noted in its treatment of divergence.[19]   Yet the "relationship" is loose and full of exceptions, if it really exists at all.   Continuing decentralization of production in many industries cannot be expected to cause closely parallel declines in company concentration.

Another likely determinant of structure is greater capital-intensity in the leading firms.   This would be expected to result from the cheaper capital (and possibly more expensive labor; see the next section) available to large and dominant firms.   Or conversely, firms may achieve dominance *because* they innovate toward best, capital-intensive techniques.   Whatever the direction of causation may be, it has become a standard assumption that leading firms are more capital intensive than their smaller rivals.   A dominant firm (or firms) with *less* capital intensity than its competitors would be improbable and unusual; in such cases, the presumption might be that in fact it lags behind the rest in process innovation.

It is now possible to test this hypothesis in some detail.[20]   And it turns out that leading firms *are* more capital-intensive (or, rather, less labor-intensive) in a majority of industries—about 325 out of about 417.[21]   But in only 25 of these is the difference really pronounced (with the leaders one-half as labor-intensive as the rest of the industry).   Moreover, these 25 industries almost all have low concentration and include virtually no heavy industries. To put it more generally, leading-firm capital-intensity bears no clear relation at all to concentration.

By contrast, in no less than 77 industries, the leading four firms are *more* labor-intensive than the rest, and in at least 27 other industries there is no significant difference.   These "unusual" cases include (1) many important industries, totalling altogether $45 billion of value-added, about one-quarter of the manufacturing total in 1963, and (2) many industries with high concentration.   Of the 77 industries, adjusted concentration was above 80 percent in 7, above 60 percent in 28, and above 40 percent in no less than 56, a clear majority.   The 77 industries focus in chemicals, primary metals, fabrication, and machinery, as well as in such low-concentration sectors as textiles, and lumber and paper products.   They include such supposedly progressive industries as general inorganic chemicals, synthetic fibers, drugs, tires and tubes, glass bottles, cement, iron and steel, copper and copper products, tin cans, many kinds of machinery, refrigerators, telephone and telegraph equipment, and shipbuilding.   No less than 26 of them are among the industries with probably substantial market power listed in Appendix Table 13.

---

[19] *Economic Concentration, Part 4*, 1730–1731.

[20] Using data given in U.S. Senate Subcommittee on Antitrust and Monopoly, *Concentration Ratios in Manufacturing Industry, 1963, Part I* (Washington, D.C.: U.S. Government Printing Office, 1966), Table 3.

[21] Actually the measure used is labor-intensity, which is inversely related to capital-intensity. More precisely, labor-intensity is shown by the ratio of the four-firm share of industry wages to the four-firm share of value-added.   Thus, for industry 3441, fabricated structural steel, the ratio is 21 : 15, which indicates relatively high labor-intensity in the leading four firms.   An accurate and direct measure of capital in firms at the four-digit industry level is not available.

Scale economies in distribution may also be important in certain industries. Distribution and sales networks are clearly important in automobiles, certain foods, soaps and toiletries, drugs, farm machinery, and computers. And advertising may raise barriers and tighten oligopoly in these and other advertising-intensive industries.[22] Some of these represent true economies, but others are dubious. If automobile dealers were allowed by custom to sell any make of car, much of the supposed "economy" of large-scale automobile production and distribution might vanish. Much soaps, toiletries, and food advertising is in itself purely repetitive and wasteful; under alternative market structures much of it, too, would probably vanish. Computer sales and support networks also are in large part a basis for effective price discrimination: again, scale economies in the usual sense of technological necessity are not clearly present.

Taken altogether, the evidence fails to substantiate economies of scale in plants and firms as a clear and consistent basis for concentration or (even less) for asymmetry.[23] In most cases, efficiency (*before* discounting for pecuniary advantages) may be roughly comparable in both large and small firms, although large units seem recently to be giving way in many industries. And concentration continues, in most industries, to exceed by far the levels which efficient scale of production would prescribe.

In Research and Innovation

While greater size may not afford superior efficiency in production in a large number of industries, there may be genuine scale economies in research, invention, and innovation. This is part (though not all) of the Schumpeter-Galbraith hypothesis, taken up by proponents of large corporations generally. With careful distinctions between inventive, innovative, and imitative acts, and with the right data, one could subject the hypothesis to a definitive test. In part the question is simply one of company (or laboratory) size—does research, as a general activity, show increasing returns to scale (that is, a *rising* net payoff from additional expenditures)? In part, also, the question is one of *relative* size among competitors—in any industry x, will the specific technical conditions favor large-scale rather than small-scale research and innovative effort?[24]

Until the last five years, the common answer to both questions was "yes," virtually without limit, and Galbraith apparently still holds to this view. But expert discussion and research has now shifted sharply toward

---

[22] See William S. Comanor and Thomas A. Wilson, "Advertising, Market Structure and Performance," *Review of Economics and Statistics*, XLIX (November 1967), 423–440, and references cited there.

[23] The consensus on this is clear from *Economic Concentration, Part 2* (1965) through *Part 7*; and Joe S. Bain, *Industrial Organization*, rev. ed. (New York: Wiley, 1968).

[24] Market structure as a possible cause of innovation, rather than an effect, is treated below in Chapter 14.

smallish and medium-size organizations as "optimum," for three reasons. First, many research problems can be farmed out to specialized research laboratories, rather than requiring a research establishment (of any size) on the premises. Company size is, in such cases, largely irrelevant. Second, reappraisals have shown that many major twentieth-century innovations have originated in small shops, not mammoth laboratories in or outside of large firms.[25] Third, econometric analysis has begun to suggest that net research productivity reaches a peak in middle-size firms, and dwindles in the very largest.[26] More work, using better data, is needed to make the point conclusively, but the burden of proof has now shifted against the larger corporations.

This and related work also fails to reveal any general research superiority of leading firms *within* industries.[27] Pending further study, these patterns appear to parallel those for production-scale economies—no proven and consistent technical advantages for the largest (and leading) firms. One must seek elsewhere for systematic determinants of (and justifications for) structural monopoly.

Overhead-cost Industries

There is little precise information about the extent of overhead or floating costs, even in those industries (recall Chapter 10) where they are probably important. Since much R&D spending is of an overhead character, it is probable that such R&D-intensive industries as communications, electronics and aerospace have substantial overhead costs of this sort. Indeed, much federal R&D reimbursement for projects is systematically channeled to *newer* projects, thereby thoroughly mixing the costs of individual programs. In computers, the main overhead costs are in general development, programming, and customer support activities. Since machine production costs are only about 20 percent of the final price, the true overhead-cost element may average as high as 50 percent; 40 percent would be a conservative estimate.[28] A recent study of the various branches of the nuclear power equipment industry in 1968 was unable to determine what the costs of specific products were, largely because the companies claimed that they themselves could not determine them.[29] This strongly suggests that costs are commingled. Much new electrical and electronic equipment is similar in this respect. In drugs, manufacturing costs are a small fraction of total costs and prices; both R&D

---

[25] See *Economic Concentration, Part 3* (1965).
[26] *Ibid.*
[27] *Ibid.*; Frederic M. Scherer, "Firm Size, Market Structure, Opportunity, and the Output of Patented Inventions," *American Economic Review*, LV (December 1965), 1097–1125; and Edwin Mansfield, *Industrial Research and Technological Innovation* (New York: Norton, 1968).
[28] See "IBM's $5 Billion Gamble," *Fortune*, September and October 1967; and Chapter 15 below.
[29] Arthur D. Little, *Competition in The Nuclear-Power Supply Industry*, Report to the Atomic Energy Commission and Department of Justice (Washington, D.C.: U.S. Government Printing Office, 1968).

and selling costs are essentially overheads.[30]   In other industries with large selling costs (sales and distribution networks, and advertising) the same is true; these include particularly soaps and toiletries, and cereals.

Such conditions may enable, and induce, the leading firms to engage in substantial price discrimination, with computers as perhaps the prime example.   Dominant firms are thereby able to secure the sales which they most want, and this tends to preempt new entrants or rivals.   This has been important in computers, nuclear power equipment and drugs, to take the clearest cases, and probably also in other cases.   It goes without saying that it also has been important in such utilities as telephones, broadcasting, electric power, and railways.   The novel point is that the overhead-cost element, which tends to yield systematic price discrimination, is probably as large in several new, large and fast-growing *manufacturing* industries as it is in some utilities.   Moreover, in some cases the overhead-cost elements are growing, rather than yielding to competitive constraints.

PECUNIARY ADVANTAGES

Input prices for funds, utility services, advertising, and other purchases normally are lower for larger buyers.   There is probably only one case in which the price advantages may be reversed—labor.   Whether the lower prices to large buyers reflect either true reductions in the costs of supply or price discrimination—or both—is not at issue at this point (see also Chapter 12 below).   The question here is simply how significant the discounts are. The main kinds of inputs may be considered one by one.

By long tradition, *financial resources* draw first attention.   As Chapter 6 indicated, the advantages of size in obtaining capital funds are beyond doubt in two main respects.   First, large firms pay less per unit for their external funds; the largest firms often borrow at interest rates 2 or 3 percentage points less than for medium-size firms.   Even more important, perhaps, is the greater availability of funds for larger and leading firms, apart from their cost.   Since large-firm accounts are more eagerly competed for, the very differential competitiveness in the large-loan markets tends to favor the larger firms.   The risks of credit rationing—of being unable to obtain more funds when they are needed, even at higher costs—are usually proportionally greater for smaller firms than for large ones.   One would hardly expect otherwise.   Large and diversified firms, many of them quasi-holding companies in their own right, usually embody less risk of financial failure (as is noted in Chapters 5 and 12). Much of this is circular: security and favored financial access are mutually sustaining.   In any event, the financial advantages of size are widespread and significant.

---

[30] This was brought out dramatically at the trial of Pfizer, American Cyanamide, and Bristol-Myers for price fixing in tetracycline drugs: see *Washington Post*, November 16, 1967.

On *utility services*, too, prices are often significantly lower to large users. Effective price differentials are steepest in electricity and gas, but they are also found to some extent in telephones. Electricity, for example, may cost on the average more than one-third less to a large user than a small one.[31] The differences in unit prices are even steeper. Transport services also customarily offer a variety of quantity discounts, and discriminatory pricing of rail services has long been built into the rate structures (though not always favoring larger users).[32]

Large-contract discounts are customary also for *advertising* services of many kinds and in many media. Those for television and newspaper advertising have drawn the sharpest comment, but others in radio and magazines have probably also been significant.[33]

The large variety of *raw and semifinished inputs* naturally contains great variation in patterns, but some degree of large-order discounting is common, though not universal.[34] In some cases, as in tire purchases by major automobile companies, the large-buyer price cuts may be deep.[35] In others, they are nominal or absent. In virtually no significant cases do larger buyers pay *more* than smaller ones.

Executive talent may also belong on the list of inputs which go cheaper "per unit" to larger firms. Company size inherently offers added scope and rewards to those in charge (or hoping eventually to be). The same holds for diversification, which offers scope for advancement beyond the primary industry. Therefore, larger firms within any given industry (or with branches in them) may usually expect to attract a superior calibre of executives, at no higher corresponding cost in salary and direct benefits.[36]

---

[31] To illustrate this: small, medium (10 times bigger), and large (still twice bigger) users of electricity were specified, with average conditions of use from a typical utility, Detroit Edison. The average prices paid by the hypothetical medium user worked out at 10 percent higher than for the larger user, while the small user paid 53 percent more on average for its electricity; see Federal Power Commission, *Utility Rate Schedules*, (Washington, D.C.: U.S. Government Printing Office, revised irregularly).

[32] See the summaries in Charles F. Phillips, Jr., *The Economics of Regulation* (Homewood, Ill.: Irwin, 1965), Chapter 10 and 11.

[33] See, among others, J. M. Ferguson, *The Advertising Rate Structure in the Daily Newspaper Industry* (Englewood Cliffs, N. J.: Prentice-Hall, 1963), concerning newpaper practices. Sharp volume discounts were common in TV advertising until 1966, when they were withdrawn under criticism. Even so, some preferential features remain. See U.S. Senate Antitrust and Monopoly Subcommittee, 90th Congress, 1st Session, *Hearings on Television Advertising Rates*, (Washington, D.C.: U.S. Government Printing Office, 1967).

[34] The most famous example, purchases by the A&P Company, has been disputed by Morris A. Adelman in the *A&P Case* (Cambridge: Harvard University Press, 1959); but see also J. B. Dirlam and A. E. Kahn, "Antitrust Law and the Big Buyer: Another Look at the A&P Case," *Journal of Political Economy*, LX (April 1952), 118–132.

[35] Concerning discounts on tires, see Federal Trade Commission, *Report on the Tire Industry* (Washington, D.C., U.S. Government Printing Office, 1966). Major British sellers of communications cable have offered discounts ranging from neglible to 27 percent; Monopolies Commission, *Report on Proposed Merger between British Insulated Callender's Cables Ltd., and Pyrotenax Ltd.*, House of Commons 490 (London: Her Majesty's Stationery Office, 1967).

[36] Perhaps one indication of this is that the highest salaries in A.T.&T., the world's largest private enterprise, and in major oil firms are lower than those in many smaller firms not obviously blessed with greater market power; see "Top Men Fatten Their Pay," *Business Week*, June 7, 1969, 84–112.

There are many exceptions to this rule, especially where a smaller firm may offer more growth potential. But the average outcome can be expected to favor the larger firms in any given competitive grouping.

For *blue-collar labor services*, however, the structure of collective bargaining may tend to make larger firms pay more per unit of labor. Larger firms, especially in large industries, have proven easier to organize than small ones, in part because of their very stability and near-permanence. Also leading firms typically have higher profits (in part because other inputs are cheaper!) from which higher wages may be extracted.[37] The wage-raising effects (such as they may be) of collective bargaining therefore fall first and most heavily—or at least most directly—on larger firms.[38] This varies in degree from case to case, and uniform industry-wide collective bargaining might eliminate it entirely in many of the major markets with high market power.

Altogether, the net input-price advantages of absolute and relative bigness in industries with high market power are manifestly numerous and widespread, and in some cases they are no doubt quite substantial. They are likely to continue, at least in their present magnitudes, rather than diminish. They favor not only large firms generally, but also, within industries, the leading firms versus their lesser competitors.

INDUSTRY LIFE-CYCLE

The main troubles with the life-cycle hypothesis, as elaborated in Chapter 3, are (1) that the cycle is often impossible to observe, and (2) that there are many exceptions to it. The extremes are often quite apparent; in 1969 the nuclear equipment industry is new, the steel industry old. Yet a large number of others refuse to follow the prescribed cycle, insisting instead on being reborn repeatedly. Such may be the automobile, cereal, cigarette, electronic equipment, photographic equipment, construction, and hotel industries, not to mention motion pictures and grocery retailing.

Moreover, others are born competitive rather than monopolistic (a good example is the computer service-bureau trade), while others, such as textiles and furniture, remain fragmented even in old age. Some utilities, such as railroad and telecommunications (as of 1969) appear to progress backward along the cycle in maturity, from monopoly toward more competitive possibilities.

---

[37] This would reflect countervailing power, almost precisely as Galbraith discussed it. For one instance, the automobile industry, see H. M. Levinson, "Pattern Bargaining: A Case Study of the Automobile Workers," *Quarterly Journal of Economics*, LXXIV (May 1960), 296–317, and Levinson's *Determining Forces in Collective Wage Bargaining* (New York: Wiley, 1966).

[38] Together with cheaper capital, the labor-cost differentials might induce large and leading firms to shift toward more capital-using, labor-saving technology than smaller firms. These technical differences have been thought to be quite strong; yet they are not universal, as was noted earlier in this chapter.

All in all, the life-cyle hypothesis may be most useful as a hatrack upon which to hang the very numerous exceptions. It also helps to clarify the role of mergers, which may best be regarded as a rapid means of shifting toward equilibrium structure. Examples of this may be seen in the waves of mergers in some American industries since World War II. Sharper examples are found in several British and European industries, where the equilibrium margin of concentration has probably shifted upward in response to (1) American entry and (2) new prohibitions upon collusions.[39] Although much of the supposed appropriateness of higher concentration may actually not be true, no small part of it may well be genuine.

GROWTH AS A SOLVENT OF STRUCTURE

Evidently, the stock of knowledge about economies of scale and other determinants of structure has turned out to be thin. Moreover, some of the main outlines of industrial structure may have been set before the turn of this century, and that is largely prehistory, impenetrable to systematic research. Interest has therefore focused more recently on the possible causes of *changes* in concentration, and discussion has recently narrowed down to industry growth as a likely and primary solvent of concentration.[40] The rationale for this—that dominant firms will find it difficult, or possibly less profitable, to keep pace with smaller firms—has never been satisfactorily spelled out. Yet, in several empirical studies, industry growth has indeed seemed to be associated with declining concentration. This has encouraged further optimism that future growth will be a powerful downward pressure on concentration.

One may analyze the possible growth effect in light of other possible determinants of changing concentration. Of course many other influences are at work, including public R&D support, so one must be cautious. Yet a statistical analysis is possible—one with relatively accurate and thorough data. The findings give little support to the hypothesis (see Appendix Table 15). First, profit rates showed little or no association with concentration changes. Although high profit rates might be expected to induce rapid entry, as is conventionally supposed, they nevertheless were not associated with declines in four-firm concentration during 1947–1958. Second, there was a mild "regression" tendency, with high and low ratios in 1947 drifting gently

[39] See *Economic Concentration, Part 7*, 3682–3706; also Richard E. Caves and Associates, *Britain's Economic Prospects* (Washington, D.C.: Brookings, 1968), Ch. 7.
[40] Especially strong recent emphasis on growth may be found in Bain, *Industrial Organization, op, cit.*, 210–211; Rosenbluth, *op. cit.*, 105–108; Nelson, *op. cit.*, 50–56; Nelson and Weston in *Economic Concentration, Part 1* (1964), 265–268; E. Rotwein, "Economic Concentration and Monopoly in Japan," *Journal of Political Economy*, 1964, 246–261; and E. T. Penrose, *The Theory of the Growth of the Firm* (New York: Wiley, 1959), and other sources cited by the author in *Economic Concentration, Part 2* (1965), 638–639, and *Part 7*, 3682–3696; see also *Part 1*, 268–272.

during 1947–1958 toward the middle range. Yet this tendency was rather weak (adding only 4 percent to the "explanation"), and many major exceptions to it can be cited. Therefore, it lends little support to the view (already undermined in Chapter 7) that high concentration does not last. Third, interfirm turnover was not significantly associated with changes in concentration.

Fourth, the much-discussed association of growth with declining concentration does persist, after the other influences have been mostly factored out. But it emerges as a fragile reed on which to rely for future decreases in concentration. The association is weak, in purely statistical terms. Growth statistically "explains" no more than 10 percent of concentration changes; therefore, among the many influences on concentration, growth is relatively minor. The regression slope (.038) suggests that a doubling of employment would be associated with a decline of only 3.8 points in the concentration ratio. Since employment growth greatly understates true output growth, it clearly takes a large dose of output growth to reduce concentration even by a sliver.

Moreover, the cause-or-effect question cannot be answered clearly, given the limitations of the data. Declining concentration might have "caused" (directly or jointly with other forces) more rapid growth, rather than the other way round. Pending further and markedly different results, one must treat growth (as well as the other factors included here) as no more than a ghostly pressure toward lower concentration.[41] British patterns also fail to show growth as a thorough and consistent solvent of concentration.[42]

One may conclude this chapter with both a summary and a prediction for further research. As Chapters 7–10 showed, market structures contain widely varied mixtures of related elements, mutually evolving and interacting. In part, at least, these mixtures presumably are influenced by real and consistent determinants, rather than by mere chance. The main determinant has commonly been supposed to be technical economies of scale. Yet, as we have now seen, public R&D support and other policies intervene in a number of major industries which have unusually tight market structure. And technical scale economies remain largely untested by scientific inquiry, except perhaps in a few industries. In most industries there appears to be an approximate parity of average costs among large and small firms, over a fairly large size range. But any general superiority of large (and/or leading)

---

[41] As a further word on growth, consider the 29 industries whose concentration declined by 10 or more points. Six of these were catchall industries; of the rest only 3 had strong growth (value of shipments more than doubling). In 14 others, growth was well below the average for all manufacturing. Of the 13 growth industries, in only 7 had the concentration ratio been above 50 in 1947 (industries 2694, 2824, 3313, 3352, 3663, and 3722). Although these 7 cases combining growth and declining high concentration may be significant, they are few. See also D. R. Kamerschen, "Market Growth and Industry Concentration," *Journal of the American Statistical Association*, LXIII (March 1968), 228–241.

[42] See W. G. Shepherd, "Changes in British Industrial Concentration, 1951–1958," *op. cit.*, 130–132; a somewhat strained attempt to salvage the growth-effect hypothesis in made by K. D. George in an article with the same title as mine, "Changes in British Industrial Concentration, 1951–1958," *Journal of Industrial Economics*, LV (July 1967).

firms remains almost wholly in the realm of conjecture. Moreover, overhead costs and discriminatory pricing tend to preserve high concentration in at least several major industries.

By contrast, pecuniary advantages of size appear to be significant and widespread. Most inputs are available to the larger buyers at lower—often much lower—prices. This probably influences structure and competitive conditions in most markets. It also creates a strong presumption that (especially in markets with stable structure) dominant firms are technically inferior to their smaller rivals. This affirms the reasoning in Chapters 3 and 4, and it carries strong implications for public policy to promote competition and performance.

As for growth as a strong solvent of structure, the evidence for it is so far very weak indeed. It apparently has not significantly eroded concentration in the United States or Britain. It offers only an uncertain and slight prospect of reducing structural monopoly in the future.

All in all, there has been only modest success in explaining the structure of markets, and no new breakthrough is in sight, either in techniques or information. Attention is therefore beginning to shift toward the causes of *change* in market structure. Even though one such possible determinant—growth—has not displayed great importance (so far, at least), others may. As such research develops, it will need to embrace a multiplicity both of determinants and of structural elements. Change analysis offers several special attractions. First, the available measures of market structure are more realiable in showing change than levels, and so change analysis builds on this strength. Second, change analysis is useful for directly predicting shifts over time (rather than equilibrium states that *may* be reached, quickly or slowly), and for identifying deviant cases that may warrant policy treatment. Third, change analysis may be especially useful for policy, because it clarifies the probable trade-offs for marginal adjustments from the *status quo*. Those trade-offs are precisely the prime focus for most public policies toward markets.

Even though such research is now still embryonic, on may venture to predict that it will tend to be organized around what may be called a "competitive limit" hypothesis. This general hypothesis would be that market forces will tend to shift the various structural elements down to the limit permitted by basic cost conditions. In the general case (recall Chapter 4), this would be loose symmetrical oligopoly. Such an hypothesis would be distinctly optimistic, since much of this volume's evidence has suggested that tight oligopoly is instead the stable equilibrium state of a large share of markets. Yet change analysis could do much to clarify the processes and rates of change further and to single out the deviant cases. Perhaps its most important contribution might be to show the real causes of the present rise in market power and to indicate which counter-influences may be most effective under alternative conditions.

The most one can say now is that the "competitive limit" hypothesis has tentative support from the preliminary evidence in only a few sectors, such as textile and wood products and parts of retail distribution and services. One can also safely say that downward market pressures on many tight-oligopoly and monopoly situations are blocked by the direct or indirect effects of certain public policies. In any event a prime objective of change analysis—the trade-offs among elements and determinants—remains largely as terra incognita, and if the past is any guide, it may remain so for many years more.

Chapter 12

Effects of Market Power
on Prices and Profits

The monopolists, by keeping the market constantly
understocked, by never fully supplying the effectual demand,
sell their commodities much above the natural price, and
raise their emoluments, whether they consist in wages or
profit, greatly above their natural rate.
ADAM SMITH
The Wealth of Nations (1776)

In appraising the *effects* of market power, one ventures even further on
to research frontiers. Economists have only begun digging deep enough to
unearth systematic patterns, and the cause-and-effect status of most of them
is shaky. There is some evidence from cross-section analysis, but it is as yet
imperfect and tentative. There are also many individual cases offering
definite hints.

The direct financial effects upon price and profitability will be reviewed
in this chapter. "Real" effects on efficiency, growth, and stability are discussed in the next chapter. Technical change and distribution are covered
in Chapter 14.

It is useful to look separately at the price and profit effects, even though
they are related and may be regarded as different ways of estimating the same
thing. The profit effects tend to be masked by adjustments over time, by
accounting devices, and by the "soaking-up" effects of internal inefficiency;
these points were noted in Chapter 4. These influences do not apply so
thoroughly to the price effects, which can often be more directly observed.

In any event, both kinds of evidence are germane. Are price levels much raised and price structures much altered? Is profitability increased? Price levels, price structures, and profits as a rate of return on investment will be discussed in the following sections.

PRICE LEVELS AND MARGINS

Perhaps the best way to proceed is to note first how *widely* market power affects price levels, and second how *steep* the effects are.

Where formal structure is highly monopolistic and free of public policy constraints, price levels are almost invariably affected, and significantly so. Most obvious are utility monopolies, where direct regulation is necessary (but often not sufficient) to control prices. In some such cases, such as television stations, the effect emerges clearly in the value of the franchise; similarly with royalties on patent licenses. The price effects will last only as long as the monopoly, and this may be brief (as in commodity corners, common at the turn of this century) or long (as in such patented items as drugs, xerography, cellophane, and color film).

At the other extreme, in loose oligopoly and below, price effects are usually inconsequential. It is in the intermediate oligopoly and quasi-collusive conditions, with relatively easy entry, where the effects have been unsure, as earlier chapters noted. In these cases, "administered prices" and identical bidding are common, and they usually reflect commonality in setting and adjusting "book" prices. In the usual case, these book prices are re-vised only at intervals, and may be virtually identical among all sellers for long periods of time. In some cases, these prices rest on uniform formulas evolved and jointly applied by all of the sellers. Often, too, revisions are routinely given by a "price leader," whose entire new price book is dutifully and immediately—even magically—imitated by his competitors.

In some cases, these apparently identical prices merely reflect innocent rules of thumb, and the sellers compete intensely with covert price shading and "quality" competition.[1] In others, the uniform prices have unquestion-ably been raised and maintained by common agreement.[2] Such "adminis-tered prices" are common in the larger tighter oligopolies, and less frequent in smaller and looser oligopolies. In fact relatively high structural monopoly appears to be virtually a necessary condition for it, though not sufficient by itself.

A closely parallel phenomenon is identical bids for contracts. Virtually nothing is known about those for private contracts; those for public contracts

---

[1] See George J. Stigler, "Administered Prices and Oligopolistic Inflation," *Journal of Business*, XXXV (January 1962), 1–12, and the sources cited there.
[2] See also the further discussion in Chapter 13, below.

have been relatively frequent for electrical equipment, chemicals, and construction equipment.[3] But identical-bid patterns are only a partial indicator of probable price effects. Identical bids are undoubtedly a clumsy and inferior method of collusion, necessary only when cooperation is imperfect. A really strong and smart price ring will shade or randomize the bid patterns in some fashion, and such strategems may now enable much collusive behavior to escape public notice. Indeed, just this may account for the shrinking volume of reported identical bids on public contracts since data were first published in 1962.

Similarly, antitrust price-fixing cases have clustered on industries with intermediate degrees of power.[4] In really tight oligopolies, tacit agreement, habit, and price leadership can be quite effective without resort to telltale, tangible collusive techniques. There are also hints that asymmetry tends to affect prices. One empirical analysis suggests:

> ... making the first eight firms more equal in size apparently reduces the tendency toward tacit collusion on price. ... competitive price rivalry may require substantial industry output produced by the second four firms[5]

Norman R. Collins and Lee E. Preston conclude, in a long review, that concentration does systematically affect price-cost margins; this affirms a series of earlier, tentative findings by others.[6] Since they reflect unadjusted concentration ratios and omit other elements of structure, the results can be regarded as partial hints rather than exhaustive tests. If the other elements were allowed for, the effects on price would probably emerge somewhat more strongly than concentration alone indicates. Entry barriers, size, and informal structure are especially likely to be influential in industries with intermediate concentration; this will become clearer in the later discussion of profitability. Since informal structure is important in most intermediate oligopolies abroad, where it is not legally constrained, the price effects are likely to be significant. The same is surely endemic in corresponding American markets, particularly those which are quasi-regulated or local and are therefore outside the reach of the Sherman Act.

It is a fair summary of all of this that the price effects usually occur even in intermediate oligopolies—especially those which are large, have entry barriers, or are local trades. Among industries, those in Appendix Table 13

---

[3] U.S. Attorney General, *Identical Bidding in Public Procurement, 1962 to 1968* (Washington, D.C.: U.S. Government Printing Office, issued annually).
[4] James M. Clabault and John F. Burton, Jr., *Sherman Act Indictments, 1955–1965* (New York: Federal Legal Publications, 1966), 128–144; and *ibid., 1967 Supplement*.
[5] Richard A. Miller, "Marginal Concentration Ratios and Industrial Profit Rates: Some Empirical Results of Oligopoly Behavior," *Southern Economic Journal*, XXXIV (October 1967), 259–267.
[6] Norman R. Collins and Lee E. Preston, *Concentration and Price-Cost Margins in Manufacturing Industries* (Berkeley: University of California Press, 1968), and the references cited there—especially Bain, Weiss, and Levinson.

offer a high probability that price is above "competitive" levels at each point in time.

The *degree* and continuity of this effect have been matters of some debate. The range of price effects is wide, from negligible to sharp, and from brief to continuous. Oligopolists are commonly thought to range rather narrowly in the middle between "limit pricing" and "umbrella pricing," as we have seen in Chapters 2 and 4. Some studies have indicated that when four-firm concentration goes above 70 percent, prices tend to go up by about 10 percent.[7] Collins and Preston more recently have reported that price-cost margins increase linearly (or at least regularly) over the whole range of four-firm concentration; and, generally, each extra 10 concentration points adds 1.1 to 1.4 percent to price.[8]

Yet these findings cover only the middle range of concentration in semi-permanent industrial oligopolies; they reflect a partial tilling of one patch in a rather large garden. The boundary cases, particularly actual and near monopolies, may better clarify the possibilities. Monopolists facing highly inelastic demand have quite frequently run true to theory, setting their prices at double, triple, or higher multiples of cost. In one instance, the price of a medical testing kit was set 43 times as high as cost.[9] The drug industry offers scores of instances of prices set at multiples of total costs. A quinine cartel in the 1960's tripled the price.[10] Kodak Ltd.'s 77 percent hold on the British color films market led it to maintain prices about 35 to 55 percent above "competitive" levels.[11] After acquiring the *San Bernardino Sun*, a fringe competitor, in 1964, the *Los Angeles Times* more than doubled its classified advertising rates. The price of cellophane was raised substantially by DuPont during the many years when it held a virtual monopoly of it in the United States.[12] Collusion in a series of tight oligopolies in American electrical equipment markets probably maintained prices about 15 to 20 percent above their long-run competitive levels during the 1950's. A price ring in rock salt for clearing Chicago roads raised the price from about $8 per ton to about $16 per ton in 1964.[13] Such examples can be multiplied many times over, in many countries, sectors, and specific settings.

---

[7] See David Schwartzman, "The Effect of Monopoly on Price," *Journal of Political Economy*, LXVII (August 1959), 352–362; and "A Correction," LXIX (October 1961), 494; also Joe S. Bain, "The Relation of Profit Rate to Industry Concentration: American Manufacturing, 1936–1940," *Quarterly Journal of Economics*, LXV (August 1951), 293–324.

[8] Collins and Preston, *op. cit.*, and their *Price-Cost Margins and Industry Structure* (Berkeley: University of California, December 1968), mimeographed.

[9] Under an exclusive arrangement, Miles Laboratories produced kits for prediagnosing mental retardation in infants for about $6 apiece and sold them for $262; Washington *Post*, June 19, 1965, 3.

[10] *The New York Times*, March 24, 1967, 16.

[11] U.K. Monopolies Commission, *Color Film*, House of Commons No. 1, (London: Her Majesty's Stationery Office, April 21, 1966).

[12] See George W. Stocking and Willard F. Mueller, "The Cellophane Case and the New Competition," *American Economic Review*, XLV (March 1955), 29–63.

[13] Chicago *Sun Times*, August 24, 1966.

The whole picture, then, is that price effects are minimal in loose oligopolies but range up to very sharp in true monopolies. The effects presumably last as long as the market power does. In intermediate and tight oligopolies with entry barriers, the effects tend to range between 10 and 30 percent, and may go much higher.

PRICE STRUCTURE

Price discrimination may be initiated by the seller or be extracted by powerful buyers (recall Chapter 4). In either case, there must be monopolistic structure among the sellers and different demand elasticities among the buyers.

Do actual price patterns fit these predictions, and is discrimination sharp where it occurs? Broadly speaking, yes, but the evidence is not thorough and systematic. Some of it was already noted in Chapter 11's discussion of input-price patterns. In industrial markets, the prime case is the drug industry, where many products are virtual monopolies and buyers differ greatly in acumen and bargaining power. The price differences on many drugs are matters of multiples; typically the price at retail is three to six times the prices to such large buyers as the Veterans Administration and the New York City hospitals.[14] Many drug prices also vary sharply among international buyers. The whole pattern is of large and systematic variation, fully in line with varying competitive conditions.

The computer industry is also pervaded with price discrimination, but in less obvious ways (see also Chapter 15 below). IBM's various computer models are alleged to have had differing profit target rates—lower for the larger models facing stiffer competition (as from the Control Data Corporation Model 6600 in 1963–1964). Some "fighting machines" may even have had negative profits. Among its many thousands of individual contracts, IBM has, moreover, provided widely differing amounts of "customer support" help in programming and getting systems running. This has turned the standard list prices into covers for sharply discriminatory bargains, with IBM able to supply enough free assistance to get many contracts even against technically superior competitive machines. IBM's educational discounts, some of them very complicated and amounting to zero pricing, have also strengthened IBM's virtual monopoly position for the long run by increasing the trained clientele.

The "infant" nuclear power equipment industry also has had differential pricing by General Electric and Westinghouse in their zeal to gain particular

---

[14] See U.S. Senate Subcommittee on Antitrust and Monopoly, *Hearings on Administered Prices, Parts 14–26* (Washington, D.C.: U.S. Government Printing Office, 1959–1961), and its *Report on Drugs* (Washington, D.C.: U.S. Government Printing Office, 1961); also U.S. Senate Committee on Small Business, *Hearings on Drug Industry Prices and Profits* (Washington, D.C.: U.S. Government Printing Office, 1968).

contracts. Some of these probably involve pricing below costs.[15] Light bulb prices differ for bulk buyers and retail outlets. The main automobile firms and mail-order houses obtain tires at prices below those for retailers.[16] Indeed, a Sears, Roebuck catalog embodies price discrimination in a large number of the products it purveys, especially the larger appliances, since the same items fetch higher prices elsewhere under other brand names. Automobiles themselves are made available to Hertz, Avis, and some other fleet buyers at prices below those charged to dealers and others.

Large discrimination is evident in many services and trades, including particularly hotels, theaters, and some medical services. Banks provide varying service packages to various customers at differing real prices. Advertising rates often vary sharply among clients.

Yet even above these instances, probably the prime locus of discriminatory pricing is the utility sector, even under public regulation and some public ownership. Telephone prices are partly fitted to demand differences, as well as partly to cost conditions.[17] As Chapter 11 noted, electricity and gas pricing have become increasingly elaborate compromises between cost conditions and pricing "to meet the competition."[18] Although the degree of genuine price-cost discrimination among household, commercial and industrial users—and within each of these groups—varies and is hard to measure, the overall extent of effective price discrimation is undoubtedly substantial. Transport rates—passenger and freight—have also long had discriminatory features.[19]

In a larger perspective, systematic price discrimination is confined to several important subsets of markets, with significant market power and favorable demand conditions. In those markets where the conditions are right, discrimination is sharp and pervasive.

PROFITABILITY AS A RATE OF RETURN ON INVESTMENT

From all the foregoing indications, market power seems regularly to yield higher profitability; if not, it would hardly be sought as eagerly and universally as it is. Yet there are still occasional assertions that the profit rewards

[15] Arthur D. Little, *Competition in the Nuclear Power Equipment Industry* (Washington, D.C.: Atomic Energy Commission, 1969), is not definite, but see admissions by Westinghouse in *The New York Times*, March 9, 1969, financial section, and estimates that General Electric will lose $30 million on the Oyster Creek plant; see "GE Nuclear Giant Warms Up," *Business Week*, May 17, 1969, 46.

[16] Federal Trade Commission, *Study of the Automobile Tire Industry* (Washington, D.C.: U.S. Government Printing Office, 1966).

[17] Charles F. Phillips, Jr., *The Economics of Regulation* (Homewood, Ill.: Irwin, 1965), Chapter 11.

[18] See Phillips, *ibid.*, and references cited there; also William G. Shepherd, "Marginal-Cost Pricing in American Utilities," *Southern Economic Journal*, XXXIII (July 1966), 58–70, and a further note, *ibid.*, January 1967, 421.

[19] Phillips, *ibid.*, Chapter 11; John R. Meyer *et al.*, *The Economics of Competition in the Transportation Industries* (Cambridge: Harvard University Press, 1959).

to market power are slender and fleeting, and some empirical findings on the point have appeared to be inconclusive. Are monopoly profits really thin and precarious, as attempts to correlate unadjusted concentration ratios and profit rates have led some to believe? This will be treated here from two angles: *company size* and profitability, and *industry structure* and profitability.

No easy answers need be expected, for several reasons (some noted already in Chapter 4). Profitability embraces at least two dimensions: raw rates of return on investment, and the degree of risk in these profit rates. A low-risk profit rate of 12 percent may represent greater genuine profitability than a high-risk 24 percent. Therefore, even if market power is enormously profitable, there may be little correlation between *raw* profit rates and concentration ratios (and/or any other single element of market structure).

Moreover, high profits tend over time to get capitalized into the structure of costs, just as low profits and losses are wrung out through mergers, bankruptcy, and accounting write-offs. And the increasingly luxuriant jungle of accounting conventions and tax adjustments unavoidably entangles any attempt to compare profits among companies and industries.[20] In additon, the proper asset and revenue definition for the calculations are arguable. Is it returns on fixed assets or on all assets (including working capital) which matter? On top of all this, the profitability of separate divisions in many large firms remains secret, since most company accounts lump all divisions and activities together, no matter how disparate and distinct they are.

Since these randomizing elements are so prevalent, one should expect the available data to understate grossly whatever market power-profitability relationship may "really" exist; they would certainly not *overstate* it. The inherent downward bias of imperfect tests, noted earlier, should be especially strong here. This is borne out in the following reviews of earlier findings and new information.

Company Size and Profitability

It was clearly shown more than a generation ago that size and profit rates are positively correlated: larger firms regularly gain higher profit rates.[21] In research on more recent periods, this relationship recurs fairly consistently, but with many exceptions.[22]

When one further allows for differences in the degree of risk, the broad profitability of large firms is even more clearly superior. Small-firm profits

---

[20] A recent study by Price, Waterhouse and Co. (see *The New York Times* July 24, 1967, Financial Section) concludes that "corporate earnings are even- less indicative of actual results than the critics of accounting methods have contended;" sharp criticism indeed.

[21] W. L. Crum, *Corporate Size and Earning Power* (Cambridge: Harvard University Press, 1939).

[22] See, among others, Federal Trade Commission-Securities and Exchange Commission, *Quarterly Financial Report for Manufacturing Corporations* (Washington, D.C.: U.S. Government Printing Office, quarterly) for recent years; H. O. Stekler, *Profitability and Size of Firm* (Berkeley: University of California Press, 1963), and references noted there; and Marshall Hall and Leonard W. Weiss, "Firm Size and Profitability," *Review of Economics and Statistics*, XLIX (August 1967), 319–331.

are widely scattered around—especially below—their (lower) average levels, while large-firm profits cluster tightly around their (higher) average levels.[23] This may partly hide differing profits for divisions *within* some large companies; but that would be irrelevant to the finding that larger companies do have higher profitability *in toto*.

This higher profitability extends across all major sectors of the economy, including finance, insurance, and distribution, as well as manufacturing. In some utility lines, the vagaries of state regulation appear to complicate the pattern, but this—and special defense procurement treatment of certain suppliers—is the exception, rather than the rule. This rule, evidently, attests the relevance of size as at least a significant element of market power.

Industry Structure and Profitability

We come finally to profitability of market power in individual industries. We will look at profitability on capital, which is the best single measure of gains to market power. As on other matters, past research has focused on concentration, rather than on the whole structure of markets. Even with complete structure data, the search for relationships would be bound to be tantalizing, if not wholly barren, partly because high profits tend to get capitalized into costs or otherwise absorbed, while low profits tend to be wrung out through financial failure or merger. In addition, there is the fundamental problem that market power is held and its fruits are reaped by *firms* within industries; often (perhaps usually), the industry-wide totals and averages of profit rates will not reflect the gains to the *leading* firms within it. On the contrary, these firms' gains may often go hand-in-hand with relatively low profits for other firms in the same industry. Ideally the measure would focus only, and precisely, on the industry leaders, which actually hold market power.

For reasons such as these, reliable evidence has been developed only slowly, and much remains to be done. Yet there now can be little doubt that market shares, taken even by themselves, do breed higher returns on investment. Very broadly speaking, an additional 10 percent of concentration appears to raise industry-wide average rates of return by .8 to 1.0 percentage points (for example, from 5 to 6 per cent or 15 to 16 percent rate of return.[24] It follows that the incremental rise in profits with the rise in any one firm's market share is higher, *particularly in the range of loose to intermediate oligopoly*. For example, the rise of concentration from 30 to 40 percent would have to raise the leading firm's profit rates by about 3 percentage points, in order to lift the *entire industry* average by 1 percentage point. At

---

[23] This would probably more than offset some possible tendencies (which may be illusory) for profit rates to decline in very large size ranges; see Stekler, *op. cit.*; *per contra*, see Hall and Weiss, *op. cit.*

[24] Collins and Preston, *op. cit.*, and the many other studies summarized there.

50 percent concentration, the profit leverage would be a factor of two. In the highest concentration ranges, where the leading firms very nearly *are* the whole industry, the leverage would fade away.

This indicates that *the shift from loose to tight oligopoly tends to raise the profits of leading firms very sharply indeed.* It also suggests that, among the leading firms in asymmetric oligopolies, the larger ones tend to have significantly higher profits. In most industries, the leading four firms do usually appear to attain profit rates which are higher than those of lesser firms.[25]

This concentration-and-profit-rate kind of analysis can be further expanded in at least four directions. One is to include measures of *risk* in the data on profitability. An ingenious study has treated the degree of dispersion among company profit rates in any given time period as the index of industry risk.[26] But this will not do, because it omits other elements of risk, and it rates as "risky" many industries which have little or no real risk. For example, there has been a wide spread among profit rates of individual American drug companies, but the patterns are stable and rigid over the years, and even the "lower" profit rates have been rather high, above a 10 percent return. Therefore a high-"risk" index for this industry is quite mistaken.[27] Although new work may bring risk more adequately into the statistical analysis of profit, it has not done so thoroughly yet.

A second direction for new study is to expand the analysis to include other structural elements besides concentration. Already there are signs that entry barriers and asymmetry do tend to cause higher profits, and advertising may also yield higher profits in at least a few major advertising-intensive industries.[28] Some new results can also be derived from Stigler's profit data and a variety of figures on structure. These preliminary findings, noted in Appendix Table 16, confirm that several structural variables were at work in 1947–1956.[29] But we may consider first some simple correlation results.

[25] Federal Trade Commission, "Rates of Return for Identical Companies in Selected Manufacturing Industries, 1940, 1947–1965," (Washington, D.C.: U.S. Government Printing Office, 1967).

[26] Gordon R. Conrad and Irving H. Plotkin, *Risk and Return in American Industry: An Econometric Analysis* (Cambridge: Arthur D. Little, 1967); see U.S. Senate Select Committee on Small Business, 90th Congress, 1st and 2nd Sessions, *Hearings on Competitive Problems in the Drug Industry, Part 5* (Washington, D.C.: U.S. Government Printing Office, 1968), 1746–1784.

[27] Willard F. Mueller, in *ibid*, 1807–1861, nicely exposes these and other weaknesses of the approach. See also I. N. Fisher and G. R. Hall, "Risk and Corporate Rates of Return," *Quarterly Journal of Economics*, LXXXIII (February 1969), 79–92.

[28] H. Michael Mann, "Seller Concentration, Barriers to Entry, and Rates of Return in Thirty Industries, 1950–1960," *Review of Economics and Statistics*, XLVIII (August 1966), 296–307; Miller, *op. cit.*; and recall William S. Comanor and Thomas A. Wilson, "Advertising, Market Structure and Performance," *Review of Economics and Statistics*, XLIX (November 1967), 423–440, noted in Chapter 11 above.

[29] Unadjusted concentration ratios were used because adjusted ratios are available only for the later year of 1966. The whole range of 426 manufacturing industries was included in a stepwise multiple regression designed to show the relative importance of the various structural elements. Though the data are imperfect (the profit-rate data most of all), and the results did not show strong relationships, the findings are consistent and significant in a statistical sense. An attempt to derive risk-adjusted profits (using year-to-year shifts in profit rates to indicate "risk") was not successful.

Concentration, by itself, shows only a slight association (simple $r^2 = .06$) with profit rates. This accords with Bain's and Stigler's findings. Both the large-firm share and leading-firm stability are more closely associated than is concentration, with r^2 of .16 and .09 respectively. The positive coefficients suggest that—in accord with expectations—concentration, large-firm share, and stability all tend to be associated with higher profitability. In the joint analysis, large-firm share appears to play the largest role, though it is moderate. Concentration's role appears virtually to vanish, especially when stability of leading-firm shares is also added in. Imports appear to play a slight role in restraining profit rates.

The third direction for research is to use adjusted concentration data. Those noted in Chapter 7 and Appendix Table 8 indicate possible relationships in recent years. Recent profit data are available only for two-digit industries, and these are shown in Figure 12.1. Even this simple and broad-gauged test confirms and sharpens the other findings, based on unadjusted ratios.[30] The positive association suggests a marginal effect on profits of about 1.1 to 1.5 percentage points per 10 percent of concentration, which is slightly more than Collins and Preston found. This is accentuated by the fact that profits of leading firms in the six highest-profit groups in Figure 12.1 (autos, oil, chemicals, electrical and communications equipment, instruments, and cigarettes) have been more stable (less "risky") than has been true of the other industries. The odd results of group 33 are, as is well known, probably caused by internal inefficiency and import competition in the steel industry, both of which can be traced to inadequately competitive behavior.[31]

A fourth direction for study is to look in detail at a limited number of prominent markets, where fairly complete information can be marshalled. This harkens back to the methods of the precomputer days, when the critics focused their hostilities on steel, oil, the packers, and the American Tobacco Company. It brings out the richness of detail which may be necessary to understand the true reach and effects of market power. This tradition lived on during the 1950's in the Kefauver Subcommittee's investigations of the steel, automobile, and drug industries.

An obvious starting point here is the group of 21 prominent market-power industries noted in Chapter 10, for which some internal details of structure and profit are known. They hint, in Table 12.1, that market power may often yield to individual leading firms even more profitability than the cross-section studies suggest. In nearly all of the industries (except such older ones as metals, ships, and glass) the leaders gained relatively high and stable rates of return during the 1961–1965 expansion—well above those for lesser firms and for competitive industries generally. The most striking cases are automobiles, computers, drugs, chemicals, soaps and toiletries, and

---

[30] Weiss's average concentration ratios (noted above in Chapter 7) give the same general result.
[31] Note the discussions of this in Chapter 13 below.

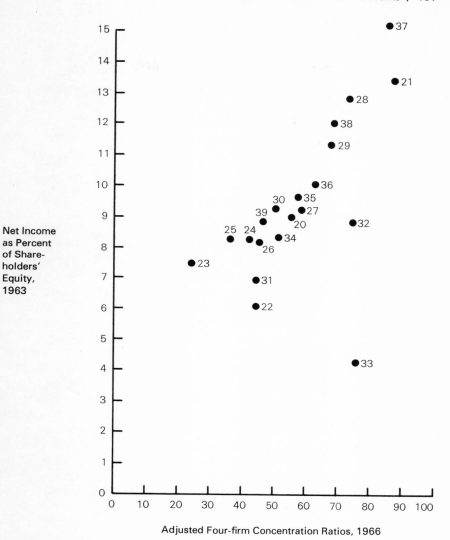

Figure 12.1 Adjusted Concentration and Profit Rates Across Broad Industry Groupings, 1963.

(Percentage)

NOTE: The number by each observation is the Census Standard Industrial Classification code number for the industry group (for industry group names, see Table 7.2). Profits for 1963 may reflect relatively typical levels during that relatively normal pre-Vietnam year. In a further study, an averaging of successive years and a factoring out of special disturbances would be useful. The present data are intended primarily for illustration.

SOURCES: Net income as a percent of shareholders' equity from Federal Trade Commission, *Rates of Return in Identical Firms in Selected Manufacturing Industries, 1940, 1947–65* (Washington, D.C.: U.S. Government Printing Office, 1967); adjusted concentration ratios from Table 7.2., *supra.*

TABLE 12.1 RATES OF PROFIT ON SHAREHOLDERS EQUITY, 1961–1965 IN SELECTED MARKETS (PERCENTAGES)

Industry and Leading Firms	Rates of Profit (Percent)	Other Firms, 1961–1965
Telephone equipment*		n.a.
Western Electric	10.8	
Motor vehicles		8.3
General Motors	21.7	
Ford Motor	13.8	
Chrysler	13.5	
Computers		7.2
IBM	19.5	
Heavy electrical equipment		11.2
General Electric	15.4	
Westinghouse	6.8	
Petroleum refining		9.3
Standard Oil (N.J.)	12.1	
Texaco	15.5	
Mobil	8.7	
Gulf	11.1	
Iron and steel		7.8
U.S. Steel	6.0	
Bethlehem	7.4	
Republic	7.7	
Armco	9.0	
Drugs		20.2
Am. Home Products	26.5	
Merck	17.1	
Pfizer	15.1	
Lilly	14.3	
Soaps		n.a.
Procter & Gamble	15.5	
Colgate	10.0	
Lever Bros.	10.2	
Industrial chemicals		14.2
DuPont	22.9	
Union Carbide	15.4	
Monsanto	11.7	
Dow	11.6	
Aircraft and engines		n.a.
United Aircraft	8.1	
General Electric	(15.4)	
Aircraft		n.a.
Boeing	14.3	
General Dynamics	19.1	
Lockheed	20.9	

TABLE 12.1—*continued*

Industry and Leading Firms	Rates of Profit (Percent)	Other Firms, 1961–1965
Glass products		7.5
P.P.G. Industries	8.6	
Libby-Owens-Ford	16.8	
Corning	18.7	
Aluminum		n.a.
Alcoa	6.8	
Kaiser	8.2	
Reynolds	7.0	
Copper		n.a.
Anaconda	5.2	
Kennecott	9.3	
Phelps Dodge	11.3	
Photographic supplies		n.a.
Eastman Kodak	18.8	
Tires and tubes		6.8
Goodyear	11.7	
Firestone	11.2	
U.S. Rubber	7.8	
Photocopying		n.a.
Xerox	29.0	
Dairy products		9.0
National Dairy	11.3	
Borden	10.9	
Carnation	11.8	
Metal containers		n.a.
American Can	9.3	
Continental Can	9.5	
Cereals		n.a.
Kellogg	21.5	
General Mills	9.2	
Soup		n.a.
Campbell	12.9	
Air transport*		n.a.
United	8.2	
American	11.0	
Pan American	14.2	
TWA	13.4	
Television broadcasting		n.a.
CBS	(18.9)	
NBC	(n.a.)	
ABC	10.1	
Banking		
New York		n.a.
Chase Manhattan	10.1	
First National City	9.6	
Manufacturers Hanover	8.9	

TABLE 12.1—*continued*

Industry and Leading Firms	Rates of Profit (Percent)	Other Firms, 1961–1965
Chicago		n.a.
Continental Illinois	10.2	
First National	9.8	
California		n.a.
Bank of America	11.2	
Safety First	9.9	
Wells Fargo	9.1	

NOTE: Figures in parentheses are estimates.
* There are indirect regulatory controls on profit rates in these industries.
SOURCE: Adapted from Federal Trade Commission, *Rates of Return on Identical Firms in Selected Manufacturing Industries, 1940, 1947–1965* (Washington, D.C.: Federal Trade Commission, 1967); and *The 500 Largest U.S. Industrial Corporations* (New York: *Fortune*, annual). The rate of return data are subject to reservations about comparability and inclusion of disparate activities. These do not, however, negate the larger differences, such as are shown by General Motors, IBM and Xerox.

photographic equipment. In them, and in many other significant industries as well, market power appears to double or triple the margin of extra profitability over bedrock minimum competitive profit levels of 6 to 8 percent. One may note also DuPont's prolonged 25 percent returns on cellophane, and Kodak Ltd.'s 27 to 55 percent returns on its virtual monopoly on color film in Britain.[32] Many of the instances noted above in the section on prices would also show extremely high profit rates.

Despite its incompleteness, the weight of evidence so far collected suggests that market power usually yields significant effects on the level of prices, on the structure of prices, and on profitability. The summary above has been painfully brief. But in contrast to the earlier reliance on simple cross-section surveys of concentration and profits, which probably led to underestimates of the actual effects, one may fairly expect new and extended research to raise the estimates of these effects still further.

---

[32] Stocking and Mueller, *op. cit.*

Chapter 13

Effects on Efficiency, Growth, and Stability

> By a perpetual monopoly, all the other subjects of the state are taxed very absurdly in two different ways; first by the high price of goods, which, in the case of a free trade, they could buy much cheaper; and, secondly, by their total exclusion from a branch of business, which it might be both convenient and profitable for many of them to carry on. It is for the most worthless of all purposes too that they are taxed in this manner. It is merely to enable the company to support the negligence, profusion, and malversation of their own servants, whose disorderly conduct seldom allows the dividend of the company to exceed the ordinary rate of profit in trades which are altogether free, and very frequently makes it fall even a good deal short of that rate.
>
> ADAM SMITH
> *The Wealth of Nations* (1776)

Along with its influences on prices and profits, market power may also affect a number of more concrete results of economic activity. Internal business efficiency may soften up. The allocation of resources among markets and sectors may be distorted. Industry growth rates may be influenced. Output, employment, and investment may fluctuate more sharply because prices are held steady. The following sections explore these possibilities.

INTERNAL INEFFICIENCY

The most straightforward problem, only too familiar to every manager of a monopoly firm, is that internal efficiency may tend to go slack in the absence of unremitting pressures on profits. To cast it in analytical terms, the managers' maximizations among various nonpecuniary preferences may be quite complex and subtle. Unfortunately, there is hardly any thorough evidence about this, so only a very approximate appraisal is possible.[1]

---

[1] See also Harvey Leibenstein, "Allocative Efficiency and X-Efficiency," *American Economic Review*, LVI (June 1966), 392–415 and the references cited there.

Whatever the effect may be, it varies widely from case to case. In recent business annals, there are many cases where market power has bred clear inefficiency, including the following examples: Curtiss-Wright's dominance on World War II aircraft-engine production led it into a long series of later blunders.[2] Parke, Davis's 20 percent-plus profits on its drugs business in the 1950's fostered lax management and innovation.[3] The protracted decline of relative efficiency in the leading firms in the American steel, meat packing, and glass industries has long been known, and it was reflected in their relative unprofitability in Table 12.1. General Dynamics' decline from feast to famine in the early 1960's reflected in part the wrong decision and weak controls which market power permitted. Kennecott Copper was for many years a secure "sleeping giant content to liquidate itself through generous contributions to its shareholders as long as its mines held out."[4] Ford Motor Company after 1925 and Douglas Aircraft in 1966 attest that market power may foster managerial softness.[5] There are many similar instances abroad, also.[6] Perhaps the wonder is that, in light of human frailties, internal inefficiency is not even more prevalent, but there can be no doubt that it often prevails; it may usually range up to 10 percent of costs, with higher cases being exceptional.[7] A conservative estimate of the average effect on efficiency would therefore be 5 percent of costs where market power is very high, and 3 percent where it is moderate. In many firms, growth-"maximizing" occurs, possibly with the effect of reducing inner slackness (as Chapter 4 noted). But the average resource waste over the whole range of enterprises with substantial market power is surely not negligible, and it may be as high as several percent of costs.

THE MISALLOCATION BURDEN

Although this "burden" has long been the prime target of economists, by 1968 only two estimates of this effect had been published. They rated the loss at an improbably low 0.1 to 0.4 percent of national income. Both

---

[2] See *Forbes*, November 15, 1967: its World War II production was also acknowledgedly in-efficient.

[3] See *Business Week*, March 2, 1968, 46–50.

[4] *Business Week*, December 7, 1968, 104–108.

[5] During 1967 alone, one business publication (*Forbes*) noted mediocre-to-poor performance in the following firms: Eastman Kodak, American Standard, Libby-Owens-Ford, Norton Company, Rohr Corporation, Remington Arms, First National Stores, Dictaphone, Wrigley, and Inter-public Advertising Company. Each was, or had been, the largest firm in its markets. The same has been true of International Paper Company, the largest U.S. paper producer (see "International Paper Sees the Forest Through the Trees," *Fortune*, March 1969, 105), and of Weyerhauser Company, the largest lumber producer (see "Weyerhauser Fells a Wooden Past," *Business Week*, June 7, 1969, 76–80.

[6] See *inter alia* the U.S. Senate Subcommittee on Antitrust and Monopoly, 90th Congress, 2nd Session, *Hearings on Economic Concentration, Part 7* (Washington, D.C.: U.S. Government Printing Office, 1968), 3441–3468, 3589–3612, and 3682–3706; and Richard E. Caves and Associates, *Britain's Economic Prospects* (Washington, D.C.: Brookings, 1968), Ch. 7.

[7] See Leibenstein, *op. cit.*

studies, resting on aggregative industry and profit data, are known to understate the effect sharply, probably by less than half.[8] Indeed, the lack of more adequate estimates is one of the more puzzling lacunae in the literature.

A reasonable estimate of the pure allocation effect would be 1 to 2 percent. This reflects the findings in Chapter 12 about market power's effects on profits and prices. Recall that profits tend, at a minimum, to be higher by more than 1 percent for each 10 concentration points. This implies that maximum concentration yields about 10 to 15 percent higher prices (this is further corroborated later in this chapter). If demand elasticities average about -1.0, which is a commonly made assumption, then output in such industries is reduced by 10 to 15 percent. At low concentration, say 25 percent, the effect is presumably negligible.

Using mainly the adjusted concentration ratios for only the industries listed in Appendix Table 13, one is led by these assumptions to an estimated welfare loss of about 3.1 percent in 1966. The degree of output restraint was assumed to vary linearly between zero at 30 percent concentration to (only) 10 percent of sales at 100 percent concentration. Adjusted concentration ratios were used for each industry, with a further upward adjustment of at most 10 percent where other structural elements were strongly reinforcing. The actual welfare loss varies between the total restraint on sales and a fraction of it. This depends on whether the burden is a matter only of reshuffling or relates also to macroeconomic output and capacity levels (recall Chapter 4).[9] The 3.1 percent misallocation in manufacturing generalizes to a 2.5 percent loss for the entire economy.[10] The loss would have grown to

---

[8] Arnold Harberger, "Monopoly and Resource Allocation," *American Economic Review*, XLIV (May, 1954), 77–87; and David Schwartzman, "The Burden of Monopoly," *Journal of Political Economy*, LXVIII (December 1960), 627–630. In particular, Harberger takes profit differentials (among rather wide industry groupings) as adequate reflections of market power. Chapter 12 has already shown that data will usually understate such a relationship. Also, both Harberger and Schwartzman ignore the capacity-increasing effect, as distinct from the simple resource-reshuffling effect, from reducing market power (see below). See also Ruth P. Mack's critical comment on Harberger's analysis, *American Economic Review*, May, 1954, 88–92; and George Stigler, "The Statistics of Monopoly and Merger," *Journal of Political Economy*, 1956, 33–40.

[9] The levels of many inputs may be quite easily expanded *in toto* in response to a reduction of market power. Labor participation may rise substantially. Raw- and semifinished-goods inputs may be greatly enlarged via imports. And, over the medium run, capital inputs may be substantially expanded. These margins of flexibility show that the fixed-capacity assumption, whereby given resources can only be reallocated, is largely if not entirely inadmissible as an assumption. Therefore much, if not most, of the output restraint may correctly be regarded as an outright loss.

Accordingly it is quite conservative to use as an approximation of the loss the proportional restraint on value-added (not gross output) in each industry. This, incidentally, also avoids the complex question of possible pyramiding of the monopoly effect at successive stages of production.

[10] In generalizing the manufacturing estimates to the rest of the economy, certain regulated utilities were excluded, on the assumption that regulatory control is actually effective in offsetting market power. Indeed, it is possible (recall Chapter 4) that capacity and production are *overexpanded* in such utilities.

The summed output loss in manufacturing was estimated at $9.3 billion of value-added, which was 7.5 percent of value-added in the market-power industries and 3.7 percent of all manufacturing value-added, in 1966. Converted to national income, the loss is about $6.9 billion. Applying the same percentage to market power in other sectors, the loss there emerges as approximately $8.8 billion of national income, which is only 2.8 percent of national income arising in all these nonmanufacturing sectors. The total burden of $15.7 billion is a shade over 2.5 percent of total national income of $617 billion in 1966.

about $17 billion in 1968. This need not be scaled down appreciably to account for large-scale economies which concentration may yield in some industries; as Chapter 11 suggested, these gains are probably relatively small and few.

By conservative estimate, then, the direct loss (distinct from X-inefficiency) is not less than 1 percent and probably between 2 and 3 percent. There are also external effects from market power in some industries. The steel industry is a prime example in the United States; its performance has added appreciably to the country's balance-of-payments problem, which has, in turn, constrained the national rates of growth and employment.[11] The same is true of automobiles, where imports in 1968 reached nearly 10 percent of all sales. A different kind of external effect stems from drug industry restriction. The extra loss is in death, disease, and pain which would have been averted by more widespread use of drugs at lower prices. These three external effects alone may have added up to the equivalent of perhaps 0.5 percent of national income. In Britain the effect via the balance of payments may be larger, perhaps on the order of 2 to 4 percent of national income. This margin has probably contributed significantly to Britain's economic problem.[12]

GROWTH

As Chapter 4 noted, there is little in economic theory to suggest that any given quantum of market power inhibits (or perhaps even promotes) growth. Yet specific claims are made so often—for example, that rapid American and West German growth can be credited chiefly to their competitiveness—that the possibility deserves a fair test.[13]

One may analyze data over the whole range of industries, in search of general relationships between structural monopoly and growth. One may also seek out individual industries whose growth has been demonstrably affected by market power. The former, statistical approach has turned up virtually blank results in several exploratory studies.[14] If market power does generally influence growth in American manufacturing industries, the pressure it exerts must be little more than atmospheric. No such effect that is statistic-

---

[11] Walter Adams and Joel B. Dirlam, "Big Steel, Invention and Innovation," *Quarterly Journal of Economics*, LXXX (May 1966), 167–189, and their "Steel Imports and Vertical Oligopoly Power," *American Economic Review*, LIV (September 1964), 626–655. In 1968, nearly one-quarter of its equipment was regarded as obsolete. See McGraw-Hill Economics Department, *How Modern is American Industry?* (New York: McGraw-Hill, 1968).

[12] See *Economic Concentration, Part 7*; and Caves, *op. cit.*

[13] See for example Egon Sohmen, "Competition and Growth: The Lesson of West Germany," *American Economic Review*, IL (December 1959) 986–1003; and comments by Roskamp, Mac-Bean and Shepherd, and Opie, *American Economic Review*, L (December 1960), 1015–1025. The topic is a hardy perennial in popular discussion.

[14] For example, see William G. Shepherd, "Trends of Concentration in American Manufacturing Industries, 1947–1958," *Review of Economics and Statistics*, XLVI (May 1964), 200–212.

ally (let alone economically) significant has yet emerged, even from relatively refined analysis.   Britain and Japan also display no clear relationship.[15]

Yet there may be *specific* markets in which growth has been sharply influenced, either upward or downward, by market power.   Among these cases, the most frequent is the slow expansion of a new market whose original seller controls supply (often through a critical patent).   Recent instances include many drugs, nylon, and cellophane.   The general pattern in new products and industries is for dominant firms to attempt to restrain growth significantly in the effort to skim off maximum profits.   Usually, only the erosion of the original structural monopoly via new entry eliminates this restraining effect, if and when it happens at all.   There are virtually no clear and proven cases of high market power actually accelerating growth.[16]

STABILITY OF PRICES, PRODUCTION, AND INVESTMENT

Concentrated industries may have relatively rigid prices and unstable production and employment, for reasons connected with both market power and accelerator theory.   The topic was sharply, but inconclusively, argued in the 1930's.   More recently the controversy has shifted and narrowed down to price "flexibility" and "administered prices."[17]   Richard Ruggles has argued that *output* price movements reflect mainly input price movements with only a small residual role for market power.[18]   George Stigler and others have noted that official price reports often mask the true frequency and amplitude of short-term price shadings and fluctuations; this, however, has little bearing on their "medium-run" movements, especially during the course of major recessions.[19]

Means, Blair, and other critics of administered prices focused their criticism on certain major concentrated industries whose prices persisted in rising even during the two recessions of the 1950's.   In the surprisingly nettlesome debate which ensued, some counter-critics (incorrectly) reinterpreted the administered price "thesis" into a straw-man claim that there is a

---

[15] See William G. Shepherd, "Changes in British Industrial Concentration, 1951–1958," *Oxford Economic Papers*, XVIII (March 1966), 126–132; and *Economic Concentration, Part 7*, 3690–3691.
[16] The lone major possible exception at the present time appears to be nuclear power equipment, where GE and Westinghouse may have been offering loss leaders on a grand scale.   But this could lead to eventual restrictiveness.
[17] See *inter alia* J. M. Blair, "Administered Prices—A Phenomenon in Search of a Theory," *American Economic Review*, XLVIII (May 1958), 431–450.
[18] See especially Richard Ruggles, "The Nature of Price Flexibility and the Determinants of Relative Price Changes in the Economy," in George J. Stigler, ed., *Business Concentration and Price Policy* (Princeton University Press, 1955).
[19] George J. Stigler, "Administered Prices and Oligopoly Inflation," *Journal of Business*, XXXV (January 1962), 1–13, and papers cited therein.

positive *general* association of secular price rises and industry *concentration*.[20] This argument would lift the burden of proof from the major industries (to justify their price rises at times of idle capacity), placing it instead upon the "administered price" critics to demonstrate that such an omni-industry relationship exists.   A study failing to find such a relationship could then be construed as rebutting the entire "administered price" thesis—indeed the whole price-output flexibility problem.   This rebuttal is exactly what DePodwin and Selden's study claimed to provide, mainly owing to "low" correlations they observed in fitting equations relating industry concentration in 1954 and price movements during 1953–1959.

This attempt at negative "proof" must be inconclusive; such a non-exhaustive "test" (using necessarily incomplete and defective data) is no test at all.   Moreover, in their haste to reach their conclusion, DePodwin and Selden overlooked the embarrassing fact that their own data actually tend to contradict their conclusion more than to support it.   As Means has already noted, the regression slopes for at least two of their equations imply no price rise for unconcentrated industries during 1953–1959, and about a 20 percent price rise for industries with maximum concentration.[21]   This would support even the misconstrued administered price thesis!

To investigate the question further, one may analyze alternative price data and additional market-structure variables.   To widen the coverage, price indexes for 1947–1949 to 1958 were assigned to 224 four-digit industry groups.[22]   Among the new possible explanatory variables were: growth, large-firm share, profit rates, and imports.

The results are complex and still statistically faint ($R^2 = .10$).   A concentration price-change association comparable to DePodwin and Selden's appears for 1947–1949 to 1958.   Low concentration goes with a 6 percent price rise, while maximum concentration goes with a 36 percent rise.   This holds despite the presence of other variables which might be expected to be influential but which were not: growth, large-firm share, and imports. The faint negative association between *changes* in concentration and prices is puzzling (perhaps spurious); conventional theory would predict a positive association.

In a further analysis, Richard Ruggles' output price indexes for 1954–1959 are "explained" substantially ($r^2 = .40$) by his *input* price indexes.[23]   Concentration shows virtually no association at all with the output price changes,

---

[20] For some of the local choler, see Stigler's "Rejoinder" to J. M. Blair's "Comment," *Journal of Business*, XXXVII, 1964.   For the new interpretation, see H. J. DePodwin and R. T. Selden, "Business Pricing Policies and Inflation," *Journal of Political Economy*, LXXI (April 1963), 116–127, reprinted in *Economic Concentration, Part 1* (1964), 477–488.   For Means' argument that this misrepresents the problem, see *ibid.*, 489–497.

[21] *Ibid.*, 496–497.

[22] These include all for which Bureau of the Census and Bureau of Labor Statistics industry definitions are reasonably congruent.   Mean values for the variables in this subset did not differ significantly for mean values for the entire set of industries, suggesting that the 224 industries are reasonably representative.

[23] I am grateful to him for making his unpublished indexes available.

not even in simple regressions. In view of Ruggles' stress on input price changes as the determinant of output price changes, the "unexplained" 60 percent residual variation of output price changes is larger than might be expected.

These results require careful interpretation. They do not deal with flexibility (either of prices or of production) during the course of the major business fluctuations, which is the real question. The structural data are incomplete, and those which exist are not very good. And the phenomenon (*if* it exists) may be inherent in only a few major industries, rather than over the whole range of industries.[24] In other words, a significant administered price effect, à la Means, in only a few major industries (such as steel, automobiles, or drugs) would rank as important, even though it might not register in cross-section studies. Evidently further testing is needed, preferably focusing on the relatively small group (perhaps 30 or 50) of industries mainly in question; these were noted in Chapter 10.

Turning to the more direct problem of stability in production and investment, there has been little published evidence since the negative "findings" about the 1930's. Postwar conditions could be studied fairly readily by measuring the degree of fluctuations of each industry about its growth trend, or during specific recession episodes, and appraising how closely this is correlated with structural monopoly.

For the whole range of American manufacturing industries, market power (especially as summarized in Chapter 10) is strongly associated with relative instability of both output and employment; this is apparent even without a detailed analysis. Similar patterns emerge for Britain and Japan, though less clearly (perhaps partly because of inferior data). Yet this also reflects something else, as Chapter 4 noted: heavy producer-goods industries typically face relatively sharp fluctuations in demand. This, rather than market power, may cause the swings in production. Segregating the industries by types and looking for monopoly-stability patterns *within* the groups may factor out this special determinant.

One such analysis does reduce the apparent monopoly-instability effect, but it does not wholly erase it.[25] Enough of it remains to suggest a presumption that market power may appreciably accentuate macroeconomic fluctuations, at least in the downward direction. If modern economic policy has

---

[24] See also Leonard W. Weiss, "Business Pricing Policies and Inflation Reconsidered," *Journal of Political Economy*, LXXIV (April 1966), 177–187, who concludes that the condition was peculiar to the late 1950's.

[25] This exploratory test by the author requires monthly indexes of real output, seasonally adjusted in order to assess the degree of cyclical fluctuations. These are available only for relatively broad groupings, in the Federal Reserve index of industrial production. Producers' equipment industries were excluded. Of the remaining broad industries, eight were (somewhat arbitrarily) rated as having high market power; nine were rated as having low market power. The average declines in each group during the 1953–1954 and 1957–1958 recessions were then tested to see if they differed significantly. They did, at the 1-percent level of confidence, but there were some wide individual variations. Although this is only primitive analysis, it does suggest the direction of difference; and available data are not likely soon to permit a really thorough analysis.

really banished the business cycle (as it seemed during 1962–1967), then market power's possible effect on instability of production may have no further effect.   But such a prophecy may be optimistic.

Investment fluctuations over time might also be affected by market power.   In an ingenious exploratory study, F. M. Scherer attempts to filter out the accelerator factor, and concludes tentatively that "investment outlays tend to be more unstable relative to their trend values in concentrated than in atomistically structured industries, *ceteris paribus*," apparently mostly because of "low decision making power dispersion."[26]   Though instability is probably only a weak negative effect of market power, the effect apparently does exist.

---

[26] F. M. Scherer, "Market Structure and the Stability of Investment," American Economic Association, *Papers and Proceedings* LIX (May 1969) 72–79.

Chapter 14

Effects on Technical
Change and Distribution

Thus, in the modern industry shared by a few large firms, size and the rewards accruing to market power combine to insure that resources for research and technical development will be available. . . . In this way market power protects the incentive to technical development.

JOHN KENNETH GALBRAITH
American Capitalism (1956)

Were it not for the miscellaneous batch of hard-bitten, shirtsleeved Texas oil-lease speculators and wildcatters that since World War I has risen on a tide of special tax privileges like science-fiction dinosaurs, it could well be said that the day of accumulating gargantuan new personal fortunes in the United States is just about ended, leaving the tubbed, scrubbed and public-relations-anointed inheritors of the nineteenth-century money scramble holding most of the chips.

FERDINAND LUNDBERG
The Rich and the Super-Rich (1968)

Among market power's possible effects, those on technical progress have recently taken a strong hold on popular and professional discussion. If market power does strongly influence the rate and direction of innovation, that impact could swamp the other effects, for good or ill. Yet this possibility (and even whether the effect is to retard or stimulate) has only begun to get definite research treatment.

The possible impact of market power on distribution has, by contrast, been neglected. Only a few economists have recently bothered to study how market power may have altered patterns of wealth and income, although this generations' distribution (as in previous ages) arises in no small part from monopoly and competition in earlier eras, and this will continue in the future. There is also the question of whether market power restricts or enlarges individual *opportunity*, especially for minority groups. These distributional effects of market power may rank in importance with, or above, any of the other effects.

TECHNICAL CHANGE

Conventional theory is (as Chapter 4 noted) inconclusive about the relation of market structure to technical change. It suggests that dominant firms in concentrated industries may—owing to possible scale economies in research and innovation, and to the security of (and eagerness to defend) their market positions—provide an optimal setting for technical advance. But such firms may also have strong incentives to impede innovation, by themselves and other firms, by maximizing profits over all investments, including older ones. The net influence of these cross-pressures will vary from case to case; generally, the greater a firm's dominance, the more likely it is that the incentives to imitate rather than innovate will influence it.[1]

In Schumpeter's view (as Chapter 2 noted), "competition," progress, and some degree of "excess" profits were intertwined in a succession of innovative disequilibria. Though Schumpeter apparently thought mainly of absolutely large firms as the innovators, this was not essential to his argument—it was the market power and its fruits which drew the process onward and, as hardly needs mentioning in this context, small markets can be dominated by small firms. Against this is the likelihood (recall Chapter 4) that loose oligopoly is closer to the general optimum for innovation.

We look first at cross-section evidence relating structure and innovation in entire industries. No close tie can be expected. Federal R&D support has played a large role in several major industries, as Table 14.1 shows (recall also Chapters 5 and 11). Moreover, as Chapter 4 noted, good measures of innovative effort and results are—like measures of market power—hard to derive. So it is not surprising that cross-section studies at essentially the two-digit industry group level have shown only traces of a possible positive association between concentration and technical change.[2] A more intensive analysis of several of the main oligopolies gives some hints of slower innovation by dominant firms than by others. Thus, Mansfield offers a variety of tests, which ". . . do not suggest that greater concentration results in a faster rate of diffusion of innovations."[3] In Scherer's view: ". . . technological vigor appears to increase with concentration at relatively low levels of concentration. When the four-firm concentration ratio exceeds 50 or 55

---

[1] See also F. M. Scherer, "R&D Resource Allocation Under Rivalry," *Quarterly Journal of Economics*, LXXXI (August 1967), 364–393.

[2] Leonard W. Weiss, "Average Concentration Ratios and Industrial Performance," *Journal of Industrial Economics*, XI (July 1963), 237–254; Almarin Phillips, "Concentration, Scale and Technological Change in Selected Manufacturing Industries, 1899–1939," *Journal of Industrial Economics*, IV (June 1956), 179–193; and F. M. Scherer, "Firm Size, Market Structure, Opportunity and the Output of Patented Inventions," *American Economic Review*, LV (December 1965), 1097–1125.

[3] Edwin Mansfield, *Industrial Research and Technological Innovation: An Econometric Analysis* (New York: Norton, 1968), 206.

TABLE 14.1 RESEARCH AND DEVELOPMENT PATTERNS IN AMERICAN INDUSTRY, 1965

	Expenditures				Largest 4 Firms	
	As Percent of Total Sales	Total Amounts ($ million)	Federal Funds	Federal as % of Total	Share of All R&D Funds in the Industry (Percent)	Share of federal R&D Funds in the Industry (Percent)
Food and kindred products	.4	150	1	1	25	*
Textiles and apparel	.4	34	*	*	46	*
Lumber and allied products	.5	13	0	*	36	0
Paper and allied products	.7	76	0	0	27	0
Chemicals and allied products	4.2	1,377	190	14	39	64
Industrial chemicals	4.6	928	147	16	58	82
Drugs and medicines	5.9	268	*	*	37	*
Other chemicals	2.3	181	*	*	46	*
Petroleum products	1.2	435	69	16	53	(74)
Rubber products	1.9	166	25	15	71	55
Stone, clay, and glass products	1.6	119	4	3	57	67
Primary metals	.8	216	8	4	42	56
Fabricated metals	1.4	145	17	11	42	70
Machinery	4.1	1,129	258	23	53	61
Electrical and communication equipment	9.4	3,167	1,978	62	53	54
Communication and components	12.2	1,912	1,253	66	55	55
Other electrical	7.0	1,255	725	58	80	93
Motor vehicles and equipment	3.1	1,238	326	26	91	92
Aircraft and missiles	28.0	5,120	4,500	88	52	51
Instruments	6.2	387	125	32	58	67
Other manufacturing	.7	67	1	2	28	0
Nonmanufacturing	*	359	255	71	35	45
All industries	4.3	$14,197	$7,759	55	21	27

* Not shown separately but included in the total.
SOURCE: Adapted from U.S. National Science Foundation, *Basic Research, Applied Research and Development in Industry, 1965,* NSF 67-12 (Washington, D.C.: U.S. Government Printing Office, 1967).

percent, additional market power is probably not conducive to more vigorous technical efforts and may be downright stultifying."[4]

Even though these and related studies have relied mainly on adjusted concentration as the indicator of market structure, and though they have not filtered out the leading-firm bias injected by much public-agency R&D support, their findings are suggestive and consistent. Altogether, the evidence about both *inputs* and *results* of innovation suggest that (1) dominant firms frequently account for a disproportionally small share of invention, and (2) loose oligopoly may be the market structure most conducive to innovation.

Yet most of these findings rely on indirect measures (such as scientists or patents) for technical progress, rather than on indexes of rising productivity itself. A direct analysis, relating technical advance to the several main structural elements (rather than just concentration) is an obvious next step, using the data for four-digit industries; but direct indexes of total productivity at this degree of detail have not yet been derived. The difficulty of specifying appropriate production functions for hundreds of disparate industries would be, in itself, great. Moreover, adequate measures of capital inputs have not been fully prepared in this degree of detail.

One might therefore revert, with admitted but calculated simplicity, to growth in value-added per worker as a proxy for total technical change. The main and obvious defects of such a labor-productivity variable are well-known, and they of course severely qualify any results of the analysis.[5] Yet, this productivity index may reflect technical change fairly sensitively. To put it briefly, capital-widening investment will not ordinarily affect average productivity, while capital-deepening (or thinning) investment will; and it is the latter which most usually involves technical change.

In light of these problems and hints from previous research, an analysis of this sort offers interesting inklings, but they need careful interpreting (see Appendix Table 17). Since the time-period (1947–1962) precedes the adjusted concentration ratios, unadjusted ratios had to be used. As Table 12.2 shows, productivity change is significantly associated with the main features of market structure (concentration, large-firm share, stability, and even slightly with changes in concentration) and with profit rates. That all of the associations are positive is at least consistent with the innovation-cum-market-power-cum-profits view of the competitive process which Schumpeter held.

---

[4] F. M. Scherer, "Market Structure and the Employment of Scientists and Engineers," *American Economic Review*, LVII (June 1967), 524–531, and Jacob Schmookler, testimony in U.S. Senate Subcommittee on Antitrust and Monopoly, *Hearings on Economic Concentration, Part 3* (Washington, D.C.: U.S. Government Printing Office, 1965) 1257–1969.
[5] Moreover, data for the full postwar period are available for only 159 industries; of these only 95 also have Gort's "stability" indexes (recall Chapter 8).

In the combined analysis, concentration and large-firm share appear to be largely interchangeable as the dominant variable. The cofficients suggest that an additional percentage point of concentration (and large-firm share) was associated approximately with an additional percentage point of worker-productivity rise during 1947–1962. The weak, positive association of increases in concentration with rising productivity provides another hint of a structure-innovation association. Even so, these variables together "explain" only about one-third of productivity changes ($R^2 = .32$).

The apparent positive associations can be reconciled with findings noted elsewhere in this volume. The government has focused R&D support in several highly monopolistic industries. Also, as Scherer, Schmookler, and others have noted, the main determinants of technical progress may lie in each industry's scientific character and opportunities rather than in market structure. Any relation between structure and progress may be fortuitous, and not an indication of cause-and-effect. Moreover, output price changes may have been focused in a narrow range of industries, in such a manner as to inflate the apparent rise of "productivity" in concentrated, large-firm-dominated, stable, and profitable industries. This would be consistent with the evidence on price trends and market structure (in Chapter 12). Alternatively, the main interaction may have been between wage trends and labor-saving investment, with market structure playing some (perhaps necessary but not sufficient) role.[6] A lagged model might, in principle, be able to decompose such an interaction, but it lies beyond the scope of the present work.

At the very most, technical change may have tended to be slightly faster in industries with some market power, though there is no proof at all that the latter has *caused* the former, in any real sense. Indeed, the test reported here suggests that even a detailed cross-section approach may fail to yield conclusive—or even useful—answers. It cannot show, for example, whether research and innovational activities have taken just the right amounts of resources at the margin, or whether dominant firms are more efficient as innovators.

The more critical question is: which firms *within* the industries do proportionally more of the innovating and do it more fruitfully? Chapter 11 already noted that recent evidence increasingly suggests that research and development activities tend to have higher net productivity in medium-size and small firms than in very large companies. In many major innovations, the industry leaders have been merely imitators, and often reluctant ones at

---

[6] See, among others, Martin Segal, "The Relation between Union Wage Impact and Market Structure," *Quarterly Journal of Economics*, LXXVIII (February 1964), 96–114; Harold M. Levinson, "Postwar Movements of Prices and Wages in Manufacturing Industries," in Joint Economic Committee, U.S. Congress, *Study of Employment, Growth and Price Levels*, Study Paper No. 21, (Washington, D.C.: U.S. Government Printing Office, 1960).

that.   Although the dynamics of invention, innovation and, imitation among firms are complicated, one would generally expect more intense innovation from the middle-range firms, as Chapter 4 noted.

Individual case studies of some major industries tend to bear out this expectation, though not conclusively.   In oil, steel, tin cans, and chemicals industries, the most active innovation during recent decades has apparently occurred in the second echelon of firms.[7]   There are many specific instances of a major innovation being forced upon the industry leader; stainless steel razor blades, synchronous satellites, and the oxygen steelmaking process are recent examples.[8]   Indeed, one may venture that it is relatively unusual for a dominant firm to persist in a disproportionally large share of inventing and innovating, as the incentives to become an imitator eventually prevail.   In the unusual cases (including some aerospace and related industries), government policies rather than spontaneous industry evolution have often been decisive.

In perspective, then, technical change may have some general association with mild structural monopoly, but this probably does not go beyond the range of loose, symmetrical oligopoly.   Within the rather few major innovating industries which tend to dominate the patterns of R&D and rapid technical change, second-level firms seem to be relatively more fruitful researchers and aggressive innovators than dominant companies.   Altogether, the sketchy evidence now available (1) confirms Chapter 4's hypotheses, and (2) truncates the Schumpeter-Galbraith position down to loose oligopoly. In the larger, tight, asymmetric oligopolies, even a skeptic may expect that dominant firms will usually have more market power than is optimum for invention and innovation.   Accordingly, the net loss of innovation from excessive market power in a number of tight-oligopoly and near-monopoly industries may be significant.

DISTRIBUTION

Turning now to the distributional impacts of market power—on wealth, income, and opportunities—we may consider them one by one.   Only on opportunities is there much really systematic evidence.

---

[7] Mansfield, *op. cit.*; Daniel Hamberg, *R&D: Essays in the Economics of Research and Development* (New York: Random House, 1966), and *Economic Concentration, Part 3*, 118–134.
[8] In Britain, a long-life light bulb (2,000 hours as against the ordinary 1,000 hours) was developed but secretly withheld from sale by the leading producers.   After discovery of it by the Monopolies Commission in December, 1968, the leading firms–British Lighting Industries, Philips and Osram–stuck to decisions not to market it, arguing that it would not be "in the public interest." A smaller producer, Crompton Parkinson (with 8 percent of the bulb market), was the first firm to go ahead with the new bulb.   See *The Economist* (January 25, 1969), 64.

Wealth

Market power usually results in gains in the capital value of the monopolistic enterprise. When the owner is also manager, he can draw off his gains either directly in current income or in capital gains by selling part or all of his share. In modern corporations, shareholders' interests may be partly at odds with management's, since the executives' payments to themselves and other input suppliers may erode the income and capital gains for shareholders.

The main lasting wealth impact of monopoly comes, in any case, through rises in the price of common stock of firms achieving and exploiting market power. The main factual questions are: How large have been the stock price rises for companies with market power (more than for competitive firms), and how widely have these gains been spread among individual holders?

On the first question, one cannot really hope to capture the effects of each *expansion* of market power, many of which took place decades ago under obscure conditions. As we have noticed, the market discounts monopoly gains, often immediately; market power attained in 1900 may still exist, but its investor gains usually will have long since been discounted. Nor can one neatly separate the capital-gains effects of market power from those of innovation, cost-cutting, and other meritorious or neutral acts.

A number of the sharpest postwar stock-price rises among major firms were for firms which (1) held key patents or other entry barriers in rapidly-growing industries, (such as IBM, drug firms, and Xerox) or (2) were especially active in mergers (such as Litton and Ling-Temco-Vought). If, as is probable, these patterns apply more generally, this would imply disequalizing effects on wealth distribution. Both of these situations usually involve and reward inside information; whatever the inventive-efficiency effects, the distributional impact is to widen the inequality of wealth holdings.

One may also use industry-wide stock indexes, comparing monopolistic with competitive industries (as noted in Chapter 10). Very broadly speaking, one finds again some apparent association of structural monopoly and capital gains; and again the risk of capital loss appears to be less in situations with market power. But this interacts also with the new-industry growth and monopoly patterns noted earlier. It has not been possible yet to factor out those patterns.

One may also compare leading firms with the others in industries with at least moderate structural monopoly. The results of a brief inspection of this sort are mixed; dominant firms in some major industries (such as steel, oil, rubber, and chemicals) have fared relatively poorly in recent years, although in a majority of cases the capital gains have been high. Industry growth is probably a main influence, and on this and other factors more and thorough analysis is evidently needed.

The persistence of such capital-gains patterns would be especially notable in the face of the probable tendency of the second-level firms to innovate more actively. Undoubtedly, too, much of the monopoly payoff was, by the 1950's, already discounted in many industries where market structure had changed little for decades. Where it *has* changed more recently, the rewards are often spectacular.

One may also approximate the total wealth effect by capitalizing the estimated extra monopoly profits currently earned by enterprises. In 1967, total corporate profits after taxes were $48 billion in the United States. Chapters 7–10 have indicated that industries presently average about 30 percent higher concentration than would be true under loose oligopoly. Chapter 12 noted that concentration alone appears to yield perhaps 1 percentage point of additional rate of return for each additional 10 concentration points in manufacturing industries. Accordingly, average profits may be 3 percentage points higher owing to market power, or perhaps 2 percent to be conservative (and to allow for possible "technological imperatives"). These 2 points are 17.1 percent of the observed average of 11.7 percent return on stockholders' equity in manufacturing in 1967, and they represent $4.9 billion in manufacturing profits. Generalized to the whole economy, the profit figure is $8.1 billion. A number of alternative formulas can be used to capitalize these flows into asset values, but all formulas will yield large figures. Using a conservative current price-earnings ratio of 12 to 1, one would estimate the capital value created by market power at $97 billion. Even if the true figure were only half of this, it would still be substantial. Yet even the $97 billion estimate (which really means perhaps $80 to $129 billion) probably understates, because it does not fully reflect the real present impact of *expected* future (and continued) market power. Thus the $42 billion of market value of IBM stock in May 1968 (at a price-earnings ratio above 50 to 1) heavily reflected expected future earnings, to flow in part from IBM's continued dominance of the computer industry. No less than $6 billion of this (and more probably $15 billion) could reasonably be attributed to IBM's market power (see also Chapter 15 below). The same logic applies on a smaller scale to many other firms as well. Therefore the $97 billion total estimate may best be regarded as distinctly on the low side, pending a more complete sifting of individual industry patterns.

As big as it may seem, the estimated impact is only about 10 percent of the total value of all corporate stock ($960 billion in 1967).[9] It is well below half of the market value of stock (about $250 billion) of just those relatively few leading firms listed in Table 10.1. It is also less than one-fourth of the total value of corporate stock held by the 4 million top wealthholders in the country.[10] From this perspective, the estimate of capital value created

---

[9] *Finance*, January 1967, extended to 1967 by the author.
[10] U.S. Treasury Department, Internal Revenue Service, *Statistics of Income, 1962*, Supplemented Report, *Personal Wealth* (Washington, D.C.: U.S. Government Printing Office, 1966, updated to 1967 by the author).

by market power appears to be a reasonable one. Note that this capital value is primarily a *redistribution*, not a pure *creation*. If, by waving a magic wand, excess market power could be made to vanish, total capital values would not simply shrink by $97 billion. Quite the contrary, the opening of better competitive opportunities would swell the capital value of *other* firms, very likely by more than the $97 billion. This reflects the fact that excess market power has reduced not only real national income but the aggregate capital value of enterprises as well.

How have these rewards to market power affected the personal distribution of wealth? If stock were more equally distributed than income, and if all investors shared equally in the gains, the end result would have been toward greater equality. In fact, neither of these conditions hold (recall Chapter 5). Therefore, market power has probably added substantially to the present and continuing inequality of wealth. Conversely, properly designed action against market power—especially in financial markets—would tend to check this effect in the future, even though past gains have become too diffused ever to correct.

The effects can, like the tip of an iceberg, be seen in the composition of the highest-wealth group of American citizens. Among 66 persons said to hold more than $150 million in 1968, some 18 represented fortunes made in the oil industry.[11] At least 12 of these were largely inherited fortunes (from the early dominant oil firms) of Rockefellers and Mellons. Five holdings (four of them Fords) stemmed from automobiles. Leading firms in chemicals, drugs, glass, and several other tight oligopolies had bred 14 more of the holdings. More than half, therefore, of the largest fortunes have arisen more or less directly from acquiring and exploiting market power. Only 9 came directly from finance and real estate. Only 2 fortunes—Edwin Land's (Polaroid) and Chester Carlson's (xerography)—represent rewards to inventive genius (the latter, of course, reflecting Xerox's monopoly). Inheritance was the main source of at least a third of the fortunes; in only a minority did the individual begin with no appreciable family funds. Many of the wealthy industrial descendants are now well placed in financial affairs.

The role of market power in all this is not easy to factor out, but it has not been small. It bears little relation to inventive contribution. Moreover, industrial fortunes, especially when they are followed through into financial affairs, tend to last and grow.

Income

Structural monopoly affects income patterns mainly through payments and benefits to the firm's employees, chiefly those at managerial levels, as

---

[11] *Fortune*, May, 1968, "America's Centimillionaires," pp. 152–156; see also Ferdinand Lundberg, *The Rich and the Super Rich* (New York: Lyle Stuart, 1968).

well as via dividend and other payments to the owners (whose wealth has just been discussed). In some degree, the managers of many large and leading firms are under only moderate constraints on their payments to themselves.[12] These contraints, both objective and subjective, may be tighter than is often thought, as Chapter 5 noted. Yet one cannot assume, at the other extreme, that managerial rewards nicely equate with marginal productivity, however that might be measured. There *are* large imperfections in the "markets" for upper management, even apart from the market power held by many firms. And firms holding market power do undeniably possess resources for very large rewards to their management.[13]

How sharply this actually affects income distribution can only be conjectured. Yet the higher-income groups in most countries are highly populated by managers and professionals in firms holding market power, and this is reinforced by extra benefits. Accordingly, the impact of market power toward inequality may be large, indeed. Since the facts presently available do not settle it, the degree of the effect must remain in doubt.

Market imperfections also affect the distribution of real purchasing power by making "the poor pay more"—often very much more.[14] Whether the differences reflect true cost-differences is irrelevant in this context. Racial and ethnic groups are the biggest losers from market imperfections and their own vulnerability, but other low-income groups suffer also. The problems are largely those of imperfect information, rather than market structure in the usual sense. Accordingly, the firms (in retailing and bill collecting) that batten on consumer ignorance and limitations often appear to be "competitive"—indeed remorselessly so. Therefore the proper remedies may lie outside the usual antitrust policies.

In any event, the total effect of market power on the distribution of wealth and income is not small A conservative estimate would be that in any year at least 3 percent of national income is redistributed mainly toward inequality, because of market power. This is not a dead economic "loss," which can be added directly to the inefficiency burdens and lost technological progress. Indeed some of it may represent incentives and rewards to individual and corporate initiative, as popular discussion commonly has it.

---

[12] For example, Edward S. Mason, *The Corporation in Modern Society* (Cambridge: Harvard University Press, 1959); Andrew Schonfield, *Modern Capitalism* (New York: Oxford University Press, 1965), 380–382. It is not clear, of course, that this situation is appreciably different from former decades. See also John K. Galbraith, *The New Industrial State* (Boston: Houghton Mifflin, 1967).

[13] Not only does executive compensation reach very high levels in many cases. In addition, there are wide variations in these levels which bear no clear relation to competitive performance; "1,700 Top Executives," *Fortune*, November, 1959, 138–143; a recent report on management compensation by McKinsey and Co., reported in *The New York Times*, September 11, 1966 Financial Section; Leonard R. Burgess, *Top Executive Pay Package* (New York: Free Press, 1963); and "Top Men Fatten Their Pay," *Business Week*, June 6, 1969, 84–112.

[14] David Caplovitz, *The Poor Pay More: Consumer Practices of Low-Income Families* (New York: Free Press, 1963); and Federal Trade Commission, *Report on Installment Credit and Retail Sales Practices of District of Columbia Retailers* (Washington, D.C.: U.S. Government Printing Office, March 1968).

Yet much of it does not.   And most of it, for whatever reason, does accentuate present inequality.   Note that it occurs within existing antitrust constraints.   A significant loosening of these constraints might increase the disequalizing effect.

Opportunities

One can say, in any case, that the economic rewards for those who reach the top are large—in fact large as never before.   The structure of opportunities does provide large prizes to many of the winners.   On an international comparison, the disparity of prizes from market activity in America has always been unusually wide.

More important, how widely are the chances to attain these big prizes distributed?   How "equal" is "opportunity," in relation to market structure and behavior?   The phenomenon eludes any precise appraisal, and the patterns are, of course, varied.   But one may assert fairly confidently that the general degree of equality (in this direction) is relatively high in this country—probably a good deal higher than in most other "competitive market" economies.   Whatever its extent and other impacts may be, market power in the United States is not generally a major source or means of personal exclusion and the preservation of social and economic privilege.

But there are some distinct exceptions to this rule.   The system does virtually exclude those whose personalities do not fit the fairly exacting and specialized competitive requirements for success in financial and corporate management, or in cornering scarce real estate or primary resources.[15]   Probably the most restricted single area is in the upper levels of financial markets, as is true virtually throughout the world.   This is doubly unfortunate because of the key importance of this sector for competition throughout the economy.   Still, the degree of this exclusiveness in the United States is probably less than is common abroad.

The other main current question about market power and opportunity involves racial and ethnic exclusion.   Chapter 5 has already noted that it tends to be relatively sharp in large enterprises.   Does it also vary in line with market power in individual industries?   The problem is acute enough to deserve a rather lengthy analysis here.[16]

Discrimination in employment may be defined as the inclusion of otherwise extraneous racial or ethnic characteristics as elements in the evaluation of job applicants and as criteria for promotions.   For firms operating under the constraints of perfect competition, any significant indulgence of such

---

[15] See, among others, W. Lloyd Warner and James Abegglen, *Big Business Leaders in America* (New York: Harper & Row, 1955), and Eugene E. Jennings, *Mobile Managers*, (Ann Arbor: Bureau of Industrial Relations, Graduate School of Business, University of Michigan, 1967).
[16] This section draws upon the author's "Market Power and Racial Discrimination in White-Collar Employment," *Antitrust Bulletin*, XIV (Spring 1969), 141–161.   For an earlier study, see Gary S. Becker, *The Economics of Discrimination* (Chicago: University of Chicago Press, 1957).

preferences would impose extra costs and therefore ultimately be incompatible with the survival of the enterprise. Hiring by firms so constrained will be "neutral;" indeed, if Negro wage rates were relatively low because of discrimination elsewhere, Negroes would tend to be substituted at the margin for white employees with equal qualifications. Of course, a majority of employees can still force racially discriminatory hiring policies upon their employers, even in firms which are under competitive constraints. This process and its results have been widely observed in blue-collar and craft jobs, often with tacit or explicit union assistance through apprenticeship programs and other devices. But such horizontally enforced discrimination is less germane to hiring for *white-collar* jobs, which are more clearly, directly, and thoroughly subject to independent management control. Therefore, white-collar employment patterns provide a sensitive and direct test of whatever role may be played by management, or "enterprise policy," under varying competitive constraints. They would be expected to be racially neutral under competition, even in firms whose employment of blue-collar workers may reflect discrimination.

By contrast with the neutral competitive outcome, the result under monopoly is not determinate, and it may run toward more discrimination or toward less. Profit-maximizing being at least partially voluntary, not mandatory, the management of a firm with market power may maximize among a variety of other preferences. The managerial preference functions may include racial or associated factors, with positive or negative trade-offs. With economic constraints eased, and assuming interracial preferences to be negative and significant for at least some managers, then one may expect that white-collar employment patterns will embody discrimination. For example, white managers would be expected to substitute white white-collar workers for Negro ones at the margin, and this margin may be a wide one.[17] Managerial preference functions also, of course, include other elements besides race, and they may differ widely in the rate and direction of trade-offs among all elements. Therefore, it is not certain that discrimination against Negroes would exceed that against applicants who are tall and gangling, or left-handed, or Doctors of Philosophy. Yet if there is any racial factor at all, it would tend in the present setting toward lesser hiring of Negroes for white-collar jobs in firms possessing market power. The strict analysis of maximizing behavior therefore predicts that discrimination, rather than neutrality, will occur under market power.

Yet, against this may be set the possibility that managers may exercise their discretion deliberately and "affirmatively" in the social interest, toward

---

[17] The few firms managed by Negroes would provide symmetrical cases. Since white ownership and management is prevalent, the overall patterns would be expected to go toward lower Negro employment.

open hiring or even "positive" discrimination.   The possible social motivation of the modern corporation might prevail in small monopolists as well as in very large oligopolists, and as the rule rather than as the exception (even though Chapter 5 has already suggested that this is not likely).   In many cases, the conflicting tendencies within a firm with market power may, at the least, yield a stand-off between these alternative directions of hiring policy. A finding of no relationship at all would not therefore indicate that no pressures at all are operating, but rather perhaps that the cross pressures are complex and varied.   And a positive relationship between market power and open hiring is entirely possible.   But it would require deliberate company efforts to reverse the natural tendency within firms holding monopoly power.

The U.S. Equal Employment Opportunity Commission has recently compiled plant data on employment patterns for two-digit industry and service groups.[18]   Although it is rather aggregative, the two-digit degree of detail may be adequate, all things considered, to reflect differing conditions of market structure.[19]   A preliminary analysis based on nine major metropolitan areas is reported here, pending a more complete combing of aggregated national total or regional subtotals for each industry.[20]   The city-based approach permits some allowance for sectional and local differences in education, labor supply, and social setting.[21]   It also focuses on the real centers in which market power in major industries may have an effect, relatively uncluttered by disparate factors (particularly in Negro labor supply) arising in the large variety of smaller towns.   Although a more exhaustive analysis is underway to clarify the patterns that are noted here, the preliminary results are suggestive enough to bear reporting.

The data on market structure incorporate some elements of estimation, and they vary somewhat in their reliability.   For the 20 manufacturing industries, weighted averages of four-digit industry ratios are used.   For the 26 nonmanufacturing groups, most of which are local markets, a very preliminary estimate of the equivalent four-firm concentration prevailing in

---

[18] The data cover only firms with 100 or more employees.   This limitation is probably, on balance, an advantage, for it focuses the analysis on policies of significant business enterprises.

[19] The industry groups do mask some of the known variations of market structure in four-digit manufacturing industries (S.I.C. 20–39), but these groups do differ fairly sharply and perhaps accurately in their average degrees of concentration.   Moreover, for *non*manufacturing groups (S.I.C. 13–19, 40–82), no systematic market structure data exist at all, so that one will have to resort to approximate estimates in any event; and trying to estimate for four-digit trades and services would be stretching things, perhaps too far.   In any case, many large firms and relevant markets transcend four-digit industries, so that quite a bit of grossing up would be appropriate even if it were not necessary.

[20] The cities are Atlanta, Chicago, Cleveland, Kansas City, Los Angeles, New Orleans, New York, San Francisco, and Washington, D.C.; see also E.E.O.C., *Nine City Minority Group Profile*, Research Report 1967–19–A, (Washington, D.C.: mimeographed).

[21] Despite their importance, intercity variations (especially between Northern and Southern cities) neither swamp nor cause the interindustry patterns of Negro employment.   The interindustry patterns are relatively stable across all of the cities; only the city-wide averages vary substantially.

larger metropolitan areas was made.[22]   These are crude and incomplete indicators of structure, but they may permit at least an outline of the phenomenon.

Employment patterns are shown primarily by Negro shares of all white-collar employees.   In addition, since the more numerous clerical jobs (many held by Negro women) dominate much of the data, patterns within the subgroups of managerial and professional employees were also isolated for a separate analysis.[23]

The basic data are summarized in Appendix Table 18.   The sharpest difference, at the outset, is between (1) public and nonprofit entities (medical, educational, etc.; S.I.C. groups 80, 82, and 86), and (2) all profit-making enterprises.   The nonprofit groups' Negro share is significantly higher on the average, by all three categories of employment.   There are some sizeable intercity variations; moreover, some of the higher shares in nonprofit entities reflect mainly clerical and technical, rather than managerial, positions. Yet the basic contrast is clear.

Three separate but related tests of detailed inter-industry patterns were made, with results as shown in Figures 14.1, 14.2 and 14.3.   First, average Negro shares in all white-collar employment were analysed against concentration.   Figure 14.1 suggests a negative association across all 46 groups, as well as within the manufacturing and nonmanufacturing subsectors separately; it is shown by the line AA in the figure.   Communications (48) is the only exceptional case, perhaps reflecting deliberate affirmative policies, by telephone systems (but confined chiefly to clerical jobs; see Figure 14.3, below). Approximately, a 20-percentage point increase in concentration is associated with a 15–20 percent reduction in the Negro share.   A fuller allowance for other structural elements would probably improve the fit.[24]   Even so, the association is closer than has come to be common in cross section analyses of the effects of market structure.   Separate tests of the Northern and Southern cities in the sample indicated that the overall pattern did not stem

---

[22] In order to avoid a false appearance of precision, a 10-decile spectrum was used to represent the range of concentration, by 10-point brackets from 0 to 100 percent.   Despite their evident artificiality, these estimations do reflect market conditions in these urban centres about as closely and reasonably as is now possible.   Although all of the ratios leave out other elements of market structure, concentration is probably of primary importance in most of them.   Also, the use of metropolitan data tends to normalize some of the other possible determinants (such as market size, urban growth rates, local educational patterns, racial composition of population, migration rates, etc.).

The chief industry information that might be added in future analysis would be industry growth, interfirm cooperation, and specialized white-collar skill requirements.   But these and other candidates pose serious measurement problems, and some of them have already turned out to lack a clear association with patterns of discrimination.   They and others are, in any case, being incorporated in further work by the author and others.

[23] Yet the consistency of the two approaches (Figures 14.1 and 14.3) suggests that the gross white-collar data are fairly reliable indicators.

[24] For example, adjustments for vertical integration and other factors in industry groups 26, 34, and 35 would probably shift them appreciably to the right in Figure 14.1.   As it stands, the r^2 is .69 for the curvilinear function.

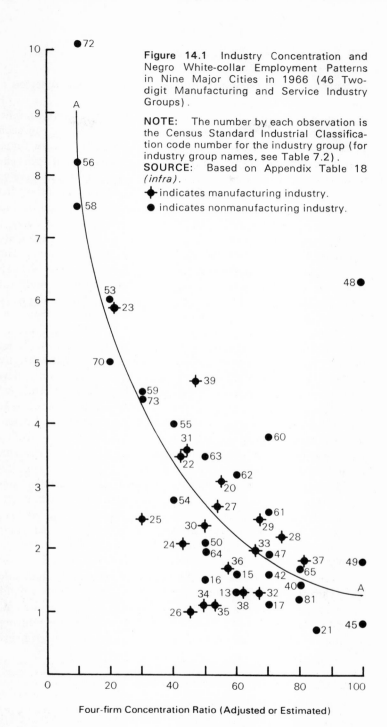

Figure 14.1 Industry Concentration and Negro White-collar Employment Patterns in Nine Major Cities in 1966 (46 Two-digit Manufacturing and Service Industry Groups).

NOTE: The number by each observation is the Census Standard Industrial Classification code number for the industry group (for industry group names, see Table 7.2).
SOURCE: Based on Appendix Table 18 *(infra)*.

✦ indicates manufacturing industry.

● indicates nonmanufacturing industry.

primarily from interregional differences, but instead reflected a true inter-industry covariation.

Second, the primary data on individual firms were searched for those firms with the *highest* Negro percentage in each industry in each city. The patterns of these "highest"-percentage firms would indicate, for each industry under local conditions, the degree to which at least some firms can exceed the average Negro share and remain viable. They might also serve as an approximate indicator of the immediate scope for rises by the other firms.[25]

These "highest"-percentage data posed some special problems of compilation and analysis, and so the results must be used cautiously. The resulting patterns are shown in Figure 14.2. A negative association emerges again with (as would be expected) rather more dispersion. The concentration-employment tradeoff is about the same as in Figure 14.1 (15–20 percent per 10 points of concentration). The observations lie well above the line fitted to the Figure 14.1 data (shown by line AA in Figure 14.2). Very broadly, the "high" percentage cases tend to range between 4 and 10 percent higher.

Some specific impressions from searching through the data may also be noted. Within industries, the smaller-firm Negro shares are more variable than leading firms' shares; but the leading firms are almost never the pace-setters, with the highest percentages. There is some tendency for Negro shares to be higher in trades where exposure to customers in a service-providing role is important, particularly in retail trades and personal services. To this extent, nondiscrimination may simply reflect clear profit-maximizing. Yet, in any case, an attempt to factor out this possible determinant would probably not alter the basic pattern.

Moreover, high-concentration industries (especially among manufacturing, some utilities, and law) show relatively constant levels of high-percentage instances among all cities. By contrast, low-concentration industries show much more intercity variety among high-percentage instances. These variations presumably reflect local differences in attitudes and labor supply, to which the high-concentration industries are less sensitive.

This further attests that the degree of monopoly does affect minority group hiring as an independent factor. Since (as noted above) public agencies and nonprofit entities are relatively high employers of white-collar Negroes, the following general conclusion appears warranted—open hiring of Negroes is found mainly in competitive industries, in some lesser firms in concentrated industries, and in nonprofit entities.

---

[25] Alan Batchelder, *Employment of Negroes in the Rubber Industry,* prepared for the U.S. Equal Employment Opportunity Commission, (Washington, D.C.: mimeographed 1967); and E.E.O.C. "White Collar Employment in 100 Major New York City Corporations," *Hearings on Discrimination in White Collar Employment* (Washington, D.C.: U.S. Government Printing Office, 1968), 582–620.

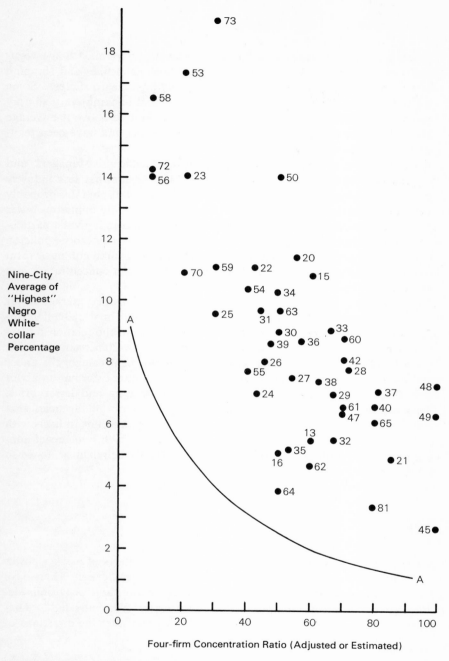

Figure 14.2 Industry Concentration and "Highest"-Percentage Patterns of Negro White-Collar Employment in Nine Major Cities in 1966.

NOTE: The number by each observation is the Census Standard Industrial Classification code number for the industry group (for industry group names, see Table 7.2).
SOURCE: Based on Appendix Table 18 (*infra*).

Regulated firms' percentages are exceptionally variable. Some regulated firms exclude Negroes almost absolutely (such as airlines and shipping firms in many cities), while others have relatively high Negro shares. Some (such as electric and gas utilities, urban transit, and banking) vary sharply from city to city. As a whole, regulated firms do not lie above the average association, even though they have high market power and have been regulated for decades "in the public interest."

The third test focuses on the employment of Officials, Managers, and Professional, with results shown in Figure 14.3. Somewhat less industry detail can be shown, owing to certain limits in the basic data; but this probably does not affect the results. This test factors out the more numerous lower white-collar positions (clerical, sales, and technical), and so it gives a particularly pointed test of the openness of hiring by those who set enterprise policies. The results strongly reaffirm the negative association, again in nonlinear form and with about the same proportional trade-off between concentration and Negro employment.

Altogether, these findings confirm earlier suggestions that market power is positively and substantially related to discrimination in white-collar employment. In the three parallel tests, the magnitudes of the relationship are consistent—for each added 10 concentration points, a 15–20 percent reduction in the Negro share of whatever white-collar employment category is under analysis. The pattern is confirmed by a variety of other information about large firms and about intracity patterns among leading and lesser firms. Generally speaking, it is in competitive firms and nonprofit agencies that employment tends to be relatively nondiscriminatory, and not in firms with market power. Evidently, firms with market power, which *could* enact nondiscriminatory employment policies, cannot normally be relied on to do so voluntarily.

ADDITIONAL EFFECTS

Although no systematic evidence about the broader effects of market power can be presented, one should not conclude that they do not exist. There have been indications that the quality of civic participation and provisions declines when major local enterprise come under control from outside.[26] That the interaction of corporate and military interests may alter the directions of

---

[26] "Small Business and Civic Welfare," Report of the Smaller War Plants Corporation to the Special Committee to Study Problems of American Small Business, U.S. Senate, 79th Congress, 2nd Session, Senate Doc. 135 (Washington, D.C.: U.S. Government Printing Office, 1946); and *Report of a Committee of the Rochester Chamber of Commerce on the Out-of-Town Acquisition of Rochester Companies,* cited in Estes Kefauver, *In a Few Hands* (New York: Random House, 1965), Ch. 5.

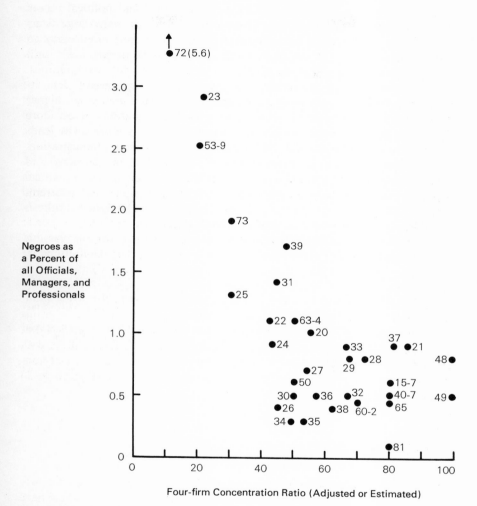

Figure 14.3 Industry Concentration and Negro Employment as Officials, Managers and Professionals in Nine Major Cities in 1966.

NOTE: The number by each observation is the Census Standard Industrial Classification code number for the industry group (for industry group names, see Table 7.2).

SOURCE: Based on Appendix Table 18 (*infra*).

national policy and affect the chances for international stability has been pointed out by Galbraith and many others.[27]

More generally, market power may provide social and political power on levels ranging from local to international. Although many large firms are reluctant to engage in local issues, their own decisions often carry so much impact that they are thrust into the center of local problems.[28] Still other firms actively use their economic leverage on individual communities. On a larger plane, high concentration of both types has appeared to lend itself to dictatorships, perhaps most evidently in Germany and Japan before and during World War II. Not only may corporate and state interest more closely combine, but, in addition, a concentrated economy more easily lends itself to control and manipulation by a determined political administration. This concern underlay the postwar trust-busting efforts in Germany and Japan.[29] No definitive proof that market power tends to encourage political absolution can ever be expected, since each case is complex and different. But the experience of Germany and Japan, as well as Italy, lend the hypothesis no small support, at least as a statement of probabilities.

Therefore few observers of the problem regard these various possible social effects lightly. Least provable of all by statistics, they may ultimately be the most important.

---

[27] Galbraith, *The New Industrial State*, 325–353; see also F. M. Scherer, "The Aerospace Industry," in Walter Adams, ed., *The Structure of American Industry*, 4th ed. (New York: Macmillan, 1970).

[28] See Carl Kaysen, "The Corporation: How Much Power? What Scope?" in Edward S. Mason, ed., *The Corporation in Modern Society* (Cambridge: Harvard University Press, 1959), Ch. 5.

[29] See T. A. Bisson, *Zaibatsu Dissolution in Japan* (Berkeley: University of California Press, 1954); and *Economic Concentration, Part 7 (1968)*, 3441–3467 and 3508–3434.

Chapter 15

Two Major Examples
of Market Power:
Computers and Automobiles

Outside the field of public utilities, the position of a
single seller can in general be conquered—and retained for
decades—only on the condition that he does not behave like
a monopolist.

From a fierce life and death struggle three [automobile]
concerns emerged that by now account for over 80 percent of
total sales.   They are under competitive pressure inasmuch
as, in spite of the advantages of an established position, an
elaborate sales and service organization and so on, any
failure to keep up and improve the quality of their products
or any attempt at monopolistic combination would call in
new competitors.

JOSEPH A. SCHUMPETER
Capitalism, Socialism and Democracy (1942)

In exploring the many forms and effects of market power, the narrative has
had to be rather fragmented and roundabout.   In order to fix the problem
in more concrete detail and to show how the elements and effects come
together in actual cases, this chapter outlines two of the most prominent
situations of market power in the United States: the leading firms in the
computer and automobile industries.   The brief accounts which follow are
intended to show the main points, even though they make no attempt at a
comprehensive treatment.

COMPUTERS

The International Business Machines company has held over 90 percent of
the tabulating machine and cards industry for more than four decades.   The
Antitrust Division brought suit against IBM in 1952, alleging monopolization

under the Sherman Act, but the case was settled by a consent decree in 1956.[1] IBM agreed to accept mild constraints, and its basic position was left intact. IBM continues to dominate the old electromechanical card-tabulating field, the so-called first generation. IBM's tabulating machines are in most significant computer installations because of this.

Meanwhile, during the early 1950's the electronic computer, pioneered largely by univac division of Remington Rand and various university scientists, entered the scene. IBM's position in tabulating machines enabled it to move (even while the 1956 decree was in negotiation) directly into dominance of this new phase of the industry, the second generation. IBM's rolling reserve of lease revenues from its tabulating equipment funded the development and introduction of the new computers, and its extensive sales and support network adapted fairly readily to the new systems. From the outset, IBM provided special bargains to university users, thereby attaching the core of computer users and trainees to IBM systems and programming languages.

Competitors began bringing out third-generation models during the early 1960's. In 1964, IBM announced in some haste its third generation of computers—the 360 line, with about eight model lines—designed to offer virtual commonality from small to large systems.[2] After some serious teething problems and delays, this array of systems seems to have assured IBM's dominance for at least the next decade, and perhaps for the rest of this century.[3] Therefore the 1956 settlement not only left the original monopoly intact; it also partially cloaked and immunized IBM's virtual monopolization of the "new" computer industry.

Most informed public estimates are that IBM has maintained at least a 70 percent share of the basic computer market, rising toward 75 precent in 1968.[4] Growing at about 17 percent yearly, the market has now become one of the largest in the economy, with no slackening of its growth yet in prospect. The three generations are shown in Figure 15.1. In the face of such extreme growth, IBM's retention of its high market share (as shown in Figure 15.2) is without parallel in modern industry. A series of major firms have had little success in challenging IBM's full-line position, even after 15 years. Most of these, including General Electric and RCA, are said to have still not broken even financially on computer activities; that is, they are apparently driven to prolonged cross-subsidizing. Only two small specialized science-oriented firms (Control Data and Scientific Data Systems) have

---

[1] The decree was Civil Action 72–344, Southern District of New York. For background on the industry's evolution, see George Schussel, "IBM vs. REMRAND," *Datamation*, XI, Nos. 5 and 6 (1965), 54–66; see also Ralph E. Miller, *The Computer Industry* (Berkeley: mimeographed, 1969).
[2] T. A. Wise, "IBM's $5 Billion Gamble," Parts 1 and 2, *Fortune*, September and October 1966, respectively.
[3] *Forbes*, March 1, 1968, 48.
[4] *EDP Industry Report and Market Review*, July 31, 1968, 1, 3, 4, 7.

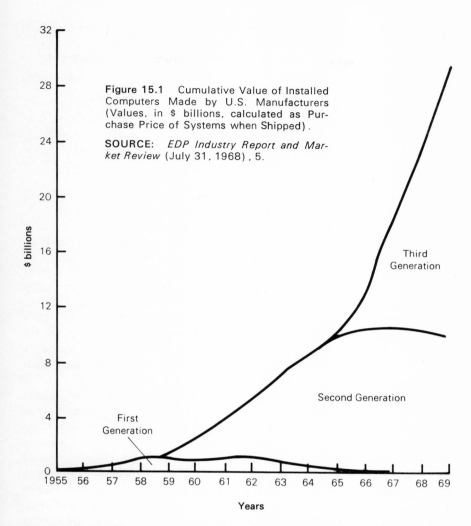

Figure 15.1 Cumulative Value of Installed Computers Made by U.S. Manufacturers (Values, in $ billions, calculated as Purchase Price of Systems when Shipped).

SOURCE: *EDP Industry Report and Market Review* (July 31, 1968), 5.

Third Generation

Second Generation

First Generation

$ billions

Years

apparently turned a profit. Several sizeable firms, (including Bendix, Raytheon and Ford-Philco) have dropped out altogether.

IBM therefore remains probably about 10 times larger than any of its seven or so "main" competitors. Asymmetry is evidently great. Divergence is probably fairly great; IBM has at least 12 locations for designing and producing computers.[5] Much of the design work has been in common; and the sales and customer-support network—that is, the retailing and leasing system—is an important element in IBM's overall success (see below). But many activities (particularly production of equipment) are decentralized.

---

[5] *Plant and Product Directory, 1965–66* (New York: *Fortune*, 1966).

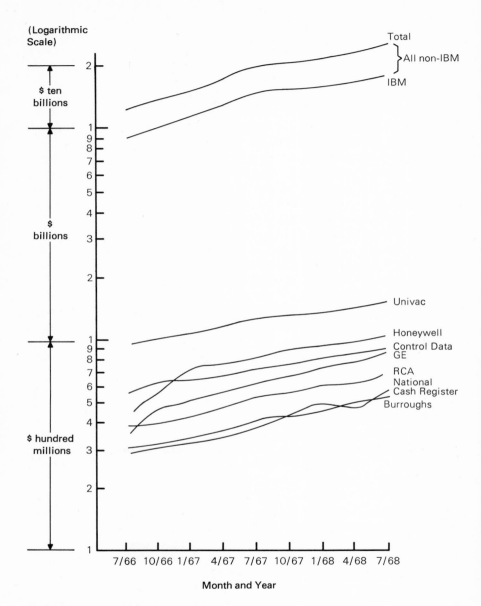

Figure 15.2 Total Value of Computers Installed by U.S. Manufacturers, 1966–1968 (Cumulative Value at Purchase Prices).

SOURCE: *EDP Industry Report and Market Review*, (July 31, 1968), 7.

Among informal elements, the most important are the very high barriers to new entry. Because IBM's pricing strategy has deliberately fostered leasing rather than selling of computers, entrants require large financial reserves to tide over the initial period of building up a stock of leased equipment.[6] Moreover, an entrant must develop a sales-and-support network capable of matching IBM's ability to provide free planning and programming for customers' systems.

IBM's relative size (seventh among all U.S. manufacturing firms in 1969) is now very large. Perhaps even more important, IBM's leasing and customer-relations policies have forestalled the emergence of major leasing firms able to exert substantial contervailing power as buyers. Only in 1968–1969 were leasing firms emerging as a significant factor.

All in all, IBM's position verges on monopoly in economic even if not in legal terms.[7] A high and steady market share is reinforced by several other major elements of market power. Further growth will probably sustain or enlarge this monopoly position, not erode it.

The original source of this position was the earlier tabulating monopoly, particularly the very large sales and support force and the lease-revenue reserves which it provided. Contrary to popular impressions carefully cultivated, IBM is not regarded professionally as a leading inventor or innovator. A series of major improvements have originated with other sources, with IBM often following developments. IBM has been outclassed in the large-scale scientific computer market, despite strenuous efforts over many years. Its 360-line announcement in 1964 was widely regarded as hasty, made under competitive pressures from superior competitive models in some lines.[8] This was confirmed by IBM's severe problems and delays in making and delivering 360 computers during 1965 and 1966. IBM has also been a follower in developing computer time-sharing systems.

Under these circumstances, IBM appears to have gained and held its market share mainly via substantial and pervasive price discrimination of several sorts. This is possible because IBM probably has large amounts of overhead or floating costs in its development and sales-support activities. Accordingly, IBM is inherently able and induced by rational profit-maximizing to engage in systematic price discrimination on a large scale. This has probably played a major role in forestalling new entry except in isolated

---

[6] Although the decree obliged IBM to sell as well as lease, the proportion of systems sold was still less than one-sixth in 1964. More recently sales have risen more rapidly, to about one-quarter, and the resulting surge in profits has cuased *concern* in IBM.

[7] This section was written before the U.S. Department of Justice brought suit against IBM on January 17, 1969, alleging monopolization of the general purpose computer industry. The basis of that suit parallels some of the analysis in this section. A full trial and disposition of the case may take at lea:t five years and more probably ten, and an earlier settlement is widely regarded as likely; see *The Wall Street Journal*, January 20, 1969. Two similar private suits, by Control Data Corporation and Data Processing Financial and General Corporation, were filed in December 1968 and January 1969. The Federal suit is *United States v. International Business Machines Corp.*, 69 CIV 200, U.S. District Court, Southern District of New York.

[8] Wise, *op. cit.*

submarkets (such as large systems) where IBM's technical inferiority is so great that it cannot be offset.

The role of overhead costs and price discrimination is important enough to deserve some elaboration here. Very roughly speaking, the production cost of computers probably averages less than 20 percent of price, while general costs for development, sales, and customer support may be more than half, according to industry analysts. IBM charges virtually all buyers standard prices for computer systems and components, so-called hardware.[9] IBM also provides varying amounts of programming and other assistance (so-called software) to customers, usually without charge. Certain buyers get access to IBM's various inventories of general programming, and in an increasing variety of industries and trades they are literally given various programs with specific industry applications, which IBM prepared and which IBM salesmen use as a major sales sweetener. Moreover, IBM has provided substantial amounts of "customer support" (that is, the personal assistance of IBM staff programmers and engineers at the customer's location) directly to buyers without charge, but with wide variations among the individual cases. Ordinarily, and understandably, this free assistance would tend to be promised and provided up to the point necessary to secure the contract which is being sought.

Therefore, the main overhead or floating costs within IBM probably have four main sources. First, as noted, the actual production costs of hardware are a small fraction of total costs (and a still smaller fraction of total revenues). Second, product development involves extensive mingling of engineering and programming resources across a whole series of systems, so that (1) a large share of hardware and software costs may be inseparably merged, and (2) in making cost assignments among individual system types (such as among the various models in the 360 series) IBM may have wide latitude for free choice.[10] Third, IBM has accumulated a large reserve of software, which it makes available free of charge, and exclusively, to users. Fourth IBM's resources in its national network of "customer engineers," its other assignable programmers, and its other sources of free customer support, may be substantial enough in themselves to yield some systematic price discrimination in marketing computers.

In these four main directions alone, IBM probably contains a large volume of overhead costs and resources, which IBM is able to assign among the individual machines and users largely at will. These overhead costs create possibilities of effective discrimination both "vertically," among the separate model series ranging from the small 1401's up through the large

---

[9] Explicit departures from standard hardware prices are made only for educational and some other nonprofit institutions. These discounts have ranged from 20 percent to 100 percent and possibly more.
[10] Thus Wise, *op. cit.*—the pricing process for the 360 line may have involved virtually "pulling cost estimates out a hat" (Part 2, p. 206).

360/95's, and "horizontally," among the different buyers for each individual machine type. In assigning these costs (if it does so) and in setting prices, IBM would inevitably be induced to pattern its prices preemptively, to "meet competition," in ways which would have the effect of undercutting prices of other firms and forestalling competition and market entry. In this, IBM would ordinarily be successful in getting sales that it really wants, because its large element of common costs and programming-support capacity would enable it to match or beat virtually any smaller rival on any particular sale (except where IBM's technical inferiority may be so great that it cannot be overcome). It would also provide leverage to improve IBM's share in related markets, in close analogy to recognized patterns of pricing and diversification by public utilities, which take advantage of their overhead cost elements.[11] This would be true whether the patterns are set deliberately and systematically at the top level, or simply arise in the course of hard-selling at grass-roots levels throughout the separate parts of the business.

Effective and systematic price discrimination would be most likely to occur in two ways. First, the models on which competition is keenest would be priced closer to direct costs than are other less competitive lines. These would, in the extreme cases, be the so-called fighting machines. There would result either a true difference in IBM's rates of return on different model lines, or at least different ratios between direct costs and average revenues on individual models.

The second possible pattern of discrimination would be in the provision of software. This subdivides into two parts. (1) Buyers are given free use of much of IBM's existing general-purpose and specific programming, whether or not they need it. This now leads to at least a partial differentiation among users in the pricing of services. (2) More directly, specific customer support varies (perhaps widely) among users, and presumably it varies systematically according to competitive conditions for each contract. Though significant, this would be only the tip of the iceberg and by itself would not lead to substantial discrimination.[12]

The whole problem and its anticompetitive effect could exist even though IBM's prices in no case actually go below direct assigned (or assignable) cost levels. This is mainly because direct costs are a relatively small share of all costs. Insofar as these pricing patterns exist, they would tend to over-price the systems to large and experienced users, while subsidizing IBM's selective efforts to capture sales to the new and less experienced users, for whom free general programming resources and programming support may

---

[11] Recall Harvey Averch and Leland L. Johnson, "Behavior of the Firm Under Regulatory Constraint," *American Economic Review*, LII (December 1962) 1052–1069, and W. G. Shepherd and T. G. Gies, *Utility Regulation* (New York: Random House, 1966), Chapter 1.
[12] In December 1968, IBM announced an intention to develop separate pricing of customer-support software and related services by June 1969. But this would not correct the major part of the floating costs and potential price discrimination, only the most readily visible part.

be critical. This involves substantial and systematic discrimination among markets and users in patterns which would tend to subsidize IBM sales and leases in the newer, growing markets. On this basis, IBM's dominant position and its continuation could not accurately be regarded as having been "thrust upon" it. These patterns would tend to preserve IBM's dominance in central equipment, not through superior technical performance, but instead because the large overhead-cost element permits and induces IBM to price preemptively and exclusionarily. This is in contrast to sporadic price discrimination in competitive markets, which is a procompetitive phenomenon.

In this context, IBM's educational discounts (which until 1969 ranged between 40 and 60 percent off standard prices) can be regarded as a magnified and explicit instance of the general pattern. IBM's assessment of the net long-run benefits obtained by maximizing the clientele which is trained and accustomed to use IBM systems had led it to offer discounts to universities which other firms could not match. This has apparently involved explicit and substantial cross-subsidizing, and, in long-run terms, it has evidently been a rational tactic for IBM, in maximizing *total* profits and market share. It has also cultivated a reliance of much of the scientific and intellectual community upon IBM "generosity." Whatever the beneficial side-effects of such research subsidies may be, the subsidies have probably been substantial and have had a significant anticompetitive effect for the long run. They have also tended to reduce competition in the related markets by limiting the training of a large share of potential customers to IBM hardware and software.

Price discrimination as outlined above tends to undercut the basis upon which other firms specializing in related equipment and software can compete and develop. It also probably has helped to prevent the emergence of strong service bureaus and leasing systems, which might otherwise have been expected to arise in a countervailing position to IBM.

These are evidently questions of degree, involving both the magnitudes of overhead cost and programming support and the sharpness with which they vary among models and users. If they are significant at all, they help preserve IBM's basic position and enhance its ability to capture a large share in the more competitive markets for software, associated equipment, and time-sharing and related services. In these related markets, the technical preconditions for competition are much more favorable, and they might otherwise serve as a basis for neutralizing IBM's ability to exploit its position or for promoting competitive new inroads against IBM's position in the central processing-equipment market.

Turning now to effects, IBM's profitability has fully reflected its market position. During 1956–1967, its return on net worth averaged 17.6 percent; only twice did the rate go below 17.0 percent, and in recent years it has risen strongly. Among the 50 largest industrials, only General Motors has shown consistently higher profit rates in recent years. IBM's risk factor is further reduced by its continuing revenue reserve from leased machines, which assures continuity in the revenue flow, and also by its dominance of most foreign computer markets as well as the domestic one. That such high profitability has induced only marginal entry indicates that entry barriers are very high indeed.

It may possibly be that IBM's policies marginally promoted the growth of the industry during the early period of the 1950's. But this development phase is now past, and it is probable that industry growth would be more rapid under looser oligopoly (such as with three or four successor IBM entities, and/or with IBM confined to only a manufacturer-seller role). If users were required to pay for all separable software services, the allocation of such activities would probably be significantly more efficient than it is now, under patterns of discrimination.

The net loss of innovation has also probably been significant. IBM, as noted, has tended to follow many technical advances, particularly time-sharing and scientific systems. A freer market, with more independent sources of innovation, would probably yield more rapid and varied advances, especially now that IBM is heavily committed to its existing 360 line. IBM's primary incentive is to sell computer time (that is, leasing of machines). This encourages its software design to be machine-time intensive. This alone has probably led to significant efficiency loss. As the largest industrial monopolist (second among American firms only to the AT&T monopoly of telephone service and production of telephone equipment), IBM inevitably faces difficulty in enforcing internal efficiency, since hierarchical control loss and the lack of competitive pressure may foster softness. There are no firm indicators of IBM's circumstances in this respect, so the issue cannot be settled precisely.

The main distributional impact of IBM's position has been toward disequalizing wealth holdings via sharp capital gains for shareowners. Of IBM's recent market value of $36 billion (recall Chapter 14), perhaps $5 billion to $8 billion reflected expectations of pure monopoly gains. Indeed, growing fears of an antitrust challenge to IBM's position helped cause in 1968 a drop from $42 billion; so at the peak, the monopoly effect on capital value was probably almost certainly $6 billion at the very least, and more likely about $15 billion. Since the challenge is at best likely to reduce the monopoly only moderately and after a long delay, a substantial monopoly element undoubtedly remains.

IBM has recently made deliberate efforts toward equal opportunity for minorities through training programs and urban improvement projects. But it is not clear that the whole structure of opportunities, including managerial positions, has been better than a more competitive setting would have yielded.

The main possible external effect has been the net advancement of science which IBM's educational discounts may have underwritten (although the net true costs to IBM have not always been as great as they have seemed to the recipients). This net effect may have been substantial, at least in some fields. But it could be paid for in other ways, such as by direct educational expenditure. The present situation raises the possibility that IBM has purchased the loyalty of the educational community while pursuing its aim of training potential users to IBM systems. An appraisal of the net costs and benefits of IBM's market position should regard the seeming promotion of knowledge with a skeptical eye.

AUTOMOBILES

The American automobile industry is virtually all held by three very large firms, with the protection of virtually absolute barriers to entry. It is the most prominent tight oligopoly in the United States—probably in the world— and its behavior fits many of the predictions for such an asymmetrical tight oligopoly.[13]

In recent years, General Motors, Ford, and Chrysler have accounted for about 97 percent of American automobile production, and about 87–90 percent of all automobile sales, including imports, in the United States. Table 15.1 shows the individual shares. It also reflects the rise of concentration in the early 1950's as several smaller firms dropped out. More recently, a resumption of the upward trend of concentration, after American Motors' brief rise during 1957–1960, has threatened the survival of American Motors also. In only a relatively few American industries of any significant size is concentration so stable and likely to rise further.

In the submarkets for medium and higher-priced models (above $2300), the Big Three's share approaches 100 percent, since American Motors' production and most imported cars generally fall in the low-price category (see Table 15.2).[14]

There is marked asymmetry among the leading firms, and General Motors' share alone has been frequently said to verge on monopoly. Clearly, General Motors sets some basic patterns of behavior for the three, as will shortly be noted. Divergence is fairly great. General Motors' five divisions —Cadillac, Buick, Oldsmobile, Pontiac, and Chevrolet (which is virtually a multiple division)—have at least 22 separate assembly plants, Ford has 17, and Chrysler has 5, as Table 15.3 shows.[15]

---

[13] See also Joe S. Bain, *Industrial Organization* (New York: Wiley, 1968), 137–138, 285–287, 346–347, and Lawrence J. White, *The American Automobile Industry in the Postwar Period* (Cambridge: Harvard University Ph.D. dissertation, 1969).

[14] Although the price ranges are not wholly separable markets, downward entry into the lower ranges (as with compact cars) is undoubtedly easier than upward-moving entry would be. Therefore the higher market-share of the three leading firms in the upper ranges has some relevance in appraising market power and the possibilities of new competition in the major markets.

[15] In 1968 General Motors announced a regrouping of some plants to centralize control over their operations. This would tend to reduce somewhat the independence and separability of the divisions. Not all of the assembly plants are easily substitutable and separable within firms, but among most of the plants the assembly operations are essentially similar.

TABLE 15.1 SHARES OF U.S. AUTOMOBILE PRODUCTION

	1940	1951	1955	1960	1961	1962	1963	1964	1965	1966	1967
General Motors	45.9	42.2	50.2	47.7	49.4	54.0	53.4	51.1	53.1	51.7	55.6
Ford	19.0	21.8	28.2	28.8	30.6	27.9	25.7	27.7	27.5	28.2	22.9
Chrysler	25.1	23.1	17.2	15.1	11.8	10.3	13.7	16.1	15.7	16.8	18.4
American Motors	4.0	4.8	1.7	7.3	6.8	6.6	6.3	5.1	3.7	3.3	3.1
Others	6.0	8.1	2.7	1.6	1.4	1.3	.9	—	—	—	—
Total	100.0	100.0	100.0	100.0	100.0	100.0	100.0	100.0	100.0	100.0	100.0
Total: GM, Ford, and Chrysler	90.0	87.1	95.6	91.1	91.8	92.1	92.8	94.9	96.3	96.7	96.9

SOURCE: Compiled from Ward's *Automotive Yearbooks* (annual).

233

TABLE 15.2   U.S. AUTO PRODUCTION BY $500 PRICE GROUPS 1966 MODEL YEAR

Factory List Price Group	Number of Autos (thousands)				Shares of Industry Total (percent)			GM, Ford and Chrysler
	GM	Ford	Chrysler	Industry Total	GM	Ford	Chrysler	
$2,000 or less	69	58	83	256	26.7	22.7	32.5	81.9
$2,001–2,500	1,294	1,179	549	3,231	40.0	36.5	17.0	93.5
$2,501–3,000	2,148	858	656	3,704	58.0	23.2	17.7	98.9
$3,001–3,500	384	250	81	715	53.7	35.0	11.3	100.0
$3,501–4,000	119	3	65	186	63.8	1.3	34.9	100.0
$4,000 and up	377	124	14	515	73.2	24.1	2.7	100.0
Total	4,390	2,472	1,448	8,606	51.0	28.7	16.8	96.6

SOURCE: Adapted from Ward's *Automotive Yearbooks* (annual).

Entry has been effectively closed for at least two decades. Kaiser's postwar attempt at entry failed, while the steady attrition of smaller firms has continued, with Studebaker the latest in 1962, and American Motors presently with hazardous prospects.[16]

Market shares of the three firms have been relatively stable, even during sharp recessions. There have been some tendencies toward joint activities, particularly on development of safety and antismog devices. Yet informal "structure" has been mostly implicit, in consciously parallel pricing, design and market behavior (see below).

The leading firms are very large; General Motors in 1968 ranks first; Ford, third; and Chrysler, fifth in sales among all American industrial corporations (ranked by assets they are second, third, and thirteenth, respectively). This strengthens entry barriers. The list of comparably large firms includes only a few oil, steel, and electrical-equipment companies. Barring radical and improbable changes in technology or other factors, it is less likely that these firms might attempt to enter automobile production than that the automobile firms might enter their industries (as indeed they have entered electrical appliances, aircraft engines, electronics, and other fields). Although they are primarily automobile manufacturers, the three firms have substantial other activities. All three have extensive activities abroad; all three are leading truck makers; and all three do a variety of appliance and

---

[16] See Harold G. Vatter, "The Closure of Entry in The American Automobile Industry," *Oxford Economic Papers*, IV (October 1952), 213–234; Joe S. Bain, *Barriers to New Competition* (Cambridge: Harvard University Press, 1956); L. W. Weiss, *Economics and American Industry* (New York: Wiley, 1961); U.S. Senate Subcommittee on Antitrust and Monopoly, 85th Congress, 2nd Session, *Report of the Study of Administered Prices in the Automobile Industry* (Washington, D.C.: U.S. Government Printing Office, 1958); and R. F. Lanzillotti, "The Automobile Industry," in W. Adams, ed., *The Structure of the American Economy*, 3rd ed. (New York: Macmillan, 1961).

TABLE 15.3 THE SIZE DISTRIBUTION OF AUTOMOBILE PLANTS, 1965–1966

Output Size Range, 1965–1966 (1,000 cars)	General Motors		Ford		Chrysler		American Motors	
	Number of Plants	Average Output (thousands)	Number of Plants	Average Output (thousands)	Number of Plants	Average Output (thousands)	Number of Plants	Average Output (thousands)
51–100	—	—	3	84	2	86	—	—
101–150	2	139	6	123	—	—	—	—
151–200	10	176	4	185	1	166	—	—
201–250	6	220	2	224	1	220	—	—
251–300	2	286	1	267	—	—	—	—
301–350	1	329	—	—	—	316	—	—
351–400	1	376	1	371	—	—	1	391
401+	—	—	—	—	1	503	—	—

NOTE: To indicate plant capacity, and to deemphasize erratic yearly fluctuations, the plant output levels are for whichever output level was higher, 1965 or 1966. This gives as reliable an indication of plant capacity in recent years as is possible with available data.
SOURCE: Compiled from Ward's *Automotive Yearbooks* (1966 and 1967).

defense work. In addition, General Motors holds virtually a monopoly in U.S. production of buses and locomotives.

As for vertical patterns, the three producers have managed to prevent the emergence of countervailing power among both their suppliers and their retailers, via common policies. Altogether, the leading automobile firms hold market power as great as in any nonregulated American industry. Their joint market power is more likely to continue growing than to recede.

The sources of this shared monopoly are of several sorts—primarily the model change and dealer-franchising policies of the major firms. Production scale economies apparently do *not* prescribe the present structure. In the mid-1950's, an annual production of 300,000 to 600,000 cars was large enough to enable a manufacturer to achieve all significant economies of scale in production.[17] There is no evidence that recent developments have substantially raised the efficient scale of assembly plant operations. Indeed, the size of production necessary to achieve scale economies may have gone down; all three firms continue to produce cars from many plants, and the newer plants are generally smaller than the older ones.[18] General Motors contains, in essentials, the equivalent of possibly three largely self-contained automobile producers, each with a full array of major-parts capacity (engines, transmissions, etc.) and assembly plants. Ford contains the equivalent of perhaps two producers.[19] Certain design and proving activities are company-wide, but these are relatively divisible and are probably not of dominant importance.

One source of the present structure is that the leading firms have established frequent model changes as the industry pattern. The practice was begun by General Motors in 1927, was accelerated during the 1950's, and still continues to be rapid. It has helped foreclose entry and penalize smaller producers, because small and new firms have been unable to spread the design and retooling costs of each model run over enough units to achieve minimum efficient size. This has sharply, and artificially, raised barriers to entry by imposing higher overhead costs.[20]

A second source is the manufacturers' distribution policy. First, the firms market their cars only through their franchised dealer network; this has prevented the emergence of automobile discounting and other forms of

---

[17] Bain, *Barriers to New Competition*, Lanzillotti, *op. cit.;* and *Report of the Study of Administered Prices*.

[18] See Table 15.2. This is shown by the underlying data on plant sizes during the last several years. No new plants are being built on the scale of the largest older plants; most of them are evidently of about 100,000 cars yearly capacity, which is well below the previous average. This may largely reflect changing transport and locational factors, but it still casts light on minimum efficient production scale.

[19] See *Plant and Product Directory* (New York: *Fortune*, 1966); and *Automotive Industries* (January 15, 1966 and January 15, and February 1, 1968).

[20] See *Report of the Study of Administered Prices*, 77–94; Bain, *Industrial Organization*; see also John A. Menge, "Style Change Costs as a Market Weapon," *Quarterly Journal of Economics*, LXXVI (November 1962), 632–647.

retailing, which could ultimately make new entry into production easier.[21] Second, the firms appear responsible for the "convention" that dealers do not sell other manufacturers' cars; in at least one instance (among Chrysler dealers) this "convention" apparently helped to drive out a small manufacturer (Studebaker).[22] There is wide agreement that a dealer system and the capital required to create one have become a major (perhaps the major) requirement for entry.[23] Yet the necessity for such a system is not based on economies of scale in distribution; on the contrary, this reflects primarily the exclusive policies governing the retailing of automobiles.

Another factor raising entry barriers is backward vertical integration into production of components and parts. Such integration has been substantial and rising in the last two decades, especially by General Motors and Ford.[24] Since entry into assembling would require full access to components and parts in a well developed market—or alternatively, it now requires the entrant to be integrated also—vertical integration has made entry more difficult.

In addition, the existing franchise system makes possible a variety of practices which restrict actual and potential competition in automobile and related areas. The manufacturers' requirement that their dealers stock "genuine" parts tends to forclose "nongenuine" parts from this important sales outlet, because efficient inventory practice makes it unattractive to stock more than one type of part, no matter how interchangeable, except at a large price differential. Similarly, the manufacturers' automobile warranty policies require use of "genuine" parts and therefore tend to tie repair work to the franchised dealer. The largely captive parts market made possible by the franchise system is reflected in a higher profitability for the major producers of parts—on the order of 20 to 35 percent of sales (and possibly more than that as a percentage of invested capital), compared to perhaps 15 to 20 percent on car sales.[25] A fair summary would be that any technical scale economies are overshadowed by the artificial "imperatives" for concentration and entry barriers which are fostered by model changes and exclusive dealer policies. The effects of the resulting market power have not been mild. Prices follow classic "administered price" patterns; manufacturers' prices are usually adjusted once a year in a delicate and swift mutual adjustment which forestalls sporadic or deep price cutting even during very

---

[21] B. Peter Pashigian, *The Distribution of Automobiles: An Economic Analysis of the Franchise System* (Englewood Cliffs N.J.: Prentice-Hall, 1961), 122. The main exception is sales to rental fleets, such as Hertz and Avis; these are handled directly by the producers. Recently a few multi-company dealers have come on the scene, but their eventual role may remain very limited; see "GM Takes the High Ground in the New Battle for Detroit," *Fortune*, May 1, 1969, 72–75, 134.

[22] See Complaint in *United States* v. *Chrysler Corp.*, Civil Action No. 1297, filed N.C. Ind., April 7, 1961.

[23] Bain, *Barriers to New Competition*, 300–302; also Bain, *Industrial Organization*.

[24] R. G. Crandall, *Vertical Integration in the U.S. Automobile Industry*, (Cambridge, M.I.T. Ph.D. Thesis, 1967).

[25] See Bain, *Industrial Organization*; and Lanzillotti, *op. cit.*, 353.

poor years.[26] Even during Chrysler's critical period in 1958 to 1963 it avoided using price as a competitive weapon.

The profitability of the automobile firms has reflected the scope of their market power. The automobile industry has been *the* most profitable of major industries in recent years. This is shown in Federal Trade Commission compilations of profit rates (see Table 15.4), which for 1962–1965 show

TABLE 15.4   PROFITS (AFTER TAX) AS A PERCENTAGE OF SHAREHOLDERS EQUITY IN AUTOMOBILES AND OTHER INDUSTRIES 1962–1965

	1962	1963	1964	1965	1962–1965
Motor vehicles	17.7	19.1	19.1	21.6	19.4
Drugs (12 firms only)	17.1	17.8	18.9	21.0	18.7
Office and computing equipment	16.1	16.2	17.6	17.5	16.8
Industrial chemicals	15.2	15.6	16.5	16.4	15.9
Soaps and related items	13.4	13.6	14.1	13.6	13.7
Cigarettes	13.9	13.7	13.1	13.6	13.6

SOURCE: Compiled from Federal Trade Commission, *Rates of Return for Identical Firms in Selected Manufacturing Industries, 1940, 1947–65* (Washington, D.C.: U.S. Government Printing Office, 1967).

the whole of "Motor Vehicles and Related Industries" averaging a 19.4 percent rate of return.[27] The next-highest profit rates were in the drug industry (at 18.7 percent) and the computer industry (at 16.8 percent), followed by industrial chemicals (at 15.9 percent). For other corporations engaged in manufacturing, average rates of return have been about 8 to 10 percent in recent years, which yield a margin of no more than 4 to 5 percent profit above the bedrock cost of capital (as shown by government bond rates). By contrast, the leading automobile firms have had *net* margins averaging about 15 percent—about three times the average for all industry. That no entry of new competitors has been induced by such remarkably high profit rates gives further affirmation that entry barriers are, in effect, high enough to prevent substantial entry.

The three firms' profitability has not been uniform. As Table 15.5 shows, rates of return on invested capital during 1962–1968 were 22.7 percent

---

[26] U.S. Senate Subcommittee Report, *op. cit.*; Lanzillotti, *op. cit.* The dealer discounts frequently offered do not eliminate the crucial role played by the yearly formal price changes.
[27] Federal Trade Commission, *Rates of Return for Identical Companies in Selected Manufacturing Industries, 1956–65* (Washington, D.C.: U.S. Government Printing Office, 1967), Table 1, p. 3. Even granted the complexities in making any profit comparisons at all, the patterns here are clear enough to support the conclusion of very high profitability.

TABLE 15.5 NET PROFIT AFTER TAXES AS A PERCENT OF INVESTED CAPITAL: GENERAL MOTORS, FORD, AND CHRYSLER, 1956–1968*

	1956	1957	1958	1959	1960	1961	1962	1963	1964	1965	1966	1967	1968	Averages 1956–1968	Averages 1962–1968
General Motors	18.5	17.2	12.6	16.3	16.5	14.8	21.9	22.4	22.8	25.8	20.6	17.6	17.8	18.8	21.4
Ford	11.9	13.2	4.5	17.3	14.9	13.1	14.1	13.1	12.6	15.7	13.0	1.8†	12.7	12.1	11.8
Chrysler	3.1	16.4	−4.9	−0.7	4.6	1.6	8.5	17.5	19.1	14.7	11.1	10.9	14.1	9.0	13.8

* Net profit is calculated after special charges or credits. Invested capital represents net worth: capital stock, surplus, and retained earnings, at year's end.
† Ford's 1967 results reflected a three-month strike which did not spread to the other producers.
SOURCE: Compiled from *The 500 Largest U.S. Industrial Corporations* (New York: *Fortune,* annual).

for General Motors, 13.6 percent for Ford, and 14.2 percent for Chrysler. The higher profitability of General Motors (including the greater stability of its profit rate) probably reflects its greater market power, its greater emphasis on the higher-price and more lucrative model lines, and the greater role of its vertical integration into parts supply. A uniformity of profit rates among the companies is not necessarily to be expected, under either formal monopoly or shared monopoly. Therefore the high total profitability confirms the exercise of large-scale market power, and the interfirm differences neither conflict with that nor lend it further support.

It bears noting that both Ford's and Chrysler's net profitability has been in the range of double the averages for competitive industry, although Chrysler has undergone serious difficulties in 1959–62 and again in 1969–70. A variety of styling mistakes and mismanagement problems took Chrysler's market share down as low as 10.3 percent in 1962, and its profits suffered sharply (see Tables 15.1 and 15.5). Chrysler's adherence to the shared-monopoly patterns of behavior, in the face of such pressures, particularly suggests a shared-monopoly interpretation of the industry.

Very roughly speaking, upwards of $1½ billion of the three firms' $3 billion of profits in recent years may well represent excess monopoly profits. This is particularly true of General Motors, whose high profit rates have been exceptionally stable.

The effects on real magnitudes have not been slight. Fluctuations in the industry's output and employment have probably been sharper than a more price-flexible, loose oligopoly would have yielded. The three firms were also able virtually to withdraw from the small-car field during the 1964–1969 period. In view of the greater profitability of the higher-price lines, a monopolist would rationally focus its production and sales effort on them, even if it entailed some loss of sales in the lower-price lines. This is what the leading firms, and particularly General Motors, have indeed done until the turnabout announced for 1970. But, absent shared-monopoly behavior, the other leading firms would be expected to enter and exploit the low-price market fully as a means of establishing a market position from which to broaden their lines. If one of the leaders were hard-pressed, it would have particularly strong incentives to exploit the low-price market, if only as a means of survival; and yet none has.[28]

In effect, Ford and Chrysler have jointly chosen during much of the 1960's (as they did in the mid-1950's) not to break the shared-monopoly ranks through innovation into the low-price markets. Instead, with General Motors, they largely abandoned it to imports. The effect of this can be seen

---

[28] In fact (as Table 15.2 notes), Chrysler does focus slightly more on lower-price cars, while General Motors focuses slightly more at the upper levels. But the differences are, in view of the cross-incentives facing the firms, remarkably small; this applies particularly to Chrysler's and Ford's lack of effort in the low-price market, now being largely served by Volkswagen and the other foreign manufacturers.

in the balance of trade in automobiles between the United States and the rest of the world. Imports have risen markedly in comparison with exports during the past five years, as they did in the 1950's before U.S. compacts were developed. During 1968, imports rose to over 10 percent of domestic sales. It has taken such sharp inroads to draw a response, finally and belatedly.

Apart from reducing and destabilizing production, the established firms' parts-supply and dealer-franchising policies may have caused significant misallocation.[29] Perhaps more costly to society have been the model-change policies. Model changes between 1949 and 1960 accounted for at least "a substantial part of expenditure on autmobiles, especially in the last half of the 1950's, our estimates running about $5 billion a year," This was about $700 in the purchase price per car, which amounts to more than 25 percent.[30] Although some of these changes responded to buyers' preferences, these preferences were at least partly formed by auto company advertising; "it is thus not easy to decide whether the costs reported in this paper were worth incurring." Given the narrow range of choice among automobiles in the market and the importance of advertising in influencing preferences, it is likely that a significant part of the cost of model changes represents dead-weight loss.

Even though innovation is particularly hard to evaluate, the patterns in the automobile industry generally conform to economic predictions of shared-monopoly conduct. The leaders' innovative performance is widely regarded as mixed and mediocre.[31] Peripheral innovations (especially styling) continue to receive heavy emphasis. Probably a disproportionate share of important innovations have come from elsewhere.[32] More recently, other smaller firms (and particularly foreign firms) have developed a variety of important safety features.[33]

The events leading to present federal and state activities to promote the use of safety features are well known. It is not possible to show conclusively that these developments have been "too slow" in some sense, although many observers believe they have been. The key point is that the leading firms took a common attitude discouraging the introduction of safety features for many years. And when compulsory action became likely, in recent years,

---

[29] Crandall, *op. cit.*
[30] F. M. Fisher, Z. Griliches, and C. Kaysen, "The Costs of Automobile Model Changes Since 1949," *Journal of Political Economy*, LXX (October 1962), 433–451.
[31] Thus, earlier, "How Strong is GM Research?" *Fortune*, June 1956, pp. 138–141 noted, "Despite the glitter of its new technical center, GM has not yet proved that it has a research laboratory of front rank. Until very recently Detroit had never done much thorough research as scientists understand it. Most of its so-called research achievements have fallen rather under the head of advanced engineering." See also Lanzillotti, *op. cit.*
[32] Weiss, *op. cit.*; Lanzillotti, *op. cit.*; *Report of the Study of Administered Prices*, pp. 18–25.
[33] An enumeration is provided in U.S. Senate Subcommittee on Antitrust and Monopoly, *Hearings on Economic Concentration, Part 3* (Washington, D.C.: U.S. Government Printing Office, 1965), 1123–1124.

242 / Causes and Effects of Market Power

they attempted to establish a *common* industry group to develop, impose, and control standards.[34] An actively competitive situation might have led at least one firm to exploit safety features more fully as a competitive tactic— particularly Chrysler during its difficult 1958–1963 period (and indeed as the Swedish Volvo has done). Instead, none of the firms, in any of their individual divisions or models, "broke the ranks." The same is true of antismog technology. The likelihood that successful devices will be made mandatory provides no small inducement for independent innovation, especially by the lesser producers. Yet the three firms have clung to a joint-venture approach, encrusted with ancillary restrictions; little or no independent moves have been made, even though the joint-venture approach has yielded little progress during 15 years.[35]

The distributional effects of the automobile industry's oligopoly have not been small. In recent years, as much as $\frac{1}{2}$ billion per year in profits may represent redistribution from at least 10 million purchasers primarily to several hundred thousand significant shareowners, with a wealth impact of as much as $4 to $8 billion. A second area of equity concerns equality of opportunity in employment and ownership. Like many other large firms, the leading automobile firms have not used their shared-monopoly advantages in a major way to promote equal opportunity, nor (as least before 1968) have they even been neutral in hiring policies. On the contrary, their hiring of minority-group members for white-collar positions has been below the average for comparable industries and for all industries and trades.[36] Moreover, General Motors has been, and remains, the most laggard of the three.[37] Perhaps the most visible manifestation of this is in franchised dealerships. Although there are over 20,000 dealerships, and a substantial share of these change hands every year, the number of Negro dealers franchised by early 1969 by the major automobile firms is no more than eight; before 1967, General Motors and Ford apparently had none.[38] A more competitive industry setting would probably yield a significant improvement in equal employment and dealer franchising practices, particularly compared to General Motors' record.[39] One evident external effect of the withdrawal

---

[34] See Harvey Levin, "The Limits of Self-Regulation," *Columbia Law Review*, LXVII (April 1967), 605–644.

[35] Further details are noted in the antitrust suit brought in January 1969 by the U.S. Department of Justice; see *The Wall Street Journal*, January 20, 1969, 3.

[36] U.S. Equal Employment Opportunity Commission, *Nine City Employment Profile*, Research Report 19, 1967 (Washington, D.C.: U.S. Government Printing Office, 1968); see also Chapter 14 above and Appendix Table 18.

[37] Herbert R. Northrup, *The Negro in the Automobile Industry* (Philadelphia: University of Pennsylvania Press, 1968).

[38] *Ibid.*, 42–44; and *The Wall Street Journal*, October 14, 1968.

[39] The recent highly-publicized moves by the firms to hire unskilled workers do not affect this point. The hirings are at the lowest levels rather than opening management opportunities. They reflect paternalism rather than well-rooted competitive motivations. They cannot be regarded as a long-run substitute for voluntary profit-maximizing choices under effective competitive constraints and inducements.

from small-car markets has been the balance-of-payments loss caused by rising imports and reduced exports. This total effect might have run as high as $200 million since the early 1960's.

Taken altogether, market power in the automobile industry is on a very large scale, and it apparently is rising. It causes a variety of important economic and social losses, compared to what would probably result from a reduction in market power.

Chapter 16

Summary and Conclusions

It is clear the combinations and partial monopolies will
play a great part in future economic history; that their effects
contain much good as well as much evil, and that to denounce
them without discrimination would be to repeat the error
which our forefathers made with regard to Protection.   If we
do not take time by the forelock, and begin early to consider
how their evil effects may be minimized and their possible
good developed, we shall miss an opportunity that will never
recur.

ALFRED MARSHALL
"Some Aspects of Competition" (*1890*)

Fragile and preliminary though much of it is, the evidence outlined in this
volume does suggest at least several broad conclusions.   Market power in
this country appears to be important and complex, more so than has come
to be commonly thought in recent years, and it appears to be increasing at
more than a glacial pace.   It tends to be a good deal greater, in most industries, than technical efficiency would require.   It levies a variety of economic
and social costs, which amount to a large and growing burden of waste and
lost opportunities.   Yet the problem is not beyond hope of correction,
because much of it is focused in a relatively few major sectors and industries.

A brief summary of the individual points may help bring them all into
focus.   The last three decades have bred many alternative concepts of
competition.   Yet the focus of research has narrowed down primarily to
concentration, so that recent findings have proably underestimated the reality
and its effects.   The postwar developments and refinements of neoclassical
theory have encouraged the neglect (and even denial) of several important
features of market power.   These characteristics include (1) some structural

elements other than concentration, such as barriers and other informal structure, relative size, vertical integration, and certain patterns of diversification; (2) the interchangeability of the elements; and (3) the likelihood that market power may spread rather than be self-containing or subject to steady erosion.

The criteria of industrial performance have similarly grown narrow and brittle, with too much focus on profits and allocational efficiency. Since a full appraisal of market power's effects needs to embrace the whole set of interrelations between two sets of variables (structure and performance), the early research returns are likely to encourage a false notion that the effects are slight, even if they have actually been large.

The main elements of market structure and of performance can be specified with some confidence, along with their likely effects. It is also possible to outline the "natural" market structure which will emerge under common preconditions, as well as a structure which would be "optimum" for fostering good industrial performance. Under general conditions, the natural structure is probably tight asymmetric oligopoly, whereas optimum structure is usually loose symmetric oligopoly. Market power will tend to grow unnecessarily large, rather than to settle spontaneously at minimal or optimal levels. Of course, antitrust and other policies may intervene to constrain structure so that it approximates the optimum. Therefore, the actual status of "the monopoly problem" is a series of open questions subject to empirical answers.

The largest firms, taken as a whole, have been encompassing a rising share of industrial activity in most advanced economies, including the United States. But they still are far from ubiquitous, and the very biggest of them are specialized types. Therefore bigness is no proven format or prerequisite for efficiency. The very large firms are, generally, more profitable and (increasingly) secure than smaller firms; much of this stems from direct governmental support for R&D and production. Their diversification is on the rise. Their "social stewardship" role is largely a myth.

These trends suggest, from their partial standpoint, a rise in market power, with no offsetting technical or social benefits, and with every likelihood that its commercial rewards will be pursued unremittingly. The trends also reflect the monopolistic character of financial markets. These markets are commonly fragmented by differing conditions of inside information; concentration is commonly high and relations with nonfinancial firms are often important. The resulting pattern of financial terms tends to favor large firms which hold market power.

Within nonfinancial markets, relatively tight oligopoly is common, verging on near-monopoly in a number of major and minor industries. Concentration has been rising more rapidly abroad than it has been in the United States, but it is still probably higher on the average in this country. High concentration has tended to last, rather than fade away, in individual markets. Asymmetry is rather high in the United States—higher than in the one country (Japan) which can be compared. In only a few industries is high concentration dictated by large sizes of efficient plants.

Entry barriers are high in many major industries. Informal structure is endemic in intermediate oligopolies, particularly in heavy industries making standardized products, which they sell partly to public agencies or regulated firms. This is reflected in the surprisingly high stability of market shares in most American industries, and it tends to accentuate formal market structure. Among the various external elements of structure, diversification tends usually to entrench leading firms rather than to strengthen lesser-ranking competitors. In partial contrast, the element of size is not so pervasively allied with the other elements; nor is vertical integration. But special buyer types (public agencies or regulated firms) definitely do cluster around some of the major monopolistic industries.

All in all, at least 35 to 45 percent of market activity in the United States appears to take place under conditions of substantial market power. In the manufacturing sector alone, the score of major industries with particularly high market power include about one-third of productive activity. In broad perspective, market power in a variety of sectors and specific forms is evidently on the increase, gradually but steadily.

In most industries, there is little or no apparent technical imperative for the present degree of monopoly, or for a further rise in it. Indeed, much market power arises purely in the pursuit of its own rewards and from the ability to acquire inputs at low prices and to secure various sorts of governmental sponsorship. Growth has not served as a strong solvent of market power, except in some new industries, nor is it likely to do so in the future. Abroad, there are growing tendencies to concentrate industries via merger; this is partly in response to American market structures and public policies, rather than from clear proof that this will genuinely promote efficiency.

Compared with the unproven, and perhaps modest, technical benefits of excess market power, its economic and social costs are large. The combined loss in efficient resource-use—internal inefficiency, misallocation, and external effects—may range upward toward 5 percent of national income. There have probably been a more than trivial retardation in innovation and an accentuation of fluctuations, in at least several major industries. Market power has also tended to sharpen economic inequality, and to accentuate racial discrimination in employment, thereby causing no small economic and social loss and indirect repercussions. These various burdens of monopoly in this country do not seem to be shrinking. They tend generally to be focused in a relatively few major industries and trades. For example, the net avoidable economic and related losses from market power in the steel, automobile, telephone equipment, computer, and drug industries alone may well exceed $6 billion annually in recent years. Needless to say, the total losses would be somewhat greater if antitrust constraints, such as they are, were not present.

That market power has many forms, is probably rising, and inflicts large costs is not a new idea. The main contours of market power have long existed, but the recent preoccupation with concentration has fostered a partial and unrealistic view of them.

The scope and character of market power, as they have emerged in this book, have a number of implications, especially for public policies toward business (including antitrust, regulation, and public ownership). These policy issues are intended for treatment in a later volume, but some technical points may deserve repeating here. Dominant firms in stable, asymmetrical oligopolies now carry a presumption of technical inferiority. Market power is strongly focused in certain sectors, but its composite forms and incidence are changeable. An important group of overhead-cost industries may require special policy treatment. There may be real, but partially unnecessary, trends toward increased structural monopoly abroad, in both national and international markets.

There is fertile ground for further research in directions which have been suggested at a number of points in the volume. Most obvious of all is the evident need for better information about structure and its effects. Even though evidence about U.S. markets is more complete in many respects than about foreign conditions, it is well short of what could be gotten with relatively little additional effort. This is particularly true of concentration, diversification, vertical relationships, and asymmetry in markets throughout the economy, not just in manufacturing. This would require some liberalizing of Census disclosure roles, which date mainly from the nineteenth century. The scope of the problem warrants such liberalization. One current proposal, to require detailed accounts from conglomerate firms, would be only a first step. More systematic information about behavior (particularly profits, technical change, and minority employment) also could be readily enlarged and processed out, on the same basis as the structural data, to facilitate an expanded analysis. Similar work abroad, now virtually in infancy, would also be important, partly to provide a comparative setting for appraising American conditions, and partly to clarify the international impact of American patterns and policies.

These improvements might enable, at last, a more reasonably reliable and thorough appraisal of market power and its effects. Moreover, it should eventually be possible to sift the data routinely and thoroughly, in order to single out the markets in which structural monopoly is unnecessarily large and damaging to performance. At the least, it is safe to say that a very large amount and variety of market power still lies hidden from view for lack of data, as well as for lack of analysis.

Market power is evidently raising new research and policy problems in a range of important markets. The process of adjusting policies and casting out unsound ones requires a large amount of data which presently are imperfect or altogether unavailable. But even perfect data would require intelligent evaluation and analysis, avoiding spurious answers and over-simple measurements. For many of the questions, no definitive answers are likely to be reached soon, if ever. For others, further study may yield answers over the course of years, although no general breakthrough in analysis or new data is presently in prospect. Therefore one will still need, as in previous decades, to proceed carefully in sifting the evidence and keeping its lessons in perspective.

Suggestions for
Further Reading

Although the reader has already been introduced to some of the surrounding literature by the footnotes in the text, it may help to single out several of the more important sources. These come under the same three main groupings that the book is divided into: concepts of market power, the extent of market power, and causes and effects of market power.

The major and classic treatises on concepts of competition and monopoly down through the years include the following: Joe S. Bain, *Industrial Organization*, rev. ed. (New York: Wiley, 1968); Carl Kaysen and Donald F. Turner, *Antitrust Policy* (Cambridge: Harvard University Press, 1959); Edward H. Chamberlin, *The Theory of Monopolistic Competition*, 8th ed. (Cambridge: Harvard University Press, 1965); William J. Fellner, *Competition Among the Few* (New York: Norton, 1949); John M. Clark, *Competition as a Dynamic Process* (Washington, D.C.: Brookings, 1962); Joseph A. Schumpeter, *Capitalism, Socialism and Democracy* (New York: Harper & Row, 1942); John K. Galbraith, *American Capitalism*, rev. ed. (Boston: Houghton Mifflin, 1956); and Corwin D. Edwards, *Maintaining Competition* (New York: McGraw-Hill, 1949). An excellent source on early views is Charles J.

Bullock, "Trust Literature: A Survey and Criticism," *Quarterly Journal of Economics*, XV (February 1901), 167–217. A good summary of neoclassical theory of market processes is in William J. Baumol, *Economic Theory and Operations Analysis*, rev. ed. (Englewood Cliffs, N.J.: Prentice-Hall, 1965).

On the extent and forms of market power, the best contemporary summary is in the U.S. Senate Subcommittee on Antitrust and Monopoly, 88th Congress, 2nd Session, and 90th Congress, 2nd Session, *Hearings on Economic Concentration, Parts 1, 2 and 7* (Washington, D.C.: U.S. Government Printing Office, 1964, 1965, and 1968). On large firms, see also Edward S. Mason, ed., *The Corporation in Modern Society* (Cambridge: Harvard University Press, 1959); and A. D. H. Kaplan, *Big Enterprise in a Competitive System*, rev. ed. (Washington, D.C.: Brookings, 1964). Major sources on industrial structure include, in rough chronological order, John Moody, *The Truth About the Trusts* (Chicago: Moody Publishing Co., 1904); Clair Wilcox, *Competition and Monopoly in American Industry*, Monograph No. 21, in Investigation of Concentration of Economic Power by the Temporary National Economic Committee, 76th Congress, 3rd Session, (Washington, D.C.: U.S. Government Printing Office, 1940); Morris A. Adelman, "The Measurement of Industrial Concentration," *Review of Economics and Statistics*, XXXIII (November 1951), 269–296; George J. Stigler, ed., *Business Concentration and Price Policy* (Princeton University Press, 1955); Joe S. Bain, *Barriers to New Competition* (Cambridge: Harvard University Press, 1956); Kaysen and Turner, *op. cit.*; Walter Adams, ed., *The Structure of American Industry*, 3rd ed. (New York: Macmillan, 1961); Michael Gort, *Diversification and Integration in American Industry* (Princeton: Princeton University Press, 1962); Joe S. Bain, *International Differences in Industrial Structure* (New Haven: Yale University Press, 1965); J. M. Guttentag and E. S. Herman, *Banking Structure and Performance*, No. 41/43, *The Bulletin*, Institute of Finance, Graduate School of Business Administration, New York University, (New York: New York University Press, 1967).

Among many sources on causes and effects of market power, one could turn first to the following: U.S. Senate Subcommittee on Antitrust and Monopoly, *Hearings on Economic Concentration, Parts 3 through 7*, 89th and 90th Congresses, (Washington, D.C.: U.S. Government Printing Office, 1965–1968); Bain, *Barriers to New Competition*; Norman R. Collins and Lee E. Preston, *Concentration and Price-Cost Margins in Manufacturing Industries* (Berkeley: University of California Press, 1968); Harvey Leibenstein, "Allocative Efficiency vs. 'X-Efficiency'," *American Economic Review*, LVI (June 1966), 392–413; Edwin Mansfield, *Industrial Research and Technological Innovation* (New York: Norton, 1968); Ferdinand Lundberg, *The Rich and the Super-Rich* (New York: Lyle Stuart, 1968); and U.S. Equal Employment Opportunity Commission, *Hearings on Discrimination in White Collar Employment* (Washington, D.C.: U.S. Government Printing Office, 1968).

Appendix

APPENDIX TABLE 1 THE SIZE RANGE OF U.S. CORPORATIONS IN 1965

	Total for all Corporations	Asset Size Classes ($ millions)						
	(Thousands)	0–0.1	0–1.0	1.0–25	25–50	50–100	100–250	Over 250
				(Number of Corporations)				
Agriculture, forestry, and fisheries	27,530	14,882	11,684	951	7	4	1	1
Mining	13,285	7,463	4,502	1,228	49	14	18	11
Construction	113,284	72,551	36,984	3,788	26	16	8	1
Manufacturing	185,924	87,379	78,244	18,971	581	317	234	198
Transport, communication, and utilities	59,676	38,338	17,879	3,047	110	82	91	129
Wholesale and retail trade	440,304	266,773	159,221	14,024	158	61	42	25
Finance, insurance, and real estate	388,428	209,275	140,158	35,018	1,879	976	671	451
Services	188,177	142,445	41,806	3,829	47	30	14	6
Total for all sectors	1,423,162	846,162	490,688	80,872	2,857	1,500	1,079	822

APPENDIX TABLE 1—*continued*

	Total for all Corporations ($ billion)	Asset Size Classes ($ millions)					
		0–0.1	0–0.1	1.0–25	25–50	50–100	100–250	Over 250
			(Percent of Assets in Each Class)					
Agriculture, forestry, and fisheries	6.8	7.9	45.5	32.9	3.1	3.8	2.2	4.6
Mining	16.5	1.4	9.0	28.3	10.7	6.3	16.3	27.9
Construction	26.7	8.7	39.7	38.4	3.3	4.6	4.4	1.0
Manufacturing	371.5	0.8	6.8	17.8	5.5	6.0	9.8	53.0
Transport, communication, and utilities	186.9	0.6	2.7	6.4	2.1	3.2	7.9	77.0
Wholesale and retail trade	125.5	7.7	35.2	30.0	4.3	3.3	5.1	14.3
Finance, insurance and real estate	955.9	0.8	4.4	18.5	6.8	7.0	10.6	51.9
Services	33.5	10.9	33.6	33.3	4.4	6.2	6.7	4.9
Total for all sectors	1,723.5	1.6	8.3	18.6	5.7	6.1	9.6	50.1

SOURCE: Adapted from U.S. Treasury Department, Internal Revenue Service, *Statistics of Income 1965, Corporation Income Tax Returns* (Washington, D.C.: U.S. Government Printing Office, 1968).

APPENDIX TABLE 2   THE LARGEST AMERICAN
MANUFACTURING
CORPORATIONS, 1947–1967

Asset Rank Among All Industrial Firms, 1967	Corporation	Main Industrial Field	Total Assets, 1967 ($ million)	Asset 1960	Rank 1947
1	Standard Oil (New Jersey)	Oil	16,786	1	1
2	General Motors	Automobiles	14,010	2	2
3	Ford Motor	Automobiles	8,953	4	4
4	Texaco	Oil	8,687	6	7
5	Gulf Oil	Oil	7,498	5	11
6	Mobil Oil	Oil	6,872	7	5
7	IBM	Computers	6,743	17	73
8	U.S. Steel	Steel	6,391	3	3
9	GT&E	Communications	6,157	88	—
10	Standard Oil (California)	Oil	5,770	10	13
11	General Electric	Electrical	5,744	11	8
12	Standard Oil (Indiana)	Oil	4,737	9	4
13	Chrysler	Automobiles	4,398	23	23
14	Shell Oil	Oil	4,230	13	22
15	ITT	Communications	4,022	55	74
16	Tenneco	Diversified	3,888	—	—
17	DuPont	Chemicals	3,289	8	6
18	Union Carbide	Chemicals	3,209	14	14
19	Bethlehem Steel	Steel	3,060	12	10
20	Phillips Petroleum	Oil	2,889	16	27
21	Western Electric	Telephone equipment	2,722	15	16
22	LTV	Diversified	2,648	335	—
23	Eastman Kodak	Photographic	2,565	33	33
24	Continental Oil	Oil	2,537	44	61
25	Atlantic Richfield	Oil	3,451	46	38

SOURCE: Compiled from *The 500 Largest Industrial Corporations* (New York: *Fortune,* May 15, 1969); and for earlier years, U.S. Senate Subcommittee on Antitrust and Monopoly, 89th and 90th Congresses, *Hearings on Economic Concentration, Part 5A* (Washington, D.C.: U.S. Government Printing Office, 1967).

APPENDIX TABLE 3 THE LARGEST AMERICAN
COMMERCIAL BANKS,
LIFE-INSURANCE AND
MERCHANDISING FIRMS, 1955–1967

Asset Rank, 1967	Name	Total Assets 1967 ($ billion)	Asset 1960	Rank 1955
	Banks			
1	Bank of America (San Fran.)	23,961	1	1
2	First National City (N.Y.)	19,355	3	3
3	Chase Manhattan (N.Y.)	19,014	2	2
4	Manufacturers Hanover (N.Y.)	10,349	6	4
5	Morgan Guaranty Trust (N.Y.)	10,370	5	5
6	Chemical Bank New York Trust	8,968	4	6
7	Bankers Trust (N.Y.)	7,653	8	8
8	Continental Illinois National (Chicago)	7,373	10	9
9	First National Bank of Chicago	6,530	9	7
10	Security First National (L.A.)	6,288	7	10
	Life Insurance			
1	Prudential	26,608	2	2
2	Metropolitan	25,840	1	1
3	Equitable Life Assurance	13,591	3	3
4	New York Life	10,026	4	4
5	John Hancock Mutual	9,318	5	5
6	Aetna	6,641	7	7
7	Northwestern Mutual	5,720	6	6
8	Connecticut General	4,435	11	14
9	Travelers	4,364	8	8
10	Massachusetts Mutual	3,934	10	10
	Merchandising			
1	Sears Roebuck	6,508	1	1
2	Marcor	2,618	2	2
3	J. C. Penney	1,187	5	7
4	F. W. Woolworth	1,134	4	4
5	Federated Department Stores	971	9	12
6	A & P	913	3	3
7	May Department Stores	826	7	8
8	Allied Stores	823	13	9
9	Safeway Stores	698	6	6
10	Gamble-Skogmo	695	—	—

SOURCE: Compiled from *The 500 Largest Industrial Corporations* (New York: *Fortune,* May 15, 1969); and for earlier years, U.S. Senate Subcommittee on Antitrust and Monopoly, *Hearings on Economic Concentration, Part 5A,* 89th and 90th Congresses, (Washington, D.C.: U.S. Government Printing Office, 1967).

APPENDIX TABLE 4 THE LARGEST FIRMS
OUTSIDE THE U.S. IN 1967

Firm	Headquarters	Main Industrial Field	Total Net Assets ($ million)	Employees (Thousands)
Royal Dutch/Shell	Netherlands; Britain	Oil, gas, chemicals	13,394	174
British Petroleum	Britain	Oil products	4,427	60
Montecatini Edison	Italy	Chemicals, fibers	4,195	119
Imperial Chemical Industries (ICI)	Britain	Chemicals	4,148	172
Finsider	Italy	Iron and steel	3,576	76
Unilever	Britain; Netherlands	Food, detergents, paper, chemicals	3,243	300
Philips' Gloeilampenfabricken	Netherlands	Electrical, chemicals	2,978	244
Ente Nazionale Idrocarburi (ENI) (publicly owned)	Italy	Oil, engineering, textiles	2,745	55
National Coal Board (publicly owned)	Britain	Coal	2,727	436
Hindustan Steel	India	Iron and steel	2,113	102
Mitsubishi Heavy Industries	Japan	Diversified	2,035	88
Charbonnage de France (publicly owned)	France	Coal	1,951	175
ERAP	France	Oil products	1,900	16
Hitachi	Japan	Electrical, machinery	1,745	131

SOURCE: Compiled from *The 500 Largest Industrial Corporations* (New York: *Fortune*, June 15, 1968); and U.S. Senate Subcommittee on Antitrust and Monopoly, 89th and 90th Congresses, *Hearings on Economic Concentration, Part 5A* (Washington, D.C.: U.S. Government Printing Office, 1967).

APPENDIX TABLE 5 FEDERAL PURCHASES AND R & D SUPPORT IN A SELECTION OF LARGE R & D-ORIENTED FIRMS, 1966–1967

Sales Rank Among all Industrial Firms, 1966	Company	Company Sales 1966	Federal Prime Contracts for Purchases, 1966–1967 ($ million)	Federal R & D Related Contracts 1966–1967	Federal Prime Contracts for Purchases As Percentage of Firm Sales 1966	Federal R & D Related Contracts 1966
1	General Motors	20,209	762	137	3.8	0.7
2	Ford	12,240	540	136	4.4	1.1
4	General Electric	7,177	2,019	729	28.2	10.2
5	Chrysler	5,650	144	79	2.5	1.4
9	IBM	4,248	410	215	9.7	5.1
11	Western Electric	3,624	117	623	30.8	17.2
12	DuPont	3,185	287	107	9.0	3.4
19	Westinghouse	2,581	651	198	24.3	7.4
20	RCA	2,549	379	111	14.9	4.4
21	Goodyear Tire & Rubber	2,476	221	66	8.9	2.7
22	GT&E	2,391	319	180	13.4	7.5
23	Boeing	2,357	1,406	494	59.7	21.0
27	Union Carbide	2,224	334	287	15.0	12.9
28	IT&T	2,121	282	27	13.3	1.3
29	Lockheed	2,085	2,558	751	122.8	36.0
30	North American Aviation	2,024	1,938	1,249	95.7	61.6
32	General Dynamics	1,797	2,368	536	132.0	29.8
34	Eastman Kodak	1,742	111	2	6.4	0.1
36	United Aircraft	1,663	1,213	116	73.0	7.0
37	Monsanto	1,612	34	34	2.1	2.1
49	Uniroyal	1,321	218	1	16.5	0.1
50	Dow Chemical	1,310	111	44	8.5	3.4
54	Allied Chemical	1,246	—	—	0	0

57	Litton	1,172	194	14	16.5	1.2
61	Textron	1,132	531	36	47.0	3.2
62	Olin Mathieson	1,117	155	1	13.9	0.1
66, 73	McDonnell-Douglas	2,109	2,593	481	123.4	22.9
67	Grumman	1,059	1,043	555	98.5	52.4
69	Bendix	1,052	539	243	51.2	23.1
80	General Tire & Rubber	1,002	448	175	44.8	17.5
87	Honeywell	914	370	56	40.4	6.1
93	TRW	864	264	143	30.6	16.6
113	Raytheon	709	403	98	56.9	13.8
120	Martin-Marietta	670	471	181	70.2	27.0
125	Zenith	625	1	1	0.4	0.4
130	Ogden	612	237	—	38.7	0
131	Hercules	610	201	6	33.0	1.0
132	Kaiser Industries	609	308	2	50.6	0.3
134	Avco	604	564	115	93.4	19.1
138	Texas Instruments	580	128	34	22.1	5.9
168	LTV	468	670	135	143.1	28.8
173	Magnavox	456	114	15	24.9	3.3
202	Collins Radio	388	216	14	55.8	3.6
223	Northrop	357	339	33	94.9	9.2
293	Teledyne	257	100	12	38.9	4.7
309	Lear Seigler	244	105	4	43.0	1.6
337	Fairchild Hiller	210	117	23	55.7	11.0
452	Curtiss-Wright	144	97	6	67.5	4.2

NOTE: The amounts of contracts have changed from year to year, and each year's amounts refer to contracts *let* rather than work performed. Moreover, these figures for prime contracts mask the substantial volume of subcontracting, which spreads the real production activity somewhat differently. In light of these points, this table is meant primarily to illustrate the general scope of the problem, not to show definitively its individual details.

SOURCES: Compiled from U.S. Defense Department, *100 Largest Prime Contracters* and *500 Largest R&D Suppliers;* NASA *Annual Procurement Report;* AEC, *Financial Report* (all Washington, D.C.: U.S. Government Printing Office, published annually); *The 500 Largest Industrial Corporations* (New York: *Fortune,* 1967).

APPENDIX TABLE 6 DISTRIBUTION OF DEFENSE PURCHASES BY "COMPETITIVE" STATUS, FISCAL YEAR 1967

Product or Service	Competition Code* ($ million)						Sum of 3, 4 plus 5 ($ millions)	Total ($ millions)	Percent of Total	
	0	1	2	3	4	5			Code 5	Codes 3, 4 plus 5
Airframes	65	632	330	477	2,394	1,596	4,467	5,495	29.0	81.2
Aircraft engines	1	183	68	42	921	332	1,295	1,548	21.4	83.5
Other aircraft	68	59	13	1	58	259	318	459	56.6	69.3
Missile systems	34	153	183	11	1,652	1,678	3,341	3,710	45.2	90.2
Ships	960	59	33	1	33	425	459	1,512	28.2	30.4
Combat vehicles	149	42	—	—	20	230	250	441	52.1	56.9
Noncombat vehicles	351	157	12	1	—	63	64	585	10.7	10.8
Weapons	21	55	3	—	4	243	247	325	74.9	75.8
Ammunition	146	575	32	85	12	2,177	2,274	3,027	71.8	75.2
Electronic plus communication equipment	250	377	210	48	288	1,376	1,712	2,549	54.0	67.1
Petroleum plus products	546	524	—	—	—	110	110	1,180	9.6	9.6
Textiles plus clothing	217	356	—	—	—	4	4	577	0.7	0.7

Military building supply	25	49	—	2	—	33	35	109	30.3	32.0
Subsistence	4	32	—	—	—	6	6	41	14.6	14.6
Construction	450	43	483	—	187	97	284	1,260	7.7	22.6
Construction equipment	29	61	—	11	—	21	32	122	17.2	26.2
Photographic equipment	6	3	8	1	14	22	36	53	41.6	68.1
All other equipment	107	272	22	15	20	149	184	584	25.4	31.5
Services	32	1,081	54	54	44	811	909	2,076	39.0	43.7
Total	3,465	4,713	1,451	748	5,647	9,632	16,027	25,656	37.5	62.2

NOTE: The amounts of contracts have changed from year to year, and each year's amounts refer to contracts *let* rather than work performed. Moreover, these figures for prime contracts mask the substantial volume of subcontracting, which spreads the real production activity somewhat differently. In light of these points, this table is meant primarily to illustrate the general scope of the problem, not to show definitively its individual details. Totals may not add up, owing to rounding.

* The competition codes are as follows:

0—Formally advertised for competitive bidding.

1—Negotiated: "price competition." More than one price quote was available.

2—Negotiated: "design and technical competition."   Price was not the decisive factor.

3—Negotiated: "Follow-on" (extension) of a code 1 contract without further competition.

4—Negotiated: "Follow-on" of a code 2 contract without further competition.

5—Negotiated directly with a single source.   No attempt at competition.

SOURCE: Computed from unpublished Defense Department listings and compilations of all prime contracts.

APPENDIX TABLE 7 THE ROLE OF GROUP 5 CONTRACTS
IN SELECTED MAJOR DEFENSE
SUPPLY FIRMS, 1966–1967

Sales Rank Among All Industrial Firms, 1966	Company	Total Sales, 1966 ($ million)	Group 5 Purchases ($ million)	Purchases As Percentage of Company Sales Total Defense	Group 5
1	General Motors	20,209	224	3.8	1.1
2	Ford	12,240	160	4.4	1.3
4	General Electric	7,177	363	28.2	5.1
5	Chrysler	5,650	116	2.5	2.1
11	Western Electric	3,624	423	30.8	11.6
19	Westinghouse	2,581	270	24.3	10.5
20	RCA	2,549	103	14.9	4.0
21	Goodyear	2,476	42	8.9	1.7
22	G T&E	2,391	39	13.4	1.6
23	Boeing	2,357	129	59.7	5.5
28	IT&T	2,121	32	13.3	1.5
29	Lockheed	2,085	535	122.8	25.6
30	North American Aviation	2,024	184	95.7	9.1
37	General Dynamics	1,797	215	132.0	12.0
34	Kodak	1,742	62	6.4	3.5
36	United Aircraft	1,663	237	73.0	14.2
52	Sperry Rand	1,280	190	47.2	14.9
57	Litton	1,172	31	16.5	2.7
61	Textron	1,132	262	47.0	23.1
62	Olin-Mathieson	1,117	94	13.9	8.5
66, 73	McDonnell-Douglas	2,109	796	123.4	37.7
67	Grumman	1,059	139	98.5	13.1
87	Honeywell	914	121	40.4	13.3
113	Raytheon	709	185	56.9	26.2
120	Martin-Marietta	670	79	70.2	11.8
131	Hercules Powder	610	144	33.0	23.7
134	Avco	604	110	93.4	18.2
168	LTV	468	126	143.1	26.9
296	Newport News Shipbuilding	254	113	47.0	44.6
452	Curtiss-Wright	144	34	67.5	23.7
	Total	84,928	5,432		

NOTE: The amounts of contracts have changed from year to year, and each year's amounts refer to contracts *let* rather than work performed. Moreover, these figures for prime contracts mask the substantial volume of subcontracting, which spreads the real production activity somewhat differently. In light of these points, this table is meant primarily to illustrate the general scope of the problem, not to show definitively its individual details.

SOURCE: Compiled from *The 500 Largest Industrial Corporations* (New York: *Fortune*, June 15, 1967); and U.S. Senate Subcommittee on Antitrust and Monopoly, 89th and 90th Congresses, *Hearings on Economic Concentration, Part 5A* (Washington, D.C.: U.S. Government Printing Office, 1967).

APPENDIX TABLE 8 1966 CONCENTRATION RATIOS FOR UNITED STATES MANUFACTURING INDUSTRIES (ADJUSTED WHERE APPROPRIATE)

Industry Code Number	Four-firm Concentration Ratio (Percent)	Factors Adjusted For*	Industry Code Number	Four-firm Concentration Ratio (Percent)	Factors Adjusted For*
2011	(40)	R	2098	31	
2013	(30–40)	R	2099	(60–70)	B
2015	(20–30)	R			
2021	(50)	R	2111	81	
2022	(60)	R, B	2121	58	
2023	(50)	R, B	2131	59	
2024	(70)	L	2141	(70–80)	B
2026	(60)	L			
2031	42		2211	(40)	B
2032	(80)	B	2221	(50)	B
2033	(40)	R, B	2231	(60)	B
2034	(50)	B	2241	23	
2035	33		2251	34	
2036	33		2252	22	
2037	(40–50)	R, B	2253	(20–30)	B
2041	(45)	R	2254	(50–60)	B
2042	(30–40)	R, B	2256	(20–30)	B
2043	87		2259	32	
2044	45		2261	44	
2045	(75)	B	2262	42	
2046	67		2269	32	
2051	(50)	R, B	2271	75	
2052	(70)	B	2272	26	
2061	50		2279	67	
2062	(40)	N	2281	(20–30)	B
2063	(40)	N	2282	51	
2071	(40–50)	B	2283	29	
2072	(85)	B	2284	62	
2073	88		2291	59	
2082	(65)	R	2292	36	
2083	41		2293	29	
2084	41	B, I	2294	45	
2085	55	B, I	2295	(50–60)	B
2086	(30–40)	L	2296	82	
2087	63		2297	63	
2091	38		2298	38	
2092	57		2299	35	
2093	53				
2094	25				
2095	(50–60)	B	2311	(20–30)	B
2096	(80–90)	L	2321	(40–50)	B
2097	(80–90)	L	2322	42	

Industry Code Number	Four-firm Concentration Ratio (Percent	Factors Adjusted For*	Industry Code Number	Four-firm Concentration Ratio (Percent)	Factors Adjusted For*
2323	20		2512	(20–30)	R, B
2327	20		2514	(20–30)	B
2328	28		2515	(40–50)	R
2329	28		2519	34	
2331	19		2521	30	
2335	(10–20)	B	2522	(40–50)	B
2337	9		2531	24	
2339	14		2541	(20–30)	R, B
2341	15		2542	22	
2342	33		2591	41	
2351	9		2599	18	
2352	36				
2361	14		2611	(75)	R
2363	15		2621	(45)	R, B, I
2369	18		2631	(30–40)	R, B, I
2371	4		2641	(50–60)	B
2381	27		2642	32	
2384	20		2643	(30–40)	B
2385	24		2644	38	
2386	24		2645	31	
2387	28		2646	(80–90)	B
2389	19		2647	(85)	B
2391	21		2649	25	
2392	(30–40)	B	2651	(30–40)	R
2393	38		2652	(20–30)	B
2394	19		2653	(30–40)	R
2395	(10–20)	B	2654	53	
2396	(70)		2655	(60–70)	B
2397	13		2661	(60–70)	R, B
2399	16				
			2711	(90)	L
2411	(40–50)	R	2721	(60)	B
2421	(50–60)	R	2731	(30–40)	B
2426	15		2732	22	
2429	17		2741	(50–60)	B
2431	(20–30)	R, B	2751	(20–30)	R, B
2432	24		2752	(20–30)	R
2433	(50–60)	R, B	2753	26	
2441	(60–70)	R, B	2761	47	
2442	(50–60)	R	2771	(80–90)	B
2443	(50–60)	R	2782	33	
2445	53		2789	(40–50)	R, B
2491	37		2791	(20–30)	R
2499	(40–50)	R, B	2793	(20–30)	R
2511	(20–30)	R, B	2794	(40–50)	R, B

Industry Code Number	Four-firm Concentration Ratio (Percent)	Factors Adjusted For*	Industry Code Number	Four-firm Concentration Ratio (Percent)	Factors Adjusted For*
2812	(70)	B	3161	(50–60)	B
2813	72		3171	11	
2814	95		3172	32	
2815	52		3199	19	
2816	(80)	B			
2818	(65)	R, B	3211	96	
2819	(70)	R, B	3221	(80)	R, B
2821	(60)	R, B	3229	(85)	R, B
2822	56		3231	40	
2823	(90)	B	3241	(80)	R
2824	(90)	B	3251	(80)	L, B
2831	46		3253	51	
2833	70		3255	(60–70)	R, B
2834	(90)	B	3259	(50–60)	R, B
2841	(90)	B	3261	56	
2842	(50–60)	B	3262	75	
2843	38		3263	61	
2844	(60)	B	3264	(60–70)	B
2851	(40–50)	B	3269	41	
2861	72		3271	(60)	L
2871	(50–60)	R, B	3272	(60)	L
2872	(40–50)	R, B	3273	(50–60)	L
2879	36		3274	31	
2891	(40–50)	R, B	3275	80	
2892	72		3281	(50–60)	L, B
2893	48		3291	(70)	B
2895	70		3292	(70)	B
2899	(50–60)	B	3293	33	
			3295	(40–50)	R, B
2911	(65)	R, B	3296	71	
2951	(40–50)	R, B	3297	(60–70)	R, B
2952	(50–60)	R, B	3299	35	
2992	(50)	R, B			
2999	80		3312	(80)	R, B
			3313	74	
3011	71		3315	(60)	R, B
3021	63		3316	(60)	R, B
3031	93		3317	(55)	R, B
3069	(40–50)	B	3321	(40–50)	R, B
3079	(20–30)	B	3322	48	
			3323	(30–40)	R, B
3111	(40–50)	R, B	3331	(80)	R, I
3121	72		3332	90	I
3131	19		3333	60	
3141	(40–50)	B	3334	95	
3142	18		3339	(60–70)	B
3151	25				

Industry Code Number	Four-firm Concentration Ratio (Percent)	Factors Adjusted For*	Industry Code Number	Four-firm Concentration Ratio (Percent)	Factors Adjusted For*
3341	(60)	B	3534	63	
3351	(60)	R, B	3535	(40)	B
3352	(80)	R, B	3536	44	
3356	46		3537	(60)	B
3357	(70)	R, B	3541	(40–50)	B
3361	(40)	R, B	3542	(30–40)	B
3362	20		3544	(30–40)	B
3369	(40–50)	B	3545	(30–40)	B
3391	(50–60)	R, B	3548	(60–70)	B
3392	78		3551	(30–40)	B
3399	(30–40)	R, B	3552	33	
			3553	(40–50)	B
3411	(90)	R	3554	37	
3421	(80–90)	R, B	3555	(50–60)	B
3423	(40–50)	B	3559	(40–50)	B
3425	55		3561	(50–60)	B
3429	(60–70)	B	3562	(70)	B
3431	47		3564	(30–40)	B
3432	(40–50)	B	3565	(20–30)	B
3433	(50–60)	B	3566	(30–40)	B
3441	(40–50)	R, B	3567	35	
3442	(30–40)	B	3569	(30–40)	B
3443	(60–70)	R, B	3571	(90)	B
3444	(40–50)	R, B	3572	(70)	B
3446	(20–30)	B	3576	50	
3449	(50–60)	B	3579	(75)	B
3451	(10–20)	B	3581	61	
3452	(30–40)	B	3582	51	
3461	(50–60)	R, B	3585	(50–60)	B
3471	(20–30)	R, B	3586	48	
3479	15		3589	(20–30)	B
3481	(50–60)	R, B	3599	(20–30)	B
3491	(50–60)	R, B			
3492	95		3611	(50)	B
3493	41		3612	(75)	B
3494	(40–50)	B	3613	(60)	B
3496	54		3621	(60)	B
3497	53		3622	(60)	B
3498	(30–40)	R, B	3623	(50)	B
3499	(40–50)	B	3624	88	
			3629	(50–60)	B
3511	(90)	B	3631	(60)	B
3519	(75)	B	3632	72	
3522	(70)	B	3633	79	
3531	(70)	B	3634	(70)	B
3532	(40–50)	B	3635	78	
3533	(50)	B			

Industry Code Number	Four-firm Concentration Ratio (Percent)	Factors Adjusted For*	Industry Code Number	Four-firm Concentration Ratio (Percent)	Factors Adjusted For*
3636	(80)	I	3822	59	
3639	(50)	B	3831	56	
3641	93		3841	(60–70)	B
3642	(30–40)	B	3842	(60)	B
3643	32		3843	(40–50)	B
3644	(30–40)	B	3851	60	
3651	(60)	B, I	3861	(80)	B, I
3652	71		3871	45	
3661	94		3872	84	
3662	(50)	B			
3671	95		3911	(30–40)	B
3672	89		3912	24	
3673	57		3913	40	
3674	51		3914	55	
3679	(40–50)	B	3931	(60)	B
3691	60		3941	22	
3692	88		3942	(40)	I
3693	67		3943	45	
3694	(85)	B	3949	(60)	B
3699	(50–60)	B	3951	46	
			3952	39	
3713	(30–40)	B	3953	26	
3715	53		3955	38	
3717	(94)	B, I	3961	25	
3721	(90)	B	3962	17	
3722	(95)	B, I	3963	27	
3723	96		3964	43	
3729	(50–60)	B	3981	32	
3731	(65)	B	3982	89	
3732	(40–50)	B	3983	69	
3741	98		3984	41	
3742	(60)	B	3987	22	
3751	(50)	B, I	3988	(60)	B
3791	21		3992	27	
3799	18		3993	(40–50)	R, B
3811	(45)	B	3995	31	
3821	(50–60)	B	3999	(40–50)	B

NOTE: Ratios in parentheses are adjusted.
* The main factors adjusted for are indicated by code letters as follows:
R: markets are mainly *regional* in scope.
L: markets are mainly *local* in scope.
B: census industry definitions are too *broad*.
N: census industry definitions are too *narrow*.
I: imports are a significant fraction of total sales.
SOURCE: Based on U.S. Bureau of the Census, "Value-of-Shipments Concentration Ratios by Industry," *Annual Survey of Manufactures, 1966*, M66(AS)-8 (Washington, D.C.: U.S. Government Printing Office, 1968), as reported or with adjustments.

APPENDIX TABLE 9 35 OLIGOPOLIES IN U.S. MANUFACTURING

1947 Census Code No.	Industry	Employment 1947	Official Census Concentration Ratios			Change in Concentration, 1947–1966	Asymmetry (Index of Disparity) 1950	Index of Market-share Stability 1947–1954
			1947	1958	1966			
2043	Cereal breakfast foods	11,276	79	83	87	+8	(high)	n.a.
2062	Cane sugar refining	17,376	70	69	(63)	(−7)	6.9	.99
2111	Cigarettes	27,674	90	79	81	−9	3.0	.97
2274	Hard-surface floor coverings	9,928	80	83	89	+9	5.5	.96
2771	Greeting cards	18,053	39	45	64	+25	8.9	.87
2825	Synthetic fibers	69,683	78	78	(85)	(+7)	(high)	.84
2826	Explosives	10,426	80	77	72	−8	12.2	.76
2841	Soap and glycerine	27,508	79	90	(90)	(+11)	5.4	.99
2898	Salt	4,809	81	81	(77)	(−4)	6.9	.99
2911	Petroleum refining	145,806	37	32	32	−5	(moderate)	n.a.
3011	Tires and inner tubes	115,657	77	74	71	−6	(moderate)	.98
3211	Flat glass	25,268	(90)	92	96	(+6)	8.3	n.a.
3241	Cement, hydraulic	35,662	30	32	30	0	(moderate)	.93
3272	Gypsum products	7,472	85	88	80	−5	7.2	1.00
3312	Blast furnaces and steel mills	536,096	50	53	49	−1	6.6	n.a.
3331	Primary copper	14,629	83	87	71	−8	(5.1)	n.a.

SIC	Product						
3333	Primary zinc	12,424	53	62	60	+7	3.9	.83
3411	Tin cans	46,760	78	80	71	−7	(high)	1.00
3521	Tractors	77,317	67	69	(71)	(+4)	3.8	.98
3522	Other farm machinery	94,144	36	38	(42)	(+6)	3.8	.96
3562	Elevators	10,227	63	62	63	0	(high)	.94
3571	Computing and related machinery	45,611	69	77	(63)	(−6)	(high)	.63
3572	Typewriters	26,604	79	79	79	0	(high)	.95
3581	Domestic laundry equipment	28,403	40	71	(79)	(+39)	(high)	.70
3593	Ball and roller bearings	52,174	62	57	56	−6	5.6	.99
3614	Electrical motors and generators	125,300	59	47	48	−11	4.7	1.00
3615	Transformers	36,635	73	71	66	−7	6.1	.97
3641	Engine electrical equipment	44,450	67	66	72	+5	5.2	.94
3651	Electric lamps	23,842	92	92	93	+1	(high)	1.00
3717	Motor vehicles and parts	645,067	56	75	79	+23	(high)	1.00
3722	Aircraft engines	50,423	72	56	58	−14	(high)	.80
3741	Locomotive and parts	30,419	91	95	98	+7	8.8	n.a.
3742	Railroad and street cars	60,851	56	58	50	−6	4.9	.78
3861	Photographic equipment	55,624	61	65	67	+6	9.6	.99
3871	Watches and clocks	34,623	41	48	45	+4	2.5	.79

NOTE: Parentheses indicate estimates.   Estimates of asymmetry are for present conditions, where known.

SOURCES: Adapted from W. G. Shepherd, "On Appraising Evidence About Market Power," *Antitrust Bulletin* XII (Spring, 1967), 65–72; and U.S. Bureau of the Census, "Value-of-shipments Concentration Ratios by Industry," *Annual Survey of Manufactures 1966*, M66 (AS)-8 (Washington, D.C.: U.S. Government Printing Office, 1968).

APPENDIX TABLE 10   CONCENTRATION AND ASYMMETRY IN THE 169 REPORTED JAPANESE INDUSTRIES IN 1963 (each entry shows the number of industries in the category)

Leading-firm Sales As a Percentage of the Next Firm	Four-Firm Concentration Ratio										
	0–9	10–19	20–29	30–39	40–49	50–59	60–69	70–79	80–89	90–99	Total
500+				1					1	3	5
400–499										1	1
300–399			1			1		1	1	4	8
200–299	1					1		2	4	2	10
150–199			5	3	6	3	4	3	7	6	37
125–149	1		2		5	5	3	2	1	7	26
100–124	2	3	12	6	14	14	8	9	11	3	82
Total	4	3	20	10	25	24	15	17	25	26	169

SOURCE: Compiled from Fair Trade Commission, *Concentration in Japanese Industries* (Tokyo: Fair Trade Commission, 1965).

ANALYSIS OF HIGH CONCENTRATION, HIGH-DIVERGENCE INDUSTRIES, 1947–1963

Industry Code Number*	Industry	1958 Concentration in Largest 8 Firms (Percent)	1958 Concentration in Largest 8 Plants (Percent)	Divergence, 1958 (Percent)	Change in Divergence 1947–1963 (Percent)	Value-added in 1958 ($ million)
	High Concentration plus High and Rising Divergence during 1947–1953					
2111	Cigarettes	99	66	33	+6	1,059
2121	Cigars	75	34	41	+15	183
2812	Alkalies and chlorine	89	51	38	+13	306
2883	Soybean oil mills	63	32	31	+13	150
3011	Tires and inner tubes	88	40	48	+12	1,155
3221	Glass containers†	93	48	45	+5	537
3229	Pressed and blown glass, n.e.c.	79	36	43	+23	312
3261	Vitreous plumbing fixtures	75	41	34	+7	87
3352	Aluminum rolling and drawing	85	44	41	(+25)	475
3411	Tin cans	89	19	70	+7	672
3491	Metal barrels, drums, and pails†	85	48	37	+4	91
3593	Ball and roller bearings	77	42	35	+9	408
3614	Motors and generators	56	26	30	+9	813
3651	Electric lamps	97	42	55	+3	270
3691	Storage batteries	81	28	53	+10	150
3692	Primary batteries	95	56	39	+9	75
3717	Motor vehicles and parts	81	20	61	(+15)	6,365
	Total					13,108

APPENDIX TABLE 11—continued

Industry Code Number*	Industry	1958 Concentration in		Divergence, 1958 (Percent)	Change in Divergence 1947–1963 (Percent)	Value-added in 1958 ($ million)
		Largest 8 Firms (percent)	Largest 8 Plants (Percent)			
	High Concentration Plus High and Falling Divergence during 1947–1953					
2011	Meat packing	46	18	28	−14	1,747
2052	Biscuits and crackers	72	32	40	−6	506
2062	Cane sugar refining	88	60	28	(−10)	185
2063	Beet sugar	94	20	74	−6	130
2085	Distilled liquor	77	40	37	−14	445
2095	Flavorings	67	24	43	−11	262
2826	Explosives	89	38	51	−5	1,687
2881	Cottonseed oil mills†	71	34	37	(−25)	64
2891	Printing ink	65	26	39	−12	109
3255	Clay refractories	61	30	31	−3	105
3351	Copper rolling and drawing	68	34	34	(−12)	458
3554	Paper industries machinery	58	27	31	−10	124
3742	Railroad and street cars	81	56	25	−11	165
	Total					5,987
	Grand Total					19,095

NOTE: High concentration equals four-firm concentration 40 percent or higher in either 1947 or 1958.
High divergence equals 30 percent or more in either 1947 or 1958.
n.e.c. means "not elsewhere classified."
Parentheses indicate estimates.
* Based on 1947 Census industry definitions.
† Based on 20-firm and 20-plant ratios in 1958, because others were not reported.
SOURCE: Compiled from U.S. Senate Subcommittee on Antitrust and Monopoly, 89th Congress, 1st Session, *Hearings on Economic Concentration, Part 4* (Washington, D.C.: U.S. Government Printing Office, 1965), 1720–1731.

THE 18 INDUSTRIES WITH HIGH CONCENTRATION AND LOW DIVERGENCE IN 1958

Industry Code Number*	Industry	1958 Concentration in		Divergence 1958 (Percent)	Change in Divergence 1947–1963 (Percent)	Value-added in 1958 ($ million)
		Largest 8 Firms (Percent)	Largest 8 Plants (Percent)			
2072	Chocolate and cocoa products	84	84	0	−3	135
2073	Chewing gum	95	92	3	0	102
2295	Coated fabric except rubberized	57	54	3	(−2)	103
2522	Metal office furniture	50	45	5	+4	174
2771	Greeting cards	62	56	6	+5	179
2824	Synthetic rubber	86	78	8	−37	198
3021	Rubber footwear	82	72	10	−1	150
3511	Steam engines and turbines	90	84	6	+7	559
3562	Elevators and escalators	71	62	9	+9	126
3565	Industrial trucks and tractors	64	56	8	−3	118
3572	Typewriters	99	96	3	−1	169
3581	Household laundry equipment	90	80	10	+3	324
3619	Welding apparatus	52	46	6	+1	139
3641	Engine electrical equipment	79	70	9	0	369
3723	Aircraft propellors	99	98	1	(−3)	112
3741	Locomotives and parts	99	97	2	−4	152
3851	Ophthalmic goods	62	58	4	+3	137
3914	Silverware and plated ware	67	57	10	−8	110
	Total					3,113

NOTE: High concentration equals 40 percent or more in 1958.
Low divergence equals 10 percent or less in 1958.
* Based on 1947 Census industry definitions.
SOURCE: Compiled from U.S. Senate Subcommittee on Antitrust and Monopoly, 89th Congress, 1st Session, *Hearings on Economic Concentration Part 4* (Washington, D.C.: U.S. Government Printing Office, 1965), 1720–1731.

APPENDIX TABLE 13   94 MANUFACTURING INDUSTRIES IN WHICH MARKET POWER WAS PROBABLY SUBSTANTIAL IN THE MIDDLE 1960's

Industry	S.I.C. Number	Internal Elements of Structure				
		Four-Firm Concentration Ratios			Asymmetry Among Firms	
		Census Reported, 1966	Adjusted 1966	Change Since 1947 (or 1954)	1–4 Firms (index)	1–4 to 5–8 Firms (percent)
Fluid milk*	2026	23	(60)	+1	6.4	(high)
Cereal preparations*	2043	87		+8	(high)	8.6
Bended and prepared flour	2045	69	(75)	n.a.	(high)	5.8
Wet corn milling*	2046	67		−10	5.8	3.2
Bread and related products*	2051	25	(50)	+9	(high)	(high)
Biscuits, crackers, and cookies*	2052	59	(70)	(−6)	6.0	6.6
Chocolate and cocoa products*	2072	78	(85)	+10	10.2	6.3
Chewing gum*	2073	88		+18	6.5	12.9
Distilled liquor*	2085	55		−20	(3.5)	3.6
Cigarettes*	2111	81	−9	−9	3.0	4.0
Pulp mills	2611	48	(75)	(+5)	3.4	2.0
Sanitary paper products	2647	64	(85)	(+12)	(4.0)	4.4
Newspapers	2711	14	(90)	(+10)	(high)	(high)
Periodicals	2721	28	(60)	−6	4.9	1.8
Alkalies and chlorine*	2812	63	(70)	−7	2.6	2.4
Industrial gases*	2813	72		−11	(high)	5.1
Intermediate coal tar products*	2815	52		−6	13.0	3.4
Inorganic pigments*	2816	64	(80)	−3	5.9	4.3
Other organic chemicals*	2818	46	(65)	−13	(moderate)	4.3
Other inorganic chemicals*	2819	29	(70)	n.a.	(moderate)	1.7
Synthetic rubber*	2822	56		+3	(low)	2.5
Cellulosic man-made fibers*	2823	85	(90)	(+9)	(moderate)	4.6

	Internal Elements of Structure			External Elements of Structure		
Divergence between 8-firm and 8-plant Concentration in 1963 (Percent)	Stability of Market Shares of Leading Firms (Index) †	Entry Barriers (Estimated)	Tariff Rate (as Percent of Value)	Size of Industry (value added in 1966 in $ million)	Diversification by Leading Firms	Special Type or Structure of Buyers?
n.a.‡	(high)	moderate	5	2,232	Yes	
16	(high)	substantial	5	443	Yes	
33	(high)	substantial	20	206	Yes	
13	—	low	5	347		
31	.88	substantial	0–5	2,658	Yes	
30	.99	low	5	713	Yes	
3	.98	substantial	5–10	180		
5	.95	substantial	10	177	Yes	
32	.98	very high	40	723		
23	.97	substantial	25	1,483	Yes	
22	—	very high	0	365	Yes	
37	(high)	substantial	5	476	Yes	
11	.98	very high	0	4,012	Yes	
11	.95	very high	0	1,706	Yes	
30	.96	substantial	10–14	467	Yes	
n.a.	(high)	substantial	0	363	Yes	
20	(high)	substantial	53	718	Yes	
25	(high)	substantial	8–20	340	Yes	
30	(high)	substantial	10–40	3,641	Yes	
16	(high)	substantial	10–25	2.149	Yes	
15	(high)	substantial	7	443	Yes	
n.a.	.94	substantial	20–50	551	Yes	

Industry	S.I.C. Number	Four-Firm Concentration Ratios			Asymmetry Among Firms	
		Census Reported, 1966	Adjusted 1966	Change Since 1947 (or 1954)	1–4 Firms (index)	1–4 to 5–8 Firms (percent)
Organic fibers, noncellulosic*	2824	85	(90)	n.a.	(moderate)	18.8
Pharmaceutical preparations*	2834	24	(90)	−4	(high)	(high)
Soap and other detergents*	2841	72	(90)	(−2)	5.4	9.0
Toilet preparations	2844	40	(60)	+15	6.3	2.7
Explosives*	2892	72		−8	12.2	5.1
Petroleum refining*	2911	32	(65)	−5	(moderate)	1.5
Tires and inner tubes*	3011	71		(−1)	(moderate)	3.7
Flat glass*	3211	96		+6	8.3	15.6
Glass containers*	3221	59	(80)	−4	7.5	3.2
Other pressed and blown glass*	3229	72	(85)	+21	5.6	5.2
Cement*	3241	30	(80)	0	(moderate)	(high)
Brick and structural tile*	3251	13	(80)	+3	(high)	(high)
Gypsum products*	3275	80		−5	7.2	6.5
Abrasive products*	3291	56	(70)	+7	5.6	6.5
Mineral wool*	3296	71		(+10)	9.3	4.2
Blast furnaces and steel mills*	3312	49	(80)	−1	6.6	2.6
Electrometallurgical products*	3313	74		−14	6.7	4.9
Cold-finished steel shapes*	3316	34	(60)	(0)	(4.0)	(high)
Steel pipe and tube*	3317	26	(55)	(−5)	4.5	(3.3)
Primary copper*	3331	71	(80)	(−12)	5.1	3.9
Primary zinc*	3333	60		+5	3.9	1.7
Primary aluminum*	3334	95		(−5)	(moderate)	(10.0)
Secondary nonferrous metals*	3341	29	(60)	(+3)	5.3	2.2
Copper rolling and drawing*	3351	43	(60)	(−14)	(4.0)	2.0
Aluminum rolling and drawing*	3352	65	(80)	(−15)	(moderate)	6.2
Nonferrous wire drawing, etc.	3357	39	(70)	(+2)	2.8	2.4
Metal cans*	3411	71	(90)	−7	(high)	6.7
Razor blades and razors	34212	(98)		(+1)	6.9	15.0

276

Internal Elements of Structure				External Elements of Structure		
Divergence between 8-firm and 8-plant Concentration in 1963 (Percent)	Stability of Market Shares of Leading Firms (Index)†	Entry Barriers (Estimated)	Tariff Rate (as Percent of Value)	Size of Industry (value added in 1966 in $ million)	Diversification by Leading Firms	Special Type or Structure of Buyers?
n.a.	(high)	substantial	15–40	1,302	Yes	
7	(high)	very high	0–20	3,447	Yes	
45	.99	very high	10	1,297	Yes	
25	(high)	substantial	5–20	1,675	Yes	
34	(high)	very high	0–30	255	Yes	Yes
34	(high)	substantial	(import controls)	4,082	Yes	Yes
50	.98	substantial	10	1,768	Yes	Yes
34	(high)	very high	0–25	431	Yes	
48	(high)	very high	10–35	763		
50	.97	very high	15–25	709	Yes	
36	.93	moderate	2	839		Yes
10	.99	low	3	275		
75	1.00	substantial	13	222		
9	.99	moderate	5–10	620	Yes	
35	(high)	moderate	15	252	Yes	
43	(high)	very high	0–15	9,644	Yes	
31	.99	moderate	0–15	198	Yes	
17	(high)	very high	5–10	307	Yes	
n.a.	(high)	very high	5	417	Yes	Yes
56	(high)	very high	5–15	363	Yes	
12	.83	substantial	10	134	Yes	
44	(high)	substantial	15	725	Yes	
28	.77	moderate	10–20	293	Yes	
34	.98	very high	15–40	898	Yes	
41	.99	substantial	15–20	862	Yes	
42	(high)	substantial	15–20	1,341	Yes	
60	1.00	substantial	10–20	1,043	Yes	
n.a.	.98	very high	5–10	(145)	Yes	

Industry	S.I.C. Number	Four-Firm Concentration Ratios			Asymmetry Among Firms	
		Census Reported, 1966	Adjusted, 1966	Change Since 1947 (or 1954)	1–4 Firms (index)	1–4 to 5–8 Firms (percent)
Transportation equipment, hardware	34291	(71)		(0)	7.8	11.8
Metal plumbing fixtures	3431	47		(−8)	5.9	2.6
Steel power boilers	34433	(82)		(+4)	9.3	8.8
Safes and vaults*	3492	95		(+8)	(high)	22.8
Steam engines and turbines	3511	87	(90)	(0)	7.9	18.6
Internal combustion engines	3519	52	(75)	(+9)	(high)	3.1
Farm machinery and equipment	3522	45	(70)	(+2)	3.8	3.6
Construction machinery	3531	45	(70)	n.a.	4.1	3.8
Elevators and moving stairways	3534	63		−2	(6.0)	5.6
Industrial trucks and tractors	3537	49	(60)	−8	9.1	5.4
Rolling mill machinery	35481	60		(+3)	7.7	4.0
Paper industries machinery	3554	37		+9	11.9	3.4
Ball and roller bearings	3562	56	(70)	−6	5.6	3.0
Computing and related machines*	3571	67	(90)	(0)	(high)	5.2
Typewriters	3572	79	(70)	−2	(high)	3.3
Transformers*	3612	66	(75)	−7	6.1	6.2
Switchgear and switchboards*	3613	52	(60)	(−4)	5.7	3.6
Motors and generators*	3621	48	(60)	−11	4.7	5.6
Industrial controls	3622	50	(60)	n.a.	(moderate)	4.3
Carbon and graphite products	3624	88		+1	(high)	9.2
Household cooking equipment	3631	54	(60)	(+11)	5.1	3.0
Household refrigerators	3632	72		(+10)	(high)	4.4
Household laundry equipment	3633	79		(+39)	(moderate)	4.5
Household vacuum cleaners*	3635	78		(0)	7.5	5.4

Internal Elements of Structure				External Elements of Structure		
Divergence between 8-firm and 8-plant Concentration in 1963 (Percent)	Stability of Market Shares of Leading Firms (Index) †	Entry Barriers (Estimated)	Tariff Rate (as Percent of Value)	Size of Industry (value added in 1966) in $ million	Diversification by Leading Firms	Special Type or Structure of Buyers?
n.a.	(high)	moderate	10–20	(700)	Yes	
9	.94	moderate	15–25	146		
(20)	(high)	substantial	14	(350)		Yes
n.a.	.99	substantial	19	64		Yes
10	.99	substantial	8–15	505	Yes	Yes
20	(high)	substantial	0–10	1,075	Yes	
27	.97	very high	0	2.057	Yes	
13	(high)	substantial	10	1,881	Yes	
10	.94	substantial	11	236	Yes	
8	.97	substantial	10	405		
n.a.	(high)	substantial	15	(260)	Yes	
7	.84	substantial	7–10	263		
30	.99	moderate	15–20	872	Yes	
36	(high)	very high	12	2,828	Yes	
7	.95	moderate	0–12	424	Yes	
29	.97	very high	13	584	Yes	Yes
33	(high)	very high	18	972	Yes	Yes
27	1.00	very high	10	1,366	Yes	Yes
7	(high)	very high	15–55	719	Yes	Yes
26	.99	very high	10–15	175	Yes	
10	(high)	substantial	8–12	254	Yes	
4	(high)	substantial	11	752	Yes	
12	(high)	substantial	12–16	416	Yes	
1	.90	moderate	14	156	Yes	

Industry	S.I.C. Number	Internal Elements of Structure				
		Four-Firm Concentration Ratios			Asymmetry Among Firms	
		Census Reported, 1966	Adjusted 1966	Change Since 1947 (or "1954)	1–4 Firms (index)	1–4 to 5–8 Firms (percent)
Sewing machines	3636	(95)	(80)	(+6)	8.3	(10.6)
Electric lamps*	3641	93		+1	(high)	23.0
Radio and TV receiving sets	3651	48	(60)	(+20)	(moderate)	2.0
Telephone and telegraph apparatus	3661	94		+4	12.3	23.0
Broadcasting equipment	3662	24	(50)	n.a.	(moderate)	1.8
Electron tubes, receiving	3671	95		+12	(moderate)	7.3
Cathode ray picture tubes*	3672	89		+21	(moderate)	22.8
Electron tubes, transmitting	3673	57		(−3)	(low)	2.1
Storage batteries	3691	60		−3	(high)	3.1
Primary batteries	3692	88		+11	11.3	9.9
X-ray apparatus and tubes	3693	67		+9	3.4	5.6
Engine electrical equipment	3694	72	(85)	+7	5.2	6.9
Motor vehicles and parts*	3717	79	(94)	+23	(high)	19.7
Aircraft	3721	67	(90)	(+8)	3.2	2.5
Aircraft engines and parts	3722	56	(95)	−11	(high)	2.7
Aircraft propellors and parts	3723	96		+3	7.7	15.0
Shipbuilding and repairing	3731	42	(65)	−1	6.2	3.2
Locomotives and parts*	3741	98		+7	8.8	48.5
Surgical appliances and supplies	3842	45	(60)	(−10)	7.7	5.4
Photographic equipment*	3861	67	(80)	+6	9.6	4.8
Hard surface floor coverings	3982	89		+6	5.5	7.9
Total						

* Industries classified by Wilcox (as noted in Chapter 10) as "monopolized" are marked with an asterisk.
† Numerical indexes are based on 1947–1954. If there are indications that recent

Internal Elements of Structure				External Elements of Structure		
Divergence between 8-firm and 8-plant Concentration in 1963 (Percent)	Stability of Market Shares of Leading Firms (Index)†	Entry Barriers (Estimated)	Tariff Rate (as Percent of Value)	Size of Industry (value added in 1966 in $ million)	Diversification by Leading Firms	Special Type or Structure of Buyers?
1	.99	moderate	10	97	Yes	
50	1.00	very high	8	495	Yes	
18	(.84)	substantial	10–13	1,675	Yes	
n.a.	(high)	very high	(zero import quota)	1,432	Yes	Yes
n.a.	(high)	substantial	10–13	4,855	Yes	Yes
n.a.	(high)	substantial	12	244	Yes	Yes
3	(high)	substantial	12	472	Yes	Yes
20	(high)	substantial	12	252	Yes	Yes
48	.99	substantial	17	284	Yes	
38	.97	substantial	18	167	Yes	
5	.97	substantial	6	141	Yes	Yes
7	.94	moderate	10–15	753	Yes	
67	1.00	very high	6	15,450	Yes	
26	.84	very high	10	4,675	Yes	Yes
21	.80	very high	10	2,765	Yes	Yes
(1)	.88	very high	10	133	Yes	Yes
12	.86	very high	(50)	1,362	Yes	Yes
0	(high)	very high	12	318	Yes	Yes
11	.94	moderate	10–35	467	Yes	Yes
11	.99	very high	10–35	2,282	Yes	Yes
3	.96	low	10–17	135		
				$114,614		

patterns conform to the 1947–1954 index, it is underlined.   Where stability is known to be high (over .9), even lacking an actual index, it is stated so.
SOURCES: As discussed in Chapters 7, 8, and 9.
‡ n.a. means not available.

APPENDIX TABLE 14   MARKETS WITH
SUBSTANTIAL MARKET
POWER (WEIGHTED
BY 1963 SHARE OF
NATIONAL INCOME)

	S.I.C. Code Number	National Income Originating in 1963 ($ million)	
		Industries with Substantial Market Power	Sector Totals
Agriculture, forestry and fisheries			18,596
Mining			5,971
Major metal ores*	101–106 ⎫	807	
Uranium ores	1094 ⎭		
Anthracite	1111 ⎫	1,211	
Bituminous coal	1211 ⎭		
Chemicals mining*	147	(250)	
Total for listed industries		(2,268)	
Construction			24,117
General building contractors	151 ⎫		
Highway and street construction*	161 ⎬	(16,000)	
Other heavy construction*	162 ⎭		
Total for listed industries		(16,000)	
Manufacturing (see Appendix, Table 13)			
Total for listed industries (adjusted from value-added)*		69,200	
Transportation and utilities			39,931
Railroads*	401 ⎫		
Sleeping car services*	402 ⎬	6,579	
Railway express service	403 ⎭		
Local and suburban passenger transport	411 ⎫	1,724	
Taxicabs	412 ⎭		
Intercity bus lines	4131		
Water transportation	44	1,803	
Airlines	451	(1,400)	

	S.I.C. Code Number	National Income Originating in 1963 ($ million)	
		Industries with Substantial Market Power	Sector Totals
Petroleum pipe lines*	461	327	
Telephone communication*	481		
Telegraph communication	482	8,690	
Radio and television broadcasting*	483	1,137	
Electric companies and systems*	491		
Gas companies and systems*	492		
Combination companies and systems*	493	10,239	
Water supply*	494		
Sanitary services*	495		
Total for listed industries		31,899	
Wholesale trade			26,688
Drugs	5022	(728)	
Dairy products	5043	(498)	
Electrical equipment and supplies	5063	(1,020)	
Alcoholic beverages	5095	(938)	
Total for listed industries		(3,182)	
Retail trade			46,597
Lumber and building materials*	521	(1,820)	
Farm equipment	5252	(595)	
Motor vehicles*	551	(5,370)	
Sporting goods and bicycles	595	(128)	
Fuel and ice	598	(840)	
Total for listed industries		(8,753)	
Finance, insurance, and real estate *			(53,213)
Commercial banks*	602		
Trust companies*	604		
Securities brokers, dealers and flotation companies*	621	(20,000)	
Insurance carriers*	63		
Real estate operators	651		
Holding and other investment companies*	67		
Total for listed industries		(20,000)	

	S.I.C. Code Number	National Income Originating in 1963 ($ million)	
		Industries with Substantial Market Power	Sector Totals
Services			54,071
Hotels*	7011	(1,000)	
Funeral services	726	(300)	
News syndicates*	735	(70)	
Automobile rentals	751	(400)	
Motion picture production, distribution, and exhibition	78	952	
Commercial sports	794	1,984	
Physicians and surgeons	801 ⎱	12,000	
Hospitals	806 ⎰		
Legal services	81	3,416	
Accounting, auditing, and bookkeeping	893	(100)	
Total for listed industries		(20,222)	
All Sectors: Total			(413,001)
Total for listed industries		$171,524	

NOTE: Figures in parentheses are estimates.

* Industries classified by Wilcox (as noted in Chapter 10) as "monopolized" are marked with an asterisk.

† In manufacturing, value-added was $189 billion in 1963 while income originating was reported at $143 billion. The difference is mainly depreciation. Assuming no important biases in the difference, the $115 billion of value-added in market-power industries in 1966 (see Appendix Table 13) was scaled down to $69 billion as an estimate of income originating in those industries in 1963.

** The financial sector is particularly difficult to estimate. The national income figure for it is not really comparable for the present purpose, which is to represent the relative importance of the sector in the economy. Moreover, the reported figure includes a large element of imputed rent to owner-occupied dwellings. Rather than provide detailed but shaky and artificial estimates for each market, I have made an overall approximation which, though conjectural, is almost certainly on the low side. In order not to distort the meaning of the all-sector totals further, I have left the reported income-originating total for the sector as reported, even though this is not wholly satisfactory.

SOURCES (other than those discussed in Chapters 6-9) : U.S. Department of Commerce, *Survey of Current Business, 1965*, and U.S. Bureau of the Census, *Census of Business, 1963*, (both Washington, D.C.: U.S. Government Printing Office, 1965), Federal Reserve Board, *Federal Reserve Bulletin, 1966*, (Washington, D.C.: U.S. Government Printing Office, 1966).

APPENDIX TABLE 15   ANALYSIS OF CHANGES
IN CONCENTRATION 1947–1958
COEFFICIENTS OF INDEPENDENT VARIABLES

Number of Industries	Dependent Variable	Constant Term	Shipments Growth (Percent)	Employment Growth (Percent)	Concentration 1947 (Percent)	Disparity 1950 (Ratio)*	Protection 1954 (Percent)	Coefficient of Determination R²
426	Change in concentration (percentage points)	4.42	(not included)	−.038 (.006) [.09]	−100 (.020) [.06]	+.37 (.17) [.01]	−.28 (.13) [.01]	.13
426	Change in concentration (percentage points)	4.89	−.091 (.023) [.04]	(not included)	−.092 (.021) [.04]	+.38 (.17) [.01]	−.31 (.13) [.01]	.09

CORRELATION MATRIX

Mean Values	Standard Deviations	Variables	Change in Concentration	Shipments Growth	Employment Growth	Concentration 1947	Disparity	Protection	Adjusted profits	Stability (203 industries)
−.17	(9.45)	Change in concentration	1.00							
98.1	(25.40)	Shipments growth	−.20	1.00						
5.76	(66.8)	Employment growth	−.27	.64	1.00					
40.5	(22.7)	Concentration, 1947	−.19	.08	−.02	1.00				
5.1	(2.7)	Disparity	.02	.11	.04	.29	1.00			
8.0	(3.3)	Protection	−.08	.05	.08	−.16	.01	1.00		
1.66	(.89)	Adjusted profits	−.03	.06	.07	.24	.13	−.19	1.00	
.83	(.22)	Stability (203 industries)	−.08	.14	−.28	.58	.20	−.18	.24	1.00

NOTE: Figures in parentheses are standard errors or (in the correlation matrix) standard deviations. Only variables significant at the 10-percent level are included. The partial correlation coefficient for each variable is shown in square brackets.
* Disparity is a ratio, with no intrinsic units.
SOURCE: Computations by the author; see Chapter 11.

285

APPENDIX TABLE 16 AN ANALYSIS OF PROFIT RATES IN AMERICAN MANUFACTURING INDUSTRIES, 1947–1957

COEFFICIENTS OF INDEPENDENT VARIABLES

Number of Industries	Dependent Variable	Constant Term	Large-firm Share (Percent)	Protection 1954 (Percent)	Imports 1954 (Percent)	Concentration 1954 (Percent)	Stability 1947–1954 (r)	R^2
426	Average profit rate 1947–57 (per cent)	6.518	+.037 (.005) [.35]	−.08 (.03) [.14]	−.035 (.010) [.10]	+.008 (.004)	(not included)	.21
203	Average profit rate 1947–57	5.859	+.027 (.007) [.26]	−.09 (.04) [.17]	−.066 (.023) [.20]		+17.6 (6.2) [.20]	.21

CORRELATION MATRIX

Mean Values	Standard Deviations	Variables	Average Profit Rate	Concentration 1954	Employment Growth	Large-firm Share	Disparity	Protection	Imports	Stability (203 Industries)
6.88	(2.04)	Average profit rate, 1947–57	1.00	.25	.06	.40	.10	−.18	−.11	.29
40.4	(22.7)	Concentration ratio, 1954		1.00	−.11	.43	.30	−.17	.13	.53
5.76	(6.8)	Employment growth, 1947–58			1.00	.17	.04	.08	−.11	−.28
22.0	(20.5)	Large-firm share				1.00	.10	−.14	−.03	.28
5.1	(2.7)	Asymmetry ratio					1.00	.00	.08	.20
8.0	(3.3)	Protection						1.00	−.12	−.18
3.6	(.9)	Imports/domestic sales							1.00	.04
.83	(.22)	Stability (203 industries)								1.00

NOTE: Figures in parentheses are standard errors or (in the correlation matrix) standard deviations. Only variables significant at the 10-percent level are included. The partial correlation coefficient for each variable is shown in square brackets. It represents the role of the variable with all of the others held constant.
SOURCE: Computations by the author; see Chapter 12.

APPENDIX TABLE 17 ANALYSIS OF GROWTH OF PRODUCTIVITY PER WORKER, 1947–1962

COEFFICIENTS OF INDEPENDENT VARIABLES

Number of Industries	Dependent Variable	Constant Term	Concentration 1954 (Percent)	Large-firm Share (Percent)	Change in Concentration 1947–1958 (Percentage Points)	Average Profit Rate 1947–1957 (Percent)	R^2
159	Productivity change, 1947–62	50.02	+0.97 (0.20) [.13]	+0.75 (0.23) [.06]	+1.12 (0.45) [.04]		.32
95	Productivity change, 1947–62	40.79		+1.29 (0.22) [.28]	+1.38 (0.56) [.06]	+6.2 (2.4) [.07]	.36

APPENDIX TABLE 17—continued

CORRELATION MATRIXES

Mean Values	Standard Deviations	Variables	Productivity Change	Concentration 1954	Large-firm Share	Profit Rate	Change in Concentration	Stability
					For 159 Industries			
104.6	(60.4)	Productivity change	1.00					
39.5	(23.6)	Concentration	.51	1.00				
22.6	(20.9)	Large-firm share	.42	.51	1.00			
6.9	(2.1)	Profit rate	.31	.35	.34	1.00		
.68	(9.0)	Change in concentration	.12	–.01	–.17	–.01	1.00	
					For 95 Industries			
114.9	(54.5)	Productivity change	1.00					
43.2	(24.2)	Concentration, 1954	.43	1.00				
22.6	(21.1)	Large-firm share	.52	.50	1.00			
7.1	(2.0)	Profit rate	.32	.29	.19	1.00		
.77	(8.2)	Change in concentration	.15	–.01	–.12	–.00	1.00	
.81	(.24)	Stability	.25	.54	.19	.26	–.10	1.00

SOURCE: Computations by the author; see Chapter 14.
NOTE: Figures in parentheses are standard errors or (in the correlation matrix) standard deviations. Only variables significant at the 10-percent level are included. The partial correlation coefficient for each variable is shown in square brackets. It represents the role of the variable with all of the others held constant.

APPENDIX TABLE 18 SUMMARY OF NEGRO EMPLOYMENT DATA FOR NINE MAJOR CITIES IN 1966 (PERCENTAGES)

Industry group	Four-firm Concentration (Adjusted or Estimated)	Nine-city Average of Negro Share in Employment		Officials, Managers, and Professionals
		All White-Collar: All Firms	All White-Collar: Highest Percentage Case	
13 Crude oil and gas	(60)	1.3	5.5	n.a.
15 Building construction	(60) ⎤	1.6	10.8 ⎤	
16 Other construction	(50) ⎬ (60)	1.5	5.1 ⎬	0.6
17 Special trade construction	(70) ⎦	1.1	11.9 ⎦	
20 Food products	55	3.1	11.4	1.0
21 Cigarettes	85	0.7	4.9	0.9
22 Textiles	42	3.5	11.1	1.2
23 Apparel	21	5.9	14.0	2.9
24 Lumber products	43	2.1	7.0	0.9
25 Furniture and fixtures	30	2.5	9.6	1.3
26 Paper products	45	1.0	8.0	0.4
27 Printing and publishing	54	2.7	7.5	0.7
28 Chemicals	74	2.2	7.8	0.8
29 Petroleum products	67	2.5	7.0	0.8
30 Rubber products	50	2.4	9.0	0.5
31 Leather products	44	3.6	9.7	1.4
32 Stone, clay, and glass	67	1.3	5.5	0.5
33 Primary metals	66	2.0	9.1	0.9
34 Fabricated metal products	49	1.1	10.3	0.3
35 Nonelectrical machinery	53	1.1	5.2	0.3
36 Electrical machinery	57	1.7	8.7	0.5
37 Transportation equipment	81	1.8	7.1	0.9
38 Instruments	62	1.3	7.4	0.4
39 Miscellaneous	47	4.7	8.6	1.7
40 Rail transport	(80) ⎤	1.4	6.6 ⎤	
41 Transit	(*) ⎥	3.2	5.6 ⎥	
42 Trucking and warehousing	(70) ⎬ (80)	1.5	8.1 ⎬	0.5
45 Air transport	(100) ⎥	0.8	2.7 ⎥	
47 Transport services	(70) ⎦	1.7	6.4 ⎦	
48 Communications	(100)	6.3	7.3	0.8
49 Utilities	(100)	1.8	6.3	0.5
50 Wholesaling	(50)	2.1	14.0	0.6
53 General retail	(20) ⎤	6.0	17.3 ⎤	
54 Food retail	(40) ⎥	2.8	10.4 ⎥	
55 Auto services	(40) ⎥	4.0	7.7 ⎥	
56 Apparel stores	(10) ⎬ (20)	8.2	14.0 ⎬	2.5
58 Eating and drinking	(10) ⎥	7.5	16.5 ⎥	
59 Miscellaneous retail	(30) ⎥	4.5	11.1 ⎥	
60 Banking	(70) ⎦	3.8	8.8 ⎦	

		Nine-city Average of Negro Share in Employment		
Industry group	Four-firm Concentration (Adjusted or Estimated)	All White-Collar: All Firms	All white-Collar: Highest Percentage Case	Officials, Managers, and Professionals
61 Credit agencies	(70) ⎱ (70)	2.6	6.4 ⎱	0.5
62 Brokers	(60) ⎰	3.2	4.7 ⎰	
63 Insurance carriers	(50) ⎱ (50)	3.5	9.7 ⎱	1.1
64 Insurance agents	(50) ⎰	2.0	3.9 ⎰	
65 Real estate	(80)	1.7	6.1	0.5
70 Hotels and lodging	(20)	5.0	10.9	n.a.
72 Personal services	(10)	10.1	14.1	5.6
73 Miscellaneous business services	(30)	4.4	19.0	1.9
80 Medical services	(*)	11.1	29.1	9.4
81 Legal services	(80)	1.2	3.4	0.1
82 Educational services	(*)	7.1	9.2	3.8
86 Non profit organizations	(*)	5.9	15.8	n.a.
Average, all groups all nine cities		3.9	12.9	1.6

NOTE: Figures in parentheses are the estimated concentration equivalents.
* Not estimated, because partly or wholly nonprofit.
SOURCES: Compiled from unpublished U.S. Equal Employment Opportunity Commission census in 1966 of establishments with 100 or more employees.

Index

Abegglen, James, 213 n
Adams, Walter, 20 n, 46 n, 166, 198 n, 222 n
Adelman, Morris A., 73 n, 75 n, 105 n, 115 n, 116 n, 175 n
Administered prices, 14–15, 15 n, 22, 182, 199–201, 237–237
Advertising, 53, 174, 175
Aerospace industries, 76, 83–88, 109, 117 n, 118, 126, 135, 141, 142, 147, 148, 153, 157, 159, 160, 161, 165, 169, 170, 173, 208, 234
Alhadeff, C., 94 n
Alhadeff, David A., 94 n
Air transport industry, 114, 186
Aluminum industry, 53, 54, 126, 131 n, 141, 147, 153, 159, 166
American Motors Corporation, 234
American Tobacco Company, 190
Antitrust policy, 4, 12, 14, 20–21, 22–23, 33, 35, 36, 39, 43, 75, 87, 101, 122 n, 130, 153, 159, 166, 183, 223, 245, 246, 247
Archer, S. H., 44 n, 98 n
Armco Steel Corp., 104
Asymmetry, 40, 58, 63–65, 119–120, 153, 158–159, 189, 225, 232, 245–246, 247
Atomic Energy Commission, 36, 83–88
Australian patterns, 104 n, 105
Automobile industry, 35, 54, 63, 76, 77, 82–83, 84, 104, 105, 109, 117 n, 119–120, 122, 126, 141, 147, 165, 169, 172, 176, 186, 190, 194, 198, 201, 211, 232–242, 246
Averch, Harvey, 229 n

Babcock and Wilcox Co., 109
Backman, Jules, 53 n, 131 n, 135 n
Bain, Joe S., 7 n, 18, 18 n, 20 n, 21, 25 n, 30 n, 42 n, 54 n, 105 n, 125, 125 n, 167 n, 168, 169, 172 n, 177 n, 183 n, 184 n, 190, 232, 234 n, 236 n, 237 n
Balassa, Bela, 126 n
Banking industry, 77, 78–79, 81, 82, 93–98, 117 n, 119, 125, 141, 143, 186, 188, 220, 245
Barriers to entry, 32, 38, 42, 47, 63–65, 125, 141 n, 144, 158, 172, 183, 189, 227, 236–237, 238, 246

Batchelder, Alan B., 218 n
Baum, Daniel J., 94 n, 99 n
Baumol, William J., 21, 21 n, 25 n, 31 n
Becker, Gary S., 60 n, 213 n
Bell System, 108, 113–114, 116, 148, 153 n, 166, 175 n, 231
Bendix Corp., 225
Berle, Adolf A., 15, 15 n, 19 n, 77 n, 88 n
Berry, Charles H., 74 n, 82, 82 n, 144, 144 n, 145 n, 146
Bethlehem Steel Corp., 104
Bigness. *See* Size, relative total
Bisson, Thomas A., 222 n
Blair, John M., 45 n, 119, 121 n, 199, 199 n, 200 n
Bork, Robert, 20 n
Boyle, Stanley E., 135 n, 136 n
Brady, Robert A., 128 n
British patterns, 70, 79, 81, 82–83, 94, 97, 104 n, 105, 109,
    114, 117, 122, 127 n, 128, 128 n 129, 142, 158, 175 n, 177,
    178, 179, 184, 198, 199, 201
Broadcasting industry, 125, 174, 175
Bronfenbrenner, Martin, 168 n
Bullock, Charles J., 4 n, 13 n, 18 n
Burgess, Leonard R., 212 n
Burns, Arthur R., 15 n
Burton, John F., Jr., 183 n

Campbell, James S., 43 n, 146 n
Campbell Soup Co., 108
Canadian patterns, 70, 104 n, 105, 109
Capital-intensity, 171
Caplovitz, David, 212 n
Capron, William M., 114 n
Carlson, Chester F., 211
Carson, Deane, 95 n
Cartels, 41, 127–131
Caves, Richard E., 114 n, 131 n, 143 n, 148 n, 177 n, 196 n
Census Bureau, U.S., 20, 21, 246
Cereals industry, 118, 126, 132, 147, 174, 176
Chamberlin, Edward H., 15 n, 30 n
Cheit, Earl F., 88 n
Chemicals industry, 63, 82, 107, 109, 110, 117 n, 118, 119,
    121, 126, 129, 130, 135, 136, 141, 142, 145, 147, 165,
    171, 182, 190, 194, 199, 208, 209, 211, 238
Chrysler Corp., 108, 232–242
Cigarette industry, 121, 122, 126, 132, 141, 142, 143, 145,
    159, 166, 170, 176
Clabault, James M., 183 n
Clark, John B., 12 n, 13 n, 34, 34 n
Clark, John M., 16, 16 n, 38 n